COMPLETE GUIDE TO

BASIC GARDENING

Project Editor:
Michael MacCaskey

Contributing Writers:
Michael MacCaskey
Lance Walheim
Susan Chamberlin
James McNair
A. Cort Sinnes

HPBooks
a division of
PRICE STERN SLOAN
Los Angeles

Published by HPBooks
a division of Price Stern Sloan, Inc.
360 North La Cienega Boulevard
Los Angeles, California 90048
ISBN: 0-89586-325-1
Library of Congress Catalog Card Number: 85-80863
©1986 Price Stern Sloan, Inc.
Printed in U.S.A.
10 9 8 7 6 5

Project Editor:
Michael MacCaskey

Contributing Writers:
Michael MacCaskey
Lance Walheim
Susan Chamberlin
James McNair
A. Cort Sinnes

Illustrations and Cover:
Roy Jones

Additional Illustrations:
Susan Chamberlin

Photography:
Michael Landis

Additional Photography:
Max Badgley
John J. Edsall
Mark K. King
Michael MacCaskey

Editorial Consultant:
Frank Shipe

Technical Advisors:
Mike Burraston
William Nelson
Dr. Wayne S. Moore

ACKNOWLEDGMENTS

A book such as this could not be produced without the help of many people—nurserymen, landscape architects, horticulturalists and specialists in many garden-related fields. No less important are the many home gardeners who shared their first-hand gardening experience with us. We would especially like to thank the following individuals and organizations:

American Association of Nurserymen, Washington D.C.
Mike Burraston, Bountiful Nursery, Tucson, AZ
California Association of Nurserymen, Sacramento, CA
Robert Cowden, Walnut Creek, CA
Walter Doty, Los Altos, CA
Stu Edey, Agro-Meterology, Ontario, Canada
John Edsall, Edsall & Associates, Columbus, OH
Entomological Society of America, College Park, MD
Mark K. King, Gibbs Landscape Co., Smyrna, GA
Kathleen M. Johnson, Palo Alto, CA
Sondra Johnson, North Hollywood, CA
Louisiana State University, Baton Rouge, LA
Michael Macauley, Napa, CA
Nathaniel MacCaskey, Burbank, CA
National Climatic Data Center, Asheville, NC
William Nelson, Pacific Tree Farms, Chula Vista, CA
Dr. Kelly O'Hanley, Palo Alto, CA
Dr. Peter O'Hanley, Palo Alto, CA
E.N. O'Rourke, Baton Rouge, LA
Paul Uenaka, San Jose, CA
Richard M. Ray, Woodland Hills, CA
United States Department of Agriculture, Forest Service
University of California Cooperative Extension, Oakland, CA
Wertheim, Van der Ploeg & Klemeyer, Architects, San Francisco, CA

CONTENTS

INTRODUCTION

It has often been said that plants are essential to our lives. They are the source of most of our clothing and shelter, and directly or indirectly provide all of our food. Less often considered is that plants soothe our spirits, as well. Flower colors and fragrances stimulate and please our senses. The textures, forms and shades of green foliage are usually taken for granted.

Beyond the gratification of merely having plants present in our environment, great satisfaction can be derived from growing and caring for them—the practice of gardening.

A successful garden does not have to contain a wide variety of plants. Some of the most beautiful gardens consist of only a few kinds of plants, well-chosen to fit their surroundings, and arranged attractively. Gardener-writer Charles A. Lewis states, "The importance of gardens lies not in the flowers or vegetables produced, but in the personal benefits experienced by gardeners pursuing the process of gardening. Gardening teaches patience and observation—time is re-quired for a seed to germinate or a fruit to ripen. Gardens connect us to the greater rhythms of nature—and ourselves."

The size or magnificence of the garden is irrelevant. If gardening space is limited, you can utilize multi-purpose plants, such as a semidwarf apple tree that provides beauty, shade and fruit. There are dwarf and compact forms of many popular plants that can be fitted to small gardens. Container gardens also offer many possibilities where space is limited.

No matter what kind of garden you envision, success depends on raising *healthy plants*. This is the primary focus of this book.

No book can answer all of your gardening questions, but this one will teach you all of the basic cultural practices involved in growing plants. It will help you select plants best adapted to your area, provide the best possible conditions for growing them and care for them once they're planted. This book also directs you to those around you who can respond to your immedi-ate questions—nursery personnel, landscape professionals, agricultural extension agents and others.

The only way to truly learn about growing plants is to grow them. To be a successful gardener requires the awareness of plants that comes with careful and frequent observation of their growth under the conditions in *your garden*. No rules or instructions cover every situation. This book will help you be more sensitive to your own plants and effectively respond to their needs as they grow. In this con-tinuing process lies much of the enjoy-ment of gardening. If you are a beginner, use this book to guide you through your first efforts. No matter how much gardening experience you have, you'll find this a valuable refer-ence book for realizing your garden plans· and solving your gardening problems.

PLANT REQUIREMENTS
The first step toward creating a suc-cessful garden is understanding how plants grow and what they need in

---

Left: From lawns to shrubs to trees, plants greatly enhance any home. This beautiful landscape is one example.

Above: A good use of limited space, this carefully planned garden includes flowers, vegetables, fruit trees and container plants.

Gardening doesn't always require a lot of space. This small apartment garden consists mostly of container plants, which can be easily transported should their owners decide to move.

order to grow. The following is an overview of the basic requirements essential to plant growth. Specific information on how to provide these requirements is organized by topic in the chapters that follow. The essentials of plant growth are:

● Soil, in which roots can anchor and air can circulate.
● Adequate water.
● Air temperature that is neither too hot nor too cold.
● Plant nutrients present in soil and air.
● Adequate light.

All of these factors work in concert to determine whether or not a certain plant will grow in a given location.

SOIL

Soil supplies water, air, nutrients and physical support to plants. A soil's ability to supply these elements depends on its physical and chemical characteristics, how they are determined and how they can be changed to produce healthier plants. These factors are examined in the chapter Soils, Fertilizers & Water, starting on page 55.

WATER

Water is essential to plants in several ways. It provides hydrogen and oxygen required by the plant to produce food. It regulates temperature by the process of *transpiration,* described on the facing page. It acts as a medium for transporting nutrients from the soil to all parts of the plant. As water percolates through the soil, it draws air to the plant roots.

Different plants need different amounts of water. The reasons are usually related to the environment in which the plant evolved. Root systems of some arid-climate clovers extend 6 to 12 feet into the soil. They are highly drought tolerant. Conversely, the root system of celery, a plant native to swamps, is shallow and requires frequent and abundant watering. Although the root systems of many drought-tolerant cacti and succulents are also shallow, these plants have the ability to store water in stems and leaves, thereby enabling them to endure long, dry periods.

The amount of water available to plants depends as much on the soil as it does on rainfall or the gardener's hose. The amount of water that soaks into the soil, the ease with which it

More important than number of plants in garden is whether or not plants are healthy, as illustrated in this garden with its well-manicured lawn and carefully pruned shrubs.

soaks in and the amount the soil can hold all depend on soil texture and structure. Water enters clay soils slowly and sand soils quickly. Clay soils and soils high in organic matter hold the most water longest. Sand soils hold the least amount for the shortest period of time. One of the gardener's goals is to provide a soil structure that drains well, yet retains enough water to meet the plant's growing requirements. Water requirements and watering are discussed on pages 67-69.

Water in the air around the plant (humidity) affects, among other things, how fast water moves through the plant, called the *transpiration rate.* The type of plant and the amount of water in the soil determine the degree of influence humidity has on the transpiration rate.

Even with plenty of soil moisture, some plants wilt if humidity is too low—moisture is drawn from the plant's leaves into the air faster than the root system can replace it. This is one of the reasons why many plants adapted to arid climates have small or narrow leaves to expose the least amount of leaf surface possible to the air. Others have succulent, water-storing leaves, or hairy, gray leaves that help reduce transpiration. On the other hand, large, fleshy leaves usually indicate that the plant evolved in a shady or humid environment where a fast transpiration rate is necessary to the plant's survival. So humidity has some effect on the kind of plants you can grow in your garden.

AIR

Air supplies two elements essential to plant growth—carbon and oxygen. Plants require air circulation both above and below ground. Roots absorb oxygen and give off carbon dioxide, just as animals do by breathing.

In heavy, compacted or clay soils, the space between soil particles, called *pore space,* is small. When air in the soil is inadequate, as is common in heavy soils, or in soils where all pore space is filled with water, the roots of most plants will die. When roots begin to die, the leaves of the plant wilt, often prompting the gardener to give the plant even more water—which kills it that much faster. Soils with a crusted surface also re-

strict air circulation, as does soil that is compacted by repeated foot or vehicle traffic.

Air circulation above ground is also necessary for healthy plant growth. Lack of air circulation under moist conditions reduces water evaporation, promoting fungal diseases and mildew. Too much circulation of dry air, such as on a hot, windy day, can dry plants out.

TEMPERATURE

More than any other element of climate, temperature determines which plants will grow where. Temperature directly influences the rate of internal plant processes. The fastest growth occurs at the upper temperature limit that the particular plant tolerates.

Perhaps the most crucial temperature for gardeners is the freezing point of water, 32F (0C). Growing-season length, planting time for warm-season plants, and harvest time are all determined by the spring and fall occurrence of this temperature. Minimum winter temperature—the basis of the United States Department of

Introduction 7

Agriculture (USDA) zone map on page 13—determines which perennial plants you can grow in a given region.

Low temperatures just above freezing will often retard plant growth or prevent seed germination. The ideal temperature for plant growth is different for different plants. Seeds of cool-season plants—cabbage, onions and peas, for example—germinate at soil temperatures as low as 40F (4C). Seeds of warm-season plants, such as Bermudagrass, beans, corn, African violets and melons, will not germinate until soil temperatures reach about 60F (16C).

Temperature also affects the quality and maturity rate of many crops and has an influence on the kinds of pests and diseases likely to be troublesome.

PLANT NUTRIENTS

There are 16 elements necessary for plant growth. The plant receives three of these—carbon, hydrogen and oxygen—from air and water. The other 13 elements are received from the soil. They are: *nitrogen, potassium, calcium, magnesium, phosphorus, sulfur, iron, copper, manganese, zinc, molybdenum, boron* and *chlorine.* These elements are absorbed from moisture in the soil. Nitrogen, phosphorus and potassium are used by plants in the greatest amounts, so these three *primary nutrients* are the ones that must be replenished most frequently. The *secondary nutrients,* magnesium, sulfur and calcium, are used by plants to a lesser extent, and are usually added only when the plant shows a deficiency. The remaining nutrients, called *trace elements,* are used by plants only in minute amounts and are usually present in the soil in sufficient quantities.

Plants grow best when nutrients are present in a steady, uniform supply. Slow-growing, long-lived plants such as trees and shrubs are more adaptable than fast-growing, short-lived plants to changes in nutrient levels in the soil. They can suffer a deficiency then fully recover once the nutrient is supplied. This is why you usually wait for a sign of nutrient need before fertilizing a tree or shrub. Fast-growing, short-lived plants—annuals and most vegetables, for instance—never fully recover from an early-season nutrient deficiency. This is why you add fertilizer to the soil before planting and then at least once again during growth. For more specific information on plant nutrients and fertilizers, see pages 63-66.

LIGHT

All green plants use sunlight, carbon dioxide and water to make food. This process is known as *photosynthesis.* The food—starch or sugar—is utilized by the plant to grow. In photosynthesis, the chlorophyll in green plants uses light energy to break water down into hydrogen and oxygen. The hydrogen then combines with carbon dioxide the plant takes in from the atmosphere to form the sugars that serve as food. The oxygen from the water is released into the atmosphere.

Light—the intensity and duration of it—affects all phases of plant growth. For instance, the intensity of light a plant receives affects its growing habit. As a rule, leaves distribute themselves so that each one receives the maximum amount of light and shades the others least. Plants in too little light become tall and spindly. Abundant light results in shorter, bushier plants. Some plants require a specific amount of light to maintain good growth. Others adapt to some degree of shade or full sun.

The duration of light is one way plants have adapted themselves to the changing seasons. For example, short days and long nights trigger the bloom of chrysanthemum flowers. Other plants respond in opposite ways and some plants are not affected by light duration at all. There's more information on light and light requirements starting on page 16.

OTHER PLANT NEEDS

Plants also need a growing environment that is relatively free of pests, diseases and competition from weeds. Many garden plants also require periodic pruning to maintain healthy growth or an attractive appearance.

As opposed to plants that grow in the wild, practically all plants bred for garden use require help from the gardener to survive and remain healthy—watering, fertilizing, pest and disease control, pruning, weeding and other gardening practices described in this book. The commitment to plant care does involve work, but the better you understand plant requirements, the easier and more enjoyable that work will become.

HOW A PLANT WORKS

At right is a simplified illustration of how a plant uses soil, water and sunlight to grow. It also shows how the component parts of roots, stems and leaves function in the growing process.

1. Water and soil nutrients (in solution form) are absorbed through tiny *root hairs,* which are located in the root-hair zone just behind rapidly growing root tips.

2. The water and nutrients are then conducted up through the roots, main stem and branches through a porous tissue called *xylem,* located beneath the bark or cambium layer of the stem.

3. The xylem tissue in individual leaf stems *(petioles)* transfers the water and nutrients to leaves. Water and nutrients are conducted to flowers and fruit in a similar manner.

4. Water and nutrients are conducted through leaf veins and absorbed by leaf cells, where they are converted to a form usable by the plant, as described below. Excess moisture is transferred to the leaf surface through small pores called *stomatas,* where it evaporates in the form of water vapor. Called *transpiration,* this process works somewhat like a human's perspiration to cool the plant. This process also releases oxygen into the air.

5, 6. Within each individual plant cell occurs the process of *photosynthesis*—the utilization of the sun's energy to convert inorganic plant nutrients into sugar (food) used for plant growth. *Chloroplasts* are microscopic bodies within plant cells (6) where photosynthesis occurs. They are also what give plants their green color. Several other complex chemical processes occur within plant cells to direct the plant's growth habits, determined by genetic information contained within each cell's nucleus.

7, 8. Buds are the points where all new plant growth starts. The *terminal bud* (7) is the growing point of the main stem or trunk. Terminal buds also occur at the growing tips of side branches. *Lateral buds* (8) on the main stem develop into side branches, leaves or flowers, depending on the plant. On many plants, side branches also develop lateral buds. The positions of various types of buds on the main stem and side branches determine the plant's eventual size and shape.

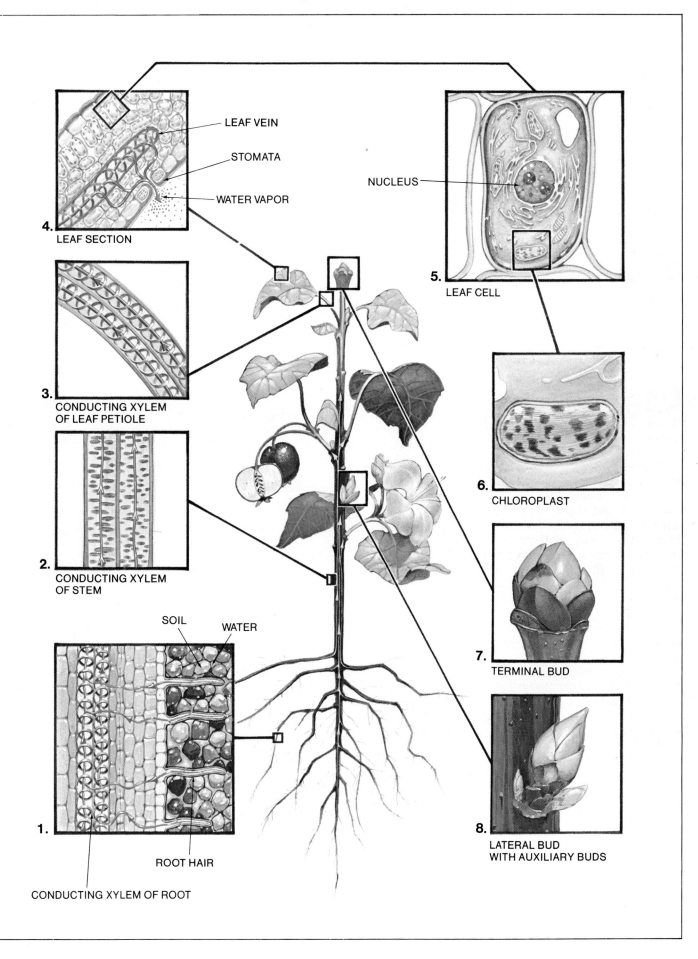

4. LEAF SECTION

LEAF VEIN

STOMATA

WATER VAPOR

5. LEAF CELL

NUCLEUS

3. CONDUCTING XYLEM OF LEAF PETIOLE

6. CHLOROPLAST

2. CONDUCTING XYLEM OF STEM

7. TERMINAL BUD

SOIL   WATER

1.

ROOT HAIR

CONDUCTING XYLEM OF ROOT

8. LATERAL BUD WITH AUXILIARY BUDS

UNDERSTANDING YOUR CLIMATE

Climate affects practically every aspect of gardening. At its gentle best, climate silently guides our gardening. The gradual warming of soil each spring determines when we plant warm-season plants. A bean seed, for example, will surely rot if planted too early when soil is too cold. At other times, climate forces us to take quick action to protect an important plant on a chilly night from an imminent frost. Our climates directly affect planting times and plant care, so it behooves any gardener to understand some climate fundamentals.

There are three basic elements of climate—*temperature, available sunshine* and *water* in the form of precipitation and humidity. The interrelationship of these three elements determines a region's climate throughout the year and what will grow where.

TEMPERATURE

This is the most influential element of climate in determining whether or not a certain type of plant will grow in your garden. Temperature affects all plant processes by controlling the rate of their internal reactions. Especially important are the expected winter minimum temperature in your area and the seasonal average time of first and last frosts.

Generally, growth begins at a certain temperature, then proceeds at a faster and faster rate until an upper limit is reached. When temperatures are either too low or too high, growth slows or stops. There are low and high temperature extremes that destroy plants outright.

The period in which temperatures are conducive to plant growth is called the *growing season*. It is the time between the last frost in spring and the first frost in winter. When the growing season ends, annual flowers and vegetables die and perennial plants begin their dormant period.

Certain *critical* or *cardinal temperatures* have been determined for a number of plants. These temperatures include the minimum, optimum and maximum temperatures for plant growth, as well as minimum and maximum lethal temperatures. As you might imagine, determining all of these temperatures is a complicated process, and they have been worked out for relatively few plants. For instance, most plants have several different sets of critical temperatures for each of their growth stages. Usually, the optimum temperature for seed germination of a plant is lower than the optimum temperature for its vegetative growth. The chart on page 148 shows minimum, optimum and maximum soil temperatures for seed germination of some common vegetables.

Annual vegetables and flowers are classified as either *cool season* or *warm season*. Most cool-season plants need a minimum soil temperature of approximately 40F (4C) to germinate and an equivalent air temperature to

---

Left: Late spring frost can destroy an entire fruit crop by killing blossoms. It can also kill newly emerging seedlings. Understanding your climate will enable you to help protect plants from such events. Polyethylene sheeting shown here is one form of frost protection. Others are described on pages 13-15 and 24-25.

Above: Simple unheated greenhouse can be used to start bedding plants early or protect cold-sensitive container plants. Surrounding hedge keeps greenhouse cool during summer months.

CLIMATE ELEMENTS

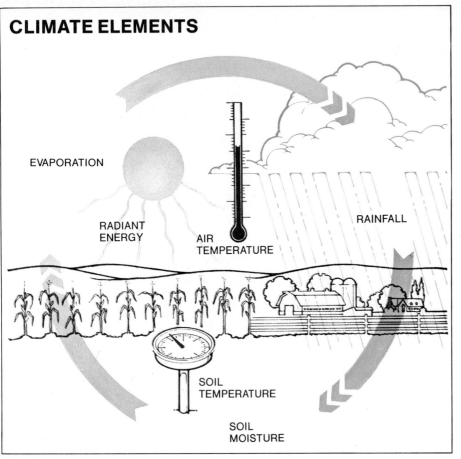

Successful gardening depends on being in tune with constant weather cycles in your area. This drawing illustrates how various weather elements work together to recycle water naturally available to plants. Amount of rainfall and when it occurs, as well as air and soil temperature, determine how much supplemental water must be given to plants.

sustain growth. Warm-season plants require temperatures some 10 degrees higher, or at least 50F (10C), to begin and sustain growth. Most perennial plants native to tropical areas are damaged by temperatures that approach freezing. A pepper plant or African violet is damaged by temperatures that fall much below 40F (4C).

Bolting—This is the premature development of a seed stalk of a biennial herb or vegetable such as celery, parsley or cilantro. Bolting frustrates beginner and expert alike. If you have ever tucked a promising celery transplant into the garden only to watch it rush to seed and die a few weeks later, you know about bolting. In this case, it happens when cool temperatures due to an unseasonably cool spring occur shortly after planting. The plant is conditioned to develop a seed stalk after exposure to the winter following a season of growth. In effect, cool weather after planting replaces winter, the entire growth cycle is compressed and the plant is useless.

Some varieties of lettuce react in an opposite way. While prevailing temperatures are cool, about 50F to 60F (10C to 16C), the edible lettuce "heads" develop. When temperatures are warm, 70F to 80F (21C to 27C), flower stalks develop rapidly at the expense of heads.

There is still more to the bolting story—some plants are triggered into flower development by a change in day length, as described on page 19.

Cold Temperatures—The freezing point of water (32F/0C) is perhaps the most familiar critical temperature. The spring and fall occurrence of this temperature establishes the length of the growing season, the planting time of warm-season annuals and the harvest time of many crops.

Equally significant is the minimum temperature of winter. The ability to adapt to temperatures below freezing varies tremendously among different kinds of plants. This ability is referred to as a plant's *hardiness*. More than any other element of climate, this

determines which plants are perennial and where. The United States Department of Agriculture (USDA) plant hardiness zone map on the facing page shows the average annual minimum temperatures in various parts of the United States and Canada. It is the most common garden climate map currently in use.

Plants are damaged by cold when ice crystals form between cells. This damage occurs due to excessive cold during winter, early-spring or late-fall frosts, or to drought because both soil water and the root system are frozen and cannot absorb water. Plants are also damaged by alternate freezing and thawing of soil (soil heaving) and by the weight of snow or ice breaking branches.

The minimum winter temperature at which a plant is damaged is not a hard and fast thing. Many factors are involved. Plants with adequate nutrient and water supplies are more tolerant of cold than identical plants not so supplied.

Duration of cold is another factor. Some plants may be able to tolerate 25F (4C) for 10 minutes, but not for 1 hour. Likewise, the rate of temperature fall can damage an otherwise cold-hardy plant. Rapidly falling temperatures can cause the bark of trees and shrubs to split apart, sometimes resulting in the death of the plant.

The time of the year cold temperature occurs is also important. If it is very early or late in the season, the plant may be less resistant than if the same or lower temperature occurred in midwinter. Also, plants protected by a mulch or blanket of snow will survive colder winters better than plants that aren't.

Most cold-temperature damage happens in spring. That is when we try to get a jump on the season by setting out tender transplants early, or when seedlings are just emerging from the soil. Also, leaf and flower buds of perennial flowers, vines, shrubs and trees are just beginning to expand. This is the reason crops of early flowering fruit trees, such as apricots, so often fail in late-frost climates where the tree itself is winter-hardy. Spring and fall frosts are most common on clear, still nights when there are no clouds to limit heat loss and no wind to prevent an air inversion.

Frost—There are two basic kinds of

PLANT HARDINESS ZONE MAP

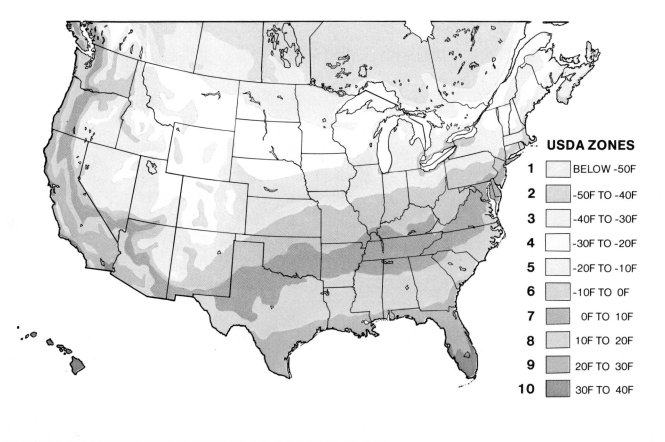

USDA ZONES

1		BELOW -50F
2		-50F TO -40F
3		-40F TO -30F
4		-30F TO -20F
5		-20F TO -10F
6		-10F TO 0F
7		0F TO 10F
8		10F TO 20F
9		20F TO 30F
10		30F TO 40F

UNITED STATES DEPARTMENT OF AGRICULTURE

This map shows average minimum winter temperature in various parts of United States and portions of Canada. Use it as a general guide to determine which perennial plants can be grown in your area. The USDA zone system is often used to indicate cold-hardiness of many perennial plants. For example, if a plant is said to be hardy to Zone 4, it can usually be expected to survive a minimum temperature between -30F to -20F. However, other factors, such as wind, sun, snow and frosts—and when these occur—also determine if a plant will survive the winter in any given location. Also, because North America has a complex climate—microclimates and variations in weather patterns from one year to the next cannot be accurately mapped—use this map as a guide only. You can get more specific information from your local weather service, county or university extension services and local nurseries.

frosts. *Air-mass frost* results from the occurence of a cold air mass with a temperature less than 32F (0C). *Radiation frost* results when plants quickly lose much more heat than they are absorbing until they reach the temperature of 32F (0C). Air-mass frosts are more likely to occur during winter and they threaten primarily half-hardy plants. Radiation frosts occur in fall or spring and threaten plants not yet fully dormant or at early, tender stages of growth.

There are variations within the two main frost types, determined by how frost affects the plant. A *white frost* or *hoarfrost* occurs when dew that has formed on a cooling leaf reaches 32F (0C). If dew does not form before the freezing temperature is reached, it is called a *dryfreeze,* or more appropriately for gardeners, a *black frost,* because there is no visible sign of frost until damaged plant tissues blacken.

A *killing freeze* is the kind that cuts the growing season short. A *hard freeze* is a freeze that kills seasonal vegetation and freezes the ground surface solid. Heavy ice forms on the surfaces of small bodies of water, such as puddles and water containers. A *light freeze* occurs when the surface tem-perature of the air drops to below freezing for a short time so that only the most tender plants are damaged.

Gardeners can do much to reduce the chances of losing plants or crops to cold winters or spring frosts. Where you plant—*site selection*—makes a significant difference. For instance, choose a wind- and overhead-protected location for a plant that is only marginally hardy. Also, south slopes and sandy soils trap more heat faster in spring. You could safely plant a vegetable garden there weeks earlier than you could on a north slope or in clay soil.

Understanding Your Climate **13**

FROST
THERMAL BELTS

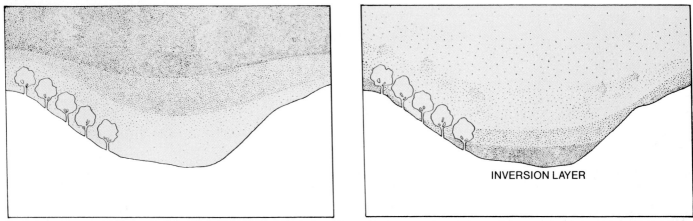

INVERSION LAYER

In the drawings on this page, darker colors represent colder temperatures. Under normal conditions, air temperatures decrease with height, as shown at left. With an *inversion layer,* cold air is trapped below a layer of warm air. This creates warmer-than-usual *thermal belts* on hillsides above low spots. Thermal belts can be ideal planting areas for plants that would normally be damaged by colder air in lower areas.

RADIATION FROST

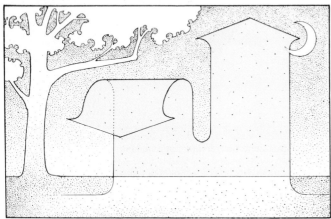

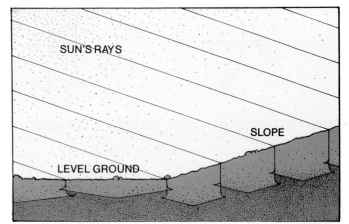

SUN'S RAYS

SLOPE

LEVEL GROUND

Heat from the sun is stored in soil during the day. At night, heat radiates back into the atmosphere. If the soil loses so much heat that it becomes colder than surrounding air, a radiation frost can occur. Objects such as trees, patio roofs or house-roof overhangs can trap radiating heat and often prevent frosts in localized areas.

A south-facing slope receives more of sun's heat than does level ground, so radiation frosts are less likely to occur in this location. Similarly, west-facing slopes receive more sun during afternoon, so soil is warmer just before nightfall.

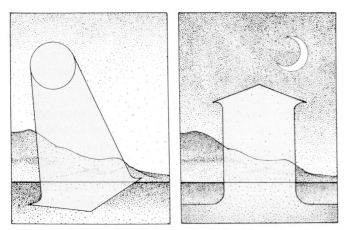

Radiation frosts are most common when night skies are clear and air is still. These conditions allow for maximum radiation of soil warmth back into atmosphere.

Cloudy nighttime skies trap soil heat radiating into atmosphere. Radiation frosts are less likely under these conditions.

Heating lamps or gasoline lanterns situated near the base of a shrub or tree are often enough to protect it from spring frosts. A plastic sheet held above the tree by long poles, by itself or in combination with a heat source, provides protection.

The way you take care of your plants has a great effect on their chances of surviving a cold winter. Raking a loose mulch of peat moss, straw, sawdust, wood shavings or leaves over the crowns of strawberries, roses and perennials will help prevent winter freeze and heaving damage. Heaving is the expansion and contraction of soil caused by alternate freezing and thawing. It damages plants by disturbing roots. In severe cases, smaller plants can be pushed out of the ground.

As previously mentioned, plants well supplied with adequate food and water will be much more cold-hardy than those that are not. Avoid heavy summer pruning and gradually reduce the amount of nitrogen fertilizer and water supplied in fall to slow growth and stimulate accumulation of food.

Innovative gardeners have discovered many methods to protect plants from untimely spring frosts by starting plants earlier, thus gaining a month or so on the growing season. There is more than pride to win from starting early—early crops are more likely to escape pest damage. Plastic sheets or wax paper draped or stretched over frames create mini-greenhouses in the garden. Minimum temperatures under such a tent are commonly warmer by 5F to 8F (-15C to -13C), which is often more than enough to make the difference. Of course, daytime temperatures under a plastic tent may rapidly become too high, so venting is often required.

Wind—This amplifies cold and has a drying effect on soil and plants. Plastic shelters are equally useful for wind protection. Seedlings and transplants will grow into vastly superior plants if protected from prevailing winds. Wood shingles are convenient for this purpose. Many commercial products are also available.

High Temperatures—Most common garden plants essentially stop growing at temperatures above 95F (35C). Among other things, high temperatures determine the quality and maturity rate of fruits and vegetables, and the kinds of pests likely to be a problem.

High temperatures restrict plants in other ways. In warm-winter climates, winters do not provide many deciduous fruit trees with enough cold to complete their physiological rest period. For instance, most peach varieties need between 600 and 900 hours of winter temperatures between 32F and 45F (0C and 7C). Fewer hours of cold result in *delayed foliation,* or weak growth, in spring. Luckily for gardeners in such climates, special *low-chill* varieties of most deciduous fruit trees are

Row cover made from translucent corrugated fiberglass panel protects tomato transplants from frost. Panel allows soil to heat during day, retains heat at night.

Raised bed in greenhouse is convenient for starting large numbers of seedlings or for growing cold-tender plants out of season.

AVERAGE GROWING-SEASON LENGTH

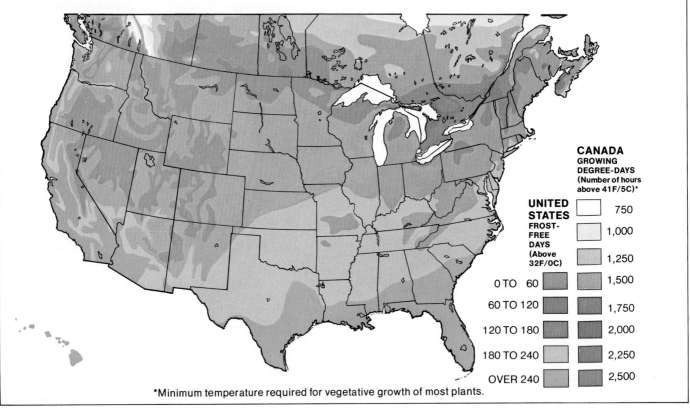

CANADA
GROWING
DEGREE-DAYS
(Number of hours
above 41F/5C)*

750	
1,000	
1,250	
1,500	
1,750	
2,000	
2,250	
2,500	

UNITED STATES
FROST-FREE DAYS
(Above 32F/0C)

0 TO 60	
60 TO 120	
120 TO 180	
180 TO 240	
OVER 240	

*Minimum temperature required for vegetative growth of most plants.

This map shows average number of freeze-free days in various portions of the United States. The freeze-free growing period is between the dates of the last 32F (0C) temperature in spring and the first 32F (0C) temperature in autumn, and is usually referred to as the *growing season*. The Canadian weather service uses a different scale to measure length of growing season: *Annual total growing degree-days above 41F (5C).* The numbers on the map indicate the sum of the number of degrees above 41F (5C) accumulated over the growing season. The higher the number, the longer the growing season.

available. See pages 166 and 167.

Pests are often more abundant when summer and winter temperatures are high. There are two reasons: First, most insects and disease organisms reproduce faster in high temperatures. Second, relatively warm winters allow more pests to survive. A really cold Minnesota winter does gardeners there more good than any pesticide used in summer.

SEASON LENGTH

The number of days between frosts determines the length of the growing season. This is important to know when planning what and how much you can grow. The maps above and at right, *Average Growing-Season Length, Last Spring Frost* and *First Fall Frost* show the variations. Growing seasons are as short as 60 freeze-free days in the coldest climates and as long as 330 or more in the mildest ones. Knowing your season length gives meaning to the information on a packet of bean seeds. When the packet says, "55 days," and your growing season is

200 days long, you can roughly figure three complete crop cycles are possible, providing temperatures remain within a favorable range. If your growing season is only 60 days long, you know you will have to work quickly to plant and harvest one crop.

In northern gardens where growing seasons are usually shortest, the sun shines longer during that time than it does farther south. All other things being equal, beans that require 55 days to mature at middle latitudes will grow faster in northern ones, sometimes needing as few as 45 days to mature. Conversely, frostless regions in middle latitudes are generally coastal areas with cool summers. The same beans there may require 70 days to mature.

SUNSHINE

Gardeners benefit by an understanding of three of the many ways sunlight influences plant growth. They are: *percent possible sunshine, light intensity* and *light duration.*

Percent Possible Sunshine—The sun is the energy source plants use to grow. Percent possible sunshine shows us how much of this basic energy is available in our climate. *Possible sunshine* is the total number of hours of sunlight a location can receive annually in the absence of clouds. *Percent possible sunshine* is the actual amount of sunshine compared to the possible sunshine.

Possible sunshine is figured on the basis of latitude. At the equator, the earth can receive 4,420 hours of sunlight annually; at 25°N, the latitude of the Florida Keys, 4,449 hours; at 49°N, the western U.S.-Canadian border, 4,486 hours. In the continental United States, the longest day—sunrise to sunset—is 16 hours and 13 minutes at 49°N and occurs about June 21. The shortest day, about December 21, occurs at the same latitude and is 8 hours and 13 minutes.

Although northern climates have longer periods of possible sunshine during the growing season, this does

LAST SPRING FROST

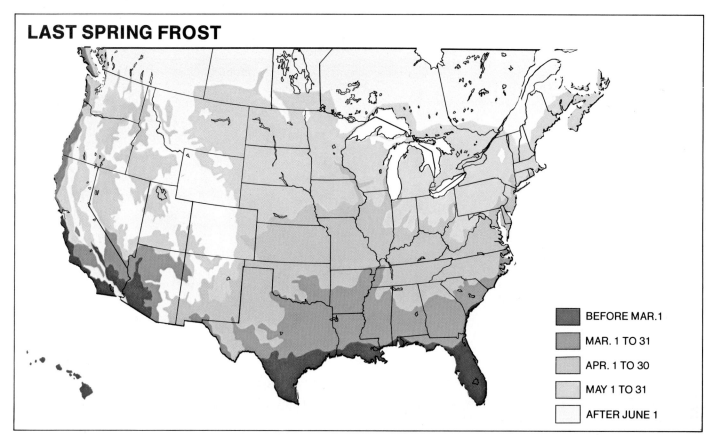

■	BEFORE MAR. 1
■	MAR. 1 TO 31
■	APR. 1 TO 30
□	MAY 1 TO 31
□	AFTER JUNE 1

This map shows average dates of last spring frost in various parts of United States and portions of Canada. Use it in conjunction with local observations to determine safe planting times.

FIRST FALL FROST

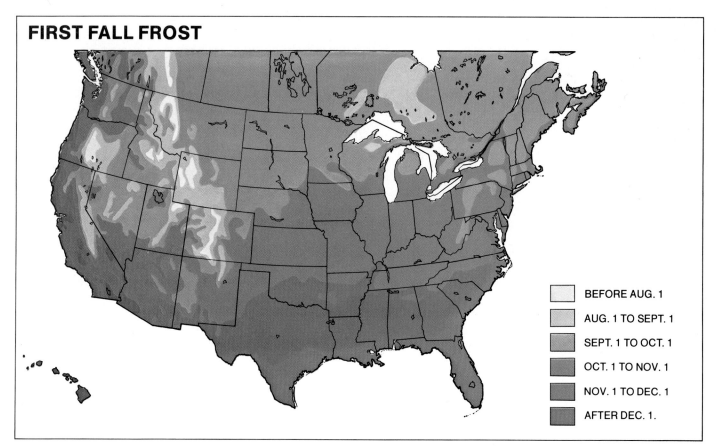

□	BEFORE AUG. 1
■	AUG. 1 TO SEPT. 1
■	SEPT. 1 TO OCT. 1
■	OCT. 1 TO NOV. 1
■	NOV. 1 TO DEC. 1
■	AFTER DEC. 1.

This map shows average dates of first fall frost in various parts of United States and portions of Canada. Use it in conjunction with local observations to determine planting and harvesting times for annual crops. For more precise information, contact local weather service or extension agent.

SUNSHINE

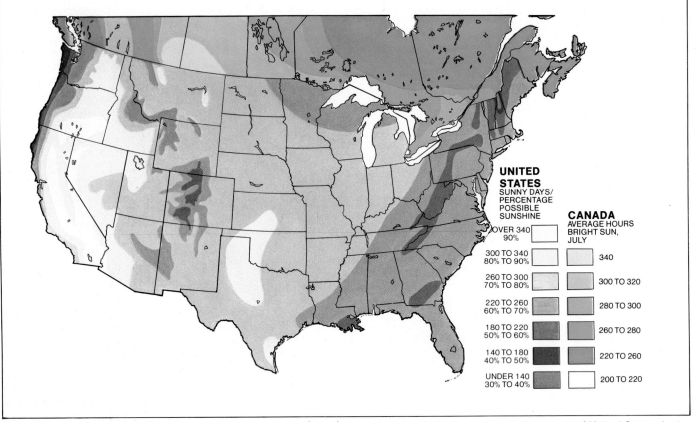

UNITED STATES
SUNNY DAYS/
PERCENTAGE
POSSIBLE
SUNSHINE

OVER 340
90%

300 TO 340
80% TO 90%

260 TO 300
70% TO 80%

220 TO 260
60% TO 70%

180 TO 220
50% TO 60%

140 TO 180
40% TO 50%

UNDER 140
30% TO 40%

CANADA
AVERAGE HOURS
BRIGHT SUN,
JULY

340

300 TO 320

280 TO 300

260 TO 280

220 TO 260

200 TO 220

This map shows average number of sunny days and average (mean) percentage possible sunshine in various parts of United States. It also shows the number of hours of bright sunlight during month of July in portions of Canada.

not necessarily mean all northern regions receive more actual sunshine than southern ones. For example, coastal areas of the Pacific Northwest receive less sunshine than the Southwest desert due to overcast.

The map above shows seven regions of roughly equal sunshine. Most of the United States receives some 300 hours of sunshine a month through summer. It is along the foggy Washington coast that the least summer sun reaches gardens, followed closely by sections of the Appalachians. The greatest monthly hours of sunshine, usually more than 400 hours a month (90% possible sunshine), occur in the San Joaquin and lower Sacramento valleys of California during June, July and August. These valleys are highly productive agricultural areas.

Here is an example of how percent possible sunshine affects plant growth: An early ripening tomato is said to require 45 days between setting out as a transplant and the first ripe fruit. But experiments in western Washington—40% to 50% possible

sunshine—showed such a tomato grown there requires twice as many days to produce fruit. Although this difference in growth rate cannot be entirely attributed to less light—the cool temperatures of western Washington are also a factor—it does prove that the amount of available sunshine has a substantial effect on the growth rate of plants and maturation of crops.

Light Intensity—Light intensity is the actual amount of light falling on a surface at any given time. Naturally, this is quite variable. Intensity varies with seasons, latitude, overcast, pollution, and shade cast by trees or buildings. One measurement of light intensity is in units called *footcandles*. A footcandle (F.C.) is defined as the density of light striking the inner surface of a sphere with all surface area 1 foot away from a standardized, 1-candle-power light source. A clear, desert day at noon may measure 12,000 F.C. while at the same moment in western Washington, light intensity measures 1,500 F.C. Light intensity in a typical, well-lighted

home will measure between 50 and 300 F.C.

There is tremendous variation in the ability of different plants to utilize light. Many of our house plants evolved in heavily shaded jungle environments, which is why they can tolerate the low light levels of a house interior. There are also a number of outdoor plants that can tolerate low light levels. A list of shade-tolerant annuals appears on page 202. Also refer to the plant lists starting on page 198 for sun/shade requirements.

Individual leaves of most plants can utilize only about 1,200 F.C. of light. But because of the way leaves are arranged on the plant to shade each other, most outdoor plants respond to a maximum of about 4,000 F.C.

Plants respond in several ways when light intensity is too low. Perhaps the first thing you will notice is they appear stretched out, with fewer, thinner leaves spaced farther apart. Seedlings grown in low light are yellowish-looking, with spindly stems and long internodes, a condition

SEASONS OF THE YEAR

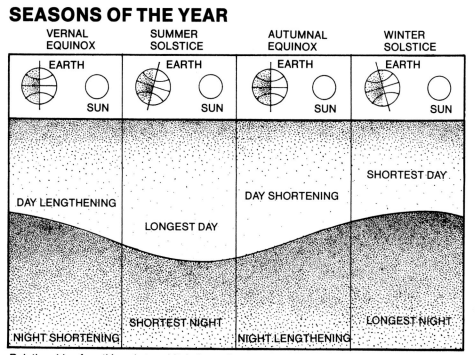

	VERNAL EQUINOX	SUMMER SOLSTICE	AUTUMNAL EQUINOX	WINTER SOLSTICE

DAY LENGTHENING — LONGEST DAY — DAY SHORTENING — SHORTEST DAY

NIGHT SHORTENING — SHORTEST NIGHT — NIGHT LENGTHENING — LONGEST NIGHT

Relationship of earth's axis to orbital plane of sun causes change in seasons and variation in day length. These changes set planting and harvesting timetables for many plants, including most vegetables.

known as *etiolation*. Leaves of plants grown in low light are not only thinner, but more succulent and darker green. Most plants situated in low light will grow slowly at best. A longer duration of exposure to light helps compensate for low light intensity.

Adjust plants slowly from one condition of light to another. A house plant such as weeping fig *(Ficus benjamina)* can adapt to either low or high levels of light. But make the shift incremental, gradually increasing or decreasing the amount of light. Leaves adapted to low light will burn if the plant is abruptly moved into strong light. Leaves adapted to high light will fall off if abruptly moved to shade—shocking the gardener as well as the plant—to be replaced with low-light leaves.

Light Duration—Duration of light, or number of daylight hours, is the guide many plants use to coordinate themselves with the seasons. The processes of flowering, bulbing, forming tubers and other shifts in plant efforts are linked to this reliable clock. The response of a plant to a particular day length (daylight hours) is called *photoperiodism*.

Chrysanthemums and poinsettias are well-known plants with specific responses to day length. They are called *short-day* plants. This means they respond to a day length shorter than a certain maximum. The shorter days of fall trigger blooming. Growers can speed blooming by covering plants to shorten their day length, or delay blooming by exposing them to artificial light to increase their day length. For details, see *How to Rebloom a Poinsettia* at right.

Spinach and onions are good examples of *long-day* plants. Spinach begins to develop a flower stalk when exposed to relatively long days. High temperatures also stimulate spinach flowering at the expense of edible leaves. When days are a certain length, spinach will flower no matter what size the plant is. Gardeners who plant spinach in late spring are much less likely to harvest a crop than those who plant when days are short in early spring or in fall.

Onions form bulbs when days are longer than a certain minimum number of hours. There are specific varieties of onions for northern and southern climates. For instance, Bermuda onions grow during the

winter in the South and begin bulbing when days reach approximately 11 hours long. They are ready to harvest in early summer. In the North, onions cannot be planted until spring. By that time, days are already long enough for the southern onion to bulb. Northern onion varieties bulb when days reach 15 hours or more in length, approximately mid-June. They are ready to harvest in fall.

Day neutral plants are not affected by day length. These are usually tropical plants accustomed to relatively unchanging day length. African violet is an example.

WATER

Water, in the form of precipitation (rainfall) and humidity, is the third critical element of climate. Usually, there is either too much or too little of it.

Water is essential to plants in more than one way. As mentioned on page 7, water is an essential plant nutrient, contributing hydrogen, which is essential to the process of photosynthesis. Water is also a solvent and carrier of the sugars manufactured in plant leaves and of mineral nutrients from the soil. And not least of all, the water that plants consume works like an air conditioner to cool the plant.

HOW TO REBLOOM A POINSETTIA

Most people treat poinsettias as annual plants, disposing of them after they bloom. They are, in fact, tender perennials that will bloom year after year under the right conditions.

After Christmas, keep the plant near a sunny window to maintain best possible growth. Water and fertilize as you would any house plant. As soon as temperatures permit, move plant outdoors, gradually adjusting it to full sun.

Begin rebloom in early November by keeping the plant in a room where only natural daylight enters. Do not expose plant to artificial light at night because as little as a few minutes of interrupted darkness will delay the flowering process. It is also possible to induce flowering by covering the entire plant at sunset with a lightproof box, then removing the box at sunrise. Any special treatment can be stopped as soon as the flower bracts show color.

RAINFALL

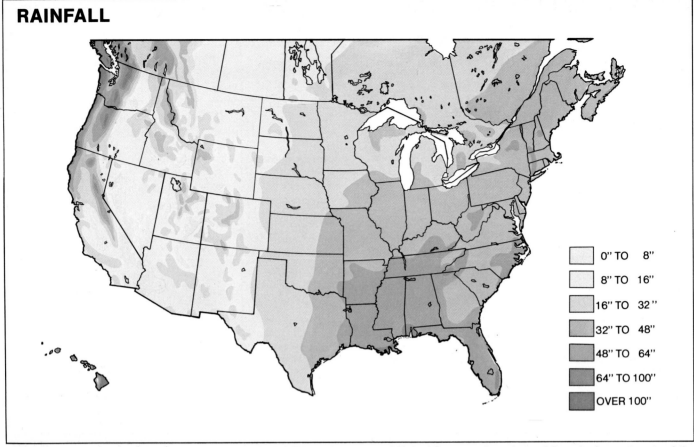

This map shows average (mean) annual amount of rainfall in various parts of United States and portions of Canada. In most parts of the country, rainfall contributes relatively little water to garden plants during growing season. However, it does have a great influence on kinds of plants you can grow in your area, as described in text below.

Gardeners must work with the amount of water naturally available from rain and the particular requirements of the plants they wish to grow. In most areas, the water provided by rainfall during the growing season is not enough to support most garden plants, so supplemental water is needed. In a few areas of the country, however, rainfall provides *too much* water for many kinds of plants. See the rainfall map above.

When rain comes is also important. An untimely rain can damage certain plants and crops. Rainfall and the high humidity that usually accompanies it are associated with several plant diseases. Scab disease of apples and crabapples is virtually unknown where the growing season is dry, but is a fact of life where it is wet. The rose disease known as *black spot* and the potato disease known as *potato blight* are similarly stimulated by moisture. Nearly ripe, high-sugar fruits such as cherries and tomatoes often crack after a rain. Rainfall patterns differ throughout the country,

some regions receiving most of their rain in summer, others in winter. These kinds of distinctions are discussed in the following text on ecosystems.

Water requirements and watering techniques are discussed on pages 67-70.

ECOSYSTEMS

So far, we have discussed individually the three major elements of climate—temperature, sunlight and rainfall. Now let's look at how *all three* factors of climate come together in an area to produce a particular climate region, or *ecosystem*. The plant and animal life of a certain region can tell us much about the climate.

Temperature is not the only factor that determines whether or not a plant will survive in a given area. A few examples comparing the southeastern and southwestern United States demonstrate this point. You'll note on the USDA zone map on page 13 that much of southern Louisiana, Mississippi and Alabama is in USDA

Zone 9, the same zone as much of California and southeastern Arizona. Most garden reference books include a USDA rating for plants, encouraging the misconception that a Zone-9 plant will grow anywhere that zone occurs. But the rating means the plant is only cold-hardy in that zone, not that it can be successfully grown in all parts of it. The plant may be completely unreliable in one part or another due to a myriad of other factors—distribution of rainfall, available sunlight, soil characteristics, regional pest problems and so on.

One example is the junipers. They are fully hardy to the expected minimum temperatures of Zone 9 but are prone to root rot when exposed to the heavy summer rainfall of the Southeast. Another example is English holly. Like many other hollies, it thrives in the Southeast but suffers and rarely lives long in the same Zone 9 of the Southwest.

The United States and southern Canada include three major types of ecosystems—forest, grassland and

ECOSYSTEMS

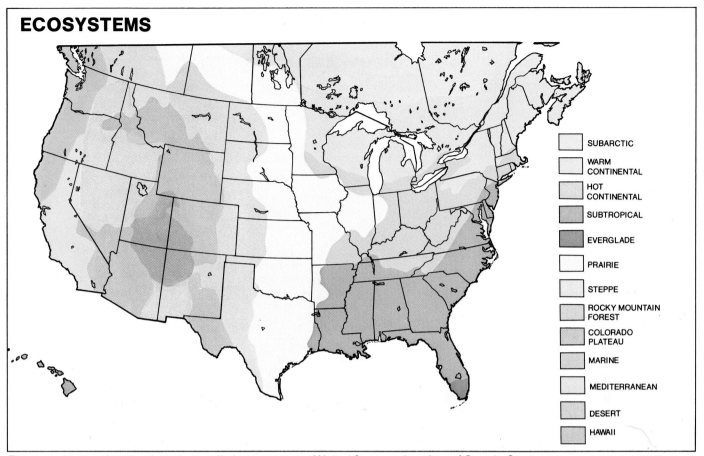

This map shows major climatic regions, called *ecosystems,* of United States and portions of Canada. Smaller ecosystems exist within these, depending on altitude, terrain, soil and climatic conditions. Observing natural vegetation in your ecosystem will give you a clue to kinds of garden plants that will do well where you live.

LEGEND: SUBARCTIC · WARM CONTINENTAL · HOT CONTINENTAL · SUBTROPICAL · EVERGLADE · PRAIRIE · STEPPE · ROCKY MOUNTAIN FOREST · COLORADO PLATEAU · MARINE · MEDITERRANEAN · DESERT · HAWAII

desert. There are subcategories of each, which appear on the map above and are described here:

Warm Continental—The climate here is generally noted by its warm, humid summers. There are 4 to 8 months of temperatures that exceed 50F (10C). There is no dry season, although most rainfall comes in summer. The natural vegetation is forest, primarily hemlock and several types of conifers that include red and white pine, spruce and fir. Deciduous trees include birches, beech, maple, basswood and the oaks. Soils tend to lack calcium, potassium and magnesium, and they are generally acid.

Hot Continental—The climate here is characteristically humid with hot summers. In the warmer regions, the frost-free growing season is 5 to 6 months long. In colder regions, growing seasons are 3 to 5 months long. In the northern portions, the dominant vegetation is forest. Trees include oaks, hickories, beech, maples, ashes, basswoods, black locust, yellow poplar and walnut. Soils are usually rich with humus.

Subtropical—Winters here are never really cold, and hot summers are humid. Rainfall comes any time of year but mostly in summer. Thunderstorms are common and hurricanes occur. Soils tend to be wet, acidic, and low in major plant nutrients. The Southeastern forest is a mix of conifers and hardwoods. It includes many kinds of pine, red cedar, gums, oaks, hickories and bald cypress.

Everglades—This is a tropical climate with most rainfall occurring during summer. The average annual temperature is approximately 73F (23C). Cypress forests are extensive and mangrove is widespread along the eastern and southern coasts. Mahogany, redbay and palmettos are found growing on *hammocks*—areas raised above surrounding, wetter land.

Prairie—The prairie is a vast, largely treeless area, variable in temperature and generally low in rainfall. The part bordering the eastern forests was once covered with tall grasses, but is now planted with corn and other crops.

Most of the 20 to 40 inches of rainfall that comes to the prairie occurs in the early part of the growing season, the reason trees are rare except in valleys and other land depressions. Soils are among the most productive of any. Wind erosion is a potential problem.

Steppe—Winters are cold and dry and summers warm to hot. The frost-free growing season ranges between 100 days in the north to more than 200 days in Texas. Summertime evaporation exceeds rainfall. Vegetation is shortgrass prairie—now planted with wheat—and semidesert. Soils tend to be salty and low in humus.

Rocky Mountain Forest—Climate is similar to semiarid steppe. Most rainfall is in winter and much of that comes as snow. Engelmann spruce grow at the upper elevations. Ponderosa pine and Douglas fir dominate at medium elevations, aspen or lodgepole pine at lower ones.

Colorado Plateau—The climate is characterized by cold winters. Summer days are usually hot, but nights are cool. Rainfall ranges between 10 and 20 inches each year, mostly in winter but occasionally with summer thundershowers. Sagebrush is abundant as are several kinds of cacti and yucca. Annual and perennial flowers appear during the summer rainy periods. Cottonwood trees grow along streams. At higher elevations, there is pinon pine, juniper, ponderosa pine, lodgepole pine and aspen.

Desert—These are areas of extreme drought coupled with extremely high air and soil temperatures. Temperature variation between day and night is also extreme. Average annual rainfall is 4 to 8 inches. Various kinds of cacti grow in some areas, as do trees such as palo verde, ironwood, mesquite and smoke trees. Shrubs include creosote bush, saltbush and desert broom. Other areas are comprised of shifting sand dunes and support no plants. Soils are low in humus and tend to be salty and generally alkaline. Deposits of calcium carbonate (caliche) are common.

Mediterranean—This is the transition zone between the dry West Coast desert and the wet, northern West Coast. The climate is characterized by cool, wet winters and hot, dry summers. Occurrence of a wet winter followed by a dry summer produces a distinctive natural vegetation of hard-leaved evergreen trees and shrubs able to withstand 2 to 4 months of drought and high temperatures. Typical trees are California live oak, tanbark oak, bay laurel and madrone. Chamise, toyon and manzanita are typical shrubs.

Marine—The climate here is temperate, rainy and humid with frequent cloud cover. Summers are relatively cool and winters are mild. Rainfall is abundant throughout the year but primarily in winter. The natural vegetation is conifer forests. Here you'll find magnificent stands of Douglas fir, red cedar and spruce. Western hemlock and Sitka spruce populate the Olympic National Forest. Grand fir, silver fir and Alaska cedar occur. Coast redwoods dominate the fog belt along the coast of northwestern California—a few of these are over 300 feet tall.

Hawaii—The climate is tropical, and due to the surrounding ocean and persistent northeast trade winds, virtually unchanging. The average January temperature is about 70F (21C)—in July it is slightly warmer. Rainfall varies between 20 and 200 inches a

PHENOLOGY

Phenology is a little known branch of climate and weather observation. The word is pronounced *fen-ALL-o-gee*, and is derived from the Greek word *phaino*, which means to show or appear. The idea is simple enough: Use events such as the flowering of particularly reliable plants as *indicators* of a season's progress. For instance, yellow-flowering forsythia *(Forsythia intermedia)* is a good indicator of the arrival of early spring, and common lilac *(Syringa vulgaris)*, of spring.

These phenological observations have some practical advantages over typical weather service records, and in any case, are a useful supplement. For example, the location of the station that records local weather records has a slightly different climate than your own backyard. The difference may not be much—a few degrees of temperature one way or another, or slightly more or less rainfall. But these small differences can be significant when determining when to do certain garden activities, such as spring planting. Perhaps more important, a signal event—once we know what to look for—in our own yard confirms seasonal changes in a more immediate, personal way. "Plant your beans when the elm leaves are as big as a penny," the oldtimers say.

Unfortunately, there is not much published on the subject of phenology. One source is the book *Phenology and Seasonality Modeling* by Helmut Leith, published by Springer-Verlag, New York, NY. If phenology interests you, begin keeping track of events in your own yard so you can gradually build your own record. Also, you need other gardeners to correlate your information with. A garden club could adapt phenology as a project.

In a sense, phenology is to meteorology what herbal remedies are to modern medicine—most of the information you're likely to find is in folklore. The following rhymes and sayings are examples:

January
A summerish January, a winterish spring
January warm, the Lord have mercy! (1)

February
When gnats dance in February,
The husbandman becomes a beggar. (1)

March
The first day of spring is one thing, and the first spring day is another. The difference between them is sometimes as great as a month. (2)

April
If it thunders on All Fool's Day
It brings good crops of corn and hay. (1)

May
A wet May
Makes a big load of hay.
A cold May is kindly
And fills the barn finely.
Let all thy joys be as the month of May. (1)

June
A cold and wet June spoils the rest of the year. (1)

July
In this month is St. Swithin's Day,
On which if that it rain they say,
Full forty days after it will
More or less some rain distill. (3)

August
August? Beware of hurricanes you must. (4)

September
By all these lovely tokens
September days are here,
With the summer's best of weather
And autumn's best of cheer. (5)

October
October gave a party;
The leaves by hundreds came:
The ashes, oaks and maples,
And those of every name. (6)

November
If All Saints' Day (Nov. 1) will bring out winter, St. Matin's Day (Nov. 11) will bring out Indian summer. (1)

December
Barnaby bright, Barnaby bright,
The longest day and the shortest night;
Lucy light, Lucy light,
The shortest day and the longest night. (4)
(Barnabas' Day is the summer solstice, St. Lucy's
Day is the winter solstice.)

1. Old English proverbs from Richard Inwards, *Weather Lore*, 1898.
2. Henry Van Dyke, *Fisherman's Luck*.
3. *Poor Robin's Almanac*, 1967.
4. Unknown origin.
5. "September" by Helen Hunt Jackson.
6. George Cooper, "October Party."

year, being heaviest on the northeast, windward side of the islands and lightest on the southwest, leeward slopes.

Subarctic—Extremely low winter temperatures prohibit the growth of most traditional garden plants unless grown in a heated greenhouse. There are few gardeners living in these regions.

ALTERING CLIMATE

Most of us live where the climate is pleasant in some respects and uncomfortable in others. Perhaps you live where it is too windy, too dry, too humid, too cool or too hot. In your house you can rely on a heater, air-conditioner or other device to maintain comfort. But you can also modify the climate outside the house.

Microclimates—These occur in small areas affected by changes in terrain or by large physical objects such as buildings or trees. Such changes or objects cause the climate immediately around them to be slightly different from the overall climate of an area. For example, a planting bed beneath a white, south-facing wall will be warmer than the surrounding garden.

Consider existing microclimates in your yard and how you can take advantage of them. You may be able to grow plants that otherwise might not do well in your area. Or, you can create microclimates to suit the kinds of plants you want to grow. Plants themselves can be used to create microclimates, such as using a tall hedge to deflect wind, or a large tree for shade.

Here are some ways to use landscape structures and plantings to create desirable microclimates around your house.

In cool-summer areas, such as near the seacoast, you can increase the warmth around your house by utilizing stone, brick or some similar material for outdoor paving. Compared to wood decking or bare soil, these materials absorb more heat during the day and hold it longer into the night. Similarly, a heavy stone or block wall can be situated where it can absorb the maximum amount of afternoon sun.

Where chilly winds are a problem, plant a windbreak of dense-growing shrubs or low trees, situated to divert the wind. If you would like more breeze or more air circulation, prune trees and shrubs to allow more air movement through them, perhaps installing sprinklers near the shrubbery to take full advantage of evaporative cooling. Regarding this entire subject, refer to HPBooks' *Hedges, Screens and Espaliers* by Susan Chamberlin. It includes many more ideas.

For outdoor cooling, few structural devices are superior to a 40-foot shade tree. If you already have such a tree, you can design your outdoor living area to take best advantage of it. If your property doesn't have a substantial shade tree in the right location, consider planting a fast-growing tree with a broad, dense canopy. Deciduous trees planted on the south or west side of the house will shade it during summer, yet allow maximum sunlight to enter during the cold season. Refer to the tree charts on pages 214-217, and ask local nursery personnel which shade trees are best adapted to your climate. Lawns, ground covers and any shade-giving structures also help cool outdoor areas.

Tall hedges and trees are one of best methods for creating microclimates within a yard. Here, hedges and trees create protected area for swimmers, offering shade, wind control and privacy.

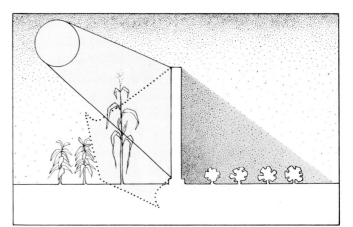

Exposure is an important aspect of selecting a planting site. Light-colored, south-facing walls reflect heat and light on soil and plants nearby. North-facing exposures receive more cooling shade. East-facing exposures are generally cooler than west-facing exposures because they receive shade during the hottest part of the day.

HELPING PLANTS THROUGH CLIMATE EXTREMES

As is usually true with anything that causes trouble in life, damage to plants from climate extremes can usually be traced to a combination of factors rather than just one influence.

Cold—Winter damage in cold northern or high-elevation climates is often caused by a combination of one or several of the following factors—wind, low temperatures, lack of soil moisture and sunlight. On a sunny or windy winter day, many evergreen plants will lose moisture through their foliage. If the ground is frozen, roots will not be able to replace the water lost. This condition is known as *physiological drought*—there's plenty of water in the ground but the plant's roots can't absorb it. Leaves, twigs and even entire branches can become desiccated and die.

Frost cracks or splits in bark occur when the west or south side of a tree trunk is warmed by winter sun. Cells on the exposed side of the tree are tricked into becoming less hardy. When the sun goes down and temperatures drop, these cells are killed and the bark cracks or splits. If severe enough, such damage can kill all the above-ground parts of a tree.

To avoid winter injury, make sure there is ample soil moisture available to plants before the ground freezes in fall. Spraying plants with anti-transpirants can also be effective in preventing winter damage. To minimize frost cracks and bark splits, paint trunks with white latex paint to help reflect warm sunlight. Light-colored tree wraps also help. With any type of winter damage, whether from frost or desiccation, wait until new growth has begun in spring before you prune out dead wood. The extent of actual damage will be more apparent at that time.

Heat—In hot, dry areas such as the deserts of California and Arizona, climate factors and growing conditions combine to pose threats similar to winter cold. High temperatures and strong winds dry out plants regardless of how much water is available in the soil. Intense light can heat bark, foliage and fruit to lethal levels. Bleached-out foliage, damaged fruit and cracked bark are common in these areas.

The first step in avoiding these problems is to choose plants well adapted to hot climates. Also, select planting locations carefully. A spot sheltered from strong winds and the hottest afternoon sun is often the key to success with less-tolerant plants.

Painting tree trunks and branches with white latex paint will help prevent sunburn. This protection is particularly important with newly planted or recently pruned trees.

Container Plants—Plants growing in containers are particularly susceptible to climate extremes. Plant roots are usually less hardy than the branches and foliage. Luckily, open soil provides the perfect insulation from the coldest temperatures. Container plants have both the roots and tops exposed and are often killed at temperatures that will not harm the same plant grown in open soil. One of the easiest way to protect container plants in winter is to group them together and cover the pots with a thick mulch. Individual plants can be tipped on their side and covered with mulch.

Plants grown in porous clay pots are highly susceptible to drying out because of the increased evaporation through the sides of the container. Small clay pots may need watering more than once a day in hot, windy weather.

Containers made of dark materials, such as black plastic, can get so hot on sunny days that they can actually kill roots growing inside. Nurseries often group dark colored containers together so they shade each other. Placing a small pot inside a larger one also works. Conversely, dark-colored pots keep roots warmer in winter, and may speed seed germination in early spring.

Painting tree trunk with white interior latex paint protects trunk from sunburn during summer and frost cracks during winter.

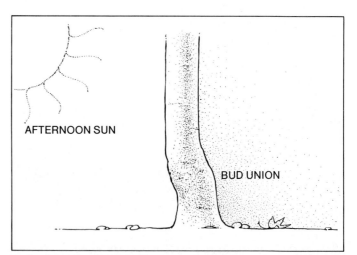

AFTERNOON SUN

BUD UNION

Bud union on young trees is more sensitive to sunburn than trunk. Plant so bud union faces away from hot afternoon sun.

COLD-PROTECTION DEVICES

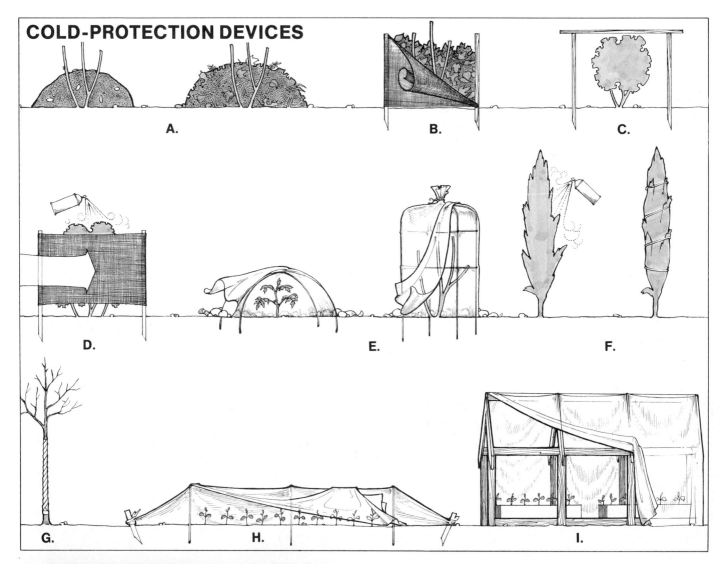

A.   B.   C.   D.   E.   F.   G.   H.   I.

Here are some methods of protecting plants against cold winter temperatures and late spring frosts:

A. Layer of mulch acts as insulation from coldest air temperatures. Exposed branches may be damaged but roots and buds below mulch will grow the following spring.

B. Wooden frame surrounded by burlap or cloth permits a deeper mulch to protect taller plants.

C. Covered frame traps heat radiating from soil and provides frost protection.

D. Winter winds desiccate plants, increasing chance of cold damage. Windbreaks and anti-transpirants are effective protective measures.

E. Wire frames covered with clear plastic can prevent frost damage to small or large plants and help you get an early start in areas with short growing seasons. The covers also act as mini-greenhouses, trapping heat and speeding growth.

F. Strong winds can increase chances of winter damage. Use anti-transpirants and secure loose branches of evergreens to minimize damage.

G. Wrap trunks of young trees with burlap or commercially available tree wraps to prevent bark cracking and winter damage.

H. A temporary row cover of wire hoops covered with clear plastic is used to protect newly emerging seedlings from late spring frosts.

I. Simple unheated greenhouse with clear-plastic cover is used to start large numbers of seedlings or provide frost protection for outdoor container plants.

Wood shingles make good shading devices for individual plants. Cool-season crops such as lettuce are particularly sensitive to hot sun.

PLANNING & NURSERY SHOPPING

This is old advice but it's still true—start with a plan and your gardening will be more effective. Planning will save time, effort and money, and result in a much more productive, more beautiful garden or landscape.

It's easy to buy plants on impulse, but if you rely on impulse alone, you may end up with no more than a collection of interesting plants that neither grow well nor look good in your garden.

Plants should fit both in terms of space and environment. The site may be too sunny or shady, or the soil may be too boggy or parched. These are important horticultural factors that determine which plants you choose. But you can modify the garden to some extent if you take the time to

study the conditions in your yard and what you can do to modify them.

Here are some examples: If you have a windy area where few plants grow, shelter it with a windbreak. If you are planting a tree, position it so that you can use its shade, not suffer from it. If you have a barren slope, cover it with an erosion-preventing ground cover. The chapters, Understanding Your Climate (pages 11-25) and Soils, Fertilizers & Water (pages 55-71), provide specific information on modifying the outdoor environment to grow a wider range of plants.

Nurseries are organized to help you find the plants you need. A typical nursery is illustrated on page 37. It is not necessary to arrive knowing exactly what plants you will buy. You can safely select as you go *if* you have

made a quick survey of your garden, noting the general kinds of plants you need—either in a list or on a rough sketch of the garden. Then choose plants that fit your general needs.

PLANNING YOUR GARDEN

Concentrate on the major elements first and keep the plan simple. Some of the most beautiful gardens are a simple combination of a few trees, one or two ground covers or a lawn, and a screen or hedge of a single type of evergreen shrub to make a private spot. After these essentials, you can begin to elaborate with the special plants you enjoy—a fragrant jasmine, a border of flowers or herbs, an espaliered fruit tree or another of your favorites.

Before you start, take a close look at

Left: This beautiful, mature landscape is result of careful planning and continuing care. A well-planned landscape is not only a pleasure to behold but much easier to maintain.

Above: Many beautiful gardens, such as this one, contain only a few different kinds of plants. The secret is knowing how to use plants effectively to create desired effect. Sloping lots allow many design opportunities. Here, golden arborvitae is framed by two different varieties of juniper.

Azaleas are intermingled with evergreen shrubs and ground covers to create well-balanced, informal landscape.

the plants growing in your neighborhood. Plants that grow well in a neighbor's yard may also work for you.

On the following pages, you'll find a series of self-contained features that will help you plan your garden. Each covers an important aspect of garden and landscape planning. Also included are two examples of well-planned landscapes, designed by professional landscapers, that you can use as sources for ideas.

If you plan on doing any major landscape work, you may want to employ professional help—a landscape architect, designer or contractor—in planning and installing your landscape.

Using Landscape Professionals—If you are undertaking a fairly large or complex landscape project, you may want to use various landscape professionals to assist you.

Landscape architects, designers and contractors are trained in the art of creating appealing and useful outdoor spaces. Each has a different area of expertise. Landscape architects and designers work in offices and make plans on paper—either as sketches or as blueprints—that give shape to possible gardens. Landscape contrac-

tors do the installation work required to carry out the plans of the architect or designer.

In addition, landscape architects are usually trained and have state certification to reshape the ground surface. This includes designing structurally sound retaining walls and devising surface and subsurface drainage systems. They also prepare contract specifications—a guarantee that all contractors bidding the job are bidding to the same standards—and oversee construction.

Landscape designers may only be concerned with planting design and site furnishing. Some landscape contractors offer a design service but most specialize in installations. There are also horticultural specialists who understand the particular needs of plants growing in a garden setting and can offer advice on plant selection.

The best way to choose a landscape professional is to find one whose work you have seen and liked. Like artists, many have a distinctive style that is reflected in their work. Some specialize is specific kinds of landscapes, such as natural, formal, contemporary, low maintenance or Oriental.

Laws vary from state to state but usually only landscape architects and contractors are licensed. A license ensures that the professional has met certain standards and is responsible to a state board should disputes arise. Landscape designers are usually not licensed, but this is not necessarily a reflection on the quality of their work. As with all landscape professionals, some do better work than others.

There are several ways you can use landscape architects and designers. You can give them full responsibility for the entire job—drawing up plans, getting permits, hiring contractors and providing follow-up services. This requires the least amount of time and effort on your part, but it can also be the most expensive way to go, at least initially. A well-designed and expertly installed landscape can often save you much time, effort and money over the years to come.

Another approach is to hire an architect or designer to design the landscape and provide finished drawings for a flat fee, then do some or all of the installation yourself. Or, if you just want some professional advice, there are many landscape architects or designers that will work with you on a consultation basis for an hourly fee.

Any agreements with architects, designers and contractors should be spelled out in a written contract. The contract should include cost, terms of payment and the date on which work is to be completed. Installation work should also include a written contract that states minimum standards for the job. These standards should be similar to the specifications a landscape architect provides, which cover lumber grades, plant material and other quality controls.

Installing It Yourself—Landscape installations consist of a number of tasks that must be accomplished in sequence. Obviously, irrigation systems are installed before the lawn is seeded. The virtues of having planting holes ready before delivery of large trees is less apparent. It is more efficient to move large trees from truck directly to hole, but only if you can provide easy access for the truck.

Allow for the unexpected, especially when the job is complex. Weather conditions and cleanup time are often overlooked. Allow more time for each phase than you think the job will actually take.

PLANNING A GARDEN

Whether you make a scale drawing of your entire landscape or simply jot down notes and ideas in a notebook, you should start with a plan for your garden or landscape. You can make your plan as complex and complete as you want, but it's usually best to keep the initial plan simple—major plantings, landscape structures, traffic paths and so on.

The first step is to consider these three basic elements:

1. Horticulture—How plants will grow in the conditions of your garden.

2. Function—The role plants perform in shaping your garden's structure.

3. Aesthetics—The subtle qualities that add interest and excitement to the garden.

SITE ANALYSIS

Start by making a quick analysis of the site. Whether you're starting with a bare yard or improving an existing landscape, this will help you successfully fit the various landscape elements into the overall picture. To make the analysis:

● Determine the sunny and shady locations, including the north, south, east and west walls of your house. Do you need more or less shade? Also check under trees and by tall hedges, screens or fences to find additional gardening space.

● Check natural slope and drainage pattern and find where water collects.

● Examine soil. Check its ability to retain or drain water. Test for pH. For more on pH, see page 60.

● Study prevailing winds so you can plan wind protection and encourage desirable breezes.

● Think about pathways you'll need—for instance, how to get the lawn mower from the garage in front to the lawn in back.

● Study existing plants you might be able to utilize in a new or revitalized landscape, either in their present location or by transplanting.

PLANNING TIPS

Consider the following when making your plan:

Plant Function—Plan for function of plants. Where do you need windbreaks? Privacy? If you include space for various outdoor activities, will you need hedges or screens for privacy or to define spaces?

Sun and Shade—Plan for solar penetration or protection. Where do you need sun or shade and at what times of the year? Deciduous trees provide summer shade and allow sun penetration during winter. Evergreens provide consistent, year-round shade. Locate trees and shrubs away from areas where shade is not wanted at a distance equal to twice their mature height.

Visual Impact—Plan for visual points of view—what the garden will look like through favorite windows or from outdoor-seating areas.

Multipurpose Plants—To get the most from your garden, use plants that serve more than one purpose. For instance, use a fruit or nut tree for a shade tree. Many perennial herbs can double as attractive borders or ground covers. Annual herbs can be mixed with flowers or vegetables in annual beds.

Low Maintenance—Plan the garden for the amount of time and effort you'll have to maintain it. Lawns usually require the most maintenance. If you want a lawn, plan for the minimum size needed, or reduce the size of your existing lawn. Install a flush concrete mowing strip around the lawn's perimeter to reduce edging chores. Ground covers, including mulch, gravel or paving, can substitute for lawn areas.

To reduce pruning chores, select slow-growing plants for formal, clipped hedges, or plant an informal hedge, allowing adequate space for growth. Use narrow, upright shrubs or trees where space is limited.

If masses of showy annuals are a chore, use flowering ground covers, shrubs or perennials for color. Use annual flowers as colorful accent plants, not as the foundation of the garden. Flowering annuals and perennials can be grown in containers and moved into showcase position during the blooming season.

To reduce watering chores, select drought-tolerant plants. Group all plants with high water requirements in a confined area with maximum visual impact.

Plant Size—Fit plants to the space available. Consider mature size of plants when planning space and making selections. How high? How wide? How fast the growth? Many people often buy more plants than they need or crowd plants too close together because young nursery plants look so tiny.

Decide where you could use some trees or shrubs, then jot down how much space you have for each. If planning a hedge, screen or windbreak, jot down how long the line should be so you can determine how many plants will be needed. For edging plants bordering a path, jot down how long the path is. Multiply by two if the path will be bordered on both sides. Allow adequate space so plants won't cover the path as they grow. For lawns and ground covers, measure the dimensions of the spaces to be filled. Figure lawn areas in square feet.

Plan for mature size when selecting and placing plants. A common mistake is to overplant for instant effect. This is especially easy to do when looking at tiny, immature plants at the nursery.

LANDSCAPE USES FOR PLANTS

There are many practical as well as esthetic uses for plants in the landscape. These two pages illustrate some of them. First consider problem areas in the yard—windy or hot areas, unsightly views beyond the property, lack of privacy, unused spaces, poor traffic circulation and so forth. Then decide what kinds of plants can be used to solve these problems and make the area more livable. Also consider how plants can be used in groupings and as accents to beautify the yard. Plants can be used for detail to highlight attractive architectural features of the house—or to mask unattractive ones or soften harsh lines.

Low shrubs or borders can be used to direct traffic. They need not serve as barriers, but simply define paths and walkways.

Choose plants that complement architectural style of house. Take advantage of architectural features that can accentuate plantings.

Plantings can be used as space shapers to define specific areas within the yard.

Use tall hedges or screens as view buffers—to hide utility or storage areas, or block unsightly views beyond the yard.

Low ground covers are used for erosion control on sloping sites.

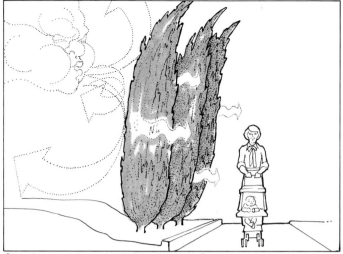

Closely spaced trees or tall hedges can deflect full force of a strong wind, turning it into gentle breeze.

Multipurpose plants, such as trees that provide both shade and fruit offer more than one benefit.

USES FOR HEDGES

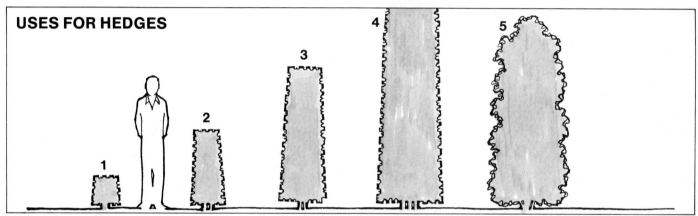

1. Border or edging: Clipped or unclipped hedge below knee height directs lines of vision. Examples are *Cratageus* and *Berberis. 2. Barrier:* Waist high or above. Dense or thorny plants make the best barriers. *3. Living wall hedge:* Clipped or unclipped, 6 feet or higher. Used for screen, backdrop, windbreak or architectural effects. Examples are Italian buckthorn, escallonia and privet. *4. Formal hedge:* Any height. Regularly pruned to tight lines or specific forms. Small-leaved plants are best. Examples are boxwood, yew, myrtle, holly, pittosporum, evergreen privet, podocarpus and beech. *5. Informal hedge:* Any height. Lightly pruned to stay in bounds, but to accentuate natural habit. Examples are quince, hibiscus and oleander.

ACCENT PLANTS

The plants shown here are used individually as visual accents or focal points in garden. Accent plants include those trained to unusual or specific forms, such as espaliers, topiary or bonsai; also *specimen plants* that hold visual interest on their own. Accent plants should be given enough space so they don't become lost in surrounding landscape.

LANDSCAPE EXAMPLES

Above: Tall, thick hedge of *Prunus lusitanica* effectively screens front yard from street. *Right:* Position plants in border so all can be seen—short ones toward front, taller ones toward back. Foliage shrubs or hedges make excellent backdrops for flowering plants. *Below:* Unusual form of this weeping hemlock makes it an excellent specimen plant that adds visual interest to garden.

Neatly trimmed hedges and well-manicured lawn provide framework of this formal garden. Trees, shrubs and bedding plants were all carefully selected and placed to complement shape created.

Shrubs, ground covers and large rocks make natural and attractive-looking retaining wall to create level areas on sloping site.

TWO WELL-PLANNED LANDSCAPES

Here are two examples of well-planned and installed landscapes. Both were designed and installed by landscape professionals. The plant materials chosen reflect the particular regions, but the design solutions—the way spaces work—are appropriate anywhere.

GEORGIA GARDEN

Clients required area for guest parking near the front of the house, a pleasant linkage between a rear parking area and the house and an unattractive garage screened. The solution involved creating a series of interesting spaces: Garage and adjoining parking area are subtly and tastefully screened with a wood fence, softened by trees and shrubs of various heights. Parking and house are linked to create a sense of continuity. The sculpture is an organizing device for the view from the arbor and the kitchen-dining area. Spaces, pedestrian circulation, plantings, and the use of color are extremely clear and create a cohesive quality to landscape. Most plants shown are also suitable for the West Coast.

Design: Gibbs Landscape Co. Inc., Smyrna, Georgia

Trees and low plantings help soften lines of wood fence that separates parking area and garage from main house and adjoining patio.

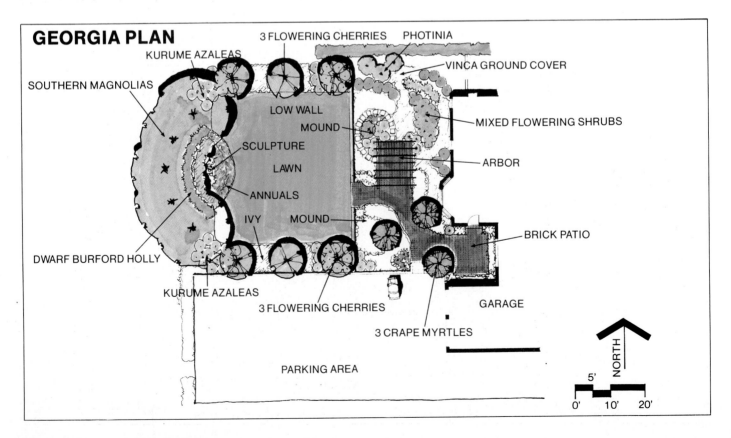

GEORGIA PLAN

3 FLOWERING CHERRIES PHOTINIA
KURUME AZALEAS
SOUTHERN MAGNOLIAS
VINCA GROUND COVER
LOW WALL
MOUND
MIXED FLOWERING SHRUBS
SCULPTURE
LAWN
ARBOR
ANNUALS
IVY   MOUND
BRICK PATIO
DWARF BURFORD HOLLY
KURUME AZALEAS
3 FLOWERING CHERRIES
GARAGE
3 CRAPE MYRTLES
PARKING AREA
NORTH
5'
0'   10'   20'

OHIO GARDEN

A young family including two children required maximum utilization of their property. The design had to be flexible enough to be adapted to changing needs as the family matured.

The design enhances the property's functional qualities for the many interests of the family and also enhances their handsome older home. New plantings complement the formal character of the house without stiffness. The landscape is generally characterized by an orderly circulation system that leaves adequate open lawn for touch football and other active games. Large existing trees are thoughtfully incorporated into the new design.

The family's desire for a vegetable garden was solved by locating it in sideyard area. Intensely developed play area for children is situated to one side of rear property, and the new rear patio is a dramatic use of a previously unimproved space. Outdoor living area is distinguished by plantings that effectively soften awkward architectural elements of the house.

Design: Edsall & Associates, Columbus, Ohio

Awkward architectural elements of house are mitigated by careful placement of trees and shrubs. Sweeping curves of lawn and borders help offset rigid, boxy appearance of house.

Separate activity areas are clearly defined by paths, lawn, low shrubs and flower beds.

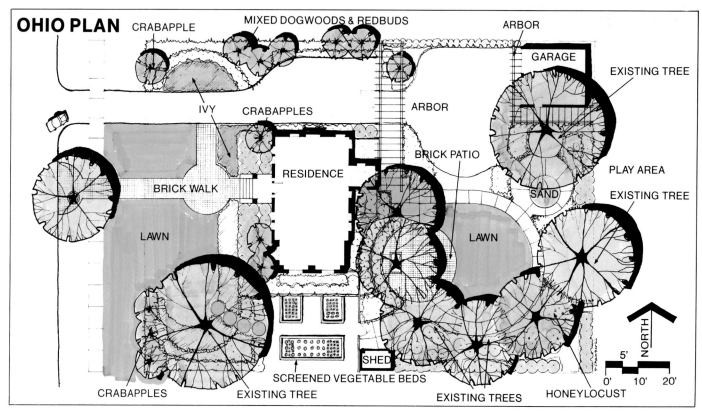

OHIO PLAN

CRABAPPLE — MIXED DOGWOODS & REDBUDS — ARBOR

GARAGE

EXISTING TREE

IVY — CRABAPPLES — ARBOR

BRICK PATIO

PLAY AREA

RESIDENCE

BRICK WALK

SAND

EXISTING TREE

LAWN

LAWN

NORTH

5'

0' 10' 20'

CRABAPPLES — EXISTING TREE — SCREENED VEGETABLE BEDS — SHED — EXISTING TREES — HONEYLOCUST

NURSERY CLOSEUP

Your local nursery is the single best garden-making resource. Each one is part display garden and part idea garden, part research center, part botanical garden. In addition to landscape plants, nurseries usually stock bulbs, seeds, soil amendments, fertilizers, tools and other garden supplies. Most nurseries welcome questions concerning gardening problems or suitable plants for specific areas.

Each nursery is different, reflecting the varying climates, communities and interests of the owners. But all nurseries have certain elements in common. Plants stocked are the most reliable for the region. Usually, a brief description including sun, soil and water requirements is either posted near each kind of plant, or appears on the plant's identification tag. Additional cultural information is available from the nursery staff.

Plants in the nursery are usually grouped according to habit and use—blocks of trees, shrubs for sun and for shade, ground covers, vegetables and herbs, bedding plants and tropicals. The drawing on the facing page shows a typical nursery layout. No other one will be exactly the same, but most share these features.

Your nursery mirrors the garden cycle in your area. Shopping tours—whether you buy or not—will familiarize you with the plants you need for a changing garden. Plants stocked vary with the seasons. For instance, bare-root roses and bare-root fruit trees come in late winter, bulbs in fall and many flowering plants in spring.

Choosing healthy plants is mostly a matter of common sense. Naturally, you wouldn't choose a plant that is showing signs of stress or one that looks stunted or sickly when compared to its neighbors. Here are some specific signs to look for when inspecting plants at the nursery:

● **Leaf Color**—Plants that show yellowing or other discoloration in leaves might indicate poor drainage, fertilizer deficiency, insect damage or disease.

● **Bud Development**—Buds on dormant plants should be firm, moist and uniformly spaced. Scratch lightly into the bark to see that the cambium or growing layer is moist and green.

● **Uniformity of Growth**—Plants in any given group should be uniform in vigor and health.

● **Plant Spacing**—Nursery plants are ideally grown and displayed with sufficient spacing to permit good development of the individual plant. Plants spaced too closely in the row or block will be tall and spindly with little, if any, side branching. Shade trees grown too close together may be extremely high headed.

● **Soil**—Plants to be balled and burlapped must be grown in soil that will hold a firm ball. If possible, check these plants to make sure root balls are not broken or loose.

● **Weeds**—Plants growing in weedy containers indicate lack of care. Plants may be in poor vigor due to weed competition. Also, you don't want to introduce weeds into the new landscape.

● **Decay**—Inspect trees for spots of decayed tissue on the trunk and branches.

● **Sunscald or Sunburn**—Damage of either kind usually appears on the side of the trunk facing the southwest. Sunburn destroys the cambium layer under the bark and increases the plant's susceptibility to various pests and diseases.

● **Abrasions on Bark**—Fresh abrasions or scrapes from handling during delivery or at the nursery are reasons to avoid a plant.

● **Girdling Roots**—These are circling roots, usually close to the soil surface, caused by poor timing or procedures in transplanting. Girdling roots tend to encircle the growing trunk and may eventually kill the plant. Any size plant that has been kept in a container too long will become rootbound. Avoid plants that seem to have outgrown their containers.

● **Improper Pruning**—Stubs left by improper pruning cause dieback into the main trunk and are common entry points for pests and diseases.

● **Frost Damage**—Long, vertical splits can occur on the south and southwest sides of young and thin-barked trees. Frost cracks are also convenient openings for various insects and diseases.

● **Signs of Injury**—Check for wilted or dead leaves, dry buds, twig or branch dieback and sunken or discolored patches in bark or stems, as well as any recent physical damage to plant.

● **Diseases**—These can take many forms. Check for abnormal growth of leaves, twigs and fruits, discoloration of leaves and bark, and unusual discharges of sap through the bark.

● **Insects**—Check for insect eggs, and evidence of damage from insect feeding on leaves, twigs, buds or other plant parts. Examine trunks of trees for holes made by boring insects.

Adequate spacing in nursery row allows for good development of individual plants.

Plants growing in weedy containers indicate lack of care.

Check bark of trees for disease, sunburn and other signs of injury. Damage to this trunk was caused by tree borer.

TYPICAL NURSERY

KEY

1. **Garden trees:** Soften lines of buildings, provide shade, may also provide flowers.
2. **Fruit trees:** For orchard or landscaping. Usually grouped into deciduous fruits and citrus.
3. **Foliage shrubs:** Provide privacy, shape spaces, soften wind, control glare, act as barriers. Can be trained as hedges or used as accents or in groupings.
4. **Flowering shrubs:** Provide color, used as accents or foundation plantings.
5. **Roses:** Add color to garden, come in many forms, from miniatures to shrubs to climbing vines. Sold bare root in winter, in containers the rest of the year.
6. **Ground covers:** Carpet large areas, prevent erosion, add color, can be used instead of lawn.
7. **Vines:** Dress up walls and fences, cover trellises and arbors to provide shade, may also provide flowers or fruit.
8. **Bedding plants:** Used for fast and easy color. Includes flowering annuals and perennials. Available in cell packs and various-size containers.
9. **Vegetables and herbs:** Available as seedlings in cell packs and individual pots. Seeds also available.

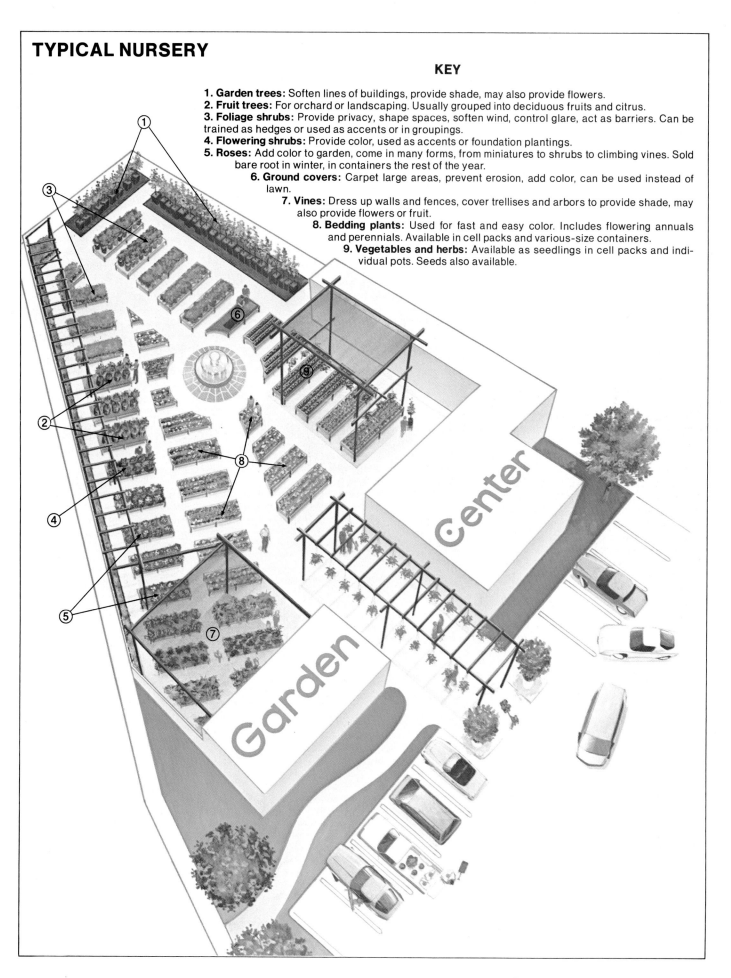

PLANTING

This chapter provides specifics on some of the most common ways of planting—sowing seeds in the garden, setting out bedding plants and seedlings, and planting container, bare-root, and balled-and-burlapped plants. It also provides instructions for transplanting established shrubs and trees and tree staking. Planting a lawn is covered on pages 122-123. Additional planting information appears in the chapters covering specific kinds of plants. See table of contents.

SOIL PREPARATION

The single most important ingredient to successful planting is soil preparation. Planting in inappropriate soil is futile.

Most garden plants require soils with good drainage yet good moisture retention, a slightly acid pH (5.5 to 6.5) and moderate fertility. Whether your thumb is green or brown, plants started in such soil will usually perform well.

If you live in farm country where topsoils are uniformly 6 to 7 feet deep, plants usually thrive with a minimum of soil preparation. But many urban and suburban gardeners live where soil was scraped level or filled and compacted just prior to construction. Most plants grow poorly, if at all, under such conditions, so the soil will need to be improved.

The easiest way to improve soil quickly is to add topsoil. Another long-term method is to add organic matter—compost, sawdust, wood chips, peat moss, sludge or any of a number of agricultural or other organic byproducts. *Note:* If you use uncomposted or *raw* wood byproducts, add nitrogen fertilizer at the rate of 1 pound *actual nitrogen* per cubic yard. Five pounds of ammonium phosphate contains 1 pound of actual nitrogen. The chart on page 64 gives the amounts of actual nitrogen contained in nitrogen fertilizers of various percentages.

Organic matter benefits soils in several ways. Most importantly, it supports the diverse and essential population of soil microbes, without which the whole soil system begins to break down.

The phrase "Add organic matter one-third by volume" is one you might have heard. Here's what it means: Assume you are going to cultivate the soil to a depth of 6 inches. Spread 2 inches of organic over the top before cultivation. The 2 inches of organic matter incorporated into 6 inches of soil is the "one-third."

Many unimproved soils are either too acid or too alkaline. East of the Mississippi River, most gardeners regularly add lime (ground limestone) to their soil to raise the *pH level*, making the soil more alkaline. See pages 59-60 for more about soil pH. The reverse—adding sulfur or similar acidifying material—is a common practice in arid regions of the West. A chart showing how much of each to use appears on page 60.

Beyond adding organic matter and adjusting pH, soils are typically deficient in nitrogen. Other necessary elements may also be in short supply—a

Left: Large container plants should be planted to same depth as they grew in the container. See page 46 for more planting tips.

Above: Planting in raised beds is one solution for gardeners who must deal with poorly draining soils.

soil test is the best way to find out. Growing and observing plants is another way. The guidance usually offered—and it's not bad advice—is to spread 5 pounds of 10-10-10 fertilizer per 100 square feet of soil before planting.

Fast-growing annual flowers and vegetables, such as petunias, lettuce and cabbage, benefit most from the addition of fertilizer before planting. They are significantly stunted by a slight shortage of essential nutrients. Perennial plants, trees and shrubs also benefit from the addition of fer-

tilizers at planting time, but are rarely irreversibly stunted. You can wait until you see deficiency symptoms, such as yellow leaves or slow growth, before fertilizing.

Gypsum, a natural mineral containing calcium and sulfur (in sulfate form), is often recommended for heavy clay soils. It is especially useful if a soil test shows excess sodium in relation to calcium. It is also useful if the soil test shows that the pH is good but calcium content is low. In these specific situations, gypsum loosens and improves clay soils.

PLANTING SEEDS

To start plants from seeds, the easiest and least time-consuming way is to plant them directly in the garden. But if you want to get a head start on the growing season, you can start seeds indoors or in a greenhouse and transplant the seedlings into the garden when the weather is favorable.

There are other advantages to starting seeds indoors: You have more control over light, temperature and moisture requirements. You can use sterile potting mixes to help prevent diseases. You can also protect delicate seedlings from insects, birds, competing weeds and other pests. Because of these factors, the germination rate of seeds grown indoors is usually higher.

Although the germination rate is usually lower with seeds planted directly in the garden, and losses to pests and diseases is higher, the plants that survive outdoor sowing are usually better adapted. Transplanting often causes shock, and many plants have to be *hardened-off*, or gradually adjusted to outdoor conditions, before they're planted.

This also is best for plants that don't transplant well during the seedling stage and those that are to be planted in quantity over a large area, such as ground covers. Raising and transplanting hundreds of seedlings can be a tedious chore.

BUY QUALITY SEEDS

Buy the highest quality seeds available. Most national seed-rack and mail-order brands are uniformly high quality. Beware: Seed that has been discounted because it is outdated is no bargain.

The newer or fresher the seed, the better. Seed companies test germination and some print the test date and germination percentage on the package. If you buy and sow the seed within 6 months of the tested date, you can assume the germination percentage is not reduced. Seed packages usually show the year they are packaged for, or give an expiration date.

If you have seeds left over from last year, you may wonder if they're still viable. Some seeds, such as sweet peas, remain viable for several years; others for only a year or less. You can test the germination rate of outdated seeds by following the instructions on page 100.

Plants that don't transplant well in seedling stage should be direct-seeded in garden.

ROW PLANTING

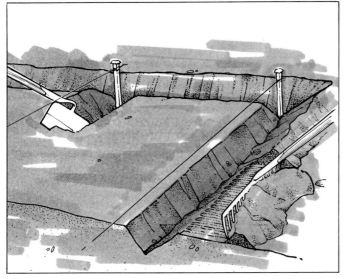

1. Use stakes and string to establish straight rows and furrows. Dig trenches as shown and rake smooth.

2. Establish mounds or hills between furrows, then make smaller trenches on top of mound for planting seeds. Follow seed-package instructions for correct planting depth of seeds.

3. Drop seeds into place, following spacing instructions on seed package. If you expect poor germination, you can plant seeds closer together, but you'll still have to thin seedlings as described in step 4.

4. Cover seeds with garden soil or potting soil, being careful not to dislodge them from their positions. Tamp soil into place over seeds. To avoid stunting plants, thin seedlings as soon as they emerge, following spacing recommendations on seed package.

Collecting Your Own Seeds—Some of the plants in your garden, including many annual flowers and some vegetables, will set viable seed that can be used for growing the same plant the following year. For information on collecting and storing seeds, see page 100.

SOWING SEEDS OUTDOORS

Timing is the most important aspect of sowing seeds outdoors. Warm-season crops such as beans, melons, squash and corn will not germinate and grow when soil is too cool.

Conversely, lettuce requires a relatively cool soil temperature for germination. Follow the seed-pack directions to determine planting times.

Soil crusting also inhibits germination of seeds. Soils with a high percentage of clay readily form a hard crust over the surface, blocking seed germination. In this case, sow seeds in trenches, then fill the trenches with a light, non-crusting material such as compost, vermiculite or peat moss.

A common error made by beginning gardeners is to plant seeds too deep. Although there are many rules of

thumb, such as "plant seeds to a depth twice their diameter," the best advice is to plant to the depth recommended on the seed package.

Hill Planting—This is a convenient way to handle spreading vegetables that require wide spacing, such as melons, cucumbers or pumpkins. Sow six to eight seeds in mounds 3 to 4 feet apart, then thin until you have three or four seedlings in each mound.

Row Planting—Most vegetables are planted in rows. Mark out straight rows by using string tied between stakes. Make a furrow of the recommended depth with your hoe. Drop seeds into the furrow, cover with soil and tamp. Sowing seeds more thickly than recommended is fine if you anticipate poor germination, and if you will thin seedlings to the required spacing as soon as they germinate. If your soil is heavy and crusting is a problem, cover seeds with potting soil mix, peat moss or vermiculite.

The typical seed-sowing sequence after soil has been prepared is illustrated on page 43.

Broadcasting—This simulates the method nature uses to sow seeds. Broadcasting, or scattering seeds by hand, is most often done to get a natural or informal effect, such as with mixed annuals or wildflowers, over a large area. Hand-broadcasting results in dense, though sometimes erratic, spacing of plants. Loosen soil thoroughly before broadcasting seeds.

Lawn seed can either be broadcast by hand or with a lawn spreader. For more on planting lawns, see pages 121-123.

STARTING SEEDS INDOORS

The basic requirements for starting seeds indoors are the same as for starting them outdoors—a light, well-draining soil mix, adequate light and water and suitable temperature. In addition, you'll need appropriate containers.

Containers — Many different kinds of containers can be used to start seeds. You can use clay pots or egg cartons, plastic pots, wooden flats, trays, peat pots and so forth. Or you can build wooden boxes or use containers found around the home —milk cartons, plastic cups or other empty food containers. Containers should have holes in the bottom to allow for drainage.

The best containers are those that can be fitted with a transparent plastic or glass cover to admit light, yet retain humidity. Commercially available seed propagators are available from mail-order nursery suppliers. These are nothing more than plastic boxes with clear-plastic lids that have holes punched in them for air circulation. Clear-plastic sweater boxes or food-storage containers make suitable substitutes for these. Such propagators can also be used to root cuttings, as described on page 101. Individual propagators can be made by placing clear-plastic picnic glasses over 4-inch plastic nursery pots.

Soil—For most home gardeners, a commercial potting mix is perhaps the most convenient and reliable medium for starting most kinds of seeds. Some gardeners prefer their own soil-mix recipes, which are usually some combination of sand, soil, an organic amendment such as ground bark or peat moss, a general-purpose fertilizer and limestone. Vermiculite or perlite is sometimes added to promote air circulation, drainage and water-holding capacity.

Garden soil should not be used unless it is first sterilized to kill weed seeds and soilborne diseases. Soil is sterilized by heating—one method is to raise the soil temperature to 212F (100C) for about 1/2 hour. This can be done in the oven, but it's a messy, smelly process, and not recommended for the home gardener.

If you need a large amount of soil mix, you can make the lightweight mix described on page 60, adjusting proportions for the desired amount.

The moist conditions required to grow seeds also fosters *damping-off*—a disease caused by soilborne fungus. Damping-off is less likely to occur with commercial potting mixes, and in containers sterilized with chlorine bleach before use. A thin layer of vermiculite or perlite placed over the soil mix will help prevent damping-off, as will a fungicide applied to the soil surface before seeds sprout. See the chart on page 220 for recommended fungicides.

How to Sow—Fill containers with soil mix, lightly firming it into place around corners and edges. Water to moisten and settle the mix in the container.

If working with very small seeds, such as petunias, impatiens or begonias, carefully level the mix and spread a 1/2-inch layer of fine-screened sphagnum moss or vermiculite over the top. Scatter seeds over the surface and do not cover them with soil mix.

For larger seeds, such as marigolds, calendulas and morning glories, use the edge of a board to press straight rows into the firmed mix. Sow the seeds to the depth and spacing recommended on the seed package. Sown too thickly, seedlings crowd each other and do not develop as well.

Watering—Mist or lightly water so that seeds are not dislodged or washed away. Let soil drain, then place the container in a location that provides optimum lighting and temperature conditions (see page 44). Cover the container with a pane of glass, a plastic bag or similar device that traps humidity.

Check the seeds each day to be sure the soil mix is moist and that seedlings have not emerged. If water is

Here are basic materials for starting seeds—sterile potting soil, various-size containers and labels. Most nurseries and garden centers carry soil mixtures especially formulated for starting seeds. Compressed peat or potting mixtures in the form of pellets (left) or squares (lower right) are a clean, easy way to start seeds.

STARTING SEEDS INDOORS

1. Plastic cell-packs are pictured in these instructions, but procedure for other types of containers is similar. Place soil mixture in planting trays or containers. Lightly compress soil and moisten with water to settle mix.

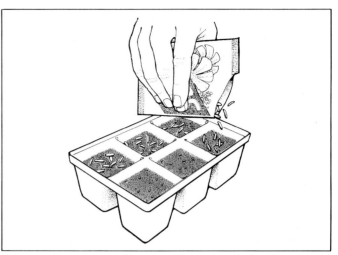

2. For small seeds, sprinkle several in each cell of cell pack or in each container. If using large trays, spread seeds evenly over soil surface.

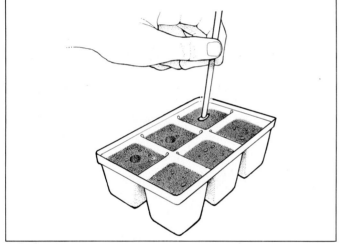

3. For large seeds, plant one or two per cell or individual container at the appropriate depth. For large trays, follow spacing directions on seed package.

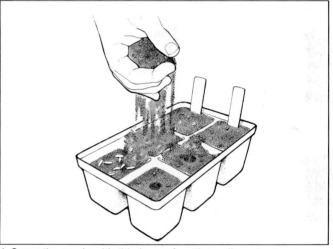

4. Cover the seeds with thin layer of potting soil, peat moss or vermiculite and label seeds appropriately.

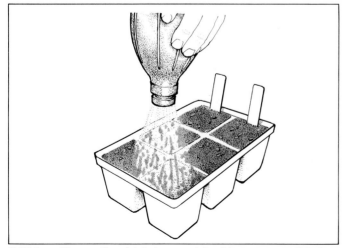

5. Water with a gentle mist, being careful not to expose or dislodge seeds.

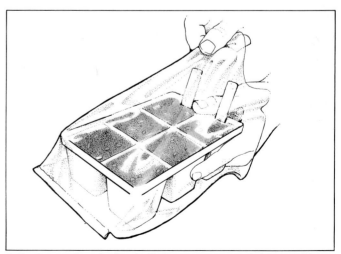

6. Enclose cell-packs in plastic bag, or cover containers and trays with clear-plastic lid or similar cover to retain moisture. Place in warm location. Do not let soil mixture dry out. When seeds germinate, move to well-lighted location. Follow directions on next page for transplanting seedlings.

Planting   **43**

TRANSPLANTING SEEDLINGS

1. If more than one seed per cell or small container germinates, gently separate seedlings as soon as possible. Or, you can thin to one seedling per container or cell. If using large trays, thin or transplant to spacing recommendations on seed package.

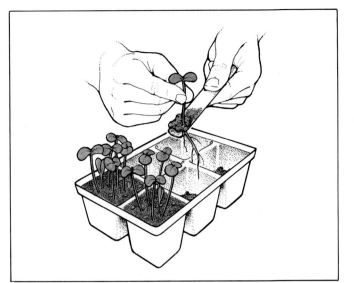

2. To transplant, use thin, flat object such as spatula or spoon handle to gently lift seedling from soil.

3. Replant each seedling in an individual cell or container. Place in soil at same or slightly deeper level. Avoid bending roots.

4. When the first true leaves appear, *harden-off* seedlings by gradually exposing to outdoor conditions.

necessary, set the container in a bowl or tray of water so that moisture can be pulled from below. Watering from the top might dislodge emerging seedlings. Of course, be sure that drainage is good, that air is able to circulate easily through the mix and that you are not overwatering.

Temperature—Most garden seeds germinate fastest at soil temperatures between 75F and 80F (24C and 27C). At lower temperatures, seeds may still germinate, but more slowly and at greater risk of damping-off disease. Heating cables or heating tapes, available at nurseries, can be placed under containers or in the bottom of flats to maintain a constant soil temperature.

The chart on page 148 gives the minimum, optimum and maximum germinating temperatures for some common garden vegetables.

Some flowering plants that prefer cool temperatures (below 65F) for germination include nemesia, larkspur, lupine, forget-me-not and phlox.

Light—Some seeds require the stimulation of minute quantities of light to begin germination. These include such vegetables as celery, witloof chicory, garden cress, dandelion and lettuce, and such flowers as ageratum, begonias, coleus, dill, feverfew, nicotiana, petunias, African violets, salvia and snapdragons. Don't cover these seeds with soil after sowing.

Seedlings require adequate light. You might be lucky enough to have a high, south- or west-facing window behind which you can line up rows of seedlings. More often, such a location is not available. Here are some alternatives: Arrange fluorescent tubes—warm white and cool white combined—about 6 inches above the tops of the seedlings and leave the lights on 16 hours a day. Or, move seedlings outdoors during the day, then back indoors at night.

TRANSPLANTING SEEDLINGS

If you've sown seeds in rows in flats, it is important to separate and replant them before they become spindly. Prepare containers or flats just as for seedlings. Lift seedlings with a spatula or knife or any similar means and place them into the new containers.

Most seedlings are best transplanted about 2 inches apart in the new containers. Spacing information is often included in seed-package instructions. Place seedlings at the same level as they were growing before, or slightly deeper.

Avoid bending roots. Or you can thin seedlings to 2 inches apart in their present container or plant in individual containers.

PLANTING BEDDING PLANTS

Bedding plants are transplant-ready seedlings, available at nurseries in wooden or plastic flats, plastic pots, peat pots, peat pellets, clay pots and most commonly, plastic cell packs. The following example describes how to plant seedlings growing in plastic cell-packs.

Press on bottom of the individual cell to push the seedling out. If it is rootbound—thickly matted with roots—free the roots by rubbing the root ball with your hands. In severe cases, use a knife to cut part way into the root ball, then spread it apart with your hands. Roots established in circles may never break out of the pattern.

Set the plant so it is slightly deeper than it was previously growing. Tomatoes and members of the cabbage family develop new roots along their stem, so they usually benefit if planted much deeper. If plants are slightly leggy, pinch off seedling leaves (cotyledons) and plant to a level just below the true leaves.

Plantable containers such as peat pots or peat pellets can be buried, but be sure their upper edges are below soil level. If not, those edges act as wicks and pull water from the rootball to the air.

BEDDING PLANTS

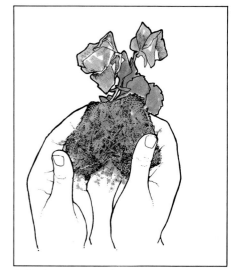

1. Remove plant from container by turning upside-down and gently tapping or squeezing container until plant and root ball fall into your hand. With cell packs, lightly press on bottom of each cell to remove plants. Gently loosen bottom of root ball as shown.

2. If plants are rootbound, gently separate root ball with fingers. For larger plants, cut into bottom of root ball with a knife and "butterfly" root ball apart, being careful not to break or damage larger roots.

3. Use trowel or hands to make hole deep enough to cover root ball, or just slightly deeper. Set plant in hole at same depth or slightly deeper than it was growing in container. Firm soil around roots and make small basin that slopes toward plant. Water to settle soil around roots.

Leave a small basin around the transplant to catch rain or irrigation water and direct it toward the roots.

Evenings or cool, cloudy days are the safest times to transplant. Hot afternoons, windy days or cold days are the least promising. Protection for the new transplant is often required. Depending on the weather, use a wood shingle to provide afternoon shade, or a hot cap for evening warmth.

You can have early crops by setting out transplants before the anticipated last frost of spring. But you will have to provide some means of protection. Plastic or glass cloches or row covers are traditional, but there are many variations on that idea available.

TRANSPLANTING TO A LARGER CONTAINER

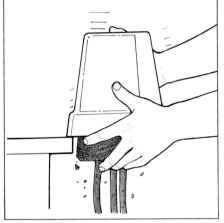

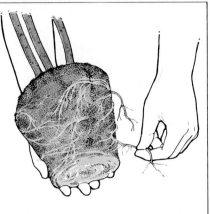

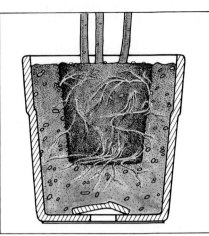

1. Hold container upside-down and gently tap rim against table edge or other flat surface until plant and root ball fall into your hand. Avoid disturbing soil around roots as much as possible.

2. Loosen encircling roots, being careful not to break them. If plant is rootbound, you may need to cut into bottom of root ball with knife and spread roots apart. The objective is to break circular pattern of roots so they will spread out into new soil.

3. Place stone or piece of broken pot over drainage hole in new container to prevent soil from leaking through. Fill container part way with potting mix and set plant in new pot. Slowly add soil, packing it lightly around roots, being careful not to bend them. Final soil level should be even with top of root ball as shown, and about 1/2 to 1 inch below rim of pot.

PLANTING TREES AND SHRUBS

Trees and shrubs are sold in three forms—*container grown, bare-root* and *balled-and-burlapped.* Planting methods and considerations common to all three are described below. See drawing sequences on following pages for specific planting instructions for each type.

Prepare Planting Hole—Dig your planting hole about 6 inches deeper and twice as wide as the rootball for balled-and-burlapped or container-grown trees, or large enough to allow ample space for the root spread of bare-root trees. In heavy or clay soils, a square hole is better than a round one because new roots will not tend to grow in a spiral manner when they reach native soil.

If the soil is heavy and shows the presence of clay, the sides of the hole may become glazed by the shovel blade and nearly impossible for the roots to penetrate. Use a hand cultivator to roughen the surface before setting the plant in the hole.

Provide Drainage—After preparing the hole, check for drainage. In some soils, water has been known to stay in the planting hole for more than 6 months, a situation deadly to plants.

First fill the planting hole with water and let it drain. After the water completely drains away, fill the hole a second time. Usually, the water from the second filling will drain within an

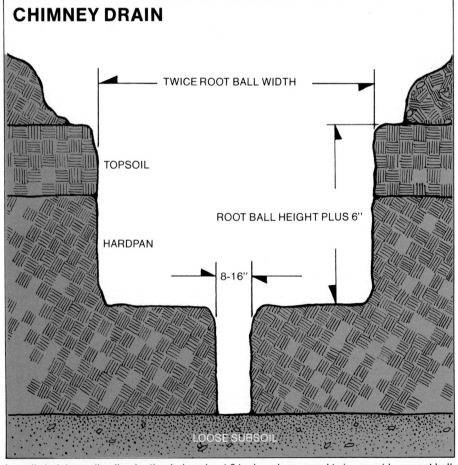

CHIMNEY DRAIN

TWICE ROOT BALL WIDTH

TOPSOIL

HARDPAN

ROOT BALL HEIGHT PLUS 6''

8-16''

LOOSE SUBSOIL

In well-draining soils, dig planting holes about 6 inches deeper and twice as wide as root ball. Where a thick hardpan layer exists, dig chimney drain for large planting holes as shown here. Post-hole digger or auger is ideal tool for making chimney drain. Fill chimney drain with fine sand, peat moss or ground bark.

Many evergreen trees and shrubs are sold balled-and-burlapped. Planting methods are similar to those for container plants, as described on pages 49-50.

Deciduous trees and shrubs are sold bare root during their dormant period. This photo shows correct planting level. Notice how longer roots have been trimmed to fit planting hole. See page 50 for planting sequence.

hour, though sometimes it takes longer. If the second filling takes more than 12 hours to empty, drainage is too slow for most plants.

Slow drainage is often caused by a layer of heavy or compacted soil below the planting hole, called *hardpan*. If such a layer is relatively thin and close to the surface, the best solution is to dig or bore a hole through it from the bottom of the planting hole.

If the hardpan isn't too thick, break through it the full width of the planting hole. Otherwise dig a narrower hole, called a chimney drain down from the hole bottom until you reach the porous stratum. See drawing on facing page. Often, a shovel can be used to dig the chimney. If the hardpan layer is very thick, a post-hole digger, auger, power auger or jackhammer may be needed.

Fill the chimney with fine sand, peat moss or ground bark. Do not use large-diameter gravel or rock that disrupts the capillary action of water movement.

Use a *slot drain* to dissipate water from poorly draining hillside planting holes. Dig a trench off to one side and downhill from the bottom of the planting hole. Then lay perforated, lightweight drain pipe in the bottom of the trench. Cap the planting-hole end of the pipe to prevent it from filling with silt.

There are situations in which nei-

ther a chimney drain nor a slot drain are practical or effective. For instance, the site might have impervious soil several feet thick. Or perhaps the situation simply does not warrant the expense or effort of providing underground drainage. In such cases, rethink the choice of your planting site, and decide if it is possible to plant the tree or shrub somewhere else where such a drainage problem does not exist. If you are committed to planting a certain shrub or tree in the chosen site, two alternatives remain.

The first alternative is to plant in an extra-large hole. Here are suggested dimensions for extra-large planting holes in poorly draining soil over hardpan: Plant 1-gallon-size plants in

Large plants usually slip easily out of plastic containers. Turn container upside-down and shake gently. Hold root ball with one hand as it slides out. Keep as much soil around root ball as possible.

Metal containers usually must be cut open to remove plant. Most nurseries will cut container for you. To remove plant, spread container apart as shown. Be careful of jagged edges where container was cut open.

PLANTS THAT TOLERATE POOR DRAINAGE

Trees
Common quince (*Chaenomeles speciosa*)
Red maple (*Acer rubrum*)
Sweet gum (*Liquidambar styraciflua*)
White alder (*Alnus rhombifolia*)
Willow (*Salix* species)

Shrubs
Pampas grass (*Cortaderia selloana*)
Papyrus (*Cyperus papyrus*)
Privet (*Ligustrum species*)
Oleander (*Nerium oleander*)

Vines
Cup-of-gold vine (*Solandra maxima*)
Hall's Japanese honeysuckle (*Lonicera japonica* 'Halliana')

Ground Covers
Corsican mint (*Mentha requienii*)
Periwinkle or myrtle (*Vinca* species)

Bulbs
Kaffir lily (*Clivia miniata*)
Iris species—Louisiana, Japanese, Siberian irises

holes 2 feet wide by 2 feet deep; plant 5-gallon-size plants in holes 4 feet wide by 3 feet deep; plant small trees in holes 5 feet wide by 3 feet deep, and plant large trees in holes 6 feet wide by 3 feet deep. Make backfill soil of one-half native soil and one-half coarse organic matter. Be careful of overwatering.

The second alternative is to raise the soil level and plant above surrounding grade level. Depending upon the situation, use an unbordered mound of soil or a rigid structure or frame to contain soil above grade level. A simple frame for a medium-size shrub or small tree can be made of 2-inch-thick lumber treated with a wood preservative that is non-toxic to plants, such as copper napthenate. Make the frame about 2 feet square and 12 inches high. That is enough to ensure the survival of most plants in situations of virtually no drainage. For larger trees, the dimensions of

the frame should be in proportion to the expected size of the plant.

Successful planting in poorly drained soil is most often achieved if the above recommendations are followed, plus one more—choose a tree or shrub that tolerates soggy soil.

Prepare Roots—Carefully remove cans from container-grown trees and shrubs. Plastic containers usually slip off easily; metal ones should be cut down the sides by the nursery attendant before leaving the nursery.

Gently remove the root ball from the container and keep it intact if possible. If any large roots are circling the ball, carefully lift them away. *Scoring* the rootball means cutting 1 or 2 inches into the root ball—usually with your planting shovel—to sever circling roots. If this is difficult, cut these roots with sharp shears or a knife, disturbing the root mass as little as possible. An important exception to this general ''rough-up the roots''

CONTAINER PLANTS (INCLUDES BALLED-AND-BURLAPPED PLANTS)

1. Dig planting hole so soil line of plant, when positioned, is about 2 inches above surrounding soil level. Then angle bottom of hole out and downward, roughen soil on sides and fill with water to check drainage (see page 47). Don't dig deeper than height of root ball or trunk will sink into water-collecting cavity as soil settles.

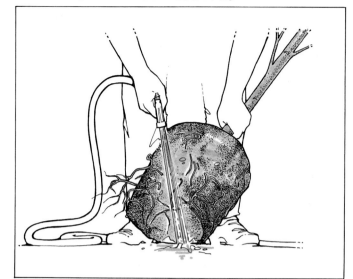

2. If roots are compacted, spray soil off outer few inches of root ball, then uncoil encircling or twisted roots. Cut off broken roots or any that seem to be permanently kinked.

3. Set plant in hole. Spread roots to direct them outward and downward. If plant is balled-and-burlapped, leave natural wrap, peel away synthetic wrap. Gradually add pulverized backfill along with water to settle soil around roots. If you use soil amendments for reasons described in text, mix it half-and-half with native soil. Check to make sure top of root ball is still 2 inches above surrounding soil level.

4. Use a trickling hose or drip emitter to apply water directly over area of original root ball. This is where soil dries fastest. Note double berm that holds water over root ball and keeps trunk dry. You can expect some settling of soil after watering. If plant has settled too deeply in hole, dig under root ball with shovel and gently lift back to correct level.

advice is bougainvillea because its root ball is characteristically delicate. Also cut off any broken or damaged roots and any roots too long to fit into the planting hole.

Inspect bare-root plants for broken or damaged roots and cut off back to healthy tissue. See *Nursery Closeup* on page 36.

Untie the cord from balled-and-burlapped shrubs and peel back the top of the burlap about half way. Remove cord if it comes out easily, otherwise bury it with the roots. If the wrapping is natural burlap, leave it in place. If the wrapping is non-biodegradable, remove as much of it as possible once the plant is correctly

positioned in the planting hole.
Place in Planting Hole—Center the tree or shrub in the planting hole. Never plant it deeper than it was in the container. Look for the change in color on the trunk above the highest root on bare-root trees—that's the original soil line. Bare-root trees usually settle, so you should position the

BARE ROOT TREES AND SHRUBS

1. If planting bare-root orchard trees, measure and mark all hole positions, then double-check for correct spacing. All holes can be dug at once, if desired.

2. Dig hole just wide enough to accommodate roots, and about 6 inches deeper than root system. Fill hole with water twice to check drainage. Correct drainage problems, if any, as described on pages 47-48.

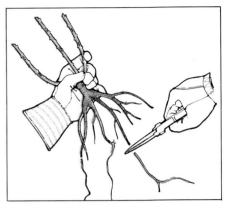

3. Prune off roots that are dried, broken, discolored or too long to fit into hole without bending.

4. Make a cone of soil in bottom of planting hole on which to spread the roots. If gophers or moles are a problem, place hand-fashioned basket of chicken wire in hole to protect tree roots.

5. Place tree in hole at original planting depth. Original soil line will appear as a dark to light color change on trunk below bud union. Spread roots over mounded earth in bottom of hole. If planting more than one plant in a hole, position them equal distances apart and slant them slightly outward.

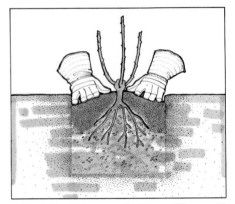

6. Backfill hole, gradually settling soil around roots with trickle of water. Firm soil around roots and double-check planting depth. Backfill in hole should be slightly higher than surrounding soil. Make water basin slightly larger than planting hole and water to settle soil. Basin should direct water over root zone but away from trunk. If tree has settled too deeply in planting hole, gently lift by the trunk back to correct height.

old soil line on the tree about 1 inch above the new soil line.

Build a cone of backfill in the bottom of the planting hole for bare-root trees. Spread the roots out evenly onto the cone and gently push the tap-root (if present) into the center of the cone. Position bare-root trees so they will be at the same soil line as they were grown—the top of the root ball should be about 2 inches above the surface of the final soil line, to allow for settling of backfill.

If the hole was dug deeper than the height of the root ball, container-grown plants should be situated high in the planting soil. Again, allow about 2 inches for settling of the back-

fill soil so that the final planting level is the same as, or slightly higher than, the original planting level.

Backfill—Backfill the planting hole with the native soil that you removed when you dug the hole. When the hole is about half filled, water thoroughly to eliminate air pockets and to settle soil around the roots.

Amendments such as planting mix, peat moss or sawdust are not always necessary but it does help to add them to backfill to increase water retention.

There are two kinds of soil that require amendments. One exception is *sterile soil*. If the upper soil layer was scraped when the site was developed, use a good grade topsoil as backfill.

Another is *decomposed granite or sandy soil*. These soils drain water so fast that it is difficult to establish plants. Amended backfill provides both nutrients and water-holding capacity.

Root Protection—If you live where gophers and moles are frequent and expected pests, it is a good idea to wrap the root ball in chicken wire or aviary netting. Gophers often chew on the roots of a young tree until nothing is left and the tree falls over.

Fertilize When Planting—Planting is the ideal time to add slow-release fertilizer tablets. Several such products are formulated especially for trees and shrubs. None burn roots and will provide nutrients to the trees or shrubs for up to 2 years.

Various "B vitamin" solutions are often offered as planting or transplanting aids. Research indicates they are of little, if any, value. Rooting aids that contain *alpha naphthaleneacetic acid (NAA)* might be helpful. These do help promote rooting.

Bare-root trees and shrubs are dormant, so skip the fertilizer at this point and add it at the beginning of spring growth. They can only use the nutrients during their growth period.

CARE AFTER PLANTING

Newly planted trees and shrubs will need frequent watering until they become fully established. Mulching will help keep soil moist and keep weeds down. Also, young trees may need staking and trunk protection.

Watering—After backfilling the planting hole, build two 3- to 4-inch-high berms around the plant. Make the smaller berm immediately beyond the trunk. The purpose of this smaller berm is to keep the trunk and crown as dry as possible so that fungus diseases are not encouraged.

Form the outer berm *slightly* outside the root system limit, and maintain this berm for the first 6 to 8 weeks after planting. In this way, water will pass through the root mass and allow

Outer berm of watering basin for newly planted shrubs and trees is 3 to 4 inches high, formed slightly outside root-system limit, as shown. Barely visible in center of photo, inner berm directs water away from trunk.

the new roots to quickly move into the backfill space.

After 6 to 8 weeks, move the outer berm to the region just beyond the tree's drip line. Or, if some system of drip irrigation is used, you can flatten the outer berm altogether. Maintain the inner berm into the next season.

Water the tree or shrub at least two or three times each week. If planting during the hotter months, the plant may need water every day, especially if you live in a dry climate. Apply water slowly and don't let it overflow the berm.

Maintain this frequent watering schedule for 6 to 8 weeks, then reduce frequency to weekly waterings for an additional 3 months. After this initial 5-month period, water needs will vary with the soil type, weather and the type of plant. In most soils, a deep watering is necessary once a week during the growing season for fruit and nut trees, once a month for most ornamentals.

Misting or wetting the plant's foliage is usually beneficial, except in regions with salty water. In those areas, salts remain after water evaporates, burning the leaves. Rain is beneficial to new plants, but keep in mind that it takes plenty of rain to replace regular irrigation. A full inch of rainfall is required to equal one deep irrigation.

Pruning—Shortly after planting, you can lightly prune a tree to encourage it to take the form you want or to encourage root development. Unless the tree is normally a multi-trunk tree, remove any leaders that compete with the main trunk. Leave on as many lower branches as possible to promote sturdy trunk growth. Some fruit and nut trees are *headed* (topped) to a specified height immediately after planting. For details, refer to the chapter Fruits, Berries, and Nuts under the appropriate heading for the tree you're planting. Shrubs generally don't require pruning when planted, except to remove dead, damaged or crossing branches, or to achieve a special effect.

Staking Trees—Support for a young tree is necessary when wind is a problem or when the trunk is too weak to support the tree. Lightly thin the top growth to reduce both weight and wind resistance, then use the minimum amount of staking necessary. Thin, flexible bamboo stakes provide

INSPECTION AFTER PLANTING

The time between initial planting and the point when plants are fully acclimated to the site's growing conditions is called the plant's *establishment period*. A variety of practices may be necessary during this time, depending on planting time and the plants involved.

Watering is generally the most important practice. Fertilizing, pruning, pest control and weeding are usually necessary during the plant's establishment period.

The following checklist includes the most critical items:

- **Provide supplemental water.** If natural rainfall is insufficient—less than 1 inch of rainfall a week during summer—be sure to soak soil surrounding new plants.
- **Check plant position.** Plants often settle too deeply in their hole and require replanting to the correct level. Also, wind, large animals or other outside influences may harm the plant's position.
- **Be sure supports are firm.** Redrive tree stakes that loosen or tighten guy wires.
- **Check trunk wrapping.** Trunk wrapping on newly planted trees or shrubs must be tight and secure.
- **Check for rodent damage.** Gophers and field mice quickly damage new plants.
- **Check for suckers and broken branches.** Remove by pruning.
- **Maintain berms and watering basins.** Be sure they are working correctly. Repair and rebuild as necessary.
- **Control weeds.** Remove weeds growing around new plants.

just enough extra support for most trees.

Young trees need two stakes on opposite sides. Single staking causes the tree to lean away from the stake, resulting in trunks that do not grow straight. Anchor stakes securely into the ground, nail on a crossbar and loop rubber-lined ties around the tree and attach ends to stakes.

Shrubs may need staking if they are too top-heavy to stand alone or if the area is very windy—some degree of wind movement actually results in stronger shrubs.

Mulching—Apply a 2- to 3-inch layer of decomposed organic material under the tree after planting. Mulch keeps roots cooler, prevents soil from crusting and reduces weed growth. For more on mulches, see page 61.

Trunk Protection—Trunks of young trees fresh from the nursery row are vulnerable in ways they will not be after a few years. Bark is still thin, therefore subject to sunburn, heat and cold, pests, and bruising from a lawn mower or weed-eater. White interior latex paint is a traditional trunk protector. You can buy tree-trunk paint at nurseries and garden centers, or use ordinary white interior latex paint thinned 50% with water. Its primary virtue is reflectivity. Plastic, burlap or paper trunk protectors offer more protection, but may ultimately encourage pests by providing hiding places.

Planting Trees in Lawns—Lush lawns growing right to the trunk of stately trees are envisioned by most gardeners planting a 5-gallon-size tree in the middle of the lawn. Unfortunately it usually doesn't work out that way.

Most young trees are severely stunted if growing in the midst of lawn grasses. Water and nutrient demands of lawns and trees are quite different, and one or the other—usually the young tree—is going to suffer. Some research suggests that roots of several common lawn grasses exude chemicals poisonous to tree roots.

All this doesn't mean you can't have a tree in your lawn, only that certain allowances are necessary. Always make a wide, grass-free planting area around the young tree. For instance, around a 5-gallon tree you should maintain a grass- and weed-free area of at least 3 square feet. Also, adjust lawn sprinklers so that the tree is not automatically watered with each lawn watering.

Some mature trees, most notably those adapted to dry summers, also suffer if lawns grow near the trunk. The problem created is less one of competition than of excess, disease-promoting moisture. For young trees, maintain a lawn-free basin extending about 1 foot beyond the tree's drip line. Avoid planting shallow-rooted trees in lawns.

STAKING TREES

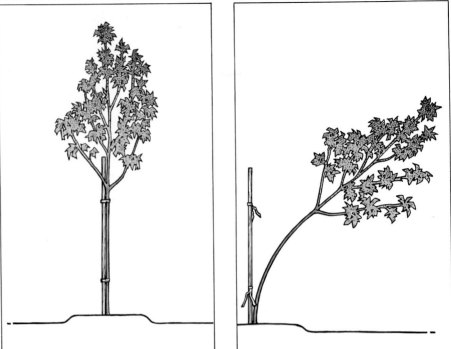

Trees require some freedom of movement in wind to develop sturdy trunk. Unfortunately, most nursery trees are tightly staked as shown here, so height growth is encouraged at expense of trunk development. Ideally you should buy an unstaked tree with enough side branches on lower part of trunk to encourage sturdy trunk growth. If you do buy a staked tree, remove stake after planting. If tree falls over, as shown at right, it will need to be staked as described below.

If unsupported tree cannot stand upright, move your hand slowly up trunk until tree straightens. When tree is straight and top returns to an upright position when bent, the level at which you're holding tree is where it should be tied to the stakes.

Place two stakes 1 foot out from opposite sides of trunk—slightly farther apart if stakes will interfere with root ball. Position stakes at a right angle to prevailing wind. Tie tree to stakes with loose, flexible loops of a non-abrasive material, such as cloth or rubber strips. Brace bottom of stakes with wood brace as shown. Ties should remain loose to allow some trunk movement in wind—check them often.

BRACE

TRANSPLANTING ESTABLISHED TREE OR SHRUB

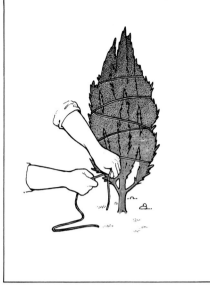

1. Prune lightly by thinning, then wrap branches to pull them together and protect them from possible damage during transplanting.

2. Cut feeder roots by slicing with shovel into soil around plant, approximately at drip line. Make root ball extra large at first—final root ball size will become apparent as roots are exposed. If transplanting plant with long taproot, or native plant well-established in soil, slice feeder roots in this fashion several months before actual transplanting and keep roots watered to encourage growth of new feeder roots to make more compact root ball.

3. Remove soil beyond root ball until you have room to dig under it with shovel. Make the final root ball as large as will hold together as you can manage.

4. Attach wrapping material—burlap, canvas, plastic, chicken wire—to one side with spikes set in root ball (as shown) if soil is heavy and spikes will hold. If soil is sandy or root ball is falling apart, wrap sides with chicken wire.

5. Undercut root ball with shovel, then pry plant in side-to-side motion until you can work wrapping underneath root ball. Try to keep root ball intact—if it begins to disintegrate, slide section of chicken wire underneath, fasten to sides and twist to tighten.

6. Adjust wrapping until tight so root ball holds together as you lift and move it. Set in new location in hole of equal size. Make water basin same size as transplanted root ball. Water thoroughly and spray leaves with anti-transpirant.

SOILS, FERTILIZERS & WATER

Any good gardener is also a good scientist. Granted, most experienced gardeners may not consider themselves scientists, but anyone who successfully raises plants has a good knowledge of the ways in which plants, soil, fertilizer and water all work together. While you are reading this chapter, remember that these are not isolated subjects. Soil, nutrients and water, along with climate, all work in harmony to produce vital, thriving gardens. They form the foundation for understanding all types of gardening—from indoor plants to lawns.

Before you can know how much water or fertilizer to give a plant, or how to improve the soil, you need to know how these three factors work together and what effects each have on the other.

THE BASICS

To understand how soil, nutrients and water work together, you must look at the subject relative to a plant. In the simplest terms, soil provides a structure that permits roots to grow freely, anchoring the plant in place. In most areas—the exception being ones with extremely sandy soil—the soil also contains the nutrients needed to sustain plant growth. Water, from rain or irrigation, soaks into the small spaces between individual soil particles where it becomes available to plant roots. Through the process of *transpiration*—much like a human's perspiration—water is drawn up from the roots, through the plant, and released from the surface of its leaves. Because the water is lost to the atmosphere in this process, water in the

soil must be more or less constantly replenished or the plant will wilt and eventually die of dehydration.

The small spaces between individual soil particles are an extremely important factor in any type of successful gardening. These spaces are where the roots of the plants receive the air, food and water they need to grow. And surprisingly, these small spaces—alternately filled with water, oxygen and nutrients held in a suspension of water—are hard to come by.

The two extreme soil types are clay and sand. Clay soils are made up of extremely small inorganic particles. Conversely, sandy soils are made up of comparatively large individual particles. Clay soils are often referred to as *heavy,* a term that can be misleading. Clay soils don't necessarily weigh more than sand soils, but

---

Left: Roto-tiller makes easy work of cultivating large areas.

Above: Raised beds allow more complete control over soil conditions. Soil is easier to keep free of weeds, has better drainage and warms up faster in spring for earlier planting.

they are denser and have a greater water-holding capacity.

In between these two extremes is the ideal soil type, called *loam*. It is also referred to as *loose* or *friable* soil. Loam soils contain both large and small particles, held together in small groups by a substance called *humus*, described below. When these groups, or aggregates, of different-size particles are held together by humus, they leave fairly stable air spaces in the soil. These spaces allow roots to grow freely, water to enter and room for oxygen after the water drains through—*all* of which are necessary for a healthy plant.

How do you get a soil like this? Some gardeners happen to be lucky enough to live in an area where loam is naturally present. The rest of us have to work at it. Whether you have clay or sandy soil, the key to creating a good soil is *humus*, a sticky excretion produced by microorganisms present in soil. Because there are millions of these microorganisms present in every tablespoon of soil, you may wonder what these creatures eat to produce the byproduct, humus. The answer is *organic matter*—and lots of it. Without a free supply of organic matter, the number of microorganisms present in the soil dwindles drastically, lessening the amount of humus produced. Without humus, the state of poor soil remains the same.

The organic matter may be peat moss, grass clippings, redwood compost, leaf mold, sawdust, manure or any of the other soil amendments illustrated on the facing page. One or more of these materials is commonly available at nurseries and garden centers. It doesn't really make that much difference what type of organic matter you add to the soil, as long as you add it.

In addition to producing humus, and thereby improving the quality of the soil, a thriving population of microorganisms has an important side benefit. Any organic matter (soil amendment), or organic fertilizer such as manure, bone meal, blood-meal or fish emulsion, must be processed first by the microorganisms before it can be used by the plant. If the microorganism population is low, most of the nutrients from the organic fertilizer will be leached through the soil without ever benefitting the plant.

SOIL

Dealing with your garden soil can be as simple or complex as you care to make it. Much has been written recently on the subject of soil analysis, the results of which give you an accurate evaluation of the physical make-up of your soil, its mineral deficiencies or excesses, and its pH. While a battery of sophisticated soil tests aren't essential to a successful garden, there are several you may

want to make. The most important tests are for pH and nutrient deficiencies. Most university or county extension services will test your soil for a nominal fee. You can also buy simple test kits at most nurseries and garden centers. Or you may prefer to take the advice of nursery personnel and gardeners familiar with soil conditions in your area.

If the plants in your garden are not growing as well as you think they should be, or if you're planting a new garden on bare land, you'll need to improve the soil. A soil improvement program can be divided into three main steps:

1. Improving the soil structure.
2. Providing correct nutrient levels.
3. Adjusting the soil pH, if necessary.

The materials needed to carry out such a program are readily available at nurseries and garden centers. These include soil conditioners used to improve soil structure and fertilizers to increase the nutrient levels in the soil. To adjust the pH level, you can use either lime or sulfur, depending on whether you need to increase or decrease the pH. See page 60.

IMPROVING SOIL STRUCTURE

Even those lucky enough to have naturally occurring loam soil should make yearly additions of organic matter to keep the soil in good shape. If your soil is too sandy or clayey, the following section tells you what soil conditioners you can use, when to use them and how to apply them.

WHAT TO ADD TO THE SOIL

Organic matter is available in many different forms. Peat moss, ground bark, sawdust and manure are almost universally available. Redwood soil conditioner, mushroom compost, cocoa bean, almond or rice hulls, and grape or apple pomace are usually available on a regional basis. You can buy organic matter in bags from nurseries and garden centers, or in bulk—sold by the cubic yard—from topsoil dealers. To find topsoil dealers, look under "topsoil" in the yellow pages of your telephone book.

Many studies have been conducted concerning the relative merits of different types of organic matter used as

Compost pile is good source of organic matter for improving soil. Grass border improves appearance.

SOIL AMENDMENTS

Shown here are some of the more common soil amendments used to improve soil structure. Organic amendments such as bark and peat moss enrich soil by providing *humus,* as described on page 56. Amendments such as manure also have value as a fertilizer, adding nitrogen to the soil. Sand is used to improve the structure of clay soils.

Peat moss has excellent water-holding ability and is good for sandy soils. Readily available but expensive.

Manure improves soil structure, also adds nitrogen to soil. Should be well-composted—fresh manure is high in salts, can burn plants.

Straw makes good surface mulch for weed control, can be dug into ground at end of season to enrich soil.

Sand is used along with organic amendments to improve structure of clay soils. Promotes drainage.

Leaf mold decomposes quickly in soil and is relatively short-lived, but adds important nutrients as well as improving soil structure.

Bark chips make good surface mulch, long-lasting soil conditioner.

Pine bark is one of several kinds of ground bark used as a soil conditioner.

Redwood sawdust is a popular soil conditioner in western states. Long-lasting.

COMPOST PILE

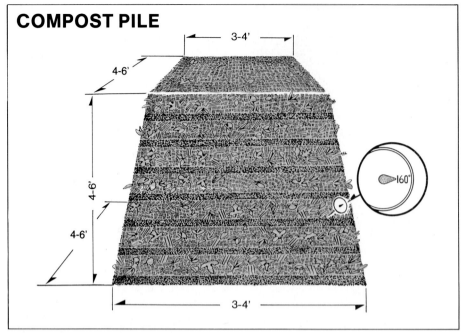

This drawing shows typical dimensions of compost pile. There must be sufficient mass in pile to keep heat at about 160F (72C). A 3'x3'x3' pile is minimum. High temperature promotes decomposition, kills any weed seeds, pests and disease organisms that could be transferred to plants.

a soil conditioner. While it's true that some are better than others, *all* of them will have a beneficial effect on the soil. The only word of caution would be concerning fresh or non-composted manure, which may contain ammonia and salts in levels high enough to damage plant growth. The following is a brief overview of the properties of commonly available organic substances used as soil conditioners:

Ground Bark—The bark of various trees, including fir, are ground into an excellent, long-lasting soil conditioner. Usually available in bags or bulk.

Homemade Compost—If you have your own compost bin or pile and can produce it in large enough quantities, homemade compost is one of the best all-around soil conditioners.

Leaf Mold—A good, although comparatively expensive, soil conditioner. Somewhat short-lived in the soil, but adds nutrients in addition to conditioning soil.

Manure—Available from nurseries in bags or in bulk, or directly from the source—chicken ranches, dairies or feed lots. Usually inexpensive, but make sure it has been composted, or *well-rotted*. Fresh manure is dangerously high in salts and should not be used around plants or in seed beds. As a soil conditioner, manure is comparatively long-lasting, and has some fertilizer value. Best when used in combination with other types of soil conditioners.

Mushroom Compost—Sold in sacks but occasionally available in bulk. A byproduct of mushroom culture, this compost is usually a combination of manure and straw, and as such, should be thoroughly composted before using in the garden. Mushroom compost is a good, comparatively long-lasting conditioner, with some fertilizer value on its own.

Peat Moss—Widely available in bulk or bags. It is an excellent conditioner with superior water-holding ability, making it especially good for use in sandy soils. When incorporated into the soil in large amounts, peat moss will also create a soil structure that permits the high level of aeration demanded by a large group of plants such as azaleas, rhododendrons, camellias and others. Peat moss is a relatively expensive amendment.

Redwood Soil Conditioner—Made from redwood sawdust, this amendment is popular and widespread in the western states. The effects of redwood soil conditioner are long-lasting. Redwood byproducts larger than sawdust can be used as mulch.

Sawdust—Various types of sawdust are often available in bulk form for garden use. They are usually comparatively inexpensive, but unless they have been "nitrogen-fortified," nitrogen will have to be added to keep the sawdust from robbing nitrogen from the soil as it breaks down.

Vermiculite and Perlite—These are considered soil amendments but instead of being organic, they are mineral elements. Vermiculite is mica which has been heated to the point where it puffs up, almost like popcorn. Perlite is pulverized volcanic stone. Both contribute no nutrients but are extremely light in weight and have a tendency to stay in the top layer of soil rather than sinking into lower layers. They are excellent for increasing the water and nutrient-holding capacity of sandy soils, and for increasing aeration in clay soils.

WHEN TO IMPROVE THE SOIL

You can add organic matter to your soil virtually any time during the year but some times are better than others. Obviously, adding organic matter to soil to benefit plants is only effective *before* you plant. Once a plant is in the ground, it is impossible to incorporate the organic matter into the soil without seriously damaging the roots of the plant.

One of the best times to do the job is early autumn, before rains or snow have begun. Apply the organic material of your choice in a thick (3 to 6 inch) layer over the area that you want to improve. It's a good idea to remove large weeds from the area before you cover it with the soil conditioner—smaller weeds will die from lack of sunlight.

Allow the organic material to stay in place through the winter. When spring rains have subsided, and the soil has dried out enough to cultivate easily, incorporate the organic matter into the soil using a tiller or shovel. Leaving the organic matter in place through the winter has two main benefits—first, it inhibits growth of weeds in early spring, and second, the effects of weather mellow the organic matter and it actually begins to compost right on the soil. If you live in a warm-winter area subject to high winds, do not use a light amendment such as peat moss as a surface dressing because it will probably be blown away from the area you're trying to amend.

The second best time to add organic matter to the soil is in spring, just prior to the beginning of the planting season. Wait until the soil has dried out enough to be workable, remove any weeds in the area and then incorporate the organic matter into the soil. This way, any plants planted at the beginning of the season will benefit from the improved soil.

HOW TO USE
SOIL CONDITIONERS

To improve large areas of soil for a lawn, vegetable garden or flower bed, add organic material in an even layer over the top of the soil and then dig in with a tiller or shovel. If you are planting large individual trees or shrubs from 5- or 10-gallon containers, you need only improve the soil in the immediate vicinity of the planting hole.

Large Areas—For an organic material to work as a soil conditioner it has to be added in significant amounts. This is especially true for large areas. The basic rule of thumb is that one third of the final mix should be organic matter. For example, if you are planning to improve the soil to a depth of 9 inches, you should add 3 inches of organic matter to the top of the soil before mixing it in. If you want to improve the soil to a depth of 12 inches, you should incorporate a 4-inch layer of organic matter into the soil.

Depending on the size of the area to be improved, this usually calls for a large amount of organic matter. Before you get started, it's a good idea to measure the area and do a little calling around to find the best value in soil conditioners. Many bulk suppliers will deliver directly to your home. Although you will want to replenish the organic matter in the soil on a regular basis in smaller amounts, rest assured that this massive addition is a one-time-only proposition.

Once you've spread the organic material over the area in a fairly even layer, you will need to incorporate it into the soil to the desired depth. If it's a large area, a power tiller does the job in little time, with the least amount of strain—but just because it's not that much trouble, don't go over the area so many times that you create a fine, powdery mixture. Overtilling the soil to the point that it's powdery and completely free of clods will cause the soil to form a crust the

Roto-tiller is best way to work organic matter into soil over a large area.

first time water is applied. It's far better to err on the side of undertilling rather than overtilling. Clods the size of half-dollars are perfectly acceptable—they can be easily dispatched when you rake the area smooth.

Small Areas—If the area is smaller, or you want some challenging exercise, the same process can be done with a shovel with far less chance of overpulverizing the soil. Spread the organic matter on top of the soil in an even layer and start turning over the soil from one end of the plot to the other. Two passes, perpendicular to each other, will be necessary to achieve a good mix.

Single Planting Holes—This procedure will work for any tree or shrub you might plant. First, dig a hole roughly twice as large as the root ball or the can from which you are taking the plant. Put the dirt from the hole in a pile, add roughly the same amount of organic matter to it and mix together.

Take the plant from the can and check to see how much improved soil you must add back to the hole to have the root ball at the same level as the surrounding soil. Add the soil back to the hole and wet thoroughly to settle. Set the plant in the hole to see if the top of the root ball is at the surrounding soil level. If it is still a little low, add more of the improved soil to

bring it up to the correct level.

Once you've added enough improved soil to the bottom of the hole, put the plant in place, and start adding soil around the root ball, tamping lightly with your hand or shovel handle as you go. After you have filled the hole, use the extra improved soil to make a small berm around the newly planted tree or shrub for a watering basin. The basin should be about the same circumference as the original hole. Water thoroughly. If the soil settles below the level of the surrounding soil, add more improved soil to bring it up to grade, and add water to settle the soil.

Special Method for Vegetable Row Crops—If you are planning an especially large vegetable garden and don't want to go to the effort of improving the soil in the entire area, you can compromise and improve only that soil where the plants are going to grow. The easiest way to accomplish this is to dig a trench, 8 to 10 inches deep and approximately 6 to 8 inches wide, and as long as you intend the row to be. Add organic matter, roughly 50% of the total volume of the soil taken out of the trench, to the soil taken from the trench and mix thoroughly. Put the improved soil back in the trench and water thoroughly. Seeds will germinate with far greater success in this mixture, and plants will get off to a much quicker start, compared to those planted in unimproved soil.

A variation of this method can be used for vegetable transplants, such as tomatoes and squash plants, using the same procedure as described for large areas.

SOIL pH

Soils in different parts of the country have different pH levels. If you're not quite sure what pH is, and why it is important to plants, don't worry. The following explanation tells you all you need to know.

The degree of acidity or alkalinity of a soil is designated by the term pH. The pH scale ranges from 0 to 14. At pH 7.0 the soil is neutral. As the values go downward from pH 7.0, the acidity increases. Conversely, as the values go upward from 7.0, the alkalinity increases. Although many plants have rather specific soil pH requirements, the best growth for a wide range of plants occurs when the

CHANGING SOIL pH

To raise pH: Here are the approximate amounts of ground limestone (dolomite) needed to raise pH (increase alkalinity) of various soils to 6.5 from various lower levels. 6.5 is considered ideal for most plants.

POUNDS OF GROUND LIMESTONE PER 1,000 SQUARE FEET*

Change in pH	Sand	Sandy Loam	Loam	Silt Loam	Clay
4.0 to 6.5	60	115	161	193	230
4.5 to 6.5	51	96	133	161	193
5.0 to 6.5	41	78	106	129	152
5.5 to 6.5	28	60	78	92	106
6.0 to 6.5	14	32	41	51	55

*In southern and coastal states, reduce amounts by approximately one half.

To lower pH: Here are approximate amounts of soil sulfur to lower pH (increase acidity) of various soils to 6.5 from various higher levels.

POUNDS OF SULFUR PER 1,000 SQUARE FEET

Change in pH	Sand	Loam	Clay
8.5 to 6.5	46	57	69
8.0 to 6.5	28	34	46
7.5 to 6.5	11	18	23
7.0 to 6.5	2	4	7

pH of the soil is approximately 6.5.

The pH of a soil affects plant growth because it has a distinct effect on the availablity of nutrients.

You can test the pH of your own soil using a simple pH test kit available from nurseries, garden centers and mail-order scientific supply houses.

Acid Soil—If you find that your particular soil is too acidic, you will want to add lime to it. How much you add depends on how acidic the soil is. Lime is a compound of calcium, and it comes in several different forms. One of the most popular forms is *dolomitic limestone,* because it adds magnesium at the same time it reduces the acidity of the soil. Refer to the above chart for the amount to add to your soil to bring it into a pH range suitable for the plants you want to grow. The best time to add lime is in autumn or spring, at the same time you add the organic matter to improve the soil structure.

Alkaline Soil—If you find your soil is too alkaline, a common problem in warm, dry areas with limited rainfall, you can bring the pH into a more acceptable range with the addition of sulfur, gypsum or lime-sulfur. All are commonly available at nurseries and garden centers. These materials are best added in the spring or any time you are adding organic material to the soil. Refer to the above chart for the amount to add to bring your soil into a pH range suitable for the plants you want to grow.

SHALLOW SOILS

Shallow soils present a real problem to gardeners, especially in some areas of the West and Southwest. You can tell that you have shallow soil if you dig a hole for a tree or shrub and you hit a seemingly impenetrable layer known as *hardpan.* If hardpan occurs within the first 18 inches, you have shallow soil.

Although you may be able to grow annual vegetables and flowers, and some perennials, the vast majority of trees and shrubs will not be able to survive in shallow soil. Some gardeners discover that the hardpan layer is actually quite thin. You can test this yourself using an earth auger, available at most large nurseries and garden centers. Once you encounter the hardpan, use the earth auger to bore through it. If you find that the hardpan is less than 12 inches thick, trees and shrubs will probably grow satisfactorily as long as you bore a hole through the hardpan in each planting hole before planting. If the hardpan is thicker than 12 inches, you'll probably have to garden in raised beds or containers, or change the garden site.

RAISED BEDS

Gardening in raised beds has become the preferred method of vegetable and flower gardening for many people—even for those without the problem of shallow soil. Perhaps the best thing about raised beds is that they can be made any size or shape, as deep as you like, and can be filled with whatever type of soil mixture you desire.

The sides of a raised bed may be built of railroad ties, bricks, 2x4s or 2x6s, or a low rock wall. How tall you make the sides depends on what types of crops you intend to grow. Deep-rooted root crops such as carrots or turnips require 10 to 12 inches of loose soil. Most other types of garden crops will make do in a raised bed with sides 6 to 8 inches tall, provided their roots can penetrate through into the natural layer of soil beneath the raised bed.

Soil in raised beds is much easier to keep free of weeds and debris. It almost always has better drainage qualities, it warms up faster in spring for earlier planting, and it gives a look of order to the garden.

In some respects a raised bed is like a gigantic, open-bottom container. As such, it needs to be filled with a lightweight soil mix that is easy and relatively inexpensive to make in large quantities. The following instructions for making a lightweight soil mix can be used both in containers or raised beds.

Lightweight Soil Mix—Over the years many different formulas or "recipes" have been developed for soil mixes. One of the most successful is equal parts fine sand, peat moss and ground bark. Do *not* use beach sand because of its high salt content. Add to this a complete dry fertilizer, such as a 5-10-10 formula, and some ground limestone in the amounts recommended on the package. The standard proportions for a large quantity (1 cubic yard) are 9 cubic feet each of sand, peat moss and ground bark, 5 pounds of complete fertilizer and 7 pounds of ground limestone.

Start the mix by dampening the peat moss. Combine in one big pile the dampened peat moss, sand and ground bark, and sprinkle the fertilizer and limestone on top. Shovel the mix from this pile into a new pile beside it, one shovelful at a time. Repeat this "pile building" process two more times, and the ingredients should be thoroughly mixed.

ORGANIC MULCHES

Many gardeners are confused by the difference between an organic soil conditioner or amendment and a *mulch*. The confusion stems from the fact that any organic soil conditioner can also be used as a mulch—the difference is not in the material, but how it is used. A soil conditioner is mixed into the soil, while a mulch is applied in a layer on top of the soil.

A 2- to 3-inch layer of an organic mulch is practically a panacea for all sorts of common garden woes. A mulch helps preserve the good structure of a soil by preventing a hard crust from forming on the soil surface. It keeps a majority of weeds from ever sprouting, and the few that do make it through are much easier to pull. A mulch conserves moisture and keeps the moisture level in the soil constant. Lastly, it keeps soil temperature cool and conducive to healthy root growth.

The best time to apply an organic mulch is in autumn after the garden has been cleaned of weeds and debris, or in spring after the soil has had a chance to warm up and dry out a bit. Good gardeners will apply a 3-inch layer of organic mulch in the autumn, then incorporate it lightly into the soil the following spring, adding an inch or so to the top of the soil to replenish the mulch. This highly recommended practice keeps the soil microorganisms well fed and the garden virtually weed-free.

Inorganic Mulches—Inorganic materials such as gravel, decorative rock and black plastic sheeting are sometimes referred to as *inorganic mulches*, because they serve many of the same purposes as an organic mulch. The difference is that they do not decompose in the soil, nor do they provide any nutritional value to plants. Gravel and rock are usually used as a more permanent form of mulch.

Black plastic is used primarily for weed control. It also absorbs heat, warming the soil and is thus sometimes used to get a head start on the growing season for warm-season crops. For this reason, it should not be used around plantings in hot climates. Because black plastic is unsightly, it's often covered with another mulch, such as gravel or bark chips.

MULCH COVERAGE

Here are the numbers of 2-cubic-foot sacks and cubic yards of mulch needed to cover various-size areas at various thicknesses.

Area in Square Feet	Mulch Thickness					
	1/8"	1/4"	1/2"	1"	2"	3"
	2-Cubic-Foot Sacks					
25	.125	.25	.5	1	2	3
50	.25	.5	1	2	4	6
100	.5	1	2	4	8	12
200	1	2	4	8	16	24
300	1.5	3	6	12	24	36
	Cubic Yards*					
1,000	.49	.8	1.5	3.1	6.25	9.4
2,000	.8	1.5	3.1	6.25	12.5	18.75
3,000	1.2	2.3	4.7	9.4	18.7	28
4,000	1.5	3.1	6.25	12.5	24	37.5
5,000	2	4	8	15.5	31.25	47

*13-1/2 sacks of 2 cubic feet equal 1 cubic yard (27 cubic feet).

Here are the numbers of cubic feet and cubic yards of mulch required to cover 1,000 square feet of area at various depths; also the number of cubic yards required to cover 1 acre at these depths.

Depth in Inches	Cubic Feet per 1,000 Square Feet	Cubic Yards per 1,000 Square Feet	Cubic Yards per Acre
1/8	10.53	0.39	17
1/4	21	0.78	34
3/8	30.5	1.17	51
1/2	42	1.56	68
5/8	52.5	1.95	85
3/4	63	2.34	102
1	84	3.12	136
2	168	6.24	272

PEAT MOSS COVERAGE

Here are the number of square feet covered by standard-size bales of compressed peat moss at various depths.

Depth in Inches	COVERAGE IN SQUARE FEET	
	4.0 Cubic Foot Compressed Bale*	5.6 Cubic Foot Compressed Bale*
1/4	345	480
1/2	172	240
1	86	120
2	43	60
3	28	40
4	21	30
6	14	20

*When loosened, compressed peat moss expands approximately 1.8 times its original volume.

USING PLASTIC MULCH FOR VEGETABLE GARDEN

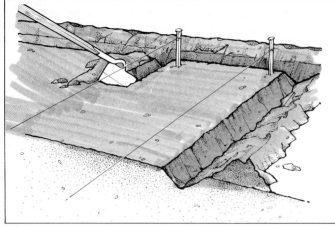

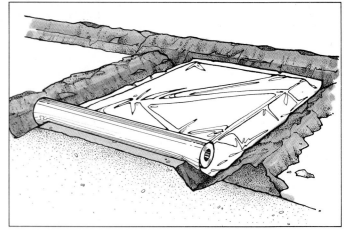

1. After preparing soil, establish straight planting rows with stakes and string. Dig furrows 6 to 8 inches deep. Plastic should be about 12 to 16 inches wider than width of planting row.

2. Unroll plastic over planting row so edges overlap into furrows.

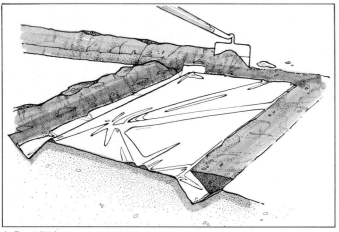

3. Backfill furrows with dirt to hold plastic in place.

4. Dig watering furrows just outside edges of plastic sheet as shown. Use hoe or shovel to punch an "X" at each plant location, then plant seedlings through cuts in plastic.

Pine needles make an attractive mulch in this bed of azaleas.

FERTILIZERS

In ideal situations, the soil naturally supplies plants with all the nutrients they need for healthy growth. Unfortunately, there are many soils where this is not the case, especially in gardens where plants are closely spaced. One example is lawns, where hundreds of thousands of individual grass plants are growing in extremely close proximity to one another, all competing for the same nutrients. Another example is container-grown plants, where nutrients in the soil are eventually leached out by repeated waterings.

There are cases where the nature of the soil itself keeps certain nutrients from being made available to the plant, or where the plant has special requirements, such as acid-loving plants like azaleas, camellias and rhododendrons, that must be met with a unique fertilizer. There are also plants, such as most of the annual vegetable crops, roses, and many citrus trees, that are naturally "heavy feeders," requiring a helping hand from the gardener.

PLANT NUTRIENTS

Before reviewing fertilizers in general, it is important to know a little about how a plant feeds itself. As listed in the introduction on page 8, there are 16 nutrients necessary for plant growth. The plant gets three of these—carbon, hydrogen and oxygen—from air and water, the other 13 nutrients from the soil. All 16 nutrients are essential to plant growth. Three of these—nitrogen, phosphorus, and potassium—are called the *primary nutrients* because they are the ones that most often need replenishing and in the greatest amounts. The *secondary nutrients,* magnesium, calcium and sulfur, are added less frequently because most soils contain adequate amounts of these elements. The remaining nutrients, called *trace elements* or *micronutrients,* are required by plants only in minute amounts and rarely have to be added to the soil.

Primary Nutrients—Nitrogen is the most important nutrient in any plant food. It is the ingredient that stimulates new growth and the ingredient usually in shortest supply in soils. Plants use it up quickly and it is rapidly leached from the soil by watering.

Nitrogen is used by plants only when they are growing—during the dormant season, the plant has no use for it. Applied at the wrong time, nitrogen can trigger tender new plant growth during periods of harsh, cold weather. So when you apply a fertilizer, remember that you want to help a plant grow during the period that it naturally wants to grow, which is usually from spring through early autumn.

The other two primary elements are phosphorus and potassium (potash). Both are used by plants to a much lesser degree than nitrogen, but more so than the trace elements.

Trace Elements—In addition to the primary and secondary nutrients, plants require minute amounts of the *trace elements,* also called *micronutrients.* Most soils contain sufficient quantities of these nutrients, but in some soils (notably alkaline ones) some of these nutrients may be "locked-up" in the form of insoluble compounds, making them unavailable to plants. Alkaline soils are often deficient in soluble iron and manganese. Acidifying the soil with sulfur, iron sulfate or ammonium sulfate "releases" these nutrients, making them available to plants.

Most complete fertilizers contain a correct portion of trace elements. Some trace elements are sold individually, but you should not use them unless a plant shows a deficiency. An oversupply of certain trace elements can be toxic to plants. Apply trace elements on their own only if they are specifically recommended to correct a condition diagnosed by your agricultural extension agent or local nursery.

FERTILIZER CHOICES

A quick look at the fertilizer section of any good-sized nursery or garden center reveals a bewildering array of general fertilizers and an even more confusing selection of specialty products. The following information should help simplify your choices and guide you to the products you really need.

Manufacturers of mixed commercial fertilizers are required by law to state on the container the guaranteed content of primary nutrients. When a fertilizer contains all three of these nutrients it is considered a *complete* fertilizer. These three nutrients are used by plants in large amounts and are likely to be deficient in the soil in varying amounts. When you buy a fertilizer, you generally buy it for its content of these materials.

The primary nutrient content of a fertilizer mixture is indicated by its *grade*—a series of three numbers separated by dashes, usually highly visible on some part of the label. The numbers show the percentage of

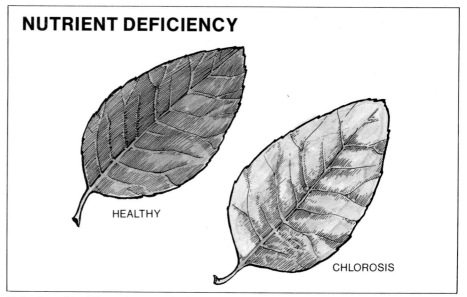

NUTRIENT DEFICIENCY

HEALTHY

CHLOROSIS

Yellowing of leaf tissue between leaf veins usually indicates a deficiency in iron, less often, zinc. Called *chlorosis,* this condition usually appears on newest growth first. Iron chlorosis is common in alkaline soils. Overall yellowing of older leaves often indicates nitrogen deficiency.

FERTILIZER APPLICATION RATES

Here are number of pounds of various-percentage nitrogen fertilizers required to equal 1 pound of actual nitrogen per 1,000 square feet for various-size areas.

		COVERAGE IN SQUARE FEET				
	500	1,000	1,500	2,000	3,000	1 acre
Percentage Nitrogen			POUNDS FERTILIZER			
40%	1.3	2.5	3.8	5	7.6	109
36%	1.4	2.75	4	5.5	8.5	121
30%	1.7	3.5	5	6.6	10	145
25%	2	4	6	8	12	180
20%	2.5	5	7.5	10	15	218
15%	3.3	6.6	10	13	20	308
10%	5	10	15	20	30	436
7%	7	14	21.5	29	43	622
6%	8.5	17	25.5	34	51	726
5%	10	20	30	40	60	870
2%	25	50	75	100	150	2,178

Here are recommended amounts of some soluble dry fertilizers added to water to make nutrient solutions*.

Nutrient	Material	Amount
Nitrogen, Sulfur	Ammonium sulfate	2-3 lbs./100 gal.
Nitrogen	Sodium nitrate	1 oz./gal.
Nitrogen, Calcium	Calcium nitrate	1.5 oz./gal.
Nitrogen, Potassium	Potassium nitrate	1.5 oz./gal.
Nitrogen	Ammonium nitrate	.25 oz./gal.
Nitrogen, Phosphorus	Monoammonium phosphate	1.5 oz./gal.
Potassium, Sulfur	Potassium sulfate	.25 oz./gal.
Magnesium, Sulfur	Magnesium sulfate	1 lb./100 gal.
Iron	Ferrous sulfate	3 lbs/100 gal.

*Adapted from O'Rourke, Louisiana State University.

Here are amounts of soluble dry fertilizers added to water to make foliar sprays to supply nutrients*

Nutrient	Material	Amount	Application
Nitrogen	Urea	.5 lb./100 gal.	Weekly until leaves green
Iron	Ferrous sulfate	.5 oz./gal.	Weekly until leaves green
Manganese	Manganese sulfate	8 oz./100 gal.	Cautiously

*Adapted from O'Rourke, Louisiana State University.

nitrogen, phosphorus and potassium, in that order, contained in the mixture. For example, a mixture with the grade 5-10-5 contains by weight 5% total nitrogen, 10% available phosphorus and 5% soluble potash.

The relative proportions of primary nutrients in a fertilizer mixture determine the suitability of the mixture for specific soils and plants. For example, lawn fertilizers are usually highest in nitrogen—the nutrient used most by lawns. Fertilizers for use on vegetables are usually highest in their proportion of phosphorus for healthy root growth. It may be wasteful, and even harmful, to use the wrong type of fertilizer. Uses for general-purpose fertilizers are customarily listed on the labels, along with recommended amounts for each kind of plant. Always follow the label directions carefully.

Specialty Fertilizers—Some fertilizers are manufactured in grades suitable for use on a specific type of plant. These include fertilizers for tomatoes, lawns, orchids, house plants, acid-loving plants, citrus and avocado, roses and others. While excellent for use on the plants for which they are intended, these are often more expensive than general formulations. Before you buy a specialty fertilizer, ask whether a more general fertilizer—one you may already have on hand—would work just as well.

The Best Deal—As a rule, fertilizers with the same relative proportions of primary nutrients can be used interchangeably. Although fertilizers may be labeled different grades, the nutrient proportions may be the same. For example, 5-10-5 and 6-12-6 are both composed of 1 part nitrogen, 2 parts phosphorus and 1 part potash, but the 6-12-6 contains the higher percentage of these nutrients. It usually is only necessary to alter the rate of application so that the desired amounts of primary nutrients are applied to the area being fed.

Frequently, the price per pound of the *nutrients* in fertilizers containing a high percentage of nutrients may be lower than the price per pound of nutrients in fertilizers containing a lower ratio of percentages. For example, 1 pound of 10-20-10 fertilizer contains the same amount of nutrients as 2 pounds of 5-10-5, yet an 80-pound bag of 10-20-10 may cost only 1/3 more than an 80 pound bag of 5-10-5. For the greatest economy, buy fertilizer for its weight of nutrients per dollar, not for its total weight.

ORGANIC VS. CHEMICAL FERTILIZERS

There has long been a debate over the relative merits of organic versus chemical fertilizers. Actually, a plant cannot tell the difference from the nitrogen contained in fish emulsion, for example, and the nitrogen contained in a manufactured chemical fertilizer. But the plant's reaction to the nutrients is only part of the story.

Generally speaking, organic fertilizers, such as composted manure, activated sewage sludge, cottonseed meal, blood meal and fish emulsion, benefit the soil as well as the plant. The organic material that contains the nutrients also provides the microorganisms in the soil with the materials they need to be active. As a rule, chemical fertilizers are beneficial to the plant only. But the nutrients found in organic formulations are usually much lower in percentages than those in manufactured chemical products. And nutrients in organic fertilizers usually are slower to act.

Most serious gardeners favor a combination of organic and chemical fertilizers—the organic for long-term, light feedings that benefit the soil, and chemical formulations for faster-acting results. In the long run, this is a wise practice.

FERTILIZER FORMS

Commercial fertilizers come in dry or liquid forms. Dry fertilizers may be granules, pellets or powder. The granulated or pelleted forms are the easiest to apply, which can be done using a spreader, and neither blow around as freely nor cake as readily as powdered forms. Dry fertilizers are favored for such wide-area large applications as lawns or ground covers.

Liquid, concentrated fertilizers can be mixed with water and applied with a hose-end sprayer or a liquid proportioner through a drip-irrigation system or sprinkler, or by hand in a bucket or watering can. Being liquid, these fertilizers go to work right away—they do not need additional water to carry nutrients into the root zone. Liquid fertilizers are favored by container gardeners—both indoors and out.

Slow-release fertilizers are available in capsules, spikes and pelleted forms in such a way that their nutrients are available over a long period of time, somewhat like a time-release cold capsule. These products can be a boon, especially for container gardeners who find it hard to remember when to feed their plants. Most of these products last for 3 to 6 months, eliminating the need for frequent feedings.

COMBINATION PRODUCTS

Fertilizer-insecticides and fertilizer-weed killers are generally designed for use on lawns. The USDA has this to say regarding these combination products: "One problem with such combinations is that chemicals are being applied that would normally be used less frequently or not at all. In some instances, fertilizers containing pre-emergence crabgrass herbicides are applied in the fall when, in fact, the herbicide should be applied in the spring. Some fertilizer-herbicide combinations injure or kill trees or shrubs when applied to grass under them. Pushing a fertilizer spreader back and forth under a tree or shrub often results in applying much more than the recommended rate of material.

"Another problem is the concentration of the ingredients. There is no way of adjusting the rate of application for different uses. Combination fertilizer and broadleaf-weed herbicides are often applied when broadleaf weeds are not present in the lawn. Also,

DRY-FERTILIZER SPREADERS

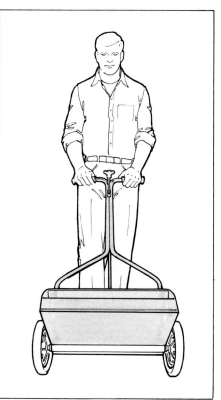

1. Drop spreaders apply accurate amounts of fertilizer to lawns in 18-inch-wide bands. Usually hold more material than other types of spreaders. Preferred if using fertilizer-herbicide combination products.

2. Broadcast spreaders distribute material in bands up to 16 feet wide. Best for large lawns.

3. Hand-held broadcast spreaders are inexpensive but must be refilled often. Good for use on flower beds, ground covers and uneven terrain.

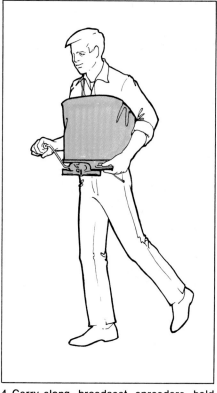

4. Carry-along broadcast spreaders hold more fertilizer than hand-held spreaders and are ideal for feeding large lawns, flower beds, ground covers and uneven areas.

Siphon attachment mixes liquid fertilizer with water at faucet connection, which allows fertilizer to be applied through drip systems, various kinds of sprinklers or other hose-end watering devices.

Root feeder applies fertilizer directly to root zone of trees and large shrubs.

and understand all label directions and precautions *before* you apply any fertilizer.

WATER

If sunlight powers the garden, then water certainly nurtures it. Unfortunately, no one subject of gardening gives as many problems to gardeners as does watering. The main problem is the number of variables that must be considered when giving advice. As soon as you've established one set of rules, you often have to turn around and practically contradict them to allow for a new set of variables. Be that as it may, there are a few truths and guidelines that can be established. These are discussed starting on page 68. But first, let's take a look at some typical problems when there is either too little or too much water.

Water Shortage—Some water is lost from the soil directly through evaporation, and some water is lost indirectly through transpiration of the plant. The combined water loss is known as *evapotranspiration* (E.T.). Whenever the E.T. rate exceeds the available amount of water in the soil, there is drought.

Too little water is probably the most common water problem in outdoor gardens. The first signs of a plant struggling for water are subtle and worth learning to spot. There is a change in plant color from a healthy green to a pale or gray-green. Also, the temperature of the leaves rises. Some farmers can tell whether or not plants need water by pressing leaves against their cheeks to feel the leaf temperature.

Of course, wilting is a clear signal of a water problem. But check first to be sure it is actually caused by too little water in the soil—watering plants that don't need it does more harm than good. Plants will also wilt when suffocating in soil that is *too full of water.* This often happens to house plants in containers with no drainage holes or in soil too heavy to allow enough air to circulate. Some plants, such as melons, commonly wilt during the hottest part of a summer day, then recover that same evening. They simply transpire more water than roots can replace, even though enough water is present in the soil.

Any plant will die if deprived of

there is a tendency to apply fertilizer with a broadleaf weed killer in the summer when cool-season grasses should not be fertilized.

"Homeowners should be aware of these problems and considerations when purchasing and applying fertilizer-insecticide or herbicide combinations. Usually, fertilizers and pesticides are best applied separately."

That may well be the case for combination products for lawn use, but the ones designed for use around roses can be particularly helpful to the home gardener. There are several combination products—fertilizer with systemic insecticide, fertilizer with weed killer, or fertilizer with both insecticide and weed killer—that are both easy to use and very effective. It is extremely important when you use any combination product that you read and follow the label directions explicitly, especially with regard to rates of application and timing.

NON-NITROGEN FERTILIZERS

Fertilizers containing no nitrogen are usually sold as *bloom or fruit enhancers* and they do improve both flower and fruit production when used correctly. Apply them in late autumn through early spring. The phosphorus and potash promote healthy root de-

velopment and increase the plant's abilities to withstand the rigors of winter. But remember that these are not complete fertilizers, and they are generally meant to be used during the dormant season only. When warm weather arrives in spring, it's time to switch to a complete fertilizer containing nitrogen.

WHAT TO DO WHEN YOU'VE APPLIED TOO MUCH

Nothing is worse than finding out after you've applied a fertilizer that you've applied too much. Although most organic forms of fertilizer are slightly more forgiving when it comes to overfertilization, both organic and chemical formulations will quickly burn or kill a plant or lawn if the concentrations are high enough.

About the only thing you can do is try to leach the nutrients through the soil with repeated heavy waterings. This is particularly effective with plants in containers where it is relatively simple to turn a hose on low and let it completely leach the fertilizer out the drain hole. In garden situations, the chances for leaching successfully are less but it may keep plants from dying completely. This is why it is extremely important to read

water long enough. But in everyday practice, water stress affects different plants in different ways. Generally, long-lived perennial plants such as trees are most tolerant of an occasional drought. Annuals—especially salad crops—are most susceptible. Some annuals will never return to optimum growth after one period of drought.

Lettuce, for example, will not be as crisp and succulent as it would have been. Hence the importance of mulching and otherwise ensuring a continuous supply of water to such crops. Although the trees fully recover, the fruit of a drought-stressed lemon or apple will be tough and stringy, and perhaps somewhat woody. A form of drought stress—extremely low humidity—is thought by some to be related to the tomato disease known as *blossom end rot*. This disease might also be caused by a calcium deficiency and fluctuations in soil temperature.

Water Excess—The problem of too much water in the soil is really the same as too little air in the soil. When water fills all the available spaces in soil, the roots suffocate. As with too little water, wilting is one of the first symptoms of waterlog.

Too much water in the soil is most often a problem with house plants, especially those growing in containers without holes for drainage. Most plants growing in containers benefit from a soil mix that allows an abundance of air circulation. A soil mix that rapidly drains excess water is virtually impossible to overwater.

Watering plants in non-draining containers is a delicate affair. First of all, try to rearrange things so that the rootball of the plant can drain into another, larger container. This is called *double potting*. If that is not possible, try to insert a narrow pipe into the soil that reaches the container bottom. Then you can use a pencil or similar object as a sort of dipstick to see if water is collecting on the bottom of the container.

Too much water in outdoor soils is less common but does occur. If you live where rainfall is more than simply "abundant," such as New Orleans, or where rainfall seems to be constant such as western Washington, you are probably aware of the problem. One of the best solutions is planting in raised mounds or beds. Raising the soil level where you plant ensures drainage at least to the level of the surrounding soil. Raised-bed planting is

Left: Wilting is an obvious sign of water shortage. Container plants dry out more quickly than plants in the ground. Right: Wilted plants usually recover about 1/2 hour after watering. If not, check for other causes. *Too much* water can also cause wilting.

also beneficial for plants that thrive only with more than average amounts of air in the soil. Azaleas and rhododendrons are in that category.

WATERING GUIDELINES

Though watering requirements vary widely, depending on climate, time of year and type of plants being grown, there are some basic rules you can follow to make sure your plants get the correct amount of water.

The first rule of watering is: *Do not let your plants get to the wilting stage before you water them.* Remember that wilting can also be a sign of too much water, so check soil before watering wilted plants to make sure the wilting is not caused by excess water.

Second, it is easy to underwater or overwater plants, given the type of soil they are planted in. Water applied to sandy soil drains through quickly, causing the gardener to pay almost constant attention to water needs of the plants.

Conversely, clay soils are notorious for their ability to retain water. In clay soils it is common for the top crust of soil to appear dry even though an inch or so under the surface there is plenty of water. The unwitting gardener sees the dry surface soil and applies water when none is needed. Loam soils

have the best drainage and retention pattern of any soil. Enough water is retained between waterings to supply the plant, while excess water drains through readily, allowing oxygen to takes its place. So the second rule is: *The best defense against overwatering and underwatering is to create a good soil.* For more information on improving your soil, see pages 56-59.

Third, climate plays an important role in the amount of water a plant needs. The same plant grown in a foggy coastline location will need far less water than one in a hot, interior valley. Hot weather combined with wind will desiccate a garden faster than you can say "sprinkler." Some regions have plentiful summer rains, while others have such little rain that it becomes nearly impossible to leave the garden to take a vacation. Watering schedules must also be adjusted as the climate changes throughout the year. The third rule is: *Adjust watering schedules and requirements according to your own climate—not to some general guidelines.*

Fourth, different plants have different water needs. In most gardens, a grass lawn has by far the greatest need for water, followed by vegetables, annual and perennial flowers, shrubs and then trees. Generally, the longer

Placing cups at regular intervals out from sprinkler will show you how much water sprinkler applies at various distances from sprinkler head. See "How Much Is Enough?" in text below.

a permanent shrub or tree has been growing, the less you'll have to water them. Newly planted trees and shrubs will have to be watered regularly during the first year of growth in your garden.

Plants native to your climate demand less water than plants imported from wetter regions. Conversely, plants native to dry areas can drown if planted in wet climates or areas where soil drains poorly. The fourth rule is: *Learn the individual needs of your plants, and water accordingly.*

Fifth, water that drains away from the root zone of the plant is wasted. Make soil basins around trees, shrubs and solitary vegetables as shown in the photo on page 51. Basins direct water to plant roots. The best size for a basin is one that extends to the plant's drip line. Be sure to enlarge the circumference of the basin around trees and shrubs as they grow. Trees and shrubs in a lawn area can get most of their water from normal lawn irrigation, but a little extra water around a tree will often help its root system develop fully and deeply.

Plant row vegetables on mounds or hills with irrigation trenches (furrows) between them. Water in the trenches will be drawn up into the hills in a siphonlike action. A trip in the countryside will dramatically illustrate the importance farmers place on furrows and basins.

When watering lawns, don't apply water faster than it can be absorbed by the soil. If water is running down sidewalks or driveways, you are applying it too fast or your sprinklers are not correctly directed. The fifth rule is: *Direct water to plant roots and do not apply more water than the soil can absorb.*

Sixth, deep-rooted plants have a larger reservoir of soil moisture to draw from. Such plants will be able to go longer between waterings and are more likely to withstand periods of drought. The final rule is: *Water deeply to encourage deep rooting.*

HOW MUCH IS ENOUGH?

One of the simplest ways to tell if you've applied enough water to a particular area is to test it with a metal probe or long screwdriver.

Irrigate until you think you've applied enough water. Turn off the water and check the depth of penetration with the probe or screwdriver. You will be able to push the rod easily into wet soil, but it will stop when it reaches dry soil. Water should have soaked down to at least two-thirds the final depth you want.

Grass roots commonly reach 24 inches into the soil, dichondra 8 inches, bedding plants 15 inches, shrubs 36 inches and trees 10 feet or more.

In a sandy loam soil, 2 inches of water should penetrate between 1 and 2 feet. Penetration will be less in clay soils, more in sandy soils. If soil is covered with lawn or weeds, penetration will be less. By using a soil probe frequently, you will be able to gauge the correct amount of water needed to completely wet the root zones.

WAYS TO APPLY WATER

There are many different ways to apply water in the garden—from the old-standby hose-end sprinklers to modern drip irrigation systems.

Hose-End Sprinklers—In any given nursery or garden center, there will probably be at least a dozen different types of sprinklers to choose from. The one you choose should correspond to the area you have to cover and also to the type of soil you have. In short, as one of our previous watering rules states, don't choose a sprinkler that applies water faster than your soil can absorb it.

Watch for signs that water is being applied too fast—puddles, streams running into other areas of the garden, and wet sidewalks or driveways.

The pattern in which water is applied is also important, especially with lawn sprinklers. Some sprinklers apply water in circular patterns, which means they miss the corners of a square lawn. Others water in square or rectangular patterns. They can be wasteful when used on circular or irregularly shaped lawns. Check the sprinkler box for the watering pattern. Your best choice is probably one with an adjustable pattern. Also check how large an area the sprinkler covers. Some sprinklers are designed for watering large areas, others are made for watering small ones. You can save a lot of time moving sprinklers if you have the right kinds.

Hose-End Water Nozzles—Hard jets or sprays of water can disturb soil and in some cases harm plants, especially newly planted transplants. So you will want to have at least one type of hose-end nozzle. Bubblers or breakers apply an even, rainlike spray which is ideal for watering delicate plants or transplants. A bubbler can be laid directly in a watering basin or furrow.

Some models have extension arms for reaching hanging baskets.

Nozzles with adjustable sprays can be very useful. They give you a choice of patterns, from a hard jet, often necessary for garden cleanup, to a fine mist for delicate plants such as ferns. The pistol-grip nozzle is one of the most popular adjustable sprayers.

Hoses—Choose a garden hose carefully. Never compromise on quality. Money you save purchasing a low-quality hose will be charged against your patience when you try to use it. Select a hose made of high-quality rubber or laminated filament that is flexible in any weather. Make sure it is long enough to reach any area in the garden. The larger the hose diameter, the more water delivered—a hose 5/8 or 3/4 of an inch in diameter is best.

Snap-On Watering Systems—Many sprinkler manufacturers are developing snap-on watering systems that simplify watering. All hoses and faucets are equipped with adaptors that allow you to snap-on all sprinklers and accessories. Nothing has to be screwed on. If you decide on one of these systems, make sure it is durable, leakproof and that the manufacturer offers all the accessories you will need. Components produced by different manufacturers are usually not interchangeable.

Drip Irrigation—Drip irrigation has revolutionized many commercial farm and ranch operations. There are small kits available for home gardeners that can take much of the labor out of watering vegetable gardens, container plants, landscape plantings and flower borders—with the added benefit of significant water savings as well.

The principle of drip irrigation is to supply small amounts of water on an almost constant basis, supplying only that water which the plant actually needs. The systems consist of a water pressure reducer and a series of gradually smaller lines, ending with very small emitters or porous tubes that supply water directly to the soil around the plant. By doing so, you reduce weeds because less soil is wet and you eliminate water puddling and runoff.

Different types of emitters are available to fit different gardening needs. They vary by the amount of water applied, usually rated in gallons per minute. In some cases, the emitters are more like mini-sprinklers than drippers like the one shown in the photo below. Some can provide a spray up to 10 feet wide By placing spray emitters on support stakes they can be combined to water large areas of ground covers or closely spaced vegetables. Other emitters yield a very fine mist, ideal for plants that like high humidity, such as ferns.

Each drip irrigation kit comes with complete instructions on how to custom design a watering system that fits your gardening needs. Some include automatic timers that are attached between your hose bib and the system to turn water on and off according to your directions.

Many hardware stores and garden centers sell drip irrigation components separately so you can design your own system, large or small. Upon request, these stores will supply helpful literature if it isn't included in the display. There are also a growing number of stores that specialize in irrigation equipment. They usually represent several manufacturers and provide valuable help and information.

Underground Watering Systems—If you have a large garden or lawn area, you might want to consider a permanent underground watering system. These consist of permanently placed sprinklers connected underground by PVC pipe tapped directly into your home water supply. Most systems consist of several networks of sprinklers that water various areas of the garden separately, according to each area's water requirements. Shrubs and trees would not necessarily be watered at the same time as the lawn. Networks usually include an automatic timer so watering becomes virtually effortless.

Many different styles of underground sprinklers are produced by a number of manufacturers. Sprinklers are available with square or circular watering patterns, and with heads designed for lawns or for landscape plants. One type used for lawns pops up out of the ground during operation, then drops back down to escape lawn mowers when not in use.

Most sprinkler manufacturers will provide do-it-yourself instructions for installing underground sprinkler systems. However, installing a large system can be complicated and time consuming—hardly a weekend project. In addition, many communities have codes dictating how the systems must be set up. If you do a large project yourself, checking your plans with a landscape contractor or irrigation specialist is money well spent.

Smaller underground systems are usually a simple project for do-it-yourselfers. You may even be able to find complete kits that contain everything needed for a small lawn system.

Hard jets of water can erode soil, disturb plant roots. Breaker attachment shown here applies a steady, gentle stream of water.

Soils, Fertilizers & Water **69**

TYPICAL DRIP-IRRIGATION LAYOUT

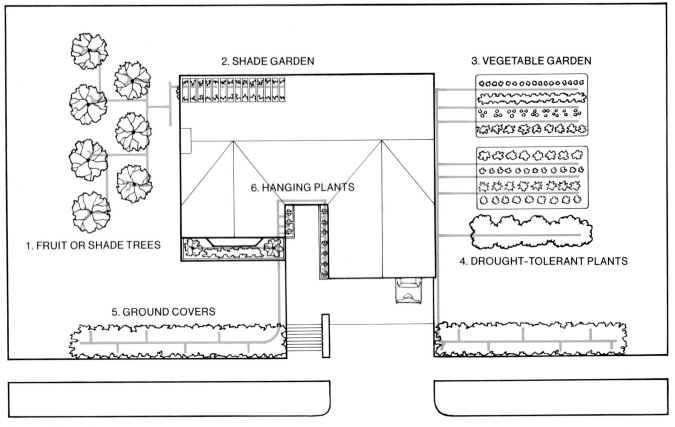

2. SHADE GARDEN

3. VEGETABLE GARDEN

6. HANGING PLANTS

1. FRUIT OR SHADE TREES

4. DROUGHT-TOLERANT PLANTS

5. GROUND COVERS

Areas on Map
1. Fruit or shade trees: Use several emitters evenly spaced under the tree canopy. Large trees need more emitters.
2. Shade garden: Use misters or sprayers for plants that like high humidity, such as ferns. Otherwise, use regular drip emitters.
3. Vegetable garden: Use emitters or ooze-tubes according to plant size and spacing. Keep system above ground for easy removal prior to tilling.
4. Drought-tolerant plants: Use drip system until plants are established, then remove system.
5. Ground covers: Use mini-sprinklers for herbaceous, spreading plants. Use grid of emitters for shrubby ground covers.
6. Hanging plants: Run main lines above plants. Suspend emitters or misters from above.

First step to installing drip-irrigation system is to draw map of your property, including all plants and their comparative water needs. Draw map to scale so you can estimate materials needed. Use map to determine drip system layout, including main lines, lateral lines, and number and kind of emitters needed. Hide or bury lines whenever possible.

Spray emitter is one of several attachments available for drip-irrigation systems. With spray patterns up to 10 feet wide, these emitters are used to cover large areas of ground cover or low plantings, such as basil shown here.

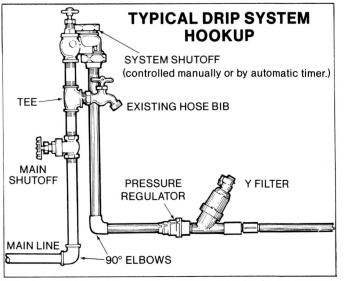

TYPICAL DRIP SYSTEM HOOKUP

SYSTEM SHUTOFF
(controlled manually or by automatic timer.)

TEE

EXISTING HOSE BIB

MAIN SHUTOFF

PRESSURE REGULATOR

Y FILTER

MAIN LINE

90° ELBOWS

This drawing shows how most drip systems are plumbed to an existing outdoor faucet. Various components shown are typical.

INSTALLING A DRIP SYSTEM

Most drip systems consist of flexible PVC pipe and fittings, and are installed as shown here. You can buy kits that come complete with instructions or buy components separately.

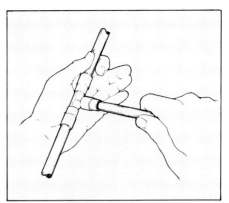

1. After installing the system shutoff, pressure regulator and filter assembly (see drawing on facing page), lay out main line.

2. Lay out lateral lines and attach to main line with tee fittings.

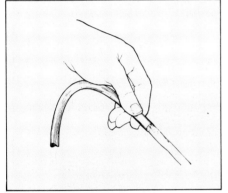

3. Turn on water to clear main and lateral lines. Attach end caps to lines.

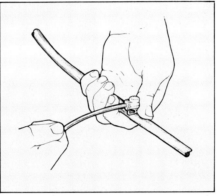

4. Assemble emitters and attach to main and lateral lines.

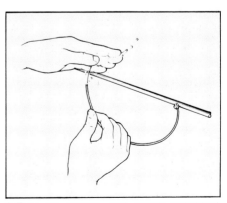

5. Complete assembly by positioning emitters in final locations. If main and lateral lines run underground, replace soil.

DRIP SYSTEM MAINTENANCE

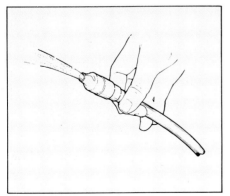

1. Remove or open end caps in main and lateral lines and flush system with water.

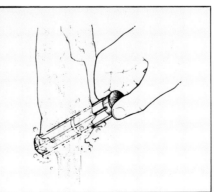

2. Remove filter and wash under running water. Replace.

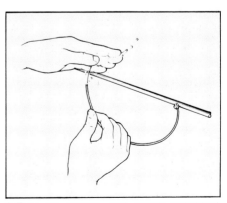

3. Turn on system and check individual emitters. If clogged, remove and clean. Replace damaged emitters, if necessary.

PRUNING

Pruning is one of the most misunderstood, therefore neglected, of all the common gardening techniques. But by understanding a few basic pruning fundamentals, you can be well on your way to becoming a truly effective director of plant growth.

The general objectives of pruning are to modify plant growth based on the conditions of the garden or your own needs and wishes. Some plants require frequent pruning, others may need little or none.

Pruning helps maintain plant health by cutting out dead, diseased or injured wood. It controls growth when an unshapely shrub or tree might otherwise result. It can increase the quality and yield of flowers or fruit, open up views or let in more sunlight. It can also train or shape plants to make a garden or landscape appear formal or informal.

TOOLS OF PRUNING

The first three tools listed below are essential and will handle most of your pruning chores. But no matter how many tools you buy, always invest in quality ones. It is penny-wise and pound-foolish to buy poorly made tools that soon break, won't hold a cutting edge or otherwise work poorly. Quality pruning tools also allow you to fully enjoy the pleasures of pruning.

Clippers—These tools are sometimes called *hand shears* or *snippers*—in England, *secateurs*. The *scissor* type has overlapping hooked and curved blades. The *anvil* type has a cutting blade that meets a flat surface. Both types are good for branches up to 1/2 inch in diameter.

Lopping Shears—This long-handled, heavy-duty tool comes with anvil or scissor type blades and is operated with two hands. Handles range from 15 to 30 inches. Use for branches up to 1-1/4 inches in diameter.

Curved Saw—This small hand saw has a narrow, curved blade with a folding or rigid handle. The saw is especially useful where growth is crowded and for branches up to 2 inches in diameter.

Bow Saw—This saw has a thin, replaceable blade with curved overhead support and handle. It comes in several sizes, and is used for quick cutting of branches over 2 inches in diameter.

Pole Saw—This long-handled version of pruning saw is used for cutting high branches up to 3 inches in diameter.

Pole Pruner—Also called a *pruning hook,* this tool has a long pole with hook for holding branches and a blade operated by a rod or rope. Use it to cut high branches. Avoid aluminum poles for both pruners and saws if you'll be pruning around overhead electrical wires.

Left: Hand clippers are the most versatile and frequently used of all pruning tools. Buy best ones you can afford.

Above: Many kinds of evergreen shrubs can be pruned to formal hedges. Here, three different kinds of shrubs meet at property line.

PRUNING TOOLS

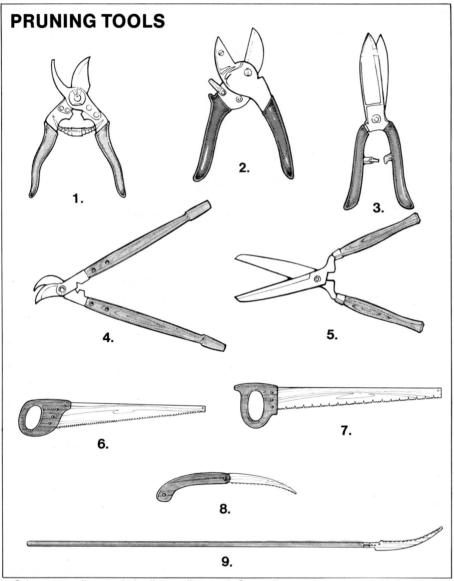

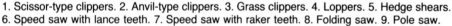

1. Scissor-type clippers. 2. Anvil-type clippers. 3. Grass clippers.
6. Speed saw with lance teeth. 7. Speed saw with raker teeth. 8. Folding saw. 9. Pole saw.
4. Loppers. 5. Hedge shears.

Chain Saw—This powerful, fast-cutting tool will do light pruning or remove entire trees. The length of the cutting bar on the saw determines the size branch that can be cut. The bar length should exceed the diameter of the branch to be cut. Some saws have interchangeable bars. These saws are dangerous to operate, so use them with extreme care. Follow all safety precautions in the owner's manual. Electric and gas-powered models are available.

Hedge Shears—Two types are available: hand-operated, long-bladed, scissor-type shears and electric shears, with a long, flat reciprocal blade in serrated housing. Used for

trimming hedges, shrubs and ground covers.

Pruning Knife—This knife has a curved blade for small pruning cuts and for smoothing the edges of large pruning wounds.

Ladder—Choose a solidly constructed ladder of sufficient height to comfortably reach branches with selected tools. It should be tall enough so you don't have to stand on the top two steps. The three-leg orchard ladder is the safest and most convenient type for garden use because it is the most stable on uneven ground. Extension ladders are used for reaching higher limbs. Four-leg household stepladders are not recommended for pruning be-

cause they are unstable on uneven ground.

WHEN TO PRUNE

Most ornamental trees and shrubs can be lightly pruned any time. It is also true that there is usually one season of the year that a particular plant is best pruned—see the chart on the facing page. Here are some important guidelines:

• Prune shrubs that flower in spring just after flowers fade.
• Prune pines in spring when the "candles" are soft.
• Prune rhododendrons and azaleas after flowers have faded and while the new growth is soft.
• Prune (shear) formal hedges whenever they begin to look ragged.
• Prune walnut, maple, and birch trees in late fall or winter to avoid excessive bleeding.
• Prune the vast majority of other vines, shrubs, and trees in late winter or early spring whenever temperatures are above 20F (7C).

Summer Pruning—We usually think of dormant seasons of fall or early spring as pruning times. However, when you want to control the size of a plant, you might choose to prune lightly in early to midsummer. You can selectively remove one or two entire branches or shorten others by cutting back one-third to one-half of their length to a side branch. Heavy cutting is followed by some new growth on the noticeably smaller plant or tree. Continue light pruning through the summer until the plant is whittled down to the desired size. Remember that woody plants can be killed by repeated summer prunings, so this should not be a regular practice.

You can prune roses during their summer blooming season to increase vigor, produce high-quality flowers and prevent seed formation. Throughout the summer, keep faded flowers clipped or pinched from roses, shrubs and other flowering plants. Removing faded or dead flowers is called *dead-heading*.

Winter Pruning—Pruning in fall or early winter just before plants become dormant increases sensitivity to freezing for at least the 2 weeks that follow. Prune early enough to allow time for healing before the first frost to prevent serious injury or death.

Late winter pruning during dorman-

WHEN TO PRUNE

	JAN	FEB	MAR	APR	MAY	JUN	JUL	AUG	SEP	OCT	NOV	DEC
CONIFERS	NO PRUNE		PRUNE	NO PRUNE			THIN				NO PRUNE	
DECIDUOUS TREES	PRUNE			LEAST PRUNE			THIN				NO PRUNE	PRUNE
EARLY-FLOWER DECIDUOUS		PRUNE			LEAST PRUNE		THIN			NO PRUNE		
LATE-FLOWER DECIDUOUS	PRUNE		LEAST PRUNE		PRUNE							PRUNE
HARDY BROAD-LEAF EVERGREEN	NO PRUNE	PRUNE			LEAST PRUNE						NO PRUNE	
TROPICALS TENDER FRUIT	NO PRUNE					PRUNE		NO PRUNE				

	DORMANT	ACTIVE GROWTH		MAXIMUM GROWTH		GROWTH SLOWDOWN		GROWTH HARDENS			DORMANT	
GROWTH CYCLE												

cy usually stimulates extensive re-growth during the active growing season. Be sure temperatures are above 20F (7C).

When damage has been caused by severe winter conditions, the dead-wood must be removed. But sometimes new growth may come from seemingly dead tissue if given ample time, often as late as midsummer. You can tell what wood is dead by slicing back a small piece of bark with a knife. If the cambium layer underneath is green, the branch is alive at that point. When new growth appears, it is easy to see where additional pruning needs to take place. When pruning at this time of year, exercise extreme caution to avoid damaging delicate new shoots.

PRUNING CUTS

All pruning cuts are either *thinning* cuts or *heading* cuts. Either kind of pruning cut can be useful, but you should know the difference and when each is appropriate.

Pruning to *thin* means to remove an entire shoot, branch or limb back to where it starts—its branch point or origin. Thinning opens up the plant to allow more light to reach interior branches.

Pruning to *head* means to shorten but not remove a shoot, branch or limb. Heading makes branches shorter and heavier, and encourages growth of side branches, resulting in a denser plant. There are many names for heading cuts for the various situations in which it is employed. *Pinching* refers

THINNING

Thinning cuts, whether for young or mature plants, remove entire branches at their point of origin. Thinning opens dense plants to more light without changing overall form.

HEADING

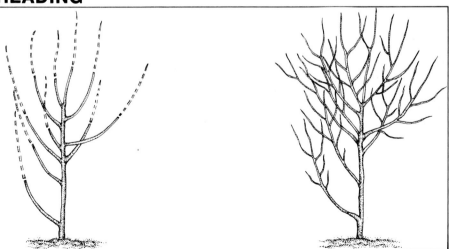

Heading cuts shorten but do not remove branches. Heading results in shorter, thicker branches and increases number of new shoots formed, encouraging side branching and denser growth.

PRUNING CUTS

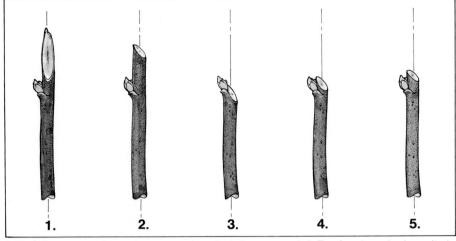

1. Too sharp an angle produces an excessively large wound. 2. Too far above bud results in dieback above cut. 3. Too close to bud damages it. 4. Just right—on a 45° angle about 1/4 inch above bud. 5. In cold climates, a slightly higher cut will help prevent bud desiccation.

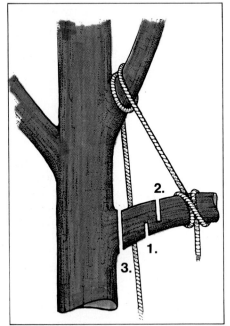

Removing large limbs takes special care and attention to safety. To prevent bark from tearing under weight of limb, secure branch with rope, if possible, and make three cuts: Make first cut (1) about 12 inches up from the final cut, and half way through bottom of limb; second cut (2) above first on upper part of limb. Limb should break away without tearing bark. Make final cut (3) close to trunk, just outside bark collar.

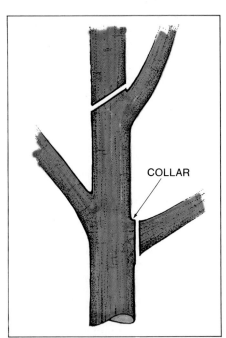

When removing dead wood from a tree, branches that have a live bark collar around the stub should be removed just outside collar.

ing branch turn upward.

When cutting off an entire shoot, hold saw or shears with cutting blade flush against the trunk or scaffold (main branch) at the top of the branch to be cut.

When removing a heavy limb, first undercut the limb a short distance from the trunk to avoid tearing bark and splitting wood. Next cut through the limb from above, just outside the point of the undercut, then trim off the stub flush with the bark collar on the trunk.

Wound Treatment—Proper care following pruning cuts ensures rapid healing and promotes callus growth to prevent decay. Avoid making wounds any larger than absolutely necessary. Use a pruning knife to trim away loose bark around the cut or press the bark into place. Use the knife, a rasp or coarse sandpaper to smooth any rough edges.

Opinions vary greatly on the use of chemical pruning compounds to seal wounds. Some tree pathologists feel these compounds are purely cosmetic while others recommend them for every pruning cut. Conclusive scientific evidence is lacking to support either extreme, although some compounds that have been used for years, such as copper and creosote, have been found harmful to living tissue. Water-soluble asphalt emulsions are thought to stimulate rapid callus

Make all cuts as close to main trunk or limb as possible. Leaving stub, as shown here, encourages growth of water sprouts.

to heading of soft plants using your thumb and forefinger to remove the current season's growth. *Snipping* is practiced to remove the growth from the previous season. *Shearing* is a type of heading where many cuts are made along a single plane using hand-operated or mechanical shears.

Correct Cuts—Unless you're removing entire limbs or shoots, always cut just above a bud at a 45° angle as shown in the drawing above.

When pruning to direct growth, cut to an outward-facing bud to help an upright branch spread outward. Cut to an upward-facing bud to help a spread-

growth, but tend to crack and provide little protection against drying. Newer compounds made with polyvinyl-acetate appear to provide a non-cracking, durable and elastic coat.

If plants are suffering from disease or pests, it may be necessary to spray wounds with appropriate chemicals. Consult with your local nursery personnel for recommendations.

Detailed instructions for pruning specific kinds of plants are given on the following pages.

ORNAMENTAL TREES

Pruning is desirable to keep trees healthy, attractive and fruitful. Ornamental trees should be pruned with attention to retaining an attractive, nearly natural appearance. Fruit trees and flowering trees are pruned to enhance productiveness. Pruning fruit trees in an ornamental garden often involves a compromise. Some beauty and some fruit production may be sacrificed to train a tree that retains some of both. Pruning ornamental trees is discussed here. Pruning fruit and nut trees is covered in the chapter Fruits, Berries and Nuts, starting on page 168.

Deciduous and Broadleaf Evergreen Trees—Begin shaping deciduous or broadleaf evergreen trees 2 or 3 years after planting them. Cut out any crossed branches and dead wood. Because lower branches remain at the same height, carefully select three or four primary scaffold branches to be left on the tree at the height you desire permanent lower branches. The strongest branches are those with 60° to 90° angles. Cut away all branches below these chosen few.

Do not prune any tips if you enjoy an open feeling to the tree. If you choose to have the tree denser, prune tips of side branches to promote fuller interior growth. Pinching back growing tips of broadleaf evergreens each spring will help control tree size and cause them to grow denser.

Most of the time, trees are only lightly pruned after they're well established. However, a severe pruning of old trees that appear worn out may give them a new lease on life. Severe pruning of mature flowering and fruit trees provides the stimulus for vigorous new growth.

Conifers—Prune conical-shaped conifers only to remove any competing leaders. Those with less symmetrical

PRUNING CONIFERS

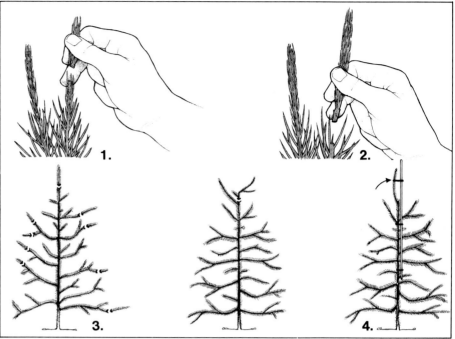

Conifers, such as pine, spruce and fir, can be kept compact by removing portions of "candles" in early spring. Removing part of candle (1) will result in moderate growth. Removing whole candle (2) results in dense, compact growth. Slightly cutting back branch tips each year (3) will keep conifers compact. If conifer looses its leader (4) remove all but one new shoot, then tie it upright to a stake.

forms can have branches pruned to create more openness and their lower branches can be removed if you want to have room underneath for other plants. All conifers will grow denser if you lightly shear off new growth each spring. To help control the size of needled evergreens, clip them back during their main growing season in spring or summer. Following are specific pruning tips for various conifers:

Pine (*Pinus* species): Pinch or cut back to lateral shoots only. Do not cut below terminal buds. Pinch candle when it expands in spring. Pines have very few non-latent buds. One exception is Canary Island pine (*Pinus canariensis*), which can take heavier pruning.

Spruce (*Picea* species), fir (*Abies* species) and Douglas fir (*Pseudotsuga menziesii*): These trees require little pruning. As the tree grows over the years, remove lower limbs for clearance. Promote density by pinching expanding lateral shoots in spring. The terminal shoot (leader) may or may not form multiple leaders when pinched. To direct growth, cut to lateral shoots or visible dormant buds.

True cedar (*Cedrus* species) and larch (*Larix* species): These usually require little pruning. Over a period of several years, remove bottom limbs for clearance. Pinch expanding shoots for denser foliage. On long shoots, cut back to lateral shoot to reduce size or direct growth. Short shoots may break into long shoot growth.

Podocarpus (*Podocarpus* species): This has few, if any, latent buds. Removal of leader may produce multistem crown. Pinch expanding shoots to create denser foliage. To direct growth or reduce size, thin to laterals or visible foliage.

Bald cypress (*Taxodium distichum*), dawn redwood (*Metasequoia glyptostroboides*), cryptomeria (*Cryptomeria* species) and giant sequoia (*Sequoiadendron giganteum*): These species have both persistent (evergreen) and annual (deciduous) shoots. Prune back to persistent shoots. To reduce size, thin to laterals or visible foliage tufts. Pinch expanding shoots to increase density.

Arborvitae (*Thuja* species), false cypress (*Chamaecyparis* species), incense cedar (*Calocedrus decurrens*) and cypress (*Cupressus* species): Thin

PRUNING SHRUBS

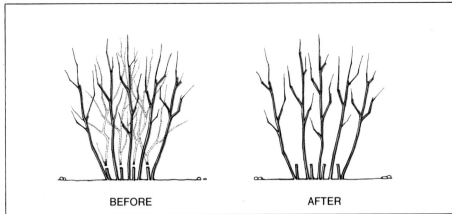

Thinning opens up shrubs by removing broken, weak or dead branches. It results in plants with softer texture and bigger, but fewer blooms.

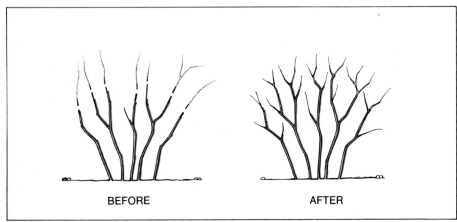

Heading in early spring and late fall results in denser, more compact plants with symmetrical shape.

Left: Frequently clipping hedges yields a compact formal appearance. Leave base slightly broader than top so light reaches edges evenly. Right: Old shrubs can often be rejuvenated by cutting back all growth. It can be done all at once, but is better to remove portions of plant over a period of 2 to 3 years.

to laterals or within visible foliage. Prune back tips to encourage dense growth. Do not prune into bare wood as these trees are slow to make new growth after pruning.

Juniper (*Juniperus* species) and yew (*Taxus* species): Thin to laterals and prune tips to direct growth and increase density. Those with needlelike foliage may not respond to pruning as well as those with awl-shaped or scale-like foliage.

Coast redwood (*Sequoia sempervirens):* Remove multiple leaders. Prune tips to increase density. Thin to laterals to direct growth or reduce size.

SHRUBS

Flowering shrubs bloom either on old or new wood. Old wood is that which has grown the year before and is darker in color and more brittle than new wood. Shrubs that bloom in early spring on old wood should be pruned within 2 weeks after the flowers fade and drop. Shrubs that bloom in late spring or early summer flower on lighter-colored new wood because the wood has grown during the current season. These should be pruned during their dormant season or just prior to early spring growth if you want newer stems, which will produce more blossoms.

Shrubs can be pruned either by thinning or heading. Entire branches are removed in thinning, converting the energy to other branches and resulting in plants that are larger and more open. Heading is cutting back only the ends of branches to a point just above a dormant bud, causing the bud to grow and resulting in plants that are smaller and denser. Heading is necessary to achieve a formal, manicured look.

The effects of heading can also be achieved with shearing and pinching. Shearing is a common pruning practice on hedges and screens because it removes many growing points at once, causing many buds near the surface to start dense growth. Pinching out growing tips of branches with your fingers forces the lateral buds near the branch end to grow, resulting in several growing points instead of one. Pinching lets you direct the growth of a developing plant or create a dense, bushy look.

For pruning instructions on roses, see page 143.

Formal hedges must be trimmed frequently to maintain neat appearance. You can use hand shears, as shown here, or make job easier with electric hedge trimmer.

Topiary is the art of pruning shrubs to specific geometric forms or recognizable shapes. It takes careful forethought to achieve desired results.

HEDGES

When planting rows of deciduous plants, cut nursery stock 1 to 2 feet tall back to 6 or 8 inches to induce low branching. Prune off half of the new growth toward the end of the first growing season or just before buds break into growth the following season. Trim off half again in the following year.

Begin shaping during the third year, trimming to the desired shape before the plants reach the desired height. Thin to prevent lower branches from being shaded. Trim mature plants closely to keep them within the dimensions you have chosen.

Do not cut back evergreen plants for hedges at the time of planting. Begin trimming lightly after a year or two, then shaping as the plants merge to form a hedge. Bear in mind that many needlelike evergreens chosen for hedges do not easily generate new growth from old wood.

Formal hedges require frequent shearing to maintain a uniform and manicured appearance.

WHEN TO PRUNE FLOWERING SHRUBS

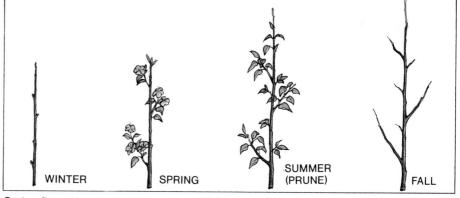

WINTER   SPRING   SUMMER (PRUNE)   FALL

Spring-flowering shrubs bloom from buds formed the previous season. Little or no growth precedes bloom. New growth occurs after flowers have faded. Dormant buds on new growth will bloom the following year. For maximum bloom the following year, prune after flowers have faded in spring. Pruning later may remove developing flower buds.

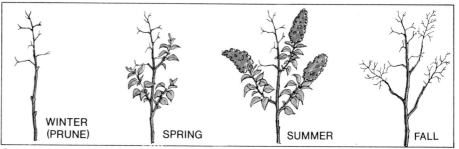

WINTER (PRUNE)   SPRING   SUMMER   FALL

Summer-flowering shrubs bloom from buds formed on current season's growth, which often occurs below previous season's bloom. Prune in fall or winter.

PRUNING WISTERIA TO TREE FORM

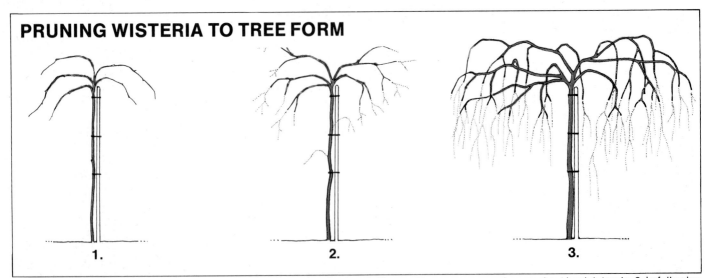

1. The first year, train vine to stake and pinch tip when it reaches the top. 2. The next year, remove suckers and cut back laterals. 3. In following years, remove suckers and cut back vigorous branches to maintain shape.

PINCHING MUMS

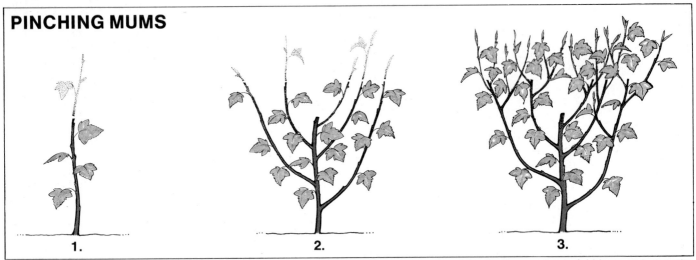

Pinching garden chrysanthemums (and other herbaceous plants) keeps them compact and bushy. For most colorful bloom and attractive plant: 1. In midsummer, pinch back one-third of growth. 2. About 1 month later, pinch back new growth again. 3. The next flush of growth will bloom in fall.

VINES

Aggressive vines such as wisteria, honeysuckle and passion vine must be pruned during their growing season to keep them under control. Some vines need to be renewed when they become tangled, overgrown or full of dead wood. This is done by cutting them back to the ground or within 1 foot of the ground. Many slow-growing vines require little, if any, pruning.

Flowering vines that bloom on wood produced the previous season should be pruned after they bloom each spring to encourage more summer growth and flower buds for the following spring.

Those that flower on growth of the current season should be pruned before growth begins each spring to stimulate growth later in spring, resulting in more flowers.

ANNUALS AND PERENNIALS

Pinching out the tips of young annuals and new growth on some perennials provides bushier plants that produce more flowers. Most plants flower more profusely the more their flowers are cut. Always pinch or cut off faded flowers to prolong blooming as well as to prevent early seed-setting. Removing dying foliage keeps plants healthier.

ESPALIERS

An espalier—pronounced *ess-PAL-yea* or *ess-PAL-yer* — is a plant trained to a single plane, usually against a wall or trellis. Formal espaliers have a predetermined recognizable geometric pattern to their branches. Informal espaliers are more free-flowing, with the final structure determined by the branching habit of the plant rather than by an intentional plan.

With these definitions in mind, your first impression of espaliers may be that they are garden art in the same category as topiary. This is true to a certain extent. Espaliers can turn a blank wall into a dramatic garden focal point. A row of espaliers forms a living fence that will stop passers-by in their tracks. But training plants as espaliers is much more than creating art. The first espaliers, created hundreds of years ago in Europe, were designed to allow gardeners to grow types of fruit not normally adapted to their climate. Espaliers permitted them to harvest bumper crops in locations too small for trees trained in traditional shapes.

Espaliers can take advantage of one of your garden's most valuable microclimates—a warm house or garden wall. Trained up against a warm, south-facing wall, citrus may receive enough reflected heat to reach new peaks of ripeness. Or, trees may receive just enough reradiated heat at night to protect them from cold damage.

Espaliers are also one of the most space-efficient methods of growing plants. For instance, espaliering may enable you to grow a particular apple tree you've always wanted but couldn't find room for.

Most espaliers require some type of trellis for support—all do initially. Branches will have to be tied in place to hold their unnatural position. Wire trellises supported by end posts are well-suited to this purpose, as are prefabricated lath trellises, available in most nurseries.

Training plants to formal shapes requires some basic understanding of plant growth and pruning responses, as well as constant attention. Starting with young plants, prune above buds that you'll want to grow into permanent scaffolds (cordons), and bend and tie as soon as possible. With wire trellises, use small wire ties to keep branches straight between wires. Raise and lower branches as needed to keep

Informal espalier of *Grewia caffra* stands in striking relief against white wall.

Most apple varieties are easily trained as espaliers. This "apple fence" is trained to wires attached to rough 4x4" posts.

the framework balanced from one side of the espalier to the other. Keep unwanted branches and shoots pinched back.

The best fruit trees for espaliers are those that bear fruit on long-lived spurs, such as apples and pears. Traditionally, they are trained in classic formal patterns such as horizontal cordons or oblique palm-ettes. Many ornamental plants make beautiful formal espaliers. Crabapples and pyracanthas are prime favorites. For a detailed discussion on espaliers and step-by-step illustrations of how to train various plants into all the classic forms, see the book *Hedges, Screens and Espaliers* by Susan Chamberlin, published by HPBooks.

PESTS & DISEASES

The following pages summarize the important points about this broad and always-changing subject. Even the largest books on pests and diseases are hardly comprehensive. This chapter outlines the basics. For the most current diagnoses or cures, it is best to rely on the advice and information provided by agricultural extension offices at state and federal levels.

Because pests and diseases are particular to certain areas, and problems with them often vary from year to year, your county extension service probably has the most useful and up-to-date information on dealing with localized pest problems.

CAUSES OF PLANT PROBLEMS

Ferreting out the cause of a plant problem is always a methodical process. Use a printed checklist like the one on page 84 until you're completely familiar with the process.

Consider the most likely causes of plant problems first—lack of water or plant nutrients, lack of light, pests and so on. Examine leaves closely—a hand lens helps. Look for patterns of symptoms and parts of plants affected.

Check stems, trunk, and if necessary, roots. Checking roots of landscape trees might mean a substantial excavation. Roots of a plant in a small container are more readily inspected.

Don't neglect background information on pesticides, weedkillers and fertilizers—many can burn plants if product is misused—and general cultural practices. Reference books, beginning with ones like this and proceeding through encyclopedias of plant problems, guide you to the most common known problems of different kinds of plants. Most plant problems fall under the general categories in the checklist on page 84.

Getting Help—With experience, you can identify most plant problems. Nursery professionals, cooperative extension agents and specialists at local colleges are all available when you need help. To show or send a sample of a damaged plant, follow this suggested procedure:

1. Wrap a fresh sample in a plastic bag.
2. Collect healthy as well as damaged plant parts. Bring more than you think necessary.
3. Make notes on all you know about the plant, such as its name, age and location in the garden. Also note possible causes of damage and recent cultural practices, such as watering schedule, fertilizing and pesticide use.

Left: Tent caterpillars are so named because communities form large webs or "tents" in trees. Severe infestations can quickly defoliate entire trees.

Above: There are many safe alternatives to pesticides. A hard water spray is often effective against aphids.

PESTS

Strictly speaking, a *pest* is any living creature that disturbs or threatens desirable plants, inadvertently or not. This not only includes tiny creatures like insects, which most people associate with the word pest, but also animals, such as gophers, deer, dogs and cats and microorganisms such as fungi, bacteria and viruses.

CULTURAL PEST CONTROL

Experienced gardeners have fewer problems with pests and diseases because they understand the basics of *cultural control* of these problems. Practices such as adequate soil preparation, fertilization and watering helps plants maintain health and resist or recover from pest and disease attack.

Seek out information from books and seed catalogs, about varieties of plants that are well-adapted to your area and ones that are resistant to common pests and diseases. For example, tomatoes advertised as "VFNT" can be expected to be resistant to the four most common tomato problems—*verticillium* and *fusarium* diseases, *nematodes* and *tobacco mosaic*. Other examples include disease-resistant fruit varieties: 'Liberty' is a scale-resistant apple, 'Moonglow' a pear that resists fireblight and 'Benton' a strawberry that resists many diseases common to the Northwest. Many ornamentals are also available in pest- and disease-resistant cultivars.

By the same token, an awareness of pest problems common to certain plants helps in early diagnosis and successful treatment. Seeking advice from local experts—agricultural extension agents, experienced gardeners, nursery personnel—before planting can save you a lot of time and aggravation later.

Generations of gardeners have advised against planting the same crop, or a closely related one, in the same place year after year. It's good advice. Pests of one kind of plant can accumulate over the years.

Companion Planting—Many gardeners also believe that certain plants will repel insect pests. For instance, marigolds and garlic are thought to discourage pests from attacking adjacent plants. Gopher spurge is so named because it is thought to repel gophers. Interplanting these plants among susceptible ones is known as *companion planting*. Sprays made from these plants are thought to be even more effective.

Garden housekeeping is important. Pest-infested plants should be cleaned up or cleaned out. Dispose completely of diseased materials—don't add them to compost. Not only do weeds compete with garden plants, reducing their ability to grow, but even more importantly, many are reservoirs of various pests and diseases.

BIOLOGICAL PEST CONTROL

All insects have several natural enemies. These enemies include parasites, predators and disease organisms (bacteria, fungi and viruses.) They are often referred to as *biological control agents*. A number of biological control agents are commercially available—there's a list of suppliers on page 223. Here are descriptions of biological control agents you should know about:

Parasites—These are usually the larval stage of insects that complete that stage of their life cycle at the expense of a particular host. Some beneficial parasites prefer a variety of pests for hosts. Tiny *Trichogramma* wasps are perhaps the most important. They lay eggs in the larvae, or plant-damaging "worm" stage of more than 200 pests, including bagworm, cutworm, tomato hornworm and codling moth. The wasp larvae use the pest larvae as hosts.

Braconid and *Ichneumen* wasps are other important parasitic wasps. *Tachinid* flies, about the size of houseflies, are parasitic on several caterpillars.

Predator Insects—These attack and consume other insects. Naturally, the beneficial kinds are those that prefer plant-eating insects. Best known are the ladybug, lacewing, syrphid fly (flower fly) and praying mantis. Beneficial parasites and predators are shown on pages 86-87.

Disease Organisms—One valuable disease organism used as a biological control is *Bacillus thuringiensis*. It attacks caterpillars and worms, and is completely non-toxic to animals and other insects. It is widely available as a liquid or a dry, wettable powder for use in sprayers. Common trade names include Dipel and Thuricide. Another disease organism, *Bacillus popillia* (milky spore), is used to control Japanese beetles.

> **PLANT PROBLEM CHECKLIST**
>
> Use this checklist to help you identify plant problems. Sometimes, damaged or poorly growing plants can be attributed to more than one cause. After identifying the symptoms, consider *all causes* below before making a diagnosis.
>
> ● **Water**—Too much water will decay roots and too little will dehydrate leaves and stems. Wilting is usually the first sign in either case. Also, even with sufficient water, some plants in hot climates may wilt in midafternoon, but usually return to normal at night. For more on watering, see pages 67-71.
>
> ● **Diseases**—Usually on leaves but sometimes below ground, damaging roots, and extending up the stem.
>
> ● **Insects**—These suck sap, chew holes or bore holes, usually on leaves but sometimes on stem, trunk and roots.
>
> ● **Nematodes**—These pests parasitize roots, gradually decreasing plant vitality.
>
> ● **Pesticides**—Herbicides can drift through the air or move through soil to damage nearby non-target plants. Insecticides applied during hot weather (over 90F/32C)—or applied excessively can damage foliage.
>
> ● **Animals**—Mice, gophers, rabbits, moles and squirrels chew on roots, stems or bark. Check for teeth marks or nearby tunnels.
>
> ● **Cold Weather**—Cold damage varies by type of plant and season. Softest, newest growth succumbs first, with damage gradually progressing to roots. Roots of container plants may suffer before the tops. See pages 24-25 for information on cold-weather protection.
>
> ● **Nutrition**—Yellowish new leaves are usually the result of iron deficiency, yellowish old leaves, the result of nitrogen deficiency. Cause may be inadequate supply of nutrients, too high or too low soil pH, or poorly functioning plant roots.
>
> ● **Air Pollution**—Various air pollutants, such as ozone, nitrous oxide and acid rain, can damage leaves of susceptible plants, such as Bermudagrass, petunias and grapes.
>
> ● **Mechanical Injury**—Limbs broken by wind or heavy fruit crops, or bark scraped by lawnmowers and filament-line grass trimmers, cause stress that encourages pests and diseases.

Predatory Animals—These include birds, and reptiles such as frogs, toads and lizards. Although birds may also damage some crops, many gardeners still value them for insect control.

INTEGRATED PEST MANAGEMENT

Integrated pest management (IPM) is the integration of the many techniques of pest control for maximum control of pests and minimum upset of existing natural controls in the environment.

Prior to the 1940s, relatively few kinds of chemical pesticides were used. Development of synthetic pesticides during World War II led to a huge increase in pesticide use over the following 30 years. Initially, pesticides were inexpensive and effective, and traditional ways of coping with plant pests were abandoned.

By the 1960s, people became aware that pesticides can be more of a problem than pests. Problems such as resistance, secondary pest outbreaks, environmental damage and health hazards were more evident.

Most pesticides kill beneficial organisms as well as pests. It is possible to destroy one kind of pest, such as caterpillars, and kill predators of spider mites at the same time. With no predators, the spider mite population explodes. This is called a *secondary pest outbreak*.

IPM is a moderate approach. It recognizes that chemical pesticides are often the only recourse, but advocates their use only when absolutely necessary and in the most specific and least-damaging manner possible.

IPM encourages techniques that reduce the need for chemical sprays. The cultural and biological controls just discussed are not the only alternatives. Hand-picking large pests such as tomato hornworms, slugs and snails can also be effective in small gardens. However, this must be done on a constant basis. Also, slugs and snails must be hunted at night.

Simple traps can also work. Both snails and earwigs are nocturnal creatures—they feed mainly at night and then hide during the day. Place a board on the ground in your garden. Use rocks or sticks to raise the board just enough so snails can crawl under it. Check under the board each morning. You should be able to dispose of quite a number. Earwigs will hide in a rolled-up newspaper.

Commercially manufactured traps using sexual hormones as bait are also available for some insect pests, such as Japanese beetle. A hard jet of water will help rid plants of aphids. A mild solution of dishwashing soap and water is even better.

Yellow Insect Traps—Insects such as aphids, whiteflies and scales are attracted to the color yellow. This is be-cause yellow and the color of green foliage—especially new foliage—look the same to them. Bright yellow sticky traps can be used to catch them. These include commercially available sticky cards or something you devise yourself, such as yellow-painted plywood covered with petroleum jelly, or yellow plastic containers cut in half and coated with something sticky. These traps are most helpful in early spring when pest numbers are low. After numbers of pests have built up, they are of little help.

INSECTS

This section describes common insect pests, their habits and common control methods. For more information on insecticides and non-chemical controls for specific insect pests, refer to the charts on pages 221-222.

Aphids are small, soft-bodied insects that suck sap through tiny needlelike mouths. Several generations develop in a single season. Colors vary. Aphids may be green, red, gray or black. They feed on soft plant parts such as new growth, and are frequently found on leaf undersides.

Control: Wash off with a strong spray of water, or snip away infested plant part. Soap sprays are effective. You can make your own by mixing approximately 2 tablespoons mild dish soap per gallon of water. Spray mix-

Continued on page 88

Japanese beetle trap uses sex attractor as bait.

Ladybugs should be encouraged in the garden—they can substantially reduce the aphid population.

BENEFICIAL INSECTS

Beneficial insects are those that feed on insect pests. There are two types—*parasites* and *predators.* Parasites are the larval stage of insects, which use live insects as hosts, eventually killing them. Predators may be either larvae or adult insects that attack and consume other insects. The most useful beneficial insects are shown here. Some of them are commercially available—refer to the retail supplier's list of beneficial organisms on page 223.

PARASITES

Larvae of tachinid fly are parasitic on several kinds of caterpillars.

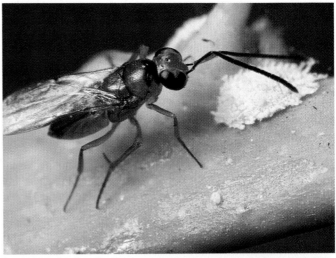

Leptomastix dactylopii preparing to lay eggs in citrus mealybug. Larval stage of wasp is an internal parasite of mealybugs. Adults feed on mealybug honeydew and nectar from flowers.

The tan, bloated aphid bodies are called *mummies.* Larvae of wasps are maturing within them. Soon they'll emerge, leaving tiny holes and these mummies as evidence of their presence.

Lysiphlebus testacipes is one of many minute parasitic wasps that use aphids as hosts. This one is *ovipositing* or laying eggs within an aphid.

PREDATORS

Larval stage of ladybird beetle, or ladybug. They eat aphids at this stage also.

Vedalia beetle (Australian ladybird beetle) feeding on cottony cushion scale. This tiny beetle saved California's fledgling citrus industry 20 years after the scale pest was unwittingly imported into California from Australia in 1869.

Adult brown lacewing *(Hemetobius* species) feeding on aphids. Brown lacewing larvae feed voraciously on all stages of spider mite.

Green lacewing larva feeding on aphid. These voracious alligatorlike larvae attack and consume a variety of soft-bodied insects—aphids, mites, mealybugs and thrips.

Adult green lacewing *(Chrysopa carnea)* feeds on all stages of spider mite as well as on soft-bodied insects, insect eggs and small larvae.

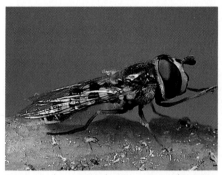

Syrphid (or flower) fly adult *(Syrphus opinator)* on flower bud of aloe plant. These flies feed on nectar and honeydew. They deposit their eggs among or near colonies of aphids. Green or tan larvae consume large numbers of aphids.

Dark and albino races of decollate snail *(Rumina decollata)* feed on brown garden snails and decaying vegetation.

Assassin bug *(Zelus* species) consuming a fly. Adults feed on a wide variety of insects.

Six-spotted thrips are tiny insects that feed on smaller soft-bodied pests such as spider mites. They are important predators of mites on strawberries.

Any gardener who has raised very many tomatoes is familiar with the tomato hornworm. It is one of many types of leaf-chewing caterpillars. Natural controls include parasitic wasps and the disease *Bacillus thuringiensis.* Malathion is an effective chemical control.

Flathead apple tree borer is larval stage of beetle. It usually attacks trees stressed by drought, recent transplanting or injury. Look for telltale holes in tree trunk.

Continued from page 85

ture on infested areas of plant, then rinse with fresh water. Or, you can use a commercial insecticidal soap spray, available at nurseries and garden centers. Follow label instructions. Many predators and parasites aid in aphid control, the most familiar being ladybugs. Nicotine sulfate, diazinon and malathion are effective chemical controls.

Beetles are hard-shelled insects. Many are solid brown or black in color, others have spots, stripes or other markings. The wormlike larvae, called *grubs,* damage plants by boring into wood, or eating roots or leaves. Adults chew leaves. Many kinds of beetles are active only at night. Common beetle pests include Japanese beetle, Colorado potato beetle, Mexican bean beetle, cucumber beetle and flea beetle.

Control: Japanese beetles can be reduced on a community-wide basis with the natural microbial insecticide *Bacillus popillia,* also known as *milky spore.* Traps containing sexual hormone baits are also available. Carbaryl, methoyxychlor and diazinon are chemical controls for all beetles. Diazinon and trichlorfon are often recommended to control beetles at the grub stage.

Borers are wormlike, larval stages of beetles (grubs) or moths (caterpillars) that tunnel into branches and stems. They are difficult to control once they infest a plant. Borers usually attack plants that are under stress from drought, recent transplanting or injury. Symptoms include small holes or soft spots on stems and branches and wilted foliage, even though soil is moist. Borers are often identified by the kind of plant they attack, such as squash vine borer or flathead apple tree borer.

Control: The best prevention is to keep plants vigorous and healthy. Avoid injuring trees with lawn mowers. Use white latex paint or tree wraps to protect young plants from sunburn. Chemical controls include lindane, chlorpyrifos and carbaryl, but they must be used exactly according to label timetables.

Caterpillars are the larvae of butterflies or moths. Most kinds chew leaves, and if enough of them are present, they can defoliate a tree or even an entire forest. Gypsy moth larvae are well-known members of this group. Some caterpillars, including borers mentioned above, bore into the plant and feed inside. Others, such as forest tent caterpillars, form webs or tents on branches and live in colonies. Many, such as the tomato hornworm, are individualistic. The corn earworm, or fruit worm, eats corn kernels and the fruits of tomatoes and squash. Also in this group are leaf rollers, cutworms, bagworms and cabbage worms.

Control: All caterpillars are susceptible to the disease *Bacillus thuringiensis.* Several parasitic wasps serve to reduce caterpillar populations. Chemical controls include carbaryl, diazinon, acephate and rotenone. Malathion is an effective control for hornworms. Cutworms, which spend daytime hours just below the soil surface, can be controlled by drenching soil with diazinon.

Earwigs are known to many people as pincher bugs because of the threatening pinchers at their posterior end. The pinchers are more bark than bite and won't hurt much if you get caught in their clamp. Earwigs feed primarily on decaying organic material, which is why compost piles are one of their

1. Chrysanthemum lacebug *(Corythocha marmorata).* 2. Shoot moth larva is leaf-chewing caterpillar common throughout North America. 3. Mites (many kinds) damage leaves by scraping and by sucking sap. 4. Flathead apple tree borer is one of many kinds of borers that attack stems of plants. 5. Adult stage of flathead apple tree borer. 6. Wingless female pea aphid. Aphids can be black, brown or yellow; some have wings. 7. Scales: Scruffy scale *(Chionapsis furfura)* at top, purple scale *(Lepidosaphes beckii)* at left, California red scale *(Aonidiella aurantii)* at right. 8. Twig girdler *(Oncideres cingulata)* does just what its name indicates—portion of plant above girdled area usually dies. 9. Peach bark beetle is common pest east of Mississippi river. 10. Root-feeding grubs attack plant roots. 11. Leaf miner damage. 12. Tent caterpillar egg mass. 13. Chewed leaves can be attributed to a wide variety of leaf-chewing insects. 14. Damage from serpentine leaf miner.

INSECT PESTS

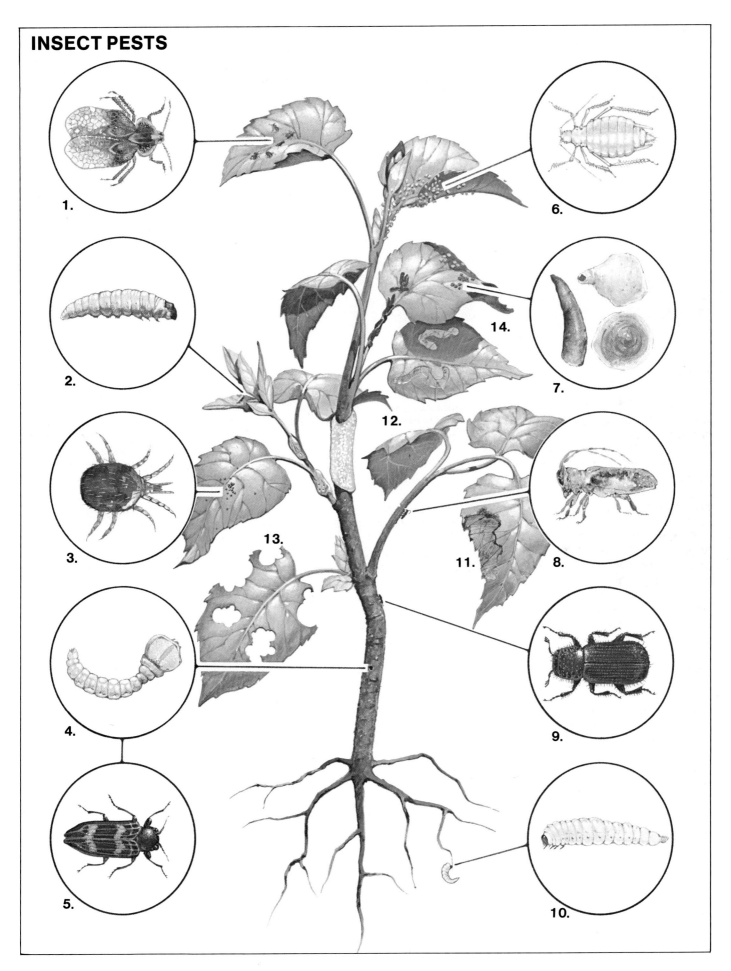

1.

2.

3.

4.

5.

6.

7.

8.

9.

10.

11.

12.

13.

14.

Grasshoppers are leaf-chewing insects. Individually, they cause minor damage. Large swarms can be devastating.

Brown specks on stem are one type of scale. Horticultural oils control scale by smothering them.

Snails chew large holes in leaves. They are usually active at night. Traps, bait and hand-picking are effective control measures.

favorite hangouts. However, some kinds also chew on soft foliage and flowers.

Control: Earwigs feed primarily at night and hide during the day. You can trap them by placing tightly rolled-up newspapers around the garden. Pick up the papers each morning and shake out earwigs into soapy water. Chemical controls include commercial earwig baits containing baygon.

Grasshoppers chew foliage on a variety of plants. In large numbers, they can cause extensive damage in the garden. The term *locust* refers to any of several species of large, migratory grasshoppers that attack areas in huge swarms, causing extreme devastation. In most cases however, grasshoppers are found in much smaller numbers, but they can still do considerable damage.

Control: Dispose of egg clusters found while cultivating soil. They look like clusters of rice. Grasshoppers are most vulnerable to sprays when young, in spring or early summer. Malathion, diazinon, sevin and chlorpyrifos are effective controls.

Leafhoppers are small grasshopper-like bugs that suck juices from many species of plants, sometimes transmitting viruses as they go. They are only about 1/4 inch long and usually green. They are not true insects, but close relatives. They're hard to see on leaves. However, when foliage of the infected plant is disturbed, they jump

around and become more visible. Infected plants often have distorted, malformed and stippled foliage. In severe cases, leaves turn brown and curl upward.

Control: Pyrethrin and rotenone can be effective. Acephate, malathion and diazinon are proven controls.

Leafminers are larvae of certain small flies, moths, or beetles. They feed inside the leaf. Damage appears as brown or discolored blotches or winding trails on the leaf. There may be more than one generation per year.

Control: Acephate controls leafminers in non-edible plants, diazinon in edible plants.

Mites are hard to see without a strong magnifying glass. Eggs, young and adults all may be present on an infested plant at the same time. Some form webs on the lower leaf surface. Mites damage plants by sucking sap. Typically, foliage becomes stippled and turns an off-green, yellow or orange. There are several generations each year.

Control: Some broad-spectrum insecticides actually encourage mite problems by killing their predators—an example is sevin. Many mites are beneficial and habitually feed on their relatives—see lists of suppliers on page 223. Horticultural oils are often useful controls. Various pesticides are used to control mites, notably kelthane.

Root-feeding grubs are the larvae

of moths or beetles. They are shaped like caterpillars, and are usually white. They feed on plant roots and crowns, weakening wood and damaging root tissues that conduct water and food. Activity of root-feeding grubs is frequently enough to destroy plants.

Control: Protected below soil level, root-feeding grubs are typically difficult pest problems to diagnose and control. If a tree or shrub is growing poorly or not at all, check with local authorities to see if grubs are a common problem of that plant.

Depending upon the severity of infestation, removing infested plants may be the best decision. Maintain healthy growth—unhealthy plants attract root-feeding grubs as well as borers. Beneficial nematodes, available from sources listed on page 223, may be helpful. Various soil-drench insecticides, including orthene or acephate, diazinon and dursban, are recommended chemical controls.

Scale are tiny insects that attach to leaves and form a hard, protective shell over their bodies. They are immobile once mature, but newly hatched scale, called *crawlers,* can move around on a plant seeking the most hospitable situations. Scale may be circular, oval or pear shaped. Large numbers form crusts on the plant, drain sap, and may deplete a plant's energy enough to kill it.

Control: Sprays of horticultural oils—mineral or refined—such as low-sulfur petroleum, are most effective. These light oils coat and smother scale insects.

Snails and slugs feed primarily at night and during cool, moist weather. Silvery slime trails on sidewalks and chewed foliage are usually all that's visible during the day while the culprits hide under rocks, leaves or other garden debris.

Control: You can walk the garden each night with a flashlight, picking them up or stepping on them as you go, or trap them under a board each morning. Removing garden debris and giving them fewer places to hide also helps decrease their population. Commercial baits containing metaldehyde or mesurol are effective chemical controls. Baits in pellet or flake form should be placed where pets won't eat them. Some dogs may eat snail and slug baits.

Thrips are tiny cream- to black-colored insects often less than 1/16-inch in length. Most feed inside flowers, where flecking of blossoms results. Others live in the growing points of plants and cause distortion or bleaching of leaves.

Control: Apply acephate or diazinon in a fine mist over flowers according to spraying schedule on label.

True bugs can occasionally be troublesome garden pests, including squash bugs, chinch bugs, stink bugs and lace bugs. Mottled or distorted foliage, flowers or fruit are usual signs of infestation.

Control: Rotenone and pyrethrin are common organic controls. Malathion, diazinon, acephate and carbaryl are proven chemical controls.

Whiteflies are small, white, fly-like insects about 1/8 inch long. They gather on the undersides of leaves and lift off as a faint white cloud if foliage is disturbed. In their larval stage they suck plant juices, causing leaves to yellow and die.

Control: Not easy because at some growth stages they are difficult to kill with pesticides. Spray frequently. Pyrethrins, acephate, malathion, diazinon, dimethoate and methoxychlor are effective sprays. A parasite of whiteflies, *Encarsia formosa*, provides effective control in enclosed areas such as greenhouses. Whiteflies are also attracted to yellow insect traps. Insecticidal soaps provide partial control.

ANIMAL PESTS

A number of common mammals can be troublesome garden pests. Rodents such as gophers, moles, voles, mice and ground squirrels are generally exterminated with traps or poisons. For practical reasons, larger animals such as rabbits, deer, dogs and cats are deterred by protecting plants with such devices as fences or wire-mesh cages.

Birds are a major threat to ripening fruits, berries and tender vegetables. The best prevention is to cover plants with bird netting (available in nurseries) or a wire covered frame. Rubber snakes, owl figures, whirlygigs and other types of scarecrows are only effective until the birds realize they're no threat.

Deer not only chew on low plants but taller ones as well. It seems everyone with a deer problem has at least one favorite method of repelling them. Some gardeners hang small bags of blood meal or human hair around the garden. Others hang something that makes a lot of noise as it blows in the wind. There are also commercially available deer repellents. However, building a deer fence is the only surefire way to keep out deer. Because deer are better high jumpers than broad jumpers, deer fences are designed so wire mesh or other light material can be attached at an angle to the fence posts. To be effective, the fence should be 5 to 6 feet tall and 5 feet wide. If deer are a common problem in your area, local fence contractors are good sources for designs.

Dogs and cats can be more of a nuisance in suburban areas than any other animal pest, especially in newly planted gardens. Commercially available odor repellents can be used to protect specific areas, but these must be applied on a regular basis. A sturdy 5- to 6-foot fence will keep dogs out of the garden. No one has yet devised a fence that will deter a cat. Wire cages can be used to protect individual plants or seedlings from dogs and cats.

Gophers are tunneling animals that leave holes, piles of dirt and mounds around the lawn and garden. Even worse, they eat bulbs and chew tender roots, often killing plants. Trapping is the most effective way to get rid of them. Cats also help. Gassing, poisons and flooding burrows are seldom completely effective and each has its drawbacks. If necessary, line the

bottom of planting holes with wire mesh to prevent gophers and moles from chewing roots.

Mice will sometimes chew the bark at the base of plants. This is especially a problem when a thick organic mulch is allowed to pile up against the trunk. The mice will burrow through the mulch and chew the bark in complete privacy until the trunk is girdled. Prevent this potentially damaging girdling by moving the mulch several inches away from the trunk. A wire mesh wrap will provide further protection.

Rabbits can do a lot of damage to garden plants, especially leafy vegetables. A fence 2 to 3 feet tall, made of chicken wire or 1-inch wire mesh will keep them out of the garden. The wire mesh should extend 6 to 8 inches into the ground to discourage rabbits from digging under the fence.

Lightweight bird netting protects ripening apricots.

Rust disease appears as small reddish-brown pustules on leaves. Common on snapdragons, roses and hollyhock (shown here.)

DISEASES

Diseases are caused by various microscopic, parasitic organisms. Most diseases are diagnosed by the symptoms they cause rather than by visual attributes of the organism itself. That's why names of many diseases are generic descriptions of their symptoms. For instance, "wilt" diseases may be caused by one of several fungi, bacteria or virus.

Fungi are the most typical cause of disease. Most fungi slowly decompose dead plants, but some attack living and healthy plants. Other causes of disease in plants are bacteria and viruses. Unlike fungi, bacteria enter plants only by wounds or other natural openings. Plants are inoculated with viruses via insects, such as aphids, leafhoppers and whiteflies. Here are some of the more common plant diseases:

Cankers are caused by a number of fungi and bacteria which enter trees and shrubs through wounds. The organisms infect areas just under the bark and cause dark, sunken areas often accompanied by oozing sap. Infection often girdles and kills branches and can kill entire trees.

Control: Minimize mechanical injury and damage from sunburn and cold. Prune carefully. Remove infected branches and cut away canker.

Sterilize pruning tools with household bleach after using.

Crown gall of roses is caused by a bacteria known as *Agrobacterium tumefaciens.* It begins as a small swelling, usually near the soil level. Galls enlarge substantially until growth is obviously stunted. Infections occur through wounds.

Control: Dispose of infected plants by burning. Sterilize soil before replanting in the same location. A bactericide known as Bacticin can eradicate gall tissue—check with your agricultural extension service.

Fire blight is a bacterial disease (*Erwinia amylovora*) common to most plants of the rose family. Pears, hawthorn, loquat, pyracantha and cotoneaster are frequent victims. Even though the organism that causes the disease is microscopic, the symptoms are distinct and easily recognizable—flowers and leaves suddenly wilt, turn dark brown or black, shrivel and die but stay connected to the stem. Bacteria survive winter in cankers on limbs. In spring, the bacteria multiply and are spread to flowers by splashing rain or water and a myriad of insects. The infection spreads from flowers down the stem, eventually clogging the conducting tissue of the stem, killing the plant.

Control: The most important means of control is to cut away blighted stems as soon as you notice them. Always cut 6 to 12 inches into apparently healthy wood and sterilize shears in household bleach between each cut. Burn prunings to thoroughly dispose of bacteria. Then spray flowers with antibacterial agent such as agricultural streptomycin or fixed copper. Finally, consider replacing susceptible plants with disease-resistant ones.

Fruit rot refers to various types of rot in ripening fruit, and sometimes blossoms, caused by any of a number of disease organisms. The most common form is *brown rot* of stone fruit such as peaches, apricots and nectarines. Firm, light brown spoiled areas begin as small spots and rapidly spread over fruit surface. Affected fruits dry leather hard (called mummies) and often hang on the tree after the leaves have fallen. Fruit rot thrives in wet conditions.

Control: Prune trees to maximize air circulation and remove mummies. Effective sprays include captan, sulfur, benomyl or fixed copper. Use according to label instructions.

Leaf spot, anthracnose and shot hole are fungal diseases that grow in warm, wet spring weather. Their symptoms are similar—small black circular spots on foliage and stems. Shot hole is slightly different in that the center of the spots fall away, leaving holes in the leaves as if the plant had been blasted with a shotgun. Various forms of these diseases attack fruit and berries, roses and many other plants.

Control: Remove and destroy infected plant parts. In severe cases, spray with fixed copper, captan, bordeaux, lime sulphur or benomyl.

Powdery mildew causes the familiar white fuzz on leaves of roses, crape myrtle, zinnias, zucchini, lilac, apple and many other plants. It does not require water on leaves to begin growing, and usually requires little humidity. Cold nights and warm days—common in spring and fall—are the only environmental trigger necessary. Crowding plants, poor air circulation and excessive shade also encourage powdery mildew.

Control: Sulfur in powder form, applied as a spray or dust, is the traditional preventative. The liquid lime-sulfur sprays (calcium polysulfides)

PLANT DISEASES

1. Powdery mildew is caused by cold nights and warm days, excessive shade and poor air circulation, rather than by moist or humid conditions. 2. Cankers are caused by bacteria or fungi entering bark wounds in trees and shrubs. 3. Fruit rot is caused by any of a number of disease organisms, usually triggered by moist conditions. 4. Crown gall in roses is caused by bacteria introduced through wounds. Enlarging galls stunt plant growth. 5. Root rot is common in moist, poorly draining soils. 6. Root knots are caused by nematodes. Other signs include wilting and stunted growth. No effective control for nematodes—remove infected plants. 7. Wilt diseases cause wilting leaves, later leaf drop and dead branches. *Verticillium wilt* is a common example. 8. Twig blight is a bacterial disease indicated by browning of leaves and dieback of twigs. Remove infected portions of plant. 9. Leaf spot is caused by any of several fungal diseases that grow in warm, humid spring weather. Use fungicides to control.

Peach leaf curl is a fungal disease that appears as a thickening, curling and blistering of leaves on peaches and nectarines. Attacks new leaves, but spores live through winter in bark and buds. Treat with lime-sulfur or fixed-copper spray when tree goes dormant in fall.

Anthracnose is a fungal disease similar to leaf spot, shown here on blackberry. Controls include lime-sulfur, fixed-copper spray and commercial fungicides.

are also effective and practical for many plants. Sprays containing cycloheximide, benomyl, folpet and triforine are other possible controls. Check the chart on page 221, and the product labels.

Root rot and crown rot are caused by constantly wet, poorly drained soils, which promote the development of several soil organisms that attack plant roots and crowns. Symptoms are often similar to stress caused by drought—wilting and yellowing of foliage. These rots can also include dieback and branches.

Control: Plants that are already infected are difficult to save. Do whatever you can to improve soil drainage and cut back on watering. Remove dead or dying plants.

Rusts are caused by fungi that thrive in wet weather. They are visible as orangish red or brown pustules on plant foliage, especially the underside of leaves. Infected foliage turns yellow and dies. Plants can become distorted and eventually die. Common on snapdragons and roses.

Control: Remove and destroy infected foliage. Avoid splashing foliage while watering. Choose resistant varieties. Spray with fungicides such as folpet, sulfur, triforine or phaltan.

Scab is a serious problem on apple trees wherever summers are wet. Dark, corky patches infect developing leaves and fruit, which gradually grow together into an unslightly, irregular infection.

Control: Old leaves and dropped fruit are the main sources of infection. Rake up and destroy all fallen leaves before trees leaf-out in spring. Choose disease-resistant varieties. Spray captan, lime-sulfur, sulphur or benomyl according to label instructions.

Wilt diseases cause, as the name implies, leaf wilting and also browning between leaf veins. Leaf drop usually begins in one branch and progresses through the tree. Common symptoms include dead and dying branches, sparseness in the crown and reduced twig growth. There are two important wilt diseases that attack shade trees. *Verticillium wilt* infects roots and *Dutch elm disease* infects trunk and branches. Verticillium wilt also attacks tomatoes and strawberries.

Control: Wilts are extremely difficult to control. If you suspect Dutch elm disease, contact your local agricultural extension service immediately. To prevent verticillium wilt, keep plants healthy and growing vigorously. Avoid planting in areas where plants were infected in previous years. Don't plant susceptible species near each other. Choose resistant varieties whenever possible. The letter "V" in VF, VFN or VFNT tomato varieties indicates resistance to verticillium wilt.

WEEDS

Weeds are usually defined as any plant growing where you do not want it to grow—along paths, in the garden or in a lawn. Sometimes weeds are just unsightly, such as when they are growing between bricks in your patio or in a vacant lot next to your house. But most of the time weeds threaten the health and survival of desirable plants. They compete for water, nutrients and sometimes even sunlight. Weeds can also harbor harmful pests and diseases.

There are basically two ways to eliminate weeds—culturally and chemically. The method you choose should depend on the severity of the problem and where the weeds are. You probably want to minimize the use of chemicals around edible plants, so cultural methods are preferred. In areas such as vacant lots or paths and driveways, you may want to take more decisive measures.

CULTURAL WEED CONTROL

Two cultural techniques are particularly effective methods of weed control—*cultivation* and *mulching*. *Cultivation* is a physical battle between you and the weeds. If you keep at it, you can win. Cultivating means turning over the soil to kill weeds before they can become established, as well as physically removing any weeds that do. It is a constant job that begins before you plant and continues through the growing season.

There are many garden tools to help. A gas driven tiller is ideal for preplanting or for use between rows of large plantings. However, a tiller should not be used to remove unwanted stoloniferous grasses, such as Bermudagrass. The tiller will chop up the roots (stolons) and spread them around. Any small piece of root left in the ground will grow a new plant.

A simple trowel is effective for cultivating between closely spaced plants such as annuals and vegetables. There are also long-handled hoes, hula hoes, swoes and other cultivating equipment that will help prevent sore backs. Cultivating soil around plants has additional advantages besides preventing weeds—it increases soil aeration and water penetration, both of which promote healthier growth.

Cultivating also includes pulling or hoeing mature weeds. Again, there are a number of weeding implements to make the job easier.

Whenever you pull weeds, make sure you get them root and all. This is especially important with perennial weeds that spread by roots. Otherwise, they may live to fight another day. Also try to remove all weeds before they set seed.

Mulching—Covering the soil with a mulch is an effective preventative method of controlling weeds. Mulches suffocate most germinating weed seeds and, in the case of organic mulches, weeds that aren't suffocated are much easier to pull.

Black plastic is by far the most effective weed-preventing mulch. Roll out sheets over the area to be planted, seal the edges with soil, and punch holes where you want to plant. A thin layer of organic mulch on top of the plastic makes it attractive as well as effective. For more on mulches and mulching, see page 61.

There are several other cultural methods that will help prevent weeds. Don't wet soil unnecessarily. Basins, furrows and drip irrigation systems direct water to roots of intended plants without wetting surrounding areas where weed seeds lie waiting to germinate. Keep plants healthy and growing vigorously. Healthy plants can usually out-compete weeds. This is particularly true with lawns, ground covers and closely spaced annuals and perennials.

In large, open areas, you may choose to keep weeds mowed or cut back rather than trying to keep them out all together. The easiest tools to use are rotary mowers or one of many models of filament-line grass cutters. Use these tools carefully, watching

Bark mulch helps prevent weed growth in rose garden.

out for stones and other hard objects hidden in the weeds. Wear heavy shoes and goggles to protect your eyes from flying objects. Weedy lots can also be cleared by hand with sickle or scythe.

CHEMICAL WEED CONTROL

Chemical weed controls are divided into *pre-emergents,* which kill weeds before they sprout, and *postemergents,* which kill growing weeds. Each type has further divisions, described on page 97.

Timing is often critical to successful weed control. Some weeds are more vulnerable to herbicides during certain times of the year. Some herbicides are only effective at certain temperatures. Always read label instructions thoroughly and follow them to the letter.

TYPES OF WEEDS

Weeds are readily categorized as *annual weeds* or *perennial weeds,* and *warm-season weeds* or *cool-season weeds.* They can also be broken down into *broadleaf weeds* and *grasses* (narrowleaf weeds). Many weedkillers are formulated to kill either broadleaf or narrowleaf weeds. Some kill both.

Annual weeds are most troublesome in home gardens. Common annual weeds in ornamental gardens include: warm-season grasses (crabgrass, foxtail, barnyardgrass) that germinate in spring and summer; cool-season

grasses (annual bluegrass) that germinate in late summer and fall; warm-season broadleaf plants (purslane, pigweed, lambsquarters) and cool-season broadleaf plants (chickweed and bittercress).

Biennial and perennial weeds are usually more problematical in areas that are rarely cultivated, such as outlying areas or plantings of ground cover. These kinds of weeds have underground plant parts that survive from year to year. Bermudagrass is perhaps the most familiar example.

Below are brief descriptions of some of the most troublesome weeds and how they can be controlled:

Annual Bluegrass—Annual cool-season grass that germinates in fall and set seeds in spring. Usually goes dormant and turns brown in summer. Control with bensulide, benefin or oxydiazon.

Bermudagrass—Perennial narrowleaf weed, which is a popular warm-season lawn grass in many areas. Spreads rapidly by wiry stems that root at the joints, underground rhizomes called *stolons* and seeds. To control, pull seedlings wherever they sprout, making sure you get entire root. Trim lawns to keep them out of beds. Spray with glyphosate or dalapon. Siduron is a pre-emergent control.

Crabgrass—Narrowleaf annual that grows during summer. It is most troublesome in poorly growing, overwatered lawns. Spreads by rooting stems.

To control, remove by hand from flower beds and vegetable gardens. Keep lawns growing vigorously and water them deeply. Apply pre-emergents such as DCPA, bensulide or benefin several weeks before seeds germinate in spring.

Oxalis—Perennial broadleaf with cloverlike leaves and yellow flowers. It spreads by creeping, rooting stems and by seed. Grows fastest in spring and fall. To control, dig out small seedlings as soon as you see them, or spot treat with glyphosate. In lawns, selectively control with 2,4-D or a combination of 2,4-D, dicamba and MCPP. Pre-emergent control with oxydiazon or siduron.

Spotted Spurge—Annual broadleaf that grows during summer. It forms a prostrate, fast-growing circular mat. Each leaflet has a red spot. Spreads quickly by seed. To control, pull small seedlings by hand or spot treat with glyphosate. In lawns, use DCPA for pre-emergent control. For selective control in grass lawns, use a combination of 2,4-D, MCPP, and dicamba—do not use these herbicides in dichondra lawns.

Dandelion—This common broadleaf weed is most often seen in thin lawns. To control, pull by hand or spot treat with glyphosate. Use 2,4-D in lawns.

Dallisgrass—Perennial, narrowleaf grass common in the Southwest and Southeast. It has a clumping habit and spreads by seed. To control, spot treat with glyphosate or dalapon. Selective control in lawns with DSMA or MSMA.

PESTICIDES AND HERBICIDES

Pesticides are chemical agents used to destroy pests. The most common kinds of pesticides are *insecticides* (kill insects), *fungicides* (kill fungi), *acaricides/miticides* (kill mites) and *nematicides* (kill nematodes). *Herbicides* kill plants.

TOXICITY

Pesticide toxicity is indicated by the *LD50 number.* The LD50 number represents the average milligrams of pesticide dose for each kilogram of body weight that kills 50% of the test organisms in laboratory tests. The dose is tested on animals in the same ways people can be affected—through the mouth (oral), through the skin (dermal), and through the respiratory system (inhalation). The higher the LD50 number, the safer the poison. There's more information about LD50 and an example in the glossary on page 230.

The *signal words* (precautions) on pesticide labels are important indicators of toxicity. The chart below shows which signal words are required for pesticides of various toxicities.

INSECTICIDES

Insecticides can be divided into two general categories—*biological* and *synthetic.* Biological insecticides are derived directly from natural sources. They include *botanical, microbial* and *hormonal* insecticides. Synthetic insecticides include various manufactured chemical formulations, described below.

Botanical Insecticides—These are extracted from plants that have evolved natural mechanisms to protect themselves from insect attacks. Most familiar are nicotine alkaloids (from tobacco), rotenoids (from the roots of some legumes), and pyrethrins (from the flowers of some chrysanthemums.)

Microbal Insecticides—These contain the organisms of common insect diseases. They are non-toxic to animals. The two most widely used microbal insecticides, *Bacillus thuringiensis* and *Bacillus popillae*, are described on page 84. Other microbial insecticides, based on parasitic viruses and fungi, are currently being developed and will probably be available to the home gardener in the near future.

Hormonal Insecticides—These utilize natural insect growth hormones to disrupt insect maturity. Most prevent reproduction, thereby reducing the numbers of insect pests. The most common is methoprene. It is used against mosquitoes, whiteflies (in greenhouses) and fleas.

Synthetic Insecticides—Most insecticides used today are called *synthetic organics.* They are separated into categories based on their chemical structures.

Chlorinated hydrocarbons are contact or stomach poisons, and they are long lasting in the environment. Contact poisons are absorbed through the skin. Well-known ones include DDT, chlordane, lindane, and methoxychlor.

Organophosphates are also contact and/or stomach poisons. They are metabolized rapidly by animals and are not chemically stable, so they do not remain in the environment as long as chlorinated hydrocarbons. Organic phosphates include some of the most toxic pesticides, as well as common home-garden insecticides such as diazinon, malathion, vapona,

---

CATEGORIES OF PESTICIDE TOXICITY

The toxicity of pesticides to humans falls into general categories, indicated by *signal words* on the pesticide label. Toxicity level is indicated by the LD50 numbers that also appears on the label. LD50 numbers are discussed in text above.

Category	Signal Word	LD50[1]
I (Highly toxic)	DANGER/POISON[2] (Skull & X-Bones)	0-200
II (Moderately toxic)	WARNING	200-2,000
III (Slightly toxic)	CAUTION	2,000-20,000
IV (Relatively non-toxic)	No signal word required[3]	Over 20,000

[1] Milligrams undiluted pesticide per kilogram body weight that kill 50% of test animals in laboratory tests—the higher the number, the lower the toxicity.

[2] Danger/Poison may also appear on the label if severe skin irritation or eye damage is possible, even if the chemical is not very toxic if ingested.

[3] "Keep Out of Reach of Children" is required on all pesticide labels, even if no signal word appears.

cygon, di-syston, meta-systox and dursban.

Carbamates are contact or stomach poisons. Sevin (carbaryl) is the most popular, and is favored for its low toxicity to mammals and broad spectrum of insect control. Various formulations of Sevin are registered for use on vegetables, fruits, lawns and shade trees. However, there are disadvantages to using Sevin. Its broad spectrum includes many beneficial predatory and parasitic insects (pages 96-97.) Spider mite invasions commonly follow use of Sevin because natural mite predators are killed. It is also toxic to honeybees, therefore not recommended for use on plants that attract them.

MITICIDES (ACARICIDES)

Mites are tiny spiders of many kinds that feed on and damage a variety of plants. Most are kept in check by other mites that feed on them. The worst mite problems can occur when predators are killed—mites are a well-known secondary pest after use of carbaryl. Kelthane and pentac are two miticides. Some insecticides are also miticidal.

FUNGICIDES

These pesticides control both fungi and bacteria. They are categorized as either *protectants* or *eradicants*. Protectants are applied in anticipation of fungus problems. Eradicants are applied after infection is established. *Systemic* fungicides are translocated in the sap stream of the plant.

HERBICIDES

These are chemicals designed to prevent, control or destroy unwanted seeds, plants or plant parts—in gardener's terms, weedkillers. There are several kinds of herbicides appropriate to various stages of plant growth.

Selective herbicides kill specific plants, enabling control of a broad range of unwanted plants on treated sites without endangering the plants to be protected.

Nonselective herbicides kill all types of plants. Use them only when you want complete removal of all plants. Many of these herbicides, such as bromacil, have residual properties. Most require a certain waiting period before you can plant.

Selective and non-selective herbicides function either on contact or by translocation.

Contact herbicides kill only the plant parts that are covered by the chemical. There is little movement of the chemical through the plant and it works quickly.

Translocated or *systemic* herbicides are absorbed through roots or leaves and transported throughout the plant. Effects may take several weeks to become apparent. These herbicides are most effective on weeds with hard-to-kill root systems.

METHODS OF APPLICATION

Pesticides are most effective when applied with the appropriate applicator. The applicator you use will depend on the type of pesticide, its dilution strength and the plants being treated. Pesticide labels usually recommend more than one application method.

Hose-End Sprayer—These are convenient and low-cost sprayers but relatively large amounts of water are applied with the pesticide and dilutions are not reliably accurate. Good for soil-drenching with insecticides because extra water carries pesticide into soil. Also good for applying contact insecticides over large areas.

Granule Spreader—Used for spreading fertilizer or pesticides over continuous areas such as lawns and ground covers. There are two basic types—drop spreaders and cyclone spreaders. Hand-held cyclone spreaders are also useful for spreading granular soil insecticides.

Compressed-Air Sprayer—These include a pressurized tank that holds a measured amount of diluted material. One type uses a manually operated pump to pressurize the tank. Larger, more expensive models use a gasoline engine powered compressor.

Slide Sprayer—This is a manually operated hydraulic sprayer with telescoping plunger, operated by two hands. Spray material is drawn from a separate container and discharged as a spray under pressure on both forward and back strokes of plunger. High pressures and increased spraying range make it ideal for trees. Nozzle adjusts to fine spray for low-growing plants.

Crank Duster—As the name indicates, it's used to apply pesticide dusts. It is manually operated, with a hopper or container for the dust and

Slide sprayer is convenient way to apply liquid pesticides over small areas.

an agitator. A high-velocity, gear-driven fan is driven by a hand-operated crank. A continuous current of air carries the dust through the discharge end. A regulator controls the volume of dust discharged, and the fan speed determines the range of carry.

SAFE USE OF CHEMICAL SPRAYS

No statements on controlling pests with chemicals are more important than the ones on safety. Almost all the sprays you will use are poisonous to humans and animals, although some are safer to use than others. Some kinds, especially in concentrated form, are deadly if used incorrectly.

Always follow label instructions exactly. Make sure you are using the right pesticide. Be sure you have correctly identified the problem and that the chemical is recommended for use on the plant you are going to spray. Use directed amounts at the directed time of year, temperature or time of day. With the exception of some herbicides, most pesticides should be sprayed on calm, windless days when there is no threat of rain.

Store chemicals safely, far out of reach of children. Always make sure chemicals are correctly labeled. Clean spray equipment with soap and water after each use. Once a sprayer has been used for applying herbicides, don't use it for other types of pesticides. Residues may harm plants.

PROPAGATION

Increasing plants is easily among the most fascinating of garden activities, whether you try seeds collected from the garden, slips on the windowsill or flats of cuttings in the greenhouse. Propagation is fun, especially when you watch your supply of a favorite plant increase. Home propagation can be economical too—fewer trips to the nursery and you might even find yourself involved in a profitable business supplying friends and neighbors with vegetable seedlings, house plants or other plants.

The various methods of propagation fall into two basic categories—*sexual* propagation and *asexual* or *vegetative* propagation. Sexual propagation reproduces a particular kind of plant from seed. Most vegetables, annuals and grasses, and some perennials, are best propagated by seed. Most trees and shrubs are not. Some kinds of flowers and vegetables grown in your garden will produce seeds that you can save for planting the following year.

Asexual or vegetative propagation involves the use of a plant part, such as a leaf, stem or root, to produce offspring identical to the parent. Methods of vegetative propagation include plant division, cuttings, layering, grafting and budding. Most perennial flowers, cacti, shrubs, trees and house plants are propagated this way.

Left: Chives are one of many clumping perennials easily propagated by division.

Above: Gloxinia and many other house plants, as well as some succulents, can be propagated by leaf cuttings. Light application of rooting hormone powder promotes root formation.

PROPAGATION BY SEED

Many garden plants will set viable seed, but resulting plants aren't always identical to the parent. If you want to propagate a specific variety of plant by seed, the plant must reproduce *true to type,* or *true from seed.*

Plants that naturally self-pollinate will reliably reproduce true to type. That is, the resulting seed will produce offspring identical to the parent plant. Self-pollinating vegetables include beans, eggplant, lima beans, peas, peppers, potatoes and many varieties of tomatoes. Self-pollinating flowers include larkspur, nicotiana and sweet peas.

Plants that naturally cross-pollinate will produce offspring different from the parent unless they are sufficiently distant from different varieties of the same species. Commercial seed growers raise such plants in controlled conditions to prevent cross-pollination with other varieties. This ensures that the seeds they sell will come true to type. In the home garden, the results are less predictable.

Some common cross-pollinating vegetables include beets, the cabbage family, cantaloupes, carrots, celery, chard, cucumbers, leeks, lettuce, okra, onions, parsley, pumpkins, radishes, spinach, squash, sweet corn, sweet potatoes and watermelons. Ornamentals include most flowers, trees and shrubs.

The *species* of many kinds of plants will reproduce true to type, but most *hybrids* will not. Most hybrid varieties either won't set viable seeds or will produce seeds that result in inferior plants. These include F-1 and F-2 hybrids (page 228.) Seeds of some F-1 hybrids may grow and produce interesting or even useful plants, but odds are overwhelming that most will be much less desirable than the parents.

SEED VIABILITY

If you harvest seeds from the garden, you may wonder if they will retain their viability until the following planting season. Similarly, you may have seed packets left over from the previous season and wonder whether to use them or throw them out. Mostly it depends on the kind of seed and how it has been stored.

The seed of some plants, such as early-fruiting trees, germinate almost immediately or quickly lose their viability. The seeds of citrus and some nut trees will not germinate if they dry out. They must be planted immediately or stored under moist conditions. If stored correctly, many flower and vegetable seeds will last from the time they're harvested to the following planting season. Some seeds, especially those with hard shells, can remain viable up to a year or more.

It is usually not worthwhile to harvest seeds of plants readily available at nurseries or through seed catalogs. It's better to start with fresh seeds that you know will come true to type. But if you're trying to propagate an unusual or hard-to-find plant, or think the seeds might produce an interesting hybrid, it takes little effort to harvest and store them.

Testing Viability—If you are ever in doubt, you can always test seed viability. Spread seeds over a moist paper towel and wait for germination. Keep seeds warm—between 70F and 80F (21C and 27C)—and maintain humidity by covering with plastic wrap or another suitable material. Calculate the germination percentage by dividing the number of seeds that germinated by the number tested.

Storage—With the exceptions noted at left, seeds are best stored at a low temperature—between 32F and 40F (0C and 14C)—and low humidity. It's a good idea to store seeds with a dehumidifying agent, such as dehydrated milk.

See pages 40-44 for instructions on planting seeds.

VEGETATIVE PROPAGATION

The different methods of vegetative propagation are useful in several ways. They are how special plant characteristics are passed from one generation to the next—a good apple or orange, or an attractive flower. These methods are also used for plants that are difficult to propagate by seed.

This section describes five basic methods of vegetative propagation—cuttings, layering, plant division, special plant parts and grafting.

CUTTINGS

The term *cutting* is applied to a portion of a plant severed from its parent and treated so that it forms roots and eventually produces a new plant. Cuttings are taken from stems, leaves, portions of leaves, tubers and roots.

Stem Cuttings—There are several ways to take stem cuttings, depending on the kind of plant. Stem cuttings of woody plants (trees and shrubs) can be taken from new growing shoots (softwood cuttings), half-ripened wood (semihardwood cuttings) or from mature wood during the dormant season (hardwood cuttings). Stem cuttings can also be taken from many herbaceous plants, including various house plants and perennials.

Softwood cuttings are usually made

Stem cuttings are best started in well-draining rooting medium that allows maximum air circulation. Good rooting medium is composed of vermiculite or perlite mixed with potting soil, peat moss or garden soil. See page 102.

from new spring growth but can be taken any time during the growing season from young, non-flowering shoots. Cuttings are taken with leaves attached. Growing shoots should be flexible but not too tender. Cuttings should be about 4 inches long and have two or more nodes (leaf buds).

Semihardwood cuttings are usually taken in mid to late summer from the newly hardened stem growth of the current season. Shrubs and vines such as azaleas, camellias, honeysuckle, pyracantha and bougainvillea can be propagated this way. Cuttings can be 3 to 6 inches long. Remove leaves from bottom end of cutting. If remaining leaves are large, cut off top half to help prevent water loss.

Hardwood cuttings are taken from older wood, usually during the dormant season. Many deciduous trees and shrubs, and a few evergreens, can be propagated this way. Cuttings are usually stored over winter, packed in moist sand, peat moss or sawdust to allow the cut ends to form calluses. The following spring they are set out in cutting beds or planted directly in the garden.

Herbaceous cuttings can be taken from many herbaceous plants, including chrysanthemums, phlox, geraniums, dianthus and delphiniums. Cuttings are usually taken from the top 4 to 6 inches of a growing shoot any time during the active growing season.

Most stem cuttings root best if the cut is made near the middle of an *internode,* usually about 1/2 inch below a node, as illustrated at right. The cut should be slightly diagonal and made with a sharp knife, pruning shears or a razor blade. If you use a knife or razor, protect your thumb with a short section of rubber hose. Take cuttings from healthy growth that is free of pests and diseases. To avoid transmitting plant diseases, keep tools, containers and work area clean when taking cuttings and rooting them.

Root Cuttings—Some of the plants that can be increased by means of root cuttings include acanthus, Japanese anemone, blackberries and raspberries, border phlox, eryngium, plumbago and oriental poppies. Root cuttings are usually taken before new growth starts in late winter or very early spring. Several roots are taken from the parent plant and cut into short (2- to 4-inch) sections. Root cut-

TYPES OF STEM CUTTINGS

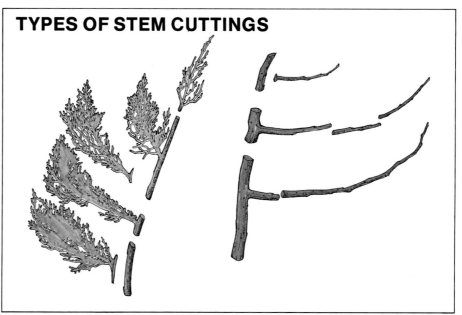

Types of stem cuttings are shown above. Where you take the cutting often depends on what type of plant you're propagating (herbaceous or woody) and when you take cutting. See text at left.

TAKING A HARDWOOD CUTTING

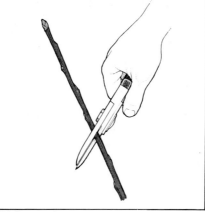

1. Make a slanted cut between nodes in dormant, 1-year-old shoot.

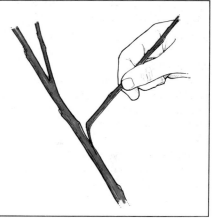

2. Or, pull shoot away with a section of older wood attached (heel cutting).

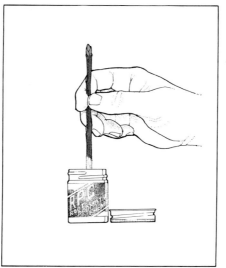

3. Brush cut end of cutting with small amount of rooting hormone.

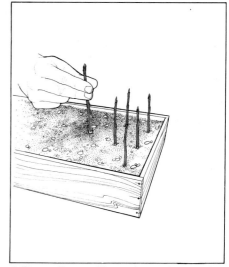

4. Place the cuttings in moist rooting medium. Cover container to retain moisture.

Propagation **101**

tings pencil-thick or thicker are placed upright in the rooting medium and covered with a 1/2-inch layer of medium. The end of the cutting that was facing the plant *crown* (trunk base) should point up. Thinner roots are laid flat in the rooting medium about 1/2 inch deep.

Leaf Cuttings—Leaf cuttings are an easy way to propagate many kinds of house plants—one of the most familiar is African violets. Succulents such as *Sedum, Echeveria, Bryophyllum* and some species of *Kalanchoe* quickly produce plantlets from leaves inserted in sandy soil. Many kinds of begonias are traditionally increased by leaf cuttings.

Rooting Cuttings—As mentioned, hardwood stem cuttings are usually stored over the winter and planted in a cutting bed or directly in the ground the following spring. All other types of cuttings are usually started in flats, pots or other containers filled with a suitable soil mix. Light, air, temperature and moisture requirements are essentially the same as for starting seeds indoors, page 42. You can start them indoors or out, providing you have control over temperature, light and humidity.

Use a soil that allows maximum air circulation and drainage of excess water. Perlite or vermiculite, often mixed with light garden soil or organic matter such as peat moss, are favorite mediums for rooting cuttings. Coarse, washed builder's sand, either by itself or mixed with peat moss, is a more traditional rooting medium. Any of these media will work well, but expect some trial and error until the right medium for your plants and your particular situation are worked out.

Cuttings can be started in wooden flats, plastic trays and pots, peat pots or any other container that allows drainage. Cuttings made from growing shoots also need a humid and bright situation. This helps leaves thrive and produce carbohydrates until roots form.

Containers that function as mini-greenhouses are especially desirable because they admit light yet retain humidity. These include transparent plastic containers with lids, such as plastic shoe boxes, sweater boxes or food-storage containers available at variety stores. You can also use commercially available plant propagators. Individual cuttings can be rooted in propagators made by placing clear-

plastic picnic glasses or plastic sandwich bags over 4-inch plastic nursery pots. You can also cover cuttings with glass jars or tumblers. Experiment with with light intensity, shading the glass or plastic cover with, lath or cheesecloth until the cuttings easily survive the hottest part of the day.

Most cuttings root faster and more successfully if the rooting medium is between 70F and 75F (21C and 24C), and air temperature is 5 to 10 degrees cooler than the soil. Estate gardeners a few generations back put their cold frames or rooting frames on top of composting manure. The heat generated by the compost was enough to speed rooting. Nowadays, electric heating cables, tapes and trays, and pipes containing hot water—all thermostatically controlled—are used for this purpose.

Mist and Fog—Automatic watering systems that spray a mist or fog over cuttings is the preferred method of watering, if such an arrangement is practical for you. This is also a good way to start seeds.

Mist systems are similar to underground watering systems. They consist of 1/2-inch-diameter, Class 200 PVC pipe with spray nozzles spaced every 4 to 5 feet. The pipe system is attached to a valve controlled by a short-duration clock. More elaborate systems control watering times with moisture- or heat-sensitive *mechanical leaf sensors.*

Fog systems use pumps to boost water pressure up to 500 to 600 pounds per square inch through Schedule 80 PVC pipe. Nozzles with tiny holes atomize water into a fine fog, not a mist.

Shelter, shade and moisture are not the only important factors in the success of cuttings made from growing shoots. The rooting medium and the care cuttings receive until roots form are equally important.

Rooting Stimulants—Three natural hormones are used to stimulate root formation. They are *indole-3-acetic acid* (IAA), *indole-3-butyric acid* (IBA), and *alpha naphthaleneacetic acid* (NAA). Preparations containing one or more of these hormones are available at most garden stores. Keep in mind that these are potent chemicals so only a minute treatment is needed. If the hormone is in powder form, lightly dust the very tip of the cutting. Too much can inhibit root formation. Rooting aids without these

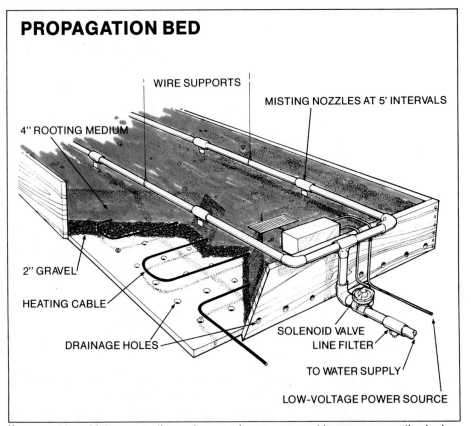

PROPAGATION BED

WIRE SUPPORTS

MISTING NOZZLES AT 5' INTERVALS

4" ROOTING MEDIUM

2" GRAVEL

HEATING CABLE

DRAINAGE HOLES

SOLENOID VALVE
LINE FILTER
TO WATER SUPPLY

LOW-VOLTAGE POWER SOURCE

If you want to get into propagation on large scale, you may want to use a propagation bed like this one. It includes overhead mist system to keep cuttings moist, and heating element to keep soil at optimum temperature. The bed pictured is a typical setup.

hormones are not as effective for starting cuttings.

Care of Cuttings—Position the cuttings in the flat, bed or container. Thoroughly soak the rooting medium to settle it around the cutting. Then close the bed or cover the cuttings (except on hot days) so air cannot escape, and keep the rooting medium moist at all times.

Transplanting—Most cuttings take between 1 and 2 months to root. Herbaceous cuttings or vigorous softwood cuttings may root in as little as 3 weeks, hardwood cuttings as long as 1 year. When new top growth forms on the cuttings, check root formation by gently lifting one plant with a spoon handle or knife and removing some of the rooting medium. When the root balls are densely branched, you can transplant the cuttings into a larger container and gradually expose them to outdoor conditions.

If cuttings were covered with a plastic or glass cover, keep the cover slightly ajar for several days to allow cuttings to acclimate to the drier air, then remove the cover completely and transplant cuttings into larger containers. If weather is warm, keep cuttings in a lightly shaded spot for about 2 weeks before planting them in the garden. Keep soil moist at all times. Protect cuttings against frost and other extremes in temperature.

LAYERS

Layering occurs when part of a stem is covered by soil and forms roots while still attached to the mother plant. Trailing and rooting plants "layer" themselves naturally. Gardeners can encourage many types of trailing and rooting plants to layer by bending stems to the ground, securing them and covering them with moist soil. See drawing above right for details. Low-growing evergreens, currants, gooseberries and many deciduous ornamental shrubs are readily propagated this way. Apple and pear rootstocks are commercially propagated by layers. Several creeping or spreading shrubs also are easily propagated by layers.

Air Layering—Rubber plants and other members of the *Ficus* family are commonly propagated using *air layers,* as are philodendrons and deciduous magnolias. Also called *marcotting,* air layering is done above ground by enclosing the section to be layered in a bag of soil mix. This often

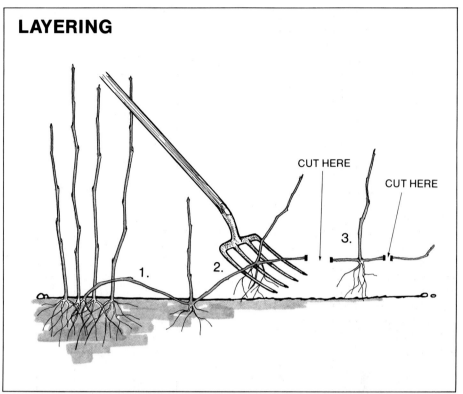

LAYERING

CUT HERE

CUT HERE

1.

2.

3.

1. To layer plant in soil, choose long, supple stem and bend to ground. Slice away small section of bark or girdle stem and treat wound with rooting hormone.

2. When roots are firmly established, gently lift layered section with pitch fork or shovel.

3. Cut new plant from parent as shown. Immediately replant in desired location.

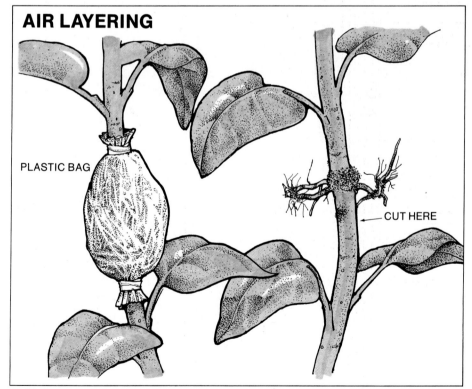

AIR LAYERING

PLASTIC BAG

CUT HERE

1. Girdle stem where you want roots to form—either remove a 1/2″ band of bark or make a small, slanting cut into the stem. Place toothpick in cut to keep it from healing.

2. Treat wounds with rooting hormone. Place handful of damp sphagnum or peat moss around the girdled area and enclose it with clear plastic.

3. Secure ends and moisten moss occasionally to prevent drying. When sufficient number of roots have formed, cut new plant from parent just below new roots. Plant immediately.

Propagation **103**

DIVIDING PERENNIALS

Division is an easy way to increase many kinds of clumping perennials. Most perennials are either divided in early spring just as new growth begins, or in fall just after topgrowth dies back.

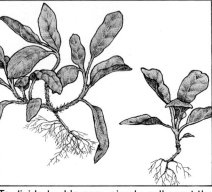
To divide lamb's ears, simply pull apart the spreading roots.

Asters are easily increased by pulling rooted shoots from main stem.

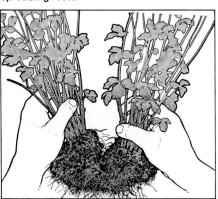
Columbines should be divided every 2 or 3 years. Pull apart root ball or cut with a sharp knife.

Separate clumps of daylilies by inserting two pitch forks back-to-back and prying apart.

Turn one hosta into many by separating individual rooted buds from established clumps.

Divide coral bells by pulling of separate divisions by hand. Discard old woody pieces and replant young, vigorous sections.

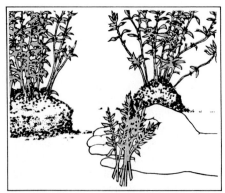
Divide perennial candytuft by cutting through roots with pruning shears. You can also propagate with cuttings.

is the best method for plants that are difficult or impossible to root by other methods.

Branches pencil size to 1 inch thick are usually best for air layering. Make a slanting cut just below a bud and use a toothpick or similar small chip to keep the wood separated. Or remove a ring of bark completely around the branch and into the stem tissue about 3/4 inch long. Lightly dust the cut area with rooting hormone. Fill a plastic bag with moistened sphagnum peat moss. Slice the bag lengthwise and hold it around the cut branch, then secure with rubber bands. Cover cut plastic with another piece of plastic and secure with more rubber bands. Keep peat moss moist until roots form, usually several months. The layered section can then be cut from the parent plant and planted.

DIVISION

Each year, clumping perennials are wider in girth, having grown new roots and stems all season. With many plants, these clumps may become too large for their alloted space or start invading nearby plants. Division helps keep these plants a manageable size—and gives you the chance to share a plant with a friend.

Another reason for division is to maintain plant health or appearance. Often, the center of the clump becomes woody or dies out, while the plant continues to produce healthy, vigorous growth around its perimeter. Dig up the plant and divide it, then replant the healthy portions.

Each root segment or division is actually a plant in itself, or is capable of becoming a new plant. Divide overgrown clumps into separate parts and you get many new plants.

Fall or early spring is the best time to divide established clumps. Fall is preferred for perennials that bloom in spring or early summer. After dividing, keep roots moist and plant as soon as possible.

Most deciduous and semideciduous perennials should be cut back to about 4 inches tall and trimmed of all dead leaves before dividing the plant.

SPECIAL PLANT PARTS

These include modified stems, roots or buds that help plants through periods of cold or drought, and in some cases, to reproduce the plant.

Bulblets and Bulbils—Many plants

that make below-ground bulbs, tubers or corms naturally propagate by division of the bulb into smaller bulbs called *bulblets* or *offset bulbs*. For instance, when a tulip plant attains maximum size, the bulb splits up into a number of smaller bulblets. Bulblets can be collected and planted. Plant bulblets to a depth three times their diameter. In the course of a few seasons, they will develop into flowering bulbs.

There are several ways to speed the process of forming bulblets on some plants. One is *scoring*—making deep vertical cuts through the base of the bulb. The other is *scooping,* done by exposing the base of the scale leaves which form the bulbs. These practices are done in summer. For example, hyacinth bulbs are scored, then planted immediately. By fall planting time, numerous small bulbils have formed along the scored surfaces.

Bulbils or *aerial bulbs* develop on the above-ground parts of several kinds of plants. Some lilies develop bulbils in their leaf axils. Onions known as *top set onions* develop bulbils at their stem tips. Bulbils can be planted like bulblets described above.

Cormels (cormlets)—These are very much like bulblets. Gladiolus and crocus are examples of common plants that propagate themselves with *corms*. New corms develop on the top of the old corm, and often the new corm is surrounded by numerous tiny cormels. Plant cormels the same as you would seeds and they will become flowering corms after two to four seasons.

Tubers and Tuberous Roots—A potato is the best example of a tuber. The potato "eyes" are actually buds, and each one can become a whole new plant. Cut the potato so that each section has two eyes, allow the cut sections to heal for 1 day and plant. For more on growing potatoes, see page 156. Tuberous-root plants such as dahlias develop buds around their root tips. Carefully cut through connected tips, leaving each root with one bud.

Rhizomes—These are underground stem parts that grow horizontally, slightly beneath the soil surface. Roots grow from the bottom of the rhizome, stems and leaves from the top. Iris is probably the most familiar example. As rhizomes grow and form branches, they can be divided with a

Left: New corm develops on top of old corm. 2-year-old corm has developed numerous tiny *cormels,* which can be removed and planted. Right: After collecting cormels, old corm is removed and discarded, new "mother" corm is replanted.

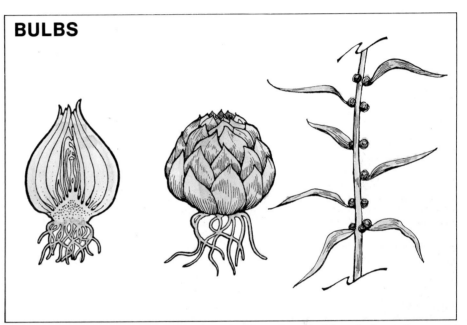

BULBS

Many bulbs split into smaller bulbs, called *bulblets.* Some bulbing plants produce aerial bulbs called *bulbils* at stem tips or in leaf axils, as shown at right.

sharp knife and replanted. Iris are divided this way after four or five seasons of growth.

Here's how to divide iris: When the plant is finished blooming, dig it up and divide rhizomes so each section has one group (fan) of leaves and a clump of roots attached. Cut back fans to about 3 inches in length to prevent water loss. Replant divisions so the root portion of the rhizome is underground and the top is exposed. The fans should point in the direction you wish the plant to grow.

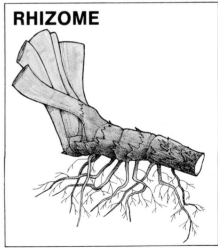

RHIZOME

Iris rhizomes are divided by cutting apart with knife. Each section should have roots and group of leaves.

T-BUDDING SEQUENCE

Also called *shield budding,* T-budding is done in late spring or early summer when bark on stock readily separates from wood. Many fruit trees and some ornamentals are budded this way. "T" describes shape of cut in stock, "shield" describes shape of bud inserted into stock.

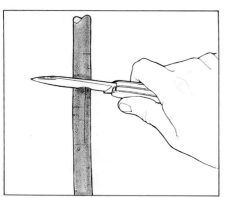

2. Make horizontal cut through bark across top of vertical cut, about 1/3 the distance around the stem.

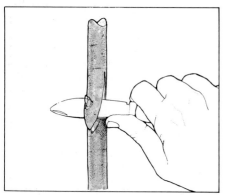

4. Slice up under bark and bud on budstick. Make slice from 1/2" below to 1" above bud.

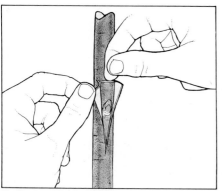

6. Push shield downward under loosened flaps of bark in T until top cuts on shield and stock are even.

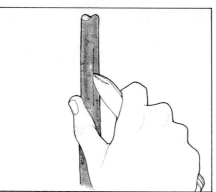

1. Make vertical cut 1" long in stock at point where it is 1/4" to 1/2" in diameter.

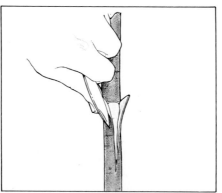

3. Try to lift corners of bark. If bark breaks or sticks tightly to wood, don't bud now—plant is too dry or it's too late in season.

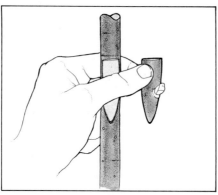

5. Crosscut into wood, 3/4" above the bud. Push shield out sidewise. Wood core in bud should stay.

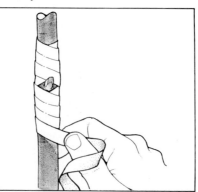

7. Wrap with plastic or rubber strip. Cover top end of strip with first full wrap, insert bottom end under last wrap.

GRAFTING

The term *grafting* is applied to methods for joining parts of two separate plants to make a single new plant. Grafting is the quickest way to have more kinds of fruit, a longer bearing season or more effective pollination. These methods are usually used to propagate plants that do not come true from seed or do not root from cuttings. Most fruit trees are in this category. For instance, shoot or twig cuttings, called *scions,* of desired apple varieties can be budded or grafted on seedling apple trees or grafted on pieces of roots of older trees.

Here are some other reasons for grafting:
● To modify the growth of the scion. This is the way many dwarf fruit trees are created.
● To adapt plants to unfavorable soil or climatic conditions, or to control or prevent pest damage to roots. For instance, graft the scion of a variety susceptible to a particular root disease on rootstock resistant to that disease.
● To change the top of a mature plant to another variety, or to have two or more varieties on the same tree. Similarly, if one fruit variety requires the pollen of a different variety to set fruit, both can be grafted on the same tree to make it self-pollinating.
● To repair tree damage caused by rodents, machinery, adverse weather or other causes.

BUDDING

This is the term used when the scion is a single bud. *T-budding (shield budding)* is the most common method of budding. "T" describes the shape of the cut in the rootstock and "shield" describes the shape of the bud inserted into the cut. See drawings at left. Roses, apples, peaches and sweet gum *(Liquidambar)* are among the plants commonly budded, usually in late spring or summer when the bark of the stock *slips,* that is, readily separates from the wood.

Patch Budding—This is the chosen budding method for plants with thick bark, such as walnuts, pecans and avocados. The double-bladed tool illustrated on the facing page is available but might be hard to find. Check with a local horticultural supplier.

T-budding and patch budding only work well if bark pulls away from the wood easily. This usually occurs during summer and early fall.

CLEFT GRAFTING

This method is used to join small scions to much larger stock. Select a section of stock branch from 2 to 4 inches in diameter that is free of knots so the split will be more consistent. Common problems are slow-healing cleft and weak graft union. The fundamentals are simple: Join similar kinds of fruits—apples to apples, pears to pears, and so on—and complete all grafts before trees begin active growth. Use twigs of the previous year's growth for your scions. Scions should be about 3/8 inch thick and 8 to 10 inches long. Two or even three scions can be grafted on one stock.

BARK GRAFTING

This method, preferred for older apples, persimmons or pears, is one of the most successful for beginners. Graft after spring growth starts and only when bark peels freely from wood beneath. Initial unions are weak and require extra support to prevent breaking.

SIDE GRAFTING

This method is used to add a branch to the side of a tree, or whenever the stock branch is too small for a bark or cleft graft, but too large for a whip graft. Unlike other methods, you don't remove top of stock.

WHIP GRAFT

Use this method in winter when joining a small scion to a small stock. Make long, sloping cuts on both the scion and stock. Tongues are made on both stock and scion by vertical cuts starting near the point of the diagonal cuts. *Wedge grafts* are similar but the scion is wedged into the middle of a split stock.

All of the above grafting methods are illustrated on the next two pages.

PATCH BUDDING

Patch budding is used for trees with thick bark, such as walnuts and pecans. The double-bladed tool shown in the drawing at right is available from horticultural supply houses and some nurseries that specialize in trees.

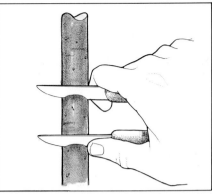

1. Use patch-budding tool to make parallel cuts 1/3 the distance around the stock, and one vertical cut, forming a rectangle.

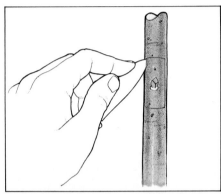

2. On budstick, make parallel cuts above and below bud, vertical connecting cuts on each side of bud.

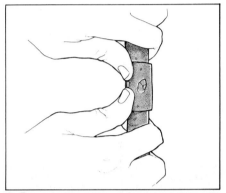

3. Press bud patch out from budstick with sideways pressure, so that the core of wood will remain in the bud.

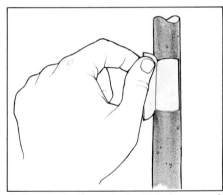

4. On stock, lift vertical edge of square C made in step 1. Bud patch will slide under this flap.

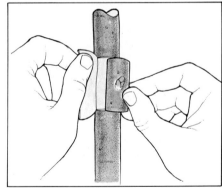

5. Slide bud patch under lifted flap until patch rests flat on bare wood. Trim overhang on flap and patch.

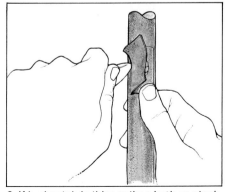

6. If bud patch is thinner than bark on stock, pare bark on stock so tying will hold patch tight.

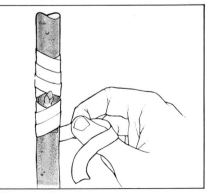

7. Tie as for T-bud. Or, secure with gummed paper tape or polyethylene tape.

CLEFT GRAFT

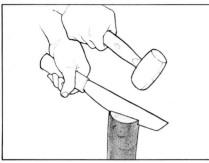

1. Select branch that is free of knots for 6'' below graft point. Cut off cleanly with saw. Split with heavy knife and mallet or stick.

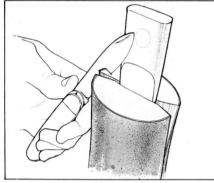

3. Use a clean, stiff, sharp knife to cut off tiny bevel of wood to accommodate upper end of scion and allow insertion to full depth.

5. Insert scion firmly to full depth into split branch, with spreading wedge still in place. Be sure thin, green cambium layers of scion and stock match along their full length.

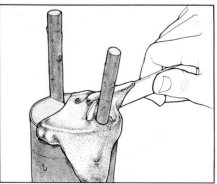

7. Cover all cut surfaces with grafting compound or wax to prevent drying out. Check frequently and repaint if compound dries and cracks.

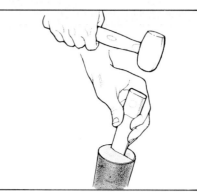

2. Drive wedge into center of split to open it 2'' to 3'' deep. **Note:** Special grafting tool may be used to split wood and hold it for steps 3 through 7.

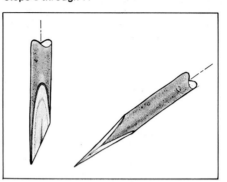

4. Hold knife blade with four fingers and rock blade slowly toward thumb to taper scion tip. Trimmed scion tapers to long point and is thicker and longer on outside edge.

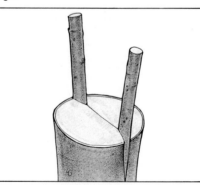

6. Insert the second scion and remove spreading wedge to firmly anchor scions.

8. New leaves indicate both grafts have taken.

BARK GRAFT

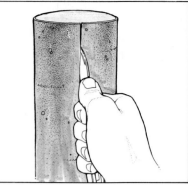

1. Cut back existing tree to main branch. Make three or four vertical cuts in bark which extend slightly into the wood.

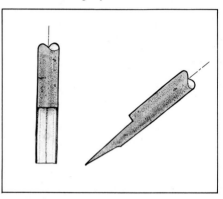

2. Cut scion so one side is wedge-shaped and the other forms a ledge as shown.

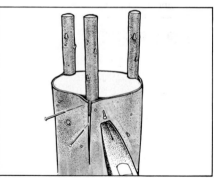

3. Slide scion under bark of stock with wedge facing out and ledge sitting on top of cut stock. Secure with three small nails—one on each side and one directly through scion.

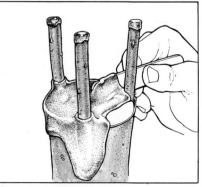

4. Seal all exposed or cut surfaces with grafting wax.

SIDE GRAFT

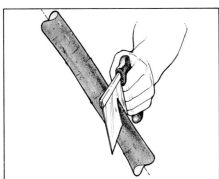

1. Use fine-tooth saw to make angled cut into stock branch.

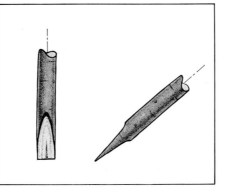

2. Shape scion tip into wedge, slanting sides longer than length of cut into stock, and longer on inner side than outer side. Lowest scion bud should face direction you want new branch to grow.

New graft is sealed with grafting tape and grafting wax.

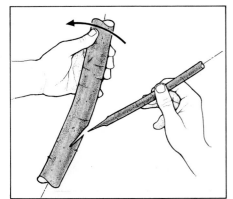

3. Push top part of stock branch to force cut open, then insert scion so cambium layers of stock and scion match.

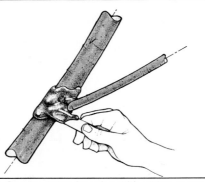

4. Secure scion by tying with string or tape and coat with grafting compound.

WHIP GRAFT

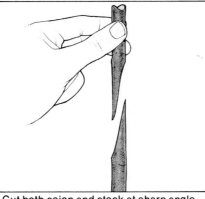

1. Cut both scion and stock at sharp angle.

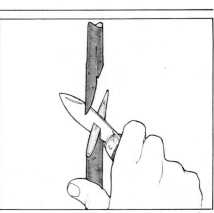

2. Make second cuts into each, starting about 1/3 the distance from opposite tips, cutting parallel to vertical length of scion.

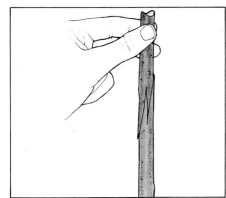

3. Fit scion and stock together as shown.

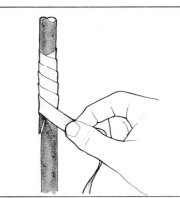

4. Wrap securely with budding tape.

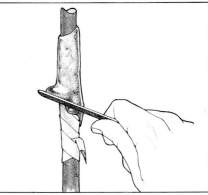

5. Coat liberally with grafting compound.

FLOWERS

Among the happiest pleasures of gardening is the yearly parade of color from plants grown primarily for flowers. Late winter ends with the first spring crocus, followed by daffodils, tulips and the many other *bulbs* that delight the gardener. Marigolds, petunias, zinnias and other *annuals* add splashes of color to the summer garden, living their entire life cycle within a year and leaving behind seed replacements. Lilies-of-the-valley, columbines, delphiniums and other *perennials* that bloom year after year add their pleasures throughout the growing seasons. Canterbury bells, foxgloves, and hollyhocks are *biennials* that take two seasons to complete their life cycle, blooming the second season.

ANNUALS

These plants germinate, develop, flower, set seed and die all within a single year. Many vegetables, weeds and grasses are annuals, but the term usually applies to those plants that are grown strictly for their flowers.

All annuals can be started from seed, although many gardeners prefer more immediate color with nursery seedlings or plants already in bloom.

In cold climates, seed should be started indoors and transplanted into prepared soil right after danger of frost has passed. Otherwise the short season may provide you with disappointing results. For more on starting plants from seeds, see pages 40-44.

If you have winters with only light frosts or no frosts at all, sow annuals in the early spring. You can also set out cool-season annuals in early autumn for winter flowering.

Most annuals need sunny locations and rich, well-draining soil that retains ample moisture. Soil preparation is a major key to success with annuals.

Before planting, read all about soils, starting on page 55.

Such short-lived plants need adequate moisture while they're growing and blooming if they are to be successful. At the same time, you must be careful not to overwater them.

Four of the most popular annuals are discussed here. A list of commonly grown garden annuals appears on pages 198-199. For more complete information on growing annuals, refer to the book *Annuals, How to Select, Grow and Enjoy* by Derek Fell, published by HPBooks.

Marigolds—These old favorites appear in many shades of yellow, gold, orange, red and white. American marigolds *(Tagetes erecta)* range from 10 to 36 inches tall, growing in a fairly vertical form. Blossoms are full and double and grow as large as 5 inches across. Look for the selections 'Climax', 'Giant Fluffy', 'Gold Coin',

---

Left: *Rudbeckia* 'Pinwheel' is showy perennial that blooms in late summer.

Above: Mixed border includes sweet alyssum *(Lobularia maritima)* at lower left, periwinkle *(Vinca minor)* at bottom, American marigolds *(Tagetes erecta)* at center and zinnias at upper right. Flowers in background include celosia, black-eyed Susans and hollyhocks. For best display, group flowers by plant height.

American marigolds have large, pompon flowers that are much larger than French marigolds.

Most gardeners are familiar with the single flower forms of petunias. Petunia 'Fanfare' mix has frilly, fully double flowers in solid colors and bicolors.

'Mellow Yellow' and the pure white 'Snowbird'.

French marigolds *(T. patula)* grow in a denser, more compact form. Small flowers, as tiny as 3/4 inch across, are single or double and may be bicolored, with petals striped or tipped in bronze or red. Recommended hybrids include the 'Boy' series, the 'Petite' series, 'Pygmy' and 'Signet'.

Triploid hybrids result from crosses between the tall American and dwarf French types, resulting in plants with a long season of vigorous blooms. Consider 'Nuggets', 'Red Seven Star', 'Copper Canyon' or 'Honey Bee'.

Signet marigolds *(T. tenuifolia)* bear profusions of tiny, single flowers that often completely cover the foliage. 'Lemon Gem' and 'Orange Gem' are excellent choices.

If you object to the typical marigold muskiness, plant 'Orange Hawaii' or 'Golden Hawaii', both odorless American marigolds.

These easy-to-grow annuals make excellent cut flowers, are easily grown in containers and have a multitude of uses in the landscape.

Petunias—You have a choice between large-flowered *grandiflora* petunias and the many-flowered *multiflora* petunias. Both are variations of *Petunia hybrida*, a half-hardy perennial commonly grown as an annual. Half-hardy perennials are those that survive the winter in warm-winter climates. Colors include all shades of purple, violet, red, pink, salmon, yellow and white. There are many bicolor selections.

Varieties of both types of petunias may have single or double blooms. Cascade hybrids are excellent subjects for trailing or in hanging containers. All are sun-loving plants that thrive in any temperate zone. Gardeners in mild-winter climates often plant them again in autumn for winter and early spring color.

Among the grandifloras, strains that are proven performers include 'Bouquet', 'Cascade', 'Titans', 'Magic' and 'Ultra'. In multifloras, start with the 'Delights', 'Joys', 'Plums' and 'Tarts'.

Snapdragons—The common name for *Antirrhinum majus* comes from the lobed and hooded flowers that snap open when you squeeze their sides. They're grouped by height—dwarf (to 8 inches), intermediate (20 to 30 inches), and tall (to 36 inches). Hybridizers have added flowers that no longer have the snapping feature, but are double, bell-shaped, butterfly-flower form, and azalea-flower form. Colors run the gamut except for blue.

Botanists continue to debate whether snapdragons are actually annuals or tender perennials. In either case, these Mediterranean natives are most often grown as annuals.

Landscape use determines the height you'll want to choose. Dwarf hybrids up to 6 inches include 'Floral Carpet', 'Pixie' and 'Tom Thumb'. In the intermediate range, 'Bright Butterflies', 'Carioca' and 'Liberty Bell' are highly favored. If you want tall snapdragons, choose 'Madame Butterfly', 'Panorama' or any of the 'Rocket' strain.

Zinnias—Summer-blooming hybrids of common zinnia *(Zinnia elegans)* and Mexican zinnia *(Z. Haageana)* come in purple, pink, red, orange, yellow, green and white, as well as bicolors. The cactus-flower form has quilled, pointed petals on double blossoms up to 6 inches across on plants 2-1/2 to 3 feet tall—look for 'Bouquet', 'Fruit Bowl' and 'Zenith'. The dahlia-flower form has rounded, flat petals, also on double blossoms up to 7 inches wide—'Envy', 'Gold Sun' and 'Red Sun' are popular hybrids. Single-flowered 'Sombrero' is a novel addition.

Both flower forms come in dwarf-size plants. The tiniest ones that grow to 6 inches tall and are good for edging include 'Creeping Zinnia', 'Mini' and 'Thumbelina'. Outstanding 1-foot-tall plants suitable for border plantings are 'Buttons', 'Cupid', 'Persian Carpet', 'Peter Pan' and 'Tom Thumb'.

Cut-and-come-again zinnias are those that produce more flowers the more they're cut. They grow about 3 feet tall with beehive-shaped flowers about 3 inches across.

Zinnia augustifolia is a spreading species that makes an attractive flowering ground cover.

Snapdragons come in wide range of colors, except blue. Familiar "snapping" flower form is shown here.

Dwarf zinnia 'Peter Pan Plum' grows about 6" high.

Hollyhocks *(Alcea rosea)* are popular biennials that bloom during second year. Most reach 4-6' in height.

Biennial foxglove *(Digitalis* species) self-sows readily and resulting plants usually come true from seed.

BIENNIALS

These are plants that take 2 years to complete their growth cycle. They germinate the first spring, develop the plant growth during the growing season, flower during the next spring or summer, then set seed and die after that flowering season. If you're impatient, purchase nursery transplants that have already gone through the developing season and are ready for their year of blooming.

Three old garden biennials usually grown as annuals are canterbury bells *(Campanula medium)*, hollyhock *(Alcea rosea)* and foxglove *(Digitalis purpurea)*.

Agapanthus is a tender perennial that grows well in mild-winter climates. In colder climates, grow in containers that can be moved indoors during winter.

Daylilies (*Hemerocallis* hybrids) are one of the most popular perennials with hundreds of varieties to choose from. Easily divided.

Pinks (*Dianthus* species) are colorful, low-growing, sweetly scented perennials, related to carnations and Sweet William. Shown here is *Dianthus* 'China Doll' mix. Often grown as annuals or biennials.

Summer-flowering purple coneflower (*Echinacea purpurea*) prefers full sun and will bloom for many weeks.

Geraniums (*Pelargonium* species) are tender perennials that grow well in mild-winter areas. Often grown as annuals in other parts of country.

PERENNIALS

This group includes flowering plants that bloom repeatedly for at least 3 years, provided they receive suitable climatic and cultural conditions. Many plants are perennial, but the term as used in flower gardening means those plants that lack woody tissue—that is, they are *herbaceous*. Most die down to the ground at the end of their growing season and start all over again at the beginning of the next growing season.

Given a suitable climate, some perennials, such as daylilies, remain evergreen. Others, such as Shasta daisies, retain only a little bit of greenery through the winter and begin more active growth with the coming of the next season. Perennials such as peonies are *deciduous*.

Short-lived perennials can be started from seed or from stem or root cuttings. Longer-lived perennials can be divided, as well as given new vigor, by digging up and separating clumps into several new plants. Summer- and autumn-flowering plants are usually divided early in spring before new growth begins. Spring-blooming plants are divided in summer or autumn.

Perennials are sold either bare-root or growing in containers. In most areas, summer- and autumn-blooming perennials, either bare-root plants or divisions, are planted in spring. Spring-blooming perennials are planted in early autumn. Container-grown perennials can be planted at any time except just before or during extremes of heat or cold. The plants will need time to adjust before facing summer heat or winter chill.

Growing requirements for some common perennials are included in the chart on pages 200-201.

To survive in cold-winter areas, perennials that retain winter foliage will need adequate mulches and a blanket of non-compacting organic material such as straw, evergreen branches and salt hay. Apply these after the soil has frozen and remove after the last freeze, but before plants begin much active growth.

Keep plants more attractive and healthy by cutting faded blooms or flower stems and removing any dead foliage. Keep dead leaves picked up to prevent them from rotting the plant or providing homes for garden pests.

A list of popular garden perennials appears on pages 200-201. For more specific information on growing a wide variety of perennials, see the book *Perennials, How to Select, Grow and Enjoy* by Pamela Harper and Frederick McGourty, published by HPBooks.

BULBS

Only a few of the flowering plants we know as "bulbs" are what botanists call *true bulbs*. These include narcissus, tulips and lilies. True bulbs are fully formed tiny plants held inside fleshy modified leaves known as *scales* or *rings* that increase in size or number each year. Roots grow from a disk or *basal plate* on the bottom of the bulb.

Crocus, freesia and gladiolus are included in the "bulbs" called *corms*. These are modified storage stems that are depleted at the end of the flowering season and replaced by a new one that grows on top of or beside the old corm. Roots grow from a basal plate on the underside.

Tubers include anemones, ranunculus, and cyclamen as well as the edible potato. Plant life is stored in these swollen underground stem parts. Roots grow from buds or *eyes* scattered over the surface of the tuber.

Plants such as begonias and dahlias grow from tuber look-alikes, known as *tuberous roots,* that are actually energy-storing swollen roots. Fibrous roots are produced during the growing season. New buds grow at the base of the old stem at the point it joined the tuberous roots.

Bearded iris is the best example of plants that grow from bulblike *rhizomes*. These are swollen underground stems that grow horizontally near the soil surface. Growth buds develop along the top side and roots grow from underneath.

What all these bulb types share in common is that they enable the plant to survive climate extremes. Bulbs are also a means by which the plants reproduce. For more information on propagating bulbs, corms, tubers and rhizomes, see page 105.

Nurseries sell bulbs in bulk or prepackaged. Some kinds are packed in moist sawdust or other material to keep them fresh, others are sold dry. Look over each bulb before buying or planting to be sure it is healthy. Discard those that are damaged or show signs of softness or rot. Lightweight bulbs are usually dehydrated and should be discarded.

To keep bulbs from drying out, they should be planted as quickly as possible after getting them. Planting times will vary with the type of plant and the climatic conditions in your area. Generally, bulbs are either classified as spring-flowering or fall-

Tulips are one of the few plants known as *true bulbs*. Number of varieties would fill a large book. Bulbs require winter chill. Shown here is tulip 'Smiling Queen'.

Naked lady *(Amaryllis belladonna)* is so named because large flowers appear in late summer after foliage has died down. Make excellent indoor container plants.

To cover large area, dig trench to correct depth, position bulbs and cover.

flowering. Gardeners in warm climates should dig up spring-flowering bulbs after blooming and store them in a cool place such as the refrigerator until warm weather is over.

Planting depth for bulbs varies according to the size of the bulb. Bulbs are generally planted at a depth equal to three times the widest point of their diameter.

For ease in planting large areas, dig up the entire area, position the bulbs and cover. Individual bulbs can be set out among other plants by digging a hole with a trowel or special bulb planter. Put the bulb in place and cover with soil, compacting by hand.

See page 202 for lists of bulbs suitable for naturalizing in the garden and bulbs for containers. For detailed information on growing a wide variety of bulbs, see *Bulbs, How to Select, Grow and Enjoy* by George Harmon Scott, published by HPBooks.

LAWNS &
GROUND COVERS

Some people cannot imagine a landscape without a luxurious expanse of green lawn. Others prefer less maintenance than a healthy lawn requires or simply like the looks of alternative ground covers.

Lawns are appropriate when you have the time to care for them and where they are in keeping with the character of the area. In dry environments or adjoining wilderness areas where grasses do not naturally grow, alongside lakes and streams that could be polluted from fertilizers or in small urban gardens, there are other ground covers that can satisfy the craving for a carpet of green.

Although this chapter deals only with plantings, ground covers do not even have to be growing. Some people may enjoy areas of gravel, decorative or native rock, organic mulches, decks or patios.

LAWNS

Today's gardener can choose from a wide range of lawn grasses. Each grass grows best under specific climatic conditions—a major consideration when choosing a grass, but not an absolute restriction. You also need to consider the individual habits of each grass, as well as recommendations for mowing heights (see the chart on page 124) and fertilizing rates (page 121) as these factors will definitely affect the time you'll spend on lawn maintenance.

Cool-season grasses are those that thrive in cool spring and fall weather, tapering off growth in the summer months while remaining green if given plenty of water. These are primarily grown in the North, but many are suitable in higher elevations or cool regions of the South.

Warm-season grasses enjoy their peak growth during hot summer months before going dormant and turning brown when cold weather arrives. Warm-season lawns are often planted *straight* or unmixed with other grass types. Most cool-season lawns are a mixture of several grasses or a blend of several varieties of one grass.

With mixtures and blends, grasses adjust to the variety of conditions usually found within a typical lawn. This allows the good features of one grass to overcome the weakness of another, creating a lawn that has a better chance of survival if hit by disease or a climatic problem. Common examples are "sun" or "shade" mixtures. Mixes blended for shady sites contain more of the shade-tolerant grasses, such as fine fescue.

In some parts of the South and Southwest, warm-season and cool-

---

Left: Large expanse of ryegrass lawn surrounds cool summer retreat.

Above: *Vinca major* is attractive, fast-growing ground cover for large areas. Can be invasive in garden.

'Tifgreen' is one of most popular varieties of improved Bermudagrass. Finer textured than common Bermudagrass but requires more fertilizer and water to maintain good appearance.

Dichondra is low, broadleaf ground cover used as lawn substitute. Requires no mowing but is sensitive to temperature extremes.

season grasses are often combined. Warm-season grasses will dominate through summer months, then, when they become dormant, cool-season grasses are planted or resume growth.

BAHIAGRASS
(Paspalum notatum)

This grass grows best in infertile, sandy soils, especially from the central coast of North Carolina to east Texas where many gardeners consider it a weed. Tall, fast-growing seedlings develop into a coarsely textured lawn that must be mowed frequently for best appearance. Low maintenance is a plus and the aggressive root system is valued for erosion control.

Although it grows best where sunshine and rainfall are plentiful and evenly distributed through the season, Bahiagrass is drought tolerant and does fairly well in shade. Problems include chlorosis (yellowing of leaves), dollar spot and mole cricket.

BENTGRASS
(Agrostis palustris)

Heavily planted in the Northeast and Pacific Northwest, bentgrass is a dense grass often used for golf courses and lawn-bowling areas where low mowing is desired. Without frequent low mowing, an extensive thatch builds up quickly. Bentgrass requires lots of water, has poor drought tolerance and needs fairly high fertilizing to maintain a good appearance. It prefers sandy-loam soils and is susceptible to several diseases.

BERMUDAGRASS, COMMON
(Cynodon dactylon)

Also known as devilgrass, manienie or wiregrass, Bermudagrass enjoys high heat, wears extremely well, requires little maintenance and tolerates heavy abuse, making it the most popular warm-season grass. It is not perfect, however, because it cannot tolerate shade, is invasive and often turns brown from fall to spring. It is often overseeded with fine fescue or ryegrass for winter lawns.

Give Bermudagrass plenty of water to keep it looking healthy during dry periods. Bermudagrass adapts best from Maryland to Florida in the East, across to Kansas and down to lower elevations of the Southwest.

BERMUDAGRASS, IMPROVED
(Cynodon hybrids and varieties)

Improved varieties and hybrids of Bermudagrass have a finer texture and a shorter dormancy than common Bermudagrass. In exchange for these improved characteristics, they require more water and fertilizer, therefore more mowing. Thatch buildup, diseases and insects can be problems. Ask local nurseries which varieties are best adapted to your area. 'Tifgreen' is one of the more popular varieties.

CENTIPEDEGRASS
(Eremochloa ophiuroides)

A coarsely textured, medium green grass with a tendency to turn yellow from chlorosis and recover slowly from damage. Among its good points are low maintenance, adaptability to poor soil, resistance to chinch bugs and its aggressiveness in choking out weeds. If you hate to mow, consider planting this grass. The shallow root system makes it drought sensitive although it recovers rapidly. Best adapted to the deep South as it is sensitive to low temperatures.

Coarse texture makes fescue a tough lawn, adaptable to a variety of situations.

Many consider Kentucky bluegrass the best of American grasses—dense, deep green and medium textured. Grows well in all northern states and southern Canada.

DICHONDRA
(Dichondra micrantha)

This is a broadleaf plant used like a grass to create a lush, bright green carpet that requires less mowing than most grasses. In warm areas, it remains green all year. It may not grow well in foggy areas and won't survive where temperatures drop below 25F (-4C). Dichondra does fairly well in shade. Both water and fertilizer needs are high and wearability is extremely poor. Tends to clump. Watch out for snails, slugs, cutworms, flea beetles and weeds. Once weeds invade they're difficult to eliminate because broadleaf weedkillers will also kill dichondra.

FESCUE, CHEWING
(Festuca rubra commutata)

A fine-textured grass that is best adapted to higher elevations or other areas where summers are cool. In warmer climates, chewing fescue is susceptible to diseases during summer. Water and fertilizer requirements are low. Often found in mixtures with Kentucky bluegrass because fescue grows well in shade and dry soils, although competitiveness with bluegrass can be a problem. Wearability is poor.

FESCUE, RED
(Festuca rubra rubra)

Also known as creeping red fescue, it isn't red at all but deep green with most of the characteristics of chewing fescue. It has poor wearability and recovery from damage is slow. Tolerates acid soil.

Fine texture of ryegrass gives lawn neat, well-manicured appearance. Both annual and perennial types available. Used for overseeding winter-dormant lawns such as Bermudagrass.

FESCUE, TALL
(Festuca arundinacea)

This is a good selection for transition zones because it is a cool-season grass that can take heat and remain green all year. Does well in partial shade and is drought tolerant. Coarse texture makes it a tough lawn that's good for playing, although wearability is not as good in summer as during spring and fall growth periods. Not a good mixer unless it dominates mix by about 90%.

KENTUCKY BLUEGRASS, COMMON
(Poa pratensis)

Considered the standard of excel-lence among American grasses, Kentucky bluegrass lawns are dense, deep green and medium textured. Needs lots of water, but little fertilizer. Some varieties can tolerate a little shade. Problems arise when grass is mowed too short and it is prone to disease during high summer heat. The northeastern and northern central United States are the best areas for bluegrass, although it grows in all northern states and southern Canada.

KENTUCKY BLUEGRASS, IMPROVED
(Poa pratensis varieties)

Improved varieties boast superior color, disease resistance and density

St. Augustinegrass is best adapted to Gulf Coast states. Prefers warm, humid summers and mild winters, is aggressive and tolerates salty soils.

to the parent. Some tolerate more shade or can be mowed shorter. Most varieties are more sensitive to drought and require more fertilizer than common bluegrass.

RYEGRASS, ANNUAL
(Lolium multiflorum)

Also known as common ryegrass or Italian ryegrass, annual ryegrass establishes itself quickly. Good for over-seeding of dormant Bermudagrass in warm-winter climates. Will grow in shade, but does not tolerate much heat or cold. Needs a lot of water and is difficult to mow evenly.

RYEGRASS, PERENNIAL
(Lolium perenne)

Like the annual, it germinates and establishes quickly and is good for overseeding. It, too, makes a tough lawn for playing, but mows smoother than the annual type. Has more heat and cold tolerance, but can't withstand cold winters. Should not comprise more than 25% of a seed mix or it will take over. Relative to other grasses, its water needs are in the medium range. Grows best in coastal regions where summers are cool and moist, and winters are mild.

ST. AUGUSTINEGRASS
(Stenotaphrum secundatum)

This adapts best in the states along the Gulf Coast and in mild areas of the Southwest. Has good tolerance for shade and salty soil. Requires a lot of water, does not wear well and has a tendency to thatch. Watch out for chinch bug and diseases such as *St. Augustinegrass Decline* (SAD) virus.

ZOYSIAGRASS
(Zoysia species)

This is another grass that grows best in the South, but is sometimes planted in the Northeast. It is slow in establishing itself and will not be successful where summers are short or cool. Assets include dense, fine-textured carpet, drought and heat tolerance, resistance to weeds and disease. Chinch bugs and thatching can be problems. Will grow in shade, but slowly. Needs moderate amount of water. Mowing must be consistent or grass blades become wiry.

PLANTING A LAWN

Lawns can be started from *seed, sod* or *sprigs*. Sometimes known as plugs, sprigs are actually pieces of grass stems. *Stolons* are similar to sprigs and planted in the same manner. No matter which method you choose, soil preparation before planting remains the same. First consider the lay of the land to be turned into lawn. You want the lawn to end up so it slopes and drains slightly away from the house. If the area is reasonably level, grading will be easy. If not, consider hiring someone with grading equipment to smooth out the area. Fill in any trenches with soil, thoroughly soak the entire area and allow time for soil

to settle before planting.

Adding organic matter to the soil improves drainage and prevents soil from becoming compacted. Compacted soil under a lawn becomes repellent to water after a few seasons. You can use leaf mold, peat moss, sawdust, ground bark, or any other locally available organic amendments. Cover the lawn site with a 2- to 3-inch layer of organic matter.

Next apply any good lawn fertilizer at the ratio recommended on the fertilizer label. Use a roto-tiller, available from rental yards, to work the organic matter and lawn food into the top 6 inches of soil until well blended. To avoid compacting soil, go easy on roto-tilling if organic matter was not added.

A heavy roller, also rentable, can be pushed over the soil, first one way, then across, to smooth out any lumps and remove air pockets. Don't use a roller if you did not add organic matter. Pick out any rocks or other debris. Use a shovel to break up clods and level down any high spots. Rake area to make the slope conform to the planned grade. If much soil was moved during leveling and grading, you might want to roll the area again before planting.

Seeding—Scatter seeds with a lawn spreader to achieve even planting. Rake in seeds and barely cover with mulch before lightly rolling with an empty roller. Keep area moist until seeds sprout.

Sodding—Roll out strips of sod in a straight line with ends staggered. Cut strips to fit corners and contoured edges. Press with hands to firm the joints together, then roll lightly and water to soak to depth of 8 inches.

Sprigging—Place sprigs or stolons 3 to 6 inches apart over the entire surface. Cover with soil, leaving tips out. Roll lightly and water well.

Plugging—Plant plugs with a trowel, small shovel or special plugging tool available at nurseries. For most grasses, plugs are spaced 12 inches apart, for zoysiagrass, 6 inches apart. Firm plugs into the soil and water well.

Watering—Adequate water is critical during the first few weeks after planting. This is especially true for sod because the heavy soil matrix that holds sod together does not absorb water readily. One dry day can kill sod. The sole water- and nutrient-gathering primary roots of newly sprouted seeds penetrate the soil to a depth of 4 to 6 inches and will need continuous moisture. In hot areas, seedlings may require several sprinklings a day with a fine spray, but be sure to turn off water before puddles form or runoff carries seed away. When the seedlings are about 1 inch high, their more-fibrous secondary roots have developed and you can begin slacking off on the water.

If you have to walk over a developing new lawn, lay down a board to walk on. Don't use weed killers or mow lawn until the grass is about 2 inches high and begins to curve. For the first mowing, set the mower blade at 1-1/2 inches and mow when the grass is dry.

After two or three mowings, begin slacking off the watering to a weekly schedule, even less in cool weather. At this time, the lawn is ready for the first feeding. By now you can use broadleaf weed killers, if necessary.

LAWN CARE

Lawns probably require more care than any other part of the garden. However, lawn care doesn't have to be the drudgery that many people think it is.

An understanding of lawn-care basics—watering, feeding, mowing and pest control—will help you maintain a healthy lawn with a minimum of effort.

Watering—Soil, season, climate, microclimate, winds, rains, grass type and numerous other factors create a wide range of lawn-watering requirements. You need to learn through on-the-lawn experience how to judge when it's time to water, as well as when it's time to vary your schedule. Surface signs indicate need for water. Footprints that leave an imprint on grass instead of bouncing right back mean a loss of resilience due to wilting. Some parts of the lawn may develop a tinge that appears smoky or bluish when water is needed.

Shallow watering leads to problems. When only the top of the soil gets watered, roots tend to stay in that area and the root system remains small, leading to the need for more frequent waterings. Wet surfaces breed diseases and encourage weeds.

When you water to the recommended depth of 6 to 8 inches, roots reach deeper, allowing lawns to go much longer between waterings. Deep waterings also cut down on growth of weeds and diseases. When lawns are

watered deeply, they can go unwatered for a week or more.

To test how deeply you are watering, use a soil-sampling tube to remove a section of soil about 12 hours after watering. This shows how deeply the roots grow and the depth to which the water has penetrated. A simpler test is to insert a long screwdriver into the ground. If it goes in easily to a depth of 6 inches, the lawn has enough moisture. The latter test will be inaccurate in very sandy soil.

As a general rule, most lawns need between 1 and 2 inches of water over the surface each week during hot weather. When you need to use that much water, it is best to run the sprinklers several times a day with 1/2-hour rest periods in between to prevent waste from water runoff.

Feeding—Lawn grasses live in a highly competitive environment that makes fertilizing essential if lawns are to be attractive and healthy.

Spring feedings help all lawns get ready to withstand summer heat and the onslaught of pests and diseases. Cool-season grasses need fall feedings to keep them green and to store food for a fast start the following spring. As long as they remain green, warm-season grasses enjoy fall feedings to help postpone brown dormancy. Dichondra needs feeding during its slow season in late spring to early summer when it sets seed and turns yellowish. Fertilizer greens it up quickly.

Nitrogen is necessary for greener leaves and fast growth. It is flushed from the soil through watering and the supply must be continuously refurbished to the growing grasses. When nitrogen is in short supply, lawns become pale or yellowish and may stop growing altogether. Phosphorous is needed for vigorous root growth. Water does not wash it away, therefore it is found in a smaller percentage in lawn foods. Potassium is necessary for hardiness and resistance to diseases. Like nitrogen, it is also washed away easily. Because most soils contain considerable amounts of potassium, lawn foods contain a lower percentage of it than of nitrogen.

The use of a complete fertilizer supplies all three of these primary nutrients. Percentages contained are displayed on the label. The first number is always nitrogen followed by phosphate and potassium. Generally, lawns require three to five times as

The type of sprinkler you choose is important to effective lawn irrigation, but kids find ways to have fun with almost any kind.

much nitrogen as phosphorous and two times as much potassium as phosphorus.

The amount of fertilizer required annually by lawn grasses is based on the nitrogen needs of the various grasses. Check the percentage of nitrogen in the complete fertilizer, then refer to the chart on page 64 to determine the amount of complete fertilizer required to furnish the needed nitrogen. This amount is divided among the feedings throughout the year.

The recommended annual amount of nitrogen per 1000 square feet of lawn varies with type of grass: 1 to 3 pounds for carpetgrass, centipedegrass and hard fescue; 2 to 4 pounds for red fescue, chewing fescue and Kentucky bluegrass (common); 4 to 6 pounds for Bahiagrass, St. Augustinegrass, zoysiagrass, tall fescue, annual ryegrass, colonial bentgrass and perennial ryegrass; 6 to 12 pounds for Bermudagrasses, dichondra, Kentucky bluegrass (improved) and creeping bentgrass. Also, application ratios for various grasses are listed on the fertilizer label. Do not exceed recommended amounts. Nitrogen fertilizers can burn lawns.

Always follow label directions when applying any fertilizer. No matter how you choose to distribute the fertilizer, first cover the ends of the lawn before going back and forth the long way in between. If you use a spreader, shut it *Continued on page 124.*

PLANTING A LAWN

1. Clean up large debris and rocks. Spread fertilizer and at least 2" to 3" of organic matter.

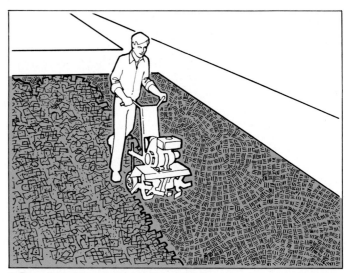

2. Roto-till soil to a depth of at least 6-8".

3. Pick up unearthed large rocks and debris.

4. Rough-level planting area.

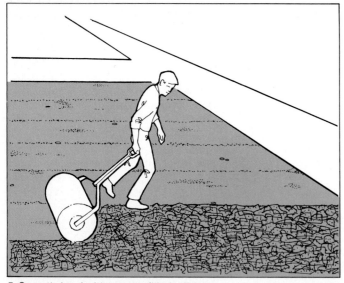

5. Smooth-level with a water-filled roller.

6. Spread seed at recommended coverage rates.

7. Lightly rake area to cover seed.

8. Apply a thin layer of organic mulch to further cover seed. Applicator shown is optional.

9. Water thoroughly.

10. Protect the area with stakes, string and cloth flags.

LAYING SOD

To lay sod, start with straight edge such as driveway or sidewalk. Stagger pieces so edges do not line up from row to row. Cover exposed edges with mulch. Roll. Water thoroughly.

PLANTING PLUGS

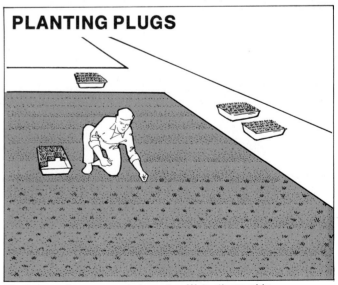

Plant plugs at recommended spacing. Water thoroughly.

MOWING HEIGHTS OF VARIOUS GRASSES

Grass	Height in Inches
Bahiagrass	2" to 3"
Bentgrass	1/4" to 1"
Bermudagrass, Common	3/4" to 1-1/2"
Bermudagrass, Improved	1/4" to 3/4"
Centipedegrass	1" to 2"
Dichondra	3/4" to 1-1/2"
Fescue, Chewing	1" to 2"
Fescue, Red	1" to 2"
Fescue, Tall	1-1/2" to 2-1/2"
Kentucky Bluegrass, Common	1-1/2" to 2-1/2"
Kentucky Bluegrass, Improved	1" to 2"
Ryegrass, Annual	1-1/2" to 2"
Ryegrass, Perennial	1" to 2"
St. Augustinegrass	1" to 2"
Zoysiagrass	3/4" to 1"

Rotary mowers are more versatile, easier to handle and less expensive than reel-type mowers but cutting is less precise. Mowing height is restricted to 1" or higher.

Continued from page 121.
off when you near the end strips.

Liquid fertilizers, applied with hose-end or hand-held sprayers, are time-consuming and prove difficult to spread easily.

Dry fertilizers can be spread by hand, but this results in uneven feeding that can cause streaks. Drop spreaders like the one illustrated on page 65 work fine on small to medium lawns when you overlap the wheels of the spreader with each new strip just enough so that no strips of lawn remain unfed. At the same time, you must be careful not to feed any strips twice or you could cause fertilizer burn.

Perhaps the easiest method of spreading dry fertilizer is the hand-held or push-wheel broadcast spreader. Fertilizer is thrown over wide areas at a time by a whirling wheel, so the spreader requires fewer passes to completely cover the lawn. As a guide, test the scattering pattern on the driveway before using.

Mowing—Good mowing is almost as important to a lawn's success as watering and feeding. Frequency of mowing depends on several factors: One is the time of year—naturally, more mowing is required during seasons of active growth. Another is your lawn-watering and feeding habits. The more luxuriant the lawn, the more the need to mow. Still another factor is the kind of grass—different grasses naturally grow at different rates and heights.

Most grasses grow best if mowed higher than most people usually allow. However, bentgrass, Bermudagrass and zoysiagrass require very low mowing to prevent thatch buildup. As a guideline, mow when the grass grows 1/4 to 1/3 taller than its recommended cut height, shown in the chart above. For example, if the chart recommends a height of 2 inches, mow when the grass reaches 2-1/2 inches. Grasses with recommended heights of less than 1 inch may grow fast enough to require mowing about every third day during active growing seasons.

Not adhering to this guideline can make all your other good lawn practices worthless. If you allow grass to get too tall and then cut it back severely, stems are suddenly exposed to sunlight that is too strong, resulting in browned leaves. Roots can go into severe shock and may require several weeks for recovery. When lawns are consistently mowed to the correct height, roots grow deeper, thereby cutting down on the amount of water needed. Not mowing low enough can bring about deterioration of the green tissue in lower leaves.

Choose a lawn mower that meets your needs. Rotary mowers are more popular because of their lower price, ease in handling and versatility. However, they require bigger motors and usually cannot mow lower than 1 inch. They are the best choice for tall-growing grasses and lawns on uneven ground. Reel mowers, available in push, gas or electric models, can be sharpened and adjusted to cut with scissorlike precision, even down to 1/4 inch in height.

If your lawn area justifies it, choose a riding mower. They come with both rotary and reel action. Riding mowers can make the work a bit more fun.

Whatever type of lawn mower you choose, follow the manufacturer's manual for correct maintenance. Be sure motor oil remains at the correct level and all fittings and gaskets are kept tight to prevent oil or gas from dripping onto the lawn and killing grasses. Mower blades should be kept sharp. Clean the mower after each use by spraying it lightly with the garden hose after the motor cools.

Sticks and stones may break mower blades as well as your bones. Always remove them before you mow. Be sure the grass is dry. Cutting wet grass results in uneven mowing and the wet clippings can compact and suffocate the grass. Clippings, wet or dry, can add to thatch accumulation or smother the roots, so it's best to use a mower

Aerating machine has long tines that punch holes in lawn to allow air and water to reach grass roots.

Thatch rake is useful for removing light thatch buildup. Thatching should be done just before most-vigorous growth period—spring for warm-season grasses, fall for cool-season grasses.

with a grass-catcher or rake up clippings after each mowing.

When you mow in the same direction every time, soil tends to compact and the lawn develops permanent patterns. This is easily prevented by alternating the mowing pattern each week. Also remember that when you move a reel mower too fast, the blade cannot make regular cuts, leaving behind a washboard effect.

Don't make radical changes in cutting height between mowings. Adjust cutting height up or down in smallest increments possible over a period of several mowings. If you lower the cutting height too much at one mowing, brown stems below the green grass blades will be exposed. This is called *scalping*. When lawn growth is fastest—spring and fall for cool-season grasses, late spring and summer for warm-season grasses—weekly mowing at the same height may result in occasional scalping. Gradually raise cutting height during this period.

Always follow the safety tips in your manufacturer's manual and exercise common sense to avoid mowing accidents.

RENOVATING A LAWN

If your lawn is worn out or thin, or struggling through a weed or pest invasion, consider renovating it.

Winter Green—Dormancy in cool weather is a natural part of the growing cycle for warm-season grasses. Some lawnkeepers choose to apply green dyes or latex paints to the dead blades. Overseeding with a fast-establishing, cool-season grass is a more organic approach. Fine fescues make good overseeders, as do annual and peren-

nial ryegrasses.

Mow your lawn closely before overseeding, removing thatch and aerating, if necessary, before scattering seeds. Top off with a thin layer of organic matter such as peat moss and keep the lawn watered until new seedlings are well established.

Just prior to the next spring's growth, mow closely and fertilize the lawn. This will reactivate growth of the permanent grass.

Patching—Unsightly or dead areas of lawn can be removed and replaced instantly with a piece of sod, or more slowly by reseeding. Always use the same grass or grass mixture as the established lawn.

To reseed, dig away the damaged area, aerating the soil underneath. If damage was caused by chemicals or gasoline, remove several inches of soil and add fresh soil up to the existing grade. Scatter seed as you would for a new lawn and keep seeded area well watered until seedlings are established.

To patch with sod, remove damaged area in the same way as for reseeding. Cut sod to fit the area, press it into place, then water it in.

Aeration—Air is as essential to roots as are water and nutrients. Heavy traffic areas often develop compacted soil which doesn't allow enough air or water to penetrate.

Special aerating machines, available from rental yards, drive hollow metal tubes into moist soil to a depth of about 4 inches, opening up the compacted areas to receive air, water and food.

Thatch Removal—Thatch consists of built-up layers of debris, stems and

roots, all slowly decomposing. A light layer of thatch can do a lawn good by reducing soil compaction from heavy traffic and working as a mulch to retard water evaporation and help control temperature. But too much thatch can be a home to insects and diseases. It can also create a barrier that inhibits penetration of water, fertilizer or pest controls. The grasses that make the thatch layer are forced to grow in it. Excess thatch also inhibits mowing, causing an uneven lawn.

Thatch should be removed just prior to the most vigorous grass-growing season, in late spring for warm-season grasses and in fall for cool-season grasses. Thatch rakes with knifelike blades, or thatch-cutting attachments for rotary mowers, will help remove thatch. Serious cases may need the aid of a sod cutter, which should only be used on grasses that have underground runners.

A vertical mower is probably the best tool for heavily thatched lawns. Unlike other mowers that cut off grass blades, a vertical mower has steel tines that slice into the turf. This thins the grass by bringing thatch to the surface, which allows you to remove the material from the lawn. Be sure that the blade is set to penetrate all the way down into the soil underneath the thatch.

PESTS

Normally, a lawn can combat a fair number of insect pests with no permanent damage. Problems arise with major infestations. The following text tells how to recognize the effects of common lawn pests and how to deal with them.

Boston fern *(Nephrolepis exaltata* 'Bostoniensis') is good, shade-tolerant ground cover for wooded areas.

GROUND COVERS

Whether they spread, creep, vine, mat or clump together, ground covers are plants that do just what the name implies. They cover bare soil. These living alternatives to lawns are among the most varied in all of nature, ranging from tiny plants only inches tall to sprawling shrubs up to several feet in height. Some are deciduous, most are evergreen. Some produce colorful berries, flowers or vibrant foliage. Ground covers are often used in lieu of lawns where conditions are harsh—windy sites, deep shade, poor soils, hillsides or under trees. They are often preferred over lawns simply because of their decorative beauty, interest and ease of maintenance. They offer a blending between various elements in the garden that no other plant group is able to achieve.

One of the most common uses of ground covers is to control erosion on steep slopes where grass or other plants would be difficult or impossible to grow or maintain. But they also have numerous other uses.

Ground covers make an excellent living mulch around shrubs that enjoy cool soil, such as clematis, azaleas and rhododendrons. Ground covers interplanted with flowering bulbs not only provide backgrounds for their flowers, but more importantly, they hide yellowing foliage after the blossoms fade.

Ground-cover possibilities vary greatly from region to region, and this book does not have space to cover the individual characteristics of every available ground cover. However, the lists on pages 204-205 describe some of the more popular ground covers and their uses. For more complete information on ground covers, refer to the book *Lawns & Ground Covers, How to Select, Grow and Enjoy* by Michael MacCaskey, published by HPBooks. Start your actual selection process with a visit to one or more local nurseries to see what is available. As you travel around your region, keep an eye out for native plants that would make potentially good ground covers.

Choose ground covers with regard to their sun or shade requirements and horticultural needs. There are many that will grow in partial or dense shade.

Whatever plants you choose, keep

When you're able to pick up a big piece of dead, soggy lawn, chances are that *grubs*—a general name for the larvae of numerous types of moths and beetles—have been eating the roots. Suspicions are confirmed if you look underneath a patch of grass and find curled-up grayish or white grubs with dark heads and hind parts. Control grubs with diazinon or dursban, watering heavily several times to flush the chemical into the soil where grubs live.

Silvery trails and ragged areas around the lawn's edge indicate nightcrawling *snails* and *slugs.* Snail bait scattered around the lawn perimeter takes care of the problem.

Small, dead patches in early spring, giving way to large brown patches by midsummer are signs of *sod webworms* at work, tunneling their way under the grass just above the thatch line. Open up damaged areas with your fingers and look for the worms or excreted tiny greenish-tan pellets left behind after a midnight supper. Control with aspon, baygon, diazinon, dursban or sevin.

Symptoms similar to those of the sod webworm are caused by the *armyworm, cutworm* and *fiery skipper,* all grubs of moths that feed on leaves. Look for them in the same way as for sod webworms. Armyworms are yellowish to white with an inverted "Y" on their heads. Cutworms are fat, smooth and usually curled up. Fiery skippers have dark brown heads at the end of a thin neck atop a yellow-brown body. Control with diazinon, dursban or sevin.

In sunny areas of the lawn, large circles of yellowish grass that appear worse toward the center indicate the presence of *chinch bugs.* They cause damage by sucking plant juices from lower leaves and stems of grass. To locate these bugs, fit a bottomless can into an area where grass is beginning to turn yellow. Fill the can with warm water and wait a few minutes to see if they float to the surface. Control with aspon, baygon, diazinon or dursban.

A bleached and unhealthy lawn or the destruction of a newly planted lawn can mean an overabundance of *leafhoppers.* These tiny green-to-gray insects will swarm when you walk through the grass. They're nearly always present in limited quantities, but when they become a problem, control with diazinon.

Pronounced small circles that turn yellowish or brownish, with stems inside the area that are easily pulled up, are symptoms of *billbugs.* Their grubs dine on roots, adults prefer late-summer stems. Baygon or diazinon are effective controls.

those for grass, described on page 120. Amend the soil and work out drainage problems *before* the plants go in. Because hillsides and other difficult sites may offer potential maintenance problems, consider installing built-in irrigation systems at the same time you are establishing the grade and improving the soil.

Although most ground covers do not need as much fertilizer as lawn grasses, many will get a better start if some nutrients are added to the soil before the plants go in. Choose a general-purpose fertilizer such as 10-10-10. If you need soil amendments to change the pH factor to suit the needs of the new plants, add them along with the fertilizer.

Some ground covers can be started from seed but transplants give much quicker results.

Plant according to the needs of the particular plants. Your local nursery staff can help you determine correct spacing and planting depth. Most ground covers naturally grow close together, and the closer you group them, the faster they cover. Take a rough garden plan with you when you shop so nursery personnel can estimate the number of flats or plants needed to cover the space.

Set out plants in your prepared soil, making a slight depression to act as a reservoir around each plant. When planting on slopes, staggered rows are better than straight ones for preventing water runoff. Spread the area with a natural-looking mulch such as bark, wood chips, hulls or gravel.

MAINTENANCE

Contrary to some popular beliefs, ground covers do require some maintenance. They need to be groomed far

Woolly thyme *(Thymus pseudolanuginosus)* is fragrant, low-growing herb that can be used to cover small areas.

Sea pink *(Armeria maritima)* has interesting mounding habit, dainty flowers. Prefers full sun and dry, sandy soil, making it excellent for warm coastal areas. Fairly heat and drought tolerant.

Cotoneaster is a medium-height, spreading ground cover. Use to cover large areas or on hillsides.

less frequently than lawns, but do require normal good gardening practices to keep them healthy and attractive.

Regular pruning or thinning controls shape, size and density of ground covers. Most benefit from an annual mowing or shearing-back of old growth to stimulate new vigor.

Weeds are more noticeable and annoying in ground-cover plantings than in lawns that are mowed frequently. Hand pulling, mulches or carefully controlled use of herbicides help keep weeds under control until the ground cover is established enough to choke them out. Before planting, consider irrigating the planting site several times to lure weeds out of hiding. Then remove them before planting the ground cover.

LANDSCAPE TREES & SHRUBS

Trees and shrubs are closely related. Both are *woody plants,* which sets them apart from all others. It is the strong, supportive woody tissue in trunks and branches that allows trees and shrubs to grow much larger than other plants. For this reason, both have similar growing requirements.

Although trees are usually considered larger plants than shrubs—over 15 feet high—some shrubs grow larger than some trees, and a few trees can be grown as shrubs. Perhaps the greatest distinction between the two is that most trees have single trunks, while shrubs have multiple trunks. By selective pruning, some trees can be kept shrublike in form by discouraging the development of the main trunk (central leader). In contrast, large shrubs can be pruned to a strong central trunk, and after a few years, will take on a treelike appearance.

TREES

Your choice of trees influences your landscape more than any other decision. They're definitely the largest, most dominant plantings, so they usually play the most important role in determining the overall character of the landscape. Give careful consideration when selecting new trees or caring for existing ones.

Deciduous or Evergreen?—All trees drop leaves. Deciduous trees are those that shed all their leaves every fall. Evergreens are those that always retain green leaves, but drop their old leaves slowly throughout the year, often unnoticed.

Choosing whether to go with deciduous or evergreen trees greatly influences any garden. Sunlight pattern and quantity change when branches are defoliated—a characteristic that may be good or bad for your garden,

depending on the needs of plants underneath and the effects of shade or sun on the interior of the house. Deciduous trees are appropriate where summer shade and winter sun are desired, such as on the south or west side of the house. Evergreens provide year-round shade. They are more suitable than deciduous trees for permanent windbreaks and privacy screens. They also add a touch of green to winter landscapes.

Tree Size and Shape—Another consideration is the anticipated ultimate growth of a tree—its height and spread at maturity. Be sure to find this out from the nursery before selecting your trees, then choose a planting site where their ultimate growth can be achieved without crowding. The size of some trees can be controlled by pruning.

Height growth is triggered from the

Left: American beech is a tall, spreading, stately shade tree.

Above: Mixed flowering and evergreen shrubs include junipers, azaleas and heathers.

TREE AND SHRUB FORMS

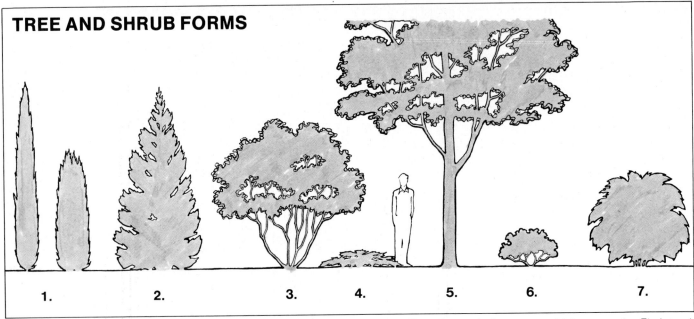

1. *Fastigate and columnar trees* are used for narrow spaces, accents or screening. Examples are Italian cypress, Irish yew, poplar, *Thuja occidentalis* and *Syzygium*. 2. *Broad conical trees* include most needled evergreens. Good for large-scale screens or as individual specimen plants. 3. *Multiple-stem trees* are often used for patio trees. Graceful. Examples are Japanese maple, *Pittosporum undulatum*, pineapple guava and several ornamental plums. 4. *Irregular shrubs* come in different plants and sizes. Examples are Hollywood juniper, rambler rose, pyracantha, bonsai plants, abutilon and prickly pear cactus. 5. *Standard trees* are broadleaf trees with single trunks. Typical street, lawn or shade tree. Examples are sycamore, magnolia, elm and apple. 6. *Mounded shrubs* are good for low hedges and borders, or for accents or mixed shrubbery. Examples are boxwood, azalea and lavender. 7. *Arching shrubs* often have multiple stems. Good for informal screens. Examples are forsythia, pyracantha and oleander.

Chinese pistache lends brilliant fall color to this yard, makes good lawn tree. As with other deciduous trees, raking leaves is annual fall chore.

Symmetrical form of blue spruce makes it focal point in yard.

Flowering dogwoods put forth prolific display of pink flowers in spring, shade drive during summer months.

Familiar shape of weeping willow imparts feeling of serenity to landscape.

tips of shoots and buds that develop shoot tips. Trees in home landscapes usually should be encouraged to develop one straight, upright trunk known as a *leader,* which determines the height and form of the tree. Shoot tips from side branches, known as *laterals,* cause the branches to elongate and produce leaves and flowers. As growth takes place, the trunk and branches develop woody cells to support the weight of the tree's crown.

Shoot tips reach toward light, therefore light affects not only growth rate, but direction and form. When planted too close together, or in the shade of another tree, young trees do not have a chance to develop their normally characteristic shape. It is therefore important to give new trees plenty of room to grow.

The form or shape of the tree is equally important as its size when determining how and where it will be used in the landscape. The drawings on the facing page show basic tree and shrub forms and list some of their applications.

Color and Texture—Consider the colors and textures the tree will lend to the garden at various times of the year. Some trees are chosen for seasonal color provided by flowers, fruit or leaves, others for year-round beauty.

Flowering trees such as crabapple, dogwood *(Cornus),* redbud *(Cercis)* and magnolia provide large-scale masses of color in spring or early summer. Deciduous fruit trees such as cherry, apple, plum and peach also

put forth beautiful flower displays during spring.

Ornamental fruit trees are valued for their colorful fruits or berries during the growing season. A few kinds, such as winterberry *(Ilex)* and chinaberry *(Melia),* retain their berries long after leaves have fallen in autumn. Many trees that produce edible fruits, berries and nuts have ornamental value, especially citrus. Pecan and English walnut are also excellent shade trees.

The color and texture of leaves or bark are the most attractive features of some trees. Consider deciduous trees whose leaves provide brilliant fall color, such as birch, shagbark hickory, maple and sumac. Birches are also known for their striking bark colors, textures and patterns. Beech, eucalyptus, madrone, paperbark maple and sycamore are other trees with interesting bark.

Landscape Uses—Trees are sometimes referred to according to their use in the landscape. *Shade trees* are large, spreading trees, usually with a dense canopy to provide deep shade. *Patio trees* are smaller trees with a neat, non-invasive habit. They do not impose on other garden plants.

Street trees are those suitable for planting along urban and suburban streets, usually in a border between the street and sidewalk. Choose a tree whose branches can be pruned to allow clearance for vehicles and pedestrian traffic without destroying the tree's natural form. Street trees in urban areas should be resistant to city

conditions, such as air pollution and reflected heat from pavement and walls.

Skyline trees are large, stately trees that help define the skyline in a neighborhood, and are best appreciated when seen at a distance. Such trees need lots of growing space. At the other extreme, *dwarf trees* are created by grafting scions (growing shoots) of standard-size trees to special dwarf rootstocks or by genetic breeding, as described on page 168. Some trees can also be miniaturized by *bonsai* methods or simply by planting them in a small container. See pages 214-217 for a list of popular garden trees and their uses.

Selecting a Nursery Tree—Once you've selected a tree type, choose the best specimen you can find from a reliable nursery. Look for medium-size, unstaked trees with straight, slightly tapered trunks. Make sure half of the foliage is located on the bottom two thirds of the trunk because the lower branches stimulate growth of the trunk's *cambium layer* or growth tissue just inside the bark. This helps strengthen the trunk as the tree grows. For this reason, don't be too anxious to remove lower branches until the tree has developed a sturdy trunk.

Be sure the tree bends easily, then returns almost upright—a good defense against wind. Bark should be blemish free and richly colored—dull bark means the tree has been previously sunburned.

Once you get the tree home, keep it

Shrubs of various heights bridge the size gap between low-growing bedding plants and tall trees to add depth to this landscape.

Bottlebrush is one of many large shrubs that can be pruned and grown as a tree.

cool and lightly moist until you can plant it, preferably within a few days. If you buy a bare-root tree, soak roots overnight in a tub of water before planting. Complete planting instructions for trees and shrubs start on page 46.

SHRUBS

Some shrubs may be grown and pruned as trees, but most remain less than 15 feet in height at maturity.

Many considerations in choosing trees also apply to shrubs—deciduous or evergreen, ultimate growth, seasonal color, privacy and wind control.

Hedges are shrubs planted closely together for special purposes. They act as borders to designate boundaries or special-use areas, as well as to direct traffic. Tall hedges act as screens for creating privacy, blocking views, breaking winds, or reducing noise or dust. They require regular pruning to maintain their function and keep their growth dense.

The uses of shrubs are determined not only by type, but by planting location and pruning methods. A single shrub can be a garden accent or focal point, while groupings of shrubs create backgrounds for flowers or a host of special effects. Shrubs can add interest to houses without any distinguishing architectural features, or block out displeasing ones.

Some shrubs are grown primarily as foliage plants, others for their flowers and some for both. Roses, azaleas, camellias and rhododendrons are popular flowering shrubs. Because of

their specific cultural requirements, these plant groups are discussed separately—roses starting on page 139, azaleas, camellias and rhododendrons starting on page 134. Many shrubs also have attractive ornamental berries.

The amount of sunlight affects the growth pattern of most shrubs. Full sun makes them grow dense and compact, while partial shade results in a more open pattern of growth. If you want shrubs to develop the patterns characteristic of the species, plant them in places that fulfill the light and other cultural requirements of the plant. See pages 206-208 for a list of popular shrubs and their cultural requirements. A local nursery can give you additional growing information on the shrubs they carry.

Selecting Shrubs—When you shop, take along cuttings of existing shrubs to help you determine what other types look good with them. If you're buying all new shrubs, find a place at the nursery where you can group together those you're considering to be sure they create the pleasing, compatible effect you want.

Like trees, shrubs may be purchased balled-and-burlapped, bare-root or in containers. Plant them when the soil can be worked easily and in seasons when the plant can fully establish itself before facing any stress from heat or cold.

Bare-root shrubs for hedges can be planted in trenches if you desire straight lines, or in individual holes if you prefer a staggered effect. Balled-

and-burlapped or container-grown shrubs for hedges do best if planted in individual holes, either in a straight or staggered line.

Pruning Shrubs—See page 78 for information on pruning shrubs and hedges.

TREE AND SHRUB CARE

Trees and shrubs require the most care during their *establishment period*—the first 5 to 6 months after planting. This is the time they are most susceptible to physical damage, pests, diseases and environmental conditions such as drought, temperature extremes and nutrient deficiencies. Special attention must be paid to watering, mulching and weeding. Young trees and shrubs may require staking and some form of trunk protection. If gophers and moles are a problem, young trees and shrubs will need root protection.

As trees and shrubs mature, they are better able to fend for themselves. They need less water, and are more resistant to pests, physical damage and climate extremes. Follow the guidelines starting on page 51 for protecting and caring for newly planted trees and shrubs.

Watering—When the new tree or shrub is planted, make a watering basin as described on page 51. As the tree or shrub grows, the watering basin should be enlarged so its perimeter remains directly beneath the drip line of the plant.

The correct amount of water is critical to newly planted trees and shrubs.

Too much is just as bad as too little, but you will probably need to water several times a week for the first month or so. Keep an eye out for wilting leaves during the heat of the day. Bare-root trees and shrubs are planted while dormant so they only need watering to settle the soil when planted—then hold off until spring growth begins.

Mature trees and shrubs need not be watered as frequently as smaller plants, but they should be watered deeply to encourage deep roots. Deep-rooted trees and shrubs are better able to withstand long periods of drought. For more on watering requirements and methods, see pages 66-71.

Fertilizing—Young trees and shrubs grow more quickly when given nitrogen-rich fertilizer. Some fertilizers are formulated especially for trees and shrubs, but general-purpose nitrogen fertilizers can also be used. Apply fertilizer at the rate given on label instructions. As a general rule, apply enough of whatever fertilizer you like so that you use actual nitrogen equal to the rate of 2 to 4 pounds per 1,000 square feet per year. Divide total amount equally into spring and summer feedings.

To determine how much area you need to cover, estimate the square footage of the area beneath the tree or shrub's leaf canopy, from the trunk to about 2 feet beyond the drip line. Fertilizer can be spread evenly over the entire area and watered in, or applied with a root feeder. See pages 63-66 for more on fertilizers and application methods.

Mature trees and many mature shrubs normally need no fertilizer unless they show a specific nutrient deficiency. However, you may choose to feed those that lack vitality or good color. Local nursery personnel or county extension agents can help you determine the right amount and time to feed different types of trees and shrubs.

Pruning—This is an often overlooked but essential part of maintaining the health and appearance of trees and shrubs. A complete guide to pruning trees and shrubs starts on page 73.

Pruning is essential to maintaining size, health and appearance of shrubs. Shrubs and climbing vines this close to the house must be carefully trained to keep from taking over.

Most young trees must be staked until they can stand upright on their own. See pages 51-52.

Viburnum makes a striking informal hedge.

Oleander is a rugged, attractive shrub that endures a variety of adverse conditions. Here it is used to screen pool area.

AZALEAS, CAMELLIAS AND RHODODENDRONS

These favorite flowering shrubs are grouped together in this chapter because all three enjoy acid soil (ph 4.5 to 5.5) that is organically rich and holds moisture, yet drains well. In their native environments, all three grow as forest understory plants where they are protected from direct sun and drying winds. Also, they all have shallow root systems that make them easy to transplant.

LANDSCAPE USES

When choosing rhododendrons, azaleas or camellias, be sure your environment comes as close to the nativelike conditions mentioned above as possible. Also keep in mind the ultimate size of the shrub. Varieties of all three can reach considerable size. Some grow tall and upright while others stay low and spreading.

The old rhododendron varieties are thought of as large shrubs that take up lots of garden space and have big leaves and showy clusters of flowers at the branch ends. They make excellent hedges, screens and backgrounds. Newer hybrids are more compact and have smaller leaves, but the flower clusters remain as large. Dwarf hybrids are more suitable to

many of today's small gardens or as plantings around house foundations.

Some azaleas can grow to considerable size and can be used like rhododendrons for borders and hedges. Groupings or mass plantings of one-color azaleas provide a bold display of spring color. Dwarf species can be effective in perennial beds or as ground covers.

The glossy foliage of camellias makes a beautiful hedge, screen or deep green background for smaller flowering plants. Single specimens are attractive garden accents. Some varieties of *C. sasanqua* are almost vinelike and can be espaliered or planted as semishady ground covers.

Azaleas, rhododendrons and camellias all are at their best when naturalized in landscapes that approximate their native environment. Plant fragrant rhododendrons and azaleas near entrances, along paths, around decks and patios or in other places where their heady aroma can be enjoyed.

RHODODENDRONS AND AZALEAS

Botanically speaking, all azaleas are members of the genus *Rhododendron,* a huge genus which includes over 10,000 named varieties of rhododendrons and azaleas. The azalea tag came from an early system of plant classification in which they were established as a separate genus. Today,

azaleas are thought of as a special series or subgenus of rhododendrons and are sold and grown as a separate group of plants.

Rhododendrons are generally more cold hardy than azaleas, grow larger and bloom later in spring. There are exceptions to these general rules. You'll find a list of popular rhododendrons on page 212.

Evergreen azaleas are hybrids of species gathered from China, Japan, Korea and Taiwan. These are the type sold by the florist industry in countless shades of purple, lavender, pink, red, orange and white. *Deciduous azaleas* are native to the coastal areas of North America, China, Japan, and southern Europe. Flowers appear on bare branches in early spring. In addition to the flower colors of the evergreen types, they also appear in bright yellow. Many produce colorful autumn foliage before their leaves drop.

Both evergreen and deciduous azaleas are divided into groups that were hybridized to meet specific requirements—cold hardiness, plant form, and flower color, form or size. Evergreen azaleas generally tolerate warmer summers and need warmer winters than deciduous azaleas. A list of popular evergreen azaleas is on page 209. It begins with the most cold hardy, and works down to the least cold hardy. A list of deciduous azaleas is on page 210.

Flower Forms—*Single* rhododendron and azalea flowers have five petals joined at the base into a tube creating a trumpet-shaped flower. In the center of each flower are stamens in multiples of five. At the base is a ring of small, green sepals that join to form a collar around the flower.

Many times, the filaments of the stamens become petal-like to create *semidouble* or *double* flowers, depending on the number of petal-like stamens. When the sepals at the base become petal-like and form a second trumpet around the main trumpet of petals, the flowers are known as *hose-in-hose.* When flowers have two trumpets or petals and petal-like stamens in the center they are known as *semidouble* and *double* hose-in-hose.

Rhododendrons flower in clusters or *trusses* which may be bell-like, elongated, ball shaped, loose, compact or dome shaped.

Azaleas belong to the same genus as rhododendrons, but are generally smaller plants.

CAMELLIAS

These flowering relatives of the tea leaf plant *(Camellia sinensis)* came to us from the Orient by way of Europe, where they arrived as early as the 1500s. The work of 19th-century breeders produced the hybrids we now enjoy. Development still continues, as evidenced by the recent introduction of fragrant varieties and the yellow-flowered varieties, *C. chrysantha* and *C. japonica* 'Golden Anniversary'.

At least 80 camellia species are recorded, but only a few are widely available to American gardeners.

Camellia japonica from Japan is the most commonly grown of all camellias, with more than 2,000 varieties. In USDA Zones 8 and 9 it is as practical for outdoor landscaping as it is beautiful. These long-lived shrubs can grow as high as 30 feet. The dense foliage is a dark, glossy green and flower colors are mostly pinks, reds and whites. Flower forms are single, semidouble, incompletely double (petal-like stamens intermixed with fertile stamens) and fully double. Overall flower shapes are further categorized as *peony, anemone* and *rose,* indicating the flowers they resemble.

Camellia sasanqua varieties are the first camellias to bloom in autumn, generally from September through December. While their individual flowers are not as impressive as those of other camellias, *C. sasanqua* is much more prolific, with flowers covering the shrub in white, pinks or reds. *C. hiemalis,* indistinguishable from most varieties of *C. sasanqua,* is usually grouped with them.

Camellia reticulata is native to China. Some varieties grow as high as 50 feet, with flowers up to 9 inches in diameter. Leaves have indented veins on sparse, open branches. Flowers are in the same color range as other camellias except there is no yellow. Plants are far less prolific than *C. japonica.* Flower petals have a silklike sheen.

See page 211 for a list of popular camellias.

COLD AND HEAT

Both summer heat and winter cold determine where rhododendrons can grow. Deciduous azaleas can take more winter cold than rhododendrons, and evergreen azaleas can

Rhododendrons flower in clusters, called *trusses.*

stand more summer heat. The best areas are those where azaleas and rhododendrons grow natively—the coastal areas of the mid-Atlantic states and the Pacific Northwest, the hills and mountains of Appalachia and the swampy areas of the South. However, growing regions are expanding because new hybrids and varieties are developed to resist heat, cold and other adverse conditions.

If you live outside the ideal areas, you may still be able to grow azaleas and rhododendrons by giving them special attention, such as winter protection or extra summer humidity and water. To many gardeners, the rewards of spring flowers make all the fuss worthwhile. Chances are, your yard may have one or more protected areas where rhododendron or azalea culture is possible. If you live in a cold-winter climate, find out the minimum average temperatures of areas around your own house and check the low-temperature tolerance of various rhododendrons and azaleas before making choices.

Camellias grow best along the Gulf, Atlantic and Pacific coasts, and inland areas where the minimum temperature doesn't fall below 10F (-12C). Some varieties can survive temperatures as low as 0F (-18C). Gardeners in outlying borders of these areas can grow camellias if they find spots in the garden protected against drying winds, freezing temperatures and direct sunlight. Growing camellias in greenhouses, or in containers that can be moved to sheltered areas during adverse weather, are two possibilities for those who live outside ideal camellia-growing areas.

Camellia 'Tomorrow'.

Even though you choose varieties that are cold hardy for your area, they may still need extra winter protection during periods of severe cold. Windbreaks can be erected around individual shrubs, using wooden stakes and stretched burlap as shown on page 25.

BUYING SHRUBS

Rhododendrons, azaleas, and camellias are available either balled-and-burlapped or growing in containers. Healthy, well-grown plants have dense foliage and are well-branched and sturdy. Spindly plants probably have root systems that are underdeveloped. In cold-winter areas, look for shrubs that are older and larger, with more woody tissue to get them through their first winter.

PLANTING SUGGESTIONS

Plant shrubs as soon as possible after you get them home from the nursery, keeping them cool, watered and shaded in the meantime. Plants in containers can be planted up to several weeks later, if necessary.

When to Plant—Spring is the best planting time in cold-winter areas. New shrubs then have a chance to become established before the hard winter sets in. In areas with mild winters (little or no freezing) and hot summers, plant in fall. This way, shrubs have a chance to get established before facing the hot, difficult summer.

Soil—Azaleas, rhododendrons and camellias prefer acid soil with a pH of 4.5 to 5.5. Soil pH is discussed on pages 59-60. Chances are rare that your soil will be too acidic for these shrubs unless you live where rainfall is exceptionally high. If you need to raise the acidity, add *ground dolomitic limestone* to the soil before planting. If your soil tests too alkaline, the condition can be improved with the addition of *ferrous sulfate* from your local garden center. Your county agricultural extension agent can recommend the right addition rate for your area.

Dig a hole at least 1-1/2 times deeper and wider than the root system. To simulate the soil found in the native habitat, mix your soil with plenty of organic amendments to improve moisture retention, drainage and aeration. Add any components necessary to balance the pH. From this point, follow the general instructions for planting shrubs, starting on page 46.

Transplanting—Because of their shallow roots, it is easy to transplant rhododendrons, azaleas and camellias. Dig out as large a rootball as possible, and replant as outlined above. Transplant at the same season as suggested for planting new shrubs.

In areas with heavy clay soil, consider raised beds for all three of these shrubs. Fill the enclosed bed with soil that drains well and is rich in organic matter.

PLANT CARE

Mulches help keep delicate roots from being damaged by temperature extremes and help retain pH level and soil moisture in the same way that decomposing leaves work in the native environment. Choose locally available organic materials and apply a thick layer around shrubs.

Water—Thoroughly soak the root system of newly planted shrubs, but be sure soil does not stay soggy. During spring growth and flowering, shrubs will need lots of water to keep them blooming longer. Water frequently if summers are dry. Begin slacking off watering in late summer to encourage dormancy necessary to prepare the shrubs for hard winters. But make sure shrubs have sufficient water before the soil freezes and cuts off their supply. They need moisture to counteract drying winter winds and sun.

Feeding—Fertilizers are not necessary if azaleas, rhododendrons and camellias are grown in rich loam and are well mulched. In the absence of such perfect conditions, apply light applications of a fertilizer recommended for acid-loving plants, or one specifically for azaleas, rhododendrons and camellias (sometimes labeled ARC). Follow label directions and apply in the early spring, then continue with light applications each month until the middle of summer.

Pruning and Dead-Heading—Little pruning is required for any of these shrubs if planted where they have plenty of growing space. Light pruning will encourage denser growth, if desired. Follow the suggestions given for pruning other shrubs, starting on page 78.

Dead-heading is good for rhododendrons and deciduous azaleas. This is the practice of removing flowers as soon as they fade, being careful not to damage nearby growth buds. Not only does the plant look better, but its energy goes into healthy new growth instead of being wasted on seed production.

Pinching and Disbudding—If you prefer a few large camellia flowers to a larger number of smaller ones, *disbud* or remove all but one of the rounded flower buds at each point along the stem where buds cluster. This is done in late summer, before buds open. Many varieties drop extra buds on their own, eliminating the need for disbudding by hand. If the plant is healthy, don't be alarmed by this normal process.

On rhododendrons and azaleas, pinching back growing tips after flowering forces more flowering shoots maintains plant shape.

Pests—Mealybugs, spider mites, and whiteflies may occasionally present a problem. See pages 90-91 for symptoms and controls. The *azalea lace bug* also attacks azaleas and rhododendrons in spring, sucking sap from leaves and leaving the shrub unsightly. They're especially troublesome on plants growing in full sun. Look for small, white specks on the underside of rhododendron leaves or rust-colored specks under azalea leaves. Treat with carbaryl, Ficam, malathion or Metasystox-R, according to label directions.

Black vine weevils can also attack azaleas and rhododendrons. They are hard-shelled, wingless beetles less than 1/2 inch long that chew leaves during the night. Their larvae feed on roots and bark, causing plants to wilt even though soil is moist. Control with Ficam or Orthene.

In areas where climate is unsuitable for growing azaleas in garden, plant in containers and put under shelter during winter months. In hot-summer climates, move container to shaded location during summer months.

ROSES

The rose is by far the most popular flower in the world, and for good reasons. Some form of rose grows everywhere except for the most frigid and most tropical regions. There is a size and form of rose for virtually any size and kind of garden. Use them individually as specimen plants or massed as bedding plants. Most important, roses unquestionably belong among the most obliging and most responsive garden plants. They involve and then reward gardeners.

The intention of this chapter is to introduce you to a wide choice of roses then briefly explore the basics of care.

KINDS OF ROSES

There are seven important categories of roses: hybrid tea, grandiflora, floribunda, miniature, climber, shrub and antique roses. But keep in mind that these categories, particularly of the hybrids, were invented for the convenience of gardeners. They overlap in many instances—a hybrid tea can look more like a floribunda, or just the reverse.

Hybrid Tea—Roses of this group most nearly match the modern idea of what a rose should be. Flowers may range impressively from soft to brilliant colors. Some are very fragrant, others are scentless. Flowers are usually borne one to a long stem—perfect for cutting—and they come in waves all season. The first wave is in spring, then, conditions granting, every 6 weeks until fall.

Plant a hybrid tea if you have room for only one rose—or plant gardens of hybrid teas if you want to fill buckets with long-stemmed, perfect flowers.

These plants that produce such a prodigious display of intense flowers are vigorous beyond the usual understanding of the word. But for all their vigor, they are susceptible to pests and diseases—primarily aphids, spider mites, thrips, black spot, mildew and rust. Luckily, there are convenient and effective solutions available.

Grandiflora—This category was created in 1949 for a very special rose. It was vigorous and prolific like a floribunda, but produced beautiful flowers like a hybrid tea.

The first grandiflora variety was named 'Queen Elizabeth', in honor of the Queen of England, and to this day remains the standard of all grandiflora roses.

Use grandiflora roses as profusely flowering background shrubs, or if pruned somewhat more severely, as you would any hybrid tea.

Floribunda—Floribundas are better understood as low-growing, low-maintenance, flowering shrubs than as a "rose." You might hear them described as "the modern landscape rose." This is not to suggest that none have beautifully formed, colored and scented flowers. Some do.

Floribundas usually grow in the 3- to 4-foot range. The plants are more branched and more shrubby looking than hybrid teas. Flowers usually come in clusters of five to seven, are a little more flat and often have fewer petals than a hybrid tea or grandiflora. On the other hand, these roses flower steadily throughout the season, so bushes are virtually never out of bloom.

Plant floribundas for low borders,

Left: Hybrid teas are perhaps the most popular of all rose types. Shown here is the variety 'Granada'.

Above: Miniature rose 'Fairy' makes a good low border along walk.

Grandiflora 'Gold Medal'.

Floribunda 'Intrigue'.

Hybrid tea 'Dainty Bess' is beautiful example of single flower form.

hedges and area dividers. Several varieties are useful for cut flowers. Check descriptions that come with the plant or choose plants in flower. Plants are somewhat more hardy and pest resistant than hybrid teas or grandifloras.

Miniature Roses—A typical miniature rose plant is about 6 inches tall. Some are a little shorter, some are taller. The larger miniature roses are often referred to as *patio roses.* Flowers are abundant and identical to the familiar rose form in every way except size. Most miniatures are somewhat less fragrant than the larger roses.

Miniature roses are as versatile as they are variable. They make excellent edging plants, especially in front of a bed of larger roses. Or use them massed in beds. They also make excellent container plants, even indoors. If you want to grow miniature roses indoors, give them a bright windowsill or fluorescent light and they will grow and flower easily.

Species Roses—These are the natural, unhybridized roses. A typical example is *Rosa banksia,* one of the best-known and most-planted roses. It is a thornless, vining, climbing rose. Another is *Rosa rugosa,* a favorite of many herb gardeners for its excellent hips. Species roses always have single (five-petal) flowers that appear once each season in spring. They also reproduce true from seed.

Antique Roses—This huge group includes primarily the popular hybrids of previous generations—in other words, they are the "modern" roses of yesterday.

There are two main groups of antique roses—the *Europeans* and the *Chinas.* The *cabbage* or *provence* roses and the *damask* roses are the fundamental European kinds. The *China* rose and the *tea* rose are the China types. These roses and their early hybrids are the classic old roses. The modern hybrid teas were developed from the tea roses.

Climbing Roses—The four main groups of climbing roses are *large-flowered climbers, climbing sports, ramblers* and *Kordessii climbers.*

Large-flowered climbers develop stout, 8- to 15-foot canes. Flowers are 2 to 6 inches in diameter and usually clustered. They usually bloom in spring. Unlike the climbing sports described at right, large-flowered climbers will produce flowers from vertically trained canes. Some offer varying degrees of repeat bloom throughout the season—check individual plant descriptions at the nursery. Large-flowered climbers are hardy to about 0F (-18 C).

You may occasionally hear the term *pillar roses.* These are actually large-flowered climbers that don't quite reach the proportions typical of a climber. About 8 to 10 feet is a stan-

Miniature roses grow well in containers. Left: 'Mary Marshall'; right 'Peaches 'n' Cream'.

dard height for pillar roses. They are important because they can be trained vertically, such as on a pillar, and still produce flowers.

Roses known as *climbing sports* are naturally occurring, extra-vigorous mutations of bush roses. They are usually discovered in a field of a few thousand bush roses, all of the same type. The grower notices a bush that is typical except for one branch that keeps growing to a length well beyond the others. A climbing sport is the result of a bud taken from that extra-long branch and grafted to its own rootstock. Most popular bush roses are available in climbing-sport forms.

It is important to understand flowering habits of climbing sports. Unlike the large-flowered climbers, climbing sports usually develop flower-bearing spurs where a branch curves over. Once the canes reach near their full length, you need to arch and tie them over. They are well adapted to training along a post-and-rail fence or over an arbor. Trained up, pillarlike, their performance will likely disappoint you.

Climbing sports are cold hardy to about 20F (-7C). Where temperatures regularly drop below that, untie and lower the canes to the ground. Then cover them with soil to protect them.

Ramblers develop long, soft, pendulous canes that will trail along the ground, climb up into and throughout a tree, or over a house. They're great for an informal cottage-garden look but not for smaller, more tailored gardens. Flowers come in spring, only on 2-year-old canes. Any canes older than that can always be removed. The best time to remove old canes is late spring, after flowering. Ramblers are hardy to -10F (-23C) and need only soil mounded over their crown to survive lower temperatures—mulches are not required to protect the plant.

Kordessii climbers are recent rose innovations, taking their class name from hybridizer Wilhelm Kordes. Compared to most climbers, they are of moderate size, have low maintenance requirements and are extremely hardy—to about -30F (-34 C). Several colors are available.

HOW TO BUY A ROSE

The best way to buy a rose is from a reputable nursery. A good nursery provides the highest quality plants of the finest varieties.

Give some thought to where you will plant the rose and what you expect from it. Descriptions of roses from nursery catalogs or books—such as HPBooks' *Roses, How to Select, Grow and Enjoy* by Richard Ray and Michael MacCaskey—include helpful information about popular roses. Think about flower color, fragrance and plant habits.

One of the most practical, up-to-date rose references is *The Handbook for Selecting Roses,* published

Climbing rose 'Royal Sunset'.

Rambler roses have long, soft canes that trail along ground, or climb into and through trees, like the variety 'Evangeline' does here.

Roses **141**

Well-planned rose garden allows plenty of room for roses to grow.

each year by the American Rose Society, Box 30,000, Shreveport, LA 71130. Cost is 25 cents. The handbook lists all the available roses and their ratings.

ARS Ratings—The members of the American Rose Society (ARS) pool their rose-growing experience to rate most available roses. Roses are rated on a scale of 1 to 10, where 10 is an ideal specimen of its type. Ratings from society members throughout the country are averaged and the result is that rose's rating. A list of high-rated roses appears on page 213.

Local Rose Societies—Local rose groups are often the best source of advice about which rose variety to buy. Unlike the ARS ratings, the experience of local rosarians is not diluted by experiences of other growers in different climates. In short, they know which roses grow best where you live. You can find your local rose society by writing to the national coordinating office of the ARS at the address given above.

PLANTING ROSES

Roses will tolerate a wide range of soil and climatic conditions—they are tougher plants than you might expect. But to grow at their best, roses prefer full sun, good air circulation and fertile, well-draining soil.

Fill the planting hole with water before setting the rose in place. If a pool of water remains after 1 hour, bore through the bottom of the hole with a water jet or post-hole digger as described on pages 46-47. Most of the time you will break through to a draining layer of soil. If you don't, and you need to plant at that location, build a raised bed at least 12 inches high.

Competing tree and shrub roots can sometimes be a problem. Root competition doesn't spell death for a rose, but it does guarantee less than optimum performance. It is possible to remove roots of nearby plants before planting, only to have them re-invade the area after a season or two. An underground barrier around plants will prevent this. Or, every few years, temporarily remove the roses during the dormant season and dig out competing roots.

Either clay soils or sandy soils are suitable, but both benefit from the addition of organic matter. Add organic matter approximately 1/3 by volume to original soil. Soil pH should be near neutral (7.0).

When to Plant—Dormant bare-root plants become available at nurseries at appropriate planting times for your area. Mail-order nurseries usually make shipments at the correct planting times for your region.

You can plant container-grown roses throughout the growing season. Beginning rose growers are encouraged to buy container-grown roses so they can see exactly what the flowers look like.

Spacing—The idea is to situate each bush far enough from its neighbor so that roots and tops have room to grow to their natural sizes. This also allows room for you to prune, spray, cut flowers and so forth.

Hybrid teas, floribundas and grandifloras—the modern bush roses—are usually positioned 3 to 4 feet apart. Old roses have a wider spread, so they need to be spaced as much 6 feet apart. But keep in mind these are guidelines for you to apply to your own situation. You can control the size of a mature rose to some extent by pruning.

Transplanting Roses—Roses can always be transplanted without difficulty. The best time is from late winter to very early spring while the plant is still dormant. First, make the plants easier to handle by pruning them back to their basic framework of three to six canes, each about 1 to 2 feet long. Carefully slice through roots with your shovel until the plant is largely free, then begin to lift. Once the plant is free, wash away clinging soil and trim away damaged or tangled roots. Replant as soon as possible, or pack in moist sawdust and store in a cool, shaded location.

HOW TO GROW ROSES

Deep, thorough watering is the first prerequisite of healthy roses. Because watering is so essential, it pays to take pains setting up the right kind of program from the beginning.

The basic rule is plenty of deep soaking, preferably without wetting the leaves. The frequency depends on your climate and weather, but a weekly watering is the general rule in most areas. Any convenient watering method is fine.

Drip systems are almost ideal because they deliver water to each rose at a rate the soil can absorb. Drip systems are most water-efficient, so they are the obvious choice in regions where water is especially precious. Where water is particularly high in salts, drip systems are beneficial because the salt in the water continually moves to the fringes of the wetted soil, away from the root system.

A hose-end bubbler is effective but can be a lot of work if you have several roses, or if the roses aren't near the hose. Keep in mind that water can come from a hose faster than the soil can absorb it, so make a good-size basin around each rose and fill each basin more than once each time you water.

Sprinklers do contribute to the spread of some rose diseases, but they have advantages too. Wetting leaves tends to keep the plants cleaner and so discourages spider mites. But if you plan to water roses with sprinklers, make an effort to water early in the morning so the plants have plenty of time to dry before evening. Also be prepared to conduct a regular spray program for pests and diseases, which is a good idea anyway.

Mulch—A layer of organic mulch, such as wood chips, compost or peat moss, encourages root growth, conserves water, and discourages weeds.

Make mulching an every-season practice, applying it around the first of June—or as soon as soil is fully warmed in your area. Remove mulch in fall to eliminate overwintering pests and diseases such as blackspot fungus and spider mites.

Feeding—Roses need regular and plentiful fertilizer to grow best. There are several fertilizers that will serve the need.

To begin with, you can rely on one of the several fertilizer products available at your nursery. Most are moderate to low in nitrogen (N), with slightly less phosphorus (P), and potassium (K). An example is a fertilizer such as 12-10-8. Many of these will also include various amounts of other essential nutrients, such as sulfur and iron. Equally important, fertilizers formulated especially for roses include helpful, specific directions on the package label. See pages 63-66 for more information on types of fertilizers and application methods.

PRUNING ROSES

There are basic principles you can apply when pruning any rose. The overall idea is to encourage new growth. After some roses are several years old, new basal growth virtually stops. New canes are produced high on a few older canes instead of arising from below ground. Prune away old canes just beyond where new canes start.

Remove dead canes all the way to the base of the plant. Dead canes are brown and shriveled inside and out. Removing dead canes is the first step in pruning any rose. Use a saw if necessary.

Remove portions of frost-damaged canes after buds begin to swell. Winter-damaged wood can be determined by cutting through a cane. Healthy wood is white all the way through. Any brown discoloration indicates frost damage. Frost-damaged portions of canes should be removed.

Remove weak, thin, spindly growth that crowds the bush's center. Prune to spread branches out, opening the center. Remove crowding stems and twigs back to their point of origin. Never leave stubs. Where two branches cross, remove the one *below* the crossing point to prevent rubbing.

Suckers—vigorous shoots that grow from the rootstock below bud unions—should be removed. They are usually easy to identify—their color and character is different from the rest of the bush. Continued growth of suckers weakens preferred rose varieties.

Always cut at an angle about 1/4 inch above an outward-facing bud, as shown in the drawing on the next page. There is a bud at every leaf. The angle of the cut should slope away from the bud. A cut made at this point heals rapidly and water drains away from the bud. Stubs, a point of disease and pest entry, will not develop if you cut close to the bud.

When to Prune—The most important time to prune roses is in early spring, just before the first burst of growth. Roses are also pruned in fall, less hard than in spring, to thin and prepare them for the rigors of winter. Where

Bark mulch keeps weeds down, looks neat and retains soil moisture.

Drip emitter is near ideal way to water roses.

Best fertilizers are those especially formulated for roses. Granular type shown here is easy to apply.

PRUNING ROSES

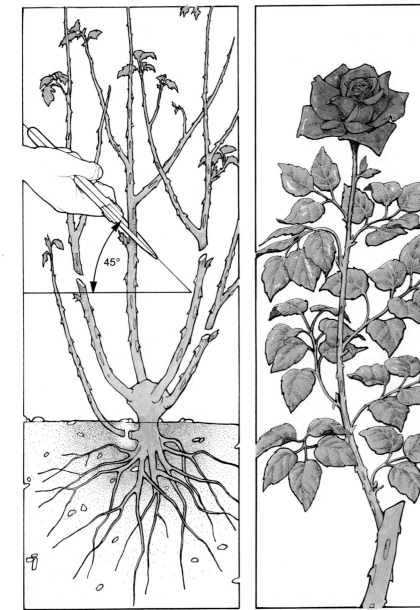

CORRECT PRUNING CUTS

1. **2.** **3.** **4.**

1. Too high. 2. Too low. 3. Too long, also made with dull blade. 4. Correct.

Left: Prune hybrid tea roses during the dormant season. Cut back vigorous canes to about half their length, but so they are all about the same height. Makes cuts at a 45° angle about 1/4 inch above a bud. Remove suckers and any dead or crowded branches. Right: New growth from buds below pruning cuts will flower the following spring.

RECOMMENDED PLANTING AND PRUNING TIMES

Region	Planting and Pruning*
Pacific Northwest	February and March
Pacific Coast	January and February
Southwest	Late December into January
South Central	Late Janaury into February
Mid South	February and March
Subtropical	December and January
North Central	April and May
Atlantic Coast	March and April
Northeast	April and May

*Heavy pruning is best done before buds open in spring. Most roses can be lightly pruned anytime. Dead-head faded flowers to encourage additional blooms.

winters are colder than 0F (-18C) roses are lightly pruned in fall, just enough so they can be wrapped or covered. Finally, roses are pruned all summer, with every flower you cut, or every wayward branch you remove.

How to Prune—Exactly how to begin varies with the situation you're facing, but the following instructions apply if you have an old, overgrown, tangled hybrid tea or grandiflora bush with lots of deadwood and, of course, wicked thorns.

Start with heavy gloves and a small folding saw to cut away the oldest, thickest canes as close to the ground as you can manage. These canes are usually brown and wrinkled. You will probably have to use loppers or strong pruning shears to reduce upper portions of these canes into smaller pieces that can be untangled. Canes you choose to keep should be the youngest, and they should be evenly arranged around the bush. As a rule, three to five canes are left to form the

structural framework of the bush.

Damage from frost or pests causes a brown staining inside the canes. Cut away a little at a time until canes are a healthy white clear through.

Next, begin to thin and shape the remaining upper growth until the bush is as symmetrical as you can make it and roughly vase-shaped. To do this, remove branches pointing toward the center of the bush, along with most of the thinnest, twiggiest growth.

As mentioned, make pruning cuts at an angle just above an eye or bud. That way no stub remains to die back, ultimately into the main cane. Choose where to make cuts largely on the location of a bud headed the direction you want growth to take.

PESTS AND DISEASES

The first rule of pest protection is to water, feed and prune so that your plants are healthy. Insect pests are inevitable, and healthy plants are least set back by attacks and best able to recover.

Secondly, make a habit of frequent and close inspections of your plants. If you are a serious enthusiast, this hardly needs mentioning—you do it anyway. If your approach is more on the practical side—"I'll do what I have to do"—the habit will pay off. You will discover diseases and pest infestations sooner, while they are more susceptible to control measures.

For general information on pests and diseases, refer to the chapter about them, beginning on page 83. Also note the listing of biological pest-control possibilities and suppliers on pages 222-223.

Here is a listing of the major rose pests and diseases, and what to do about them:

Aphids—Common in spring, aphids are usually the first pest of the season to attack roses. You'll find them clustered on the tips of soft, new growth. First try a soap-type insecticide, described on pages 85-86. Or use one of the granular systemics—often combined with a fertilizer—that you cultivate into the soil at the plant's base.

Spider Mites—These dot-size spiders thrive during hot weather. Their colonies first develop on the undersides of leaves. You can spot them with a magnifying glass. While the plants are dormant, use dormant sprays of horticultural oils and liquid lime-sulfur. That treatment destroys overwintering eggs, the main source of summer's mite problems. During the growing season, use the miticides that contain kelthane or plictran.

Thrips—These tiny insects live inside flowers, especially white ones, and chew on petals. Orthene is presently the most effective pesticide. Use it morning or evening, spraying flowers only. A fine mist of spray is most effective.

Powdery Mildew—Warm days followed by cool nights almost guarantee this mildew on rose leaves. A small amount of water, from dew for instance, is all that's needed to get it started. Powdery mildew is common in spring and fall. It won't kill the bush, but will ruin leaves, reducing the number of flowers produced. Water early in the morning so leaves can dry thoroughly before the cool part of the day. Various fungicides are useful for mildew control. Funginex is a widely available brand that also controls other important rose diseases. Actidione PM, benomyl, and Parnon are other recommended mildew-control fungicides.

Blackspot—Round, black spots appear on lower leaves first. The disease occurs in almost every climate, but is most common and most destructive in areas with frequent summer rains and high humidity. Here, regular spraying every 7 to 10 days is recommended. Use fungicides containing triforine, benomyl, folpet or maneb.

Rust—Rustlike spots on leaf undersides are sure signs of this disease. Rust is common to cool climates. Use Plantvax or fungicides containing triforine or zineb.

WINTER PROTECTION

Most roses will require protection to survive winters with temperatures below 0F (-18C). Soil heaped over the bud unions and crowns of bush roses is generally adequate. For more protection, various kinds of plastic, styrofoam, paper or cardboard cones are available to set over pruned shrubs before covering with soil. Wait until after the early frosts but just before hard freezes—before Thanksgiving in most areas.

Unfasten canes of climbing roses from their trellis and pin to the ground with stakes or wire pins before covering with 4 inches of soil. Uncover them in spring only after the possibility of spring frosts is past.

Protect tree roses by severing roots on one side of the bush, laying it over, then covering it with soil. This protection method is called *heeling-in.*

There is more information about winter protection on pages 24-25.

CUT ROSES

Here are some tips for making cut roses last longer:

● Cut between 3 p.m. and 5 p.m. Leaves and flowers have most abundant food supply at this time.

● Use a sharp knife or scissors-type pruning shears to avoid mashing stems.

● Cut while still in the bud stage. Varieties with few petals should be cut "tight," even before green sepals unfold. Varieties with 40 or more petals should be cut after a few petals have unfolded.

● Immerse cut roses up to their necks in warm water for 20 minutes, as shown in photo below. This straightens necks and helps revive wilted roses. Then move to cool, dark place for 1 to 2 hours. Before arranging, wash leaves and stems in warm, soapy water, then trim about 1 inch off stem. Cut stems underwater, if possible.

● Every day or two, change water and cut stems back about 1/2 inch. Make slanting cuts with sharp knife or shears.

● Keep arrangement in cool spot at night.

Preservatives are available that make cut flowers last longer. Check with local florist shops.

VEGETABLES

Growing vegetables is a contagious pastime. It is also one of the most enjoyable and rewarding forms of gardening. The yearning to "grow your own" usually begins soon after you taste your first home-grown tomato—bright red, incredibly juicy and sweetness and flavor like nothing you have ever found in a supermarket. It probably came from a neighbor who had lovingly nurtured the plants from early spring through summer. Your excited reaction may have brought you other treasures, such as fresh, sweet corn, tender young beans or watermelon that was out of this world.

There is more than one reason to grow your own vegetables. Done on a large scale, it may save you grocery money. It also allows you to control the types of pesticides that are sprayed on your food. But the most convincing reason is that home-grown vegetables taste so much better than those purchased at the supermarket.

Because they haven't had to be shipped long distances, they are fresher. Because the varieties you plant are developed for flavor rather than firmness during shipping, they are more tender, moister and a pleasure to eat. Because you control the harvesting, home-grown vegetables can be picked at peak quality.

The time between when you taste your first home-grown vegetables and when you actually grow your own is often more than a single season. Many first-timers appreciate the flavor of fresh vegetables but don't notice the amount of time and effort. They may experience a summer or two of failure, when the plants didn't get enough water or the soil wasn't correctly prepared beforehand. Like anything worth having, growing top-quality vegetables takes a certain amount of commitment, as well as an understanding of the plant's growing and producing requirements.

COOL-SEASON AND WARM-SEASON VEGETABLES
Vegetables are commonly divided into two types—*cool-season* vegetables and *warm-season* vegetables. Cool-season vegetables, which include broccoli, cabbage and lettuce, grow best in the cool months of spring and fall when the days are short and average daytime temperatures are low. In some mild-winter climates, cool-season vegetables can be grown throughout winter. In many northern and high-elevation areas, seasons are short and cool enough to grow cool-season vegetables all summer long. As the days become longer and warmer, many cool-season vegetables *bolt,* which means they flower and become bitter.

Warm-season vegetables, such as tomatoes, corn and peppers grow best during the hot months of summer. They will grow slowly or not produce a crop if the weather is too cool.

There is also a third group of vegetables that can't really be classified as warm-season or cool-season. These are the *perennial vegetables* which, if properly cared for, are long-lived and produce crops year after year.

Left: Zucchini is most popular type of summer squash. They are easy to grow and prolific producers.

Above: Garden of cool-season vegetables includes (left to right) carrots, leaf lettuce, turnips, cabbage, potatoes and onions.

PLANTING TIMES FOR COMMON VEGETABLES

Cold-hardy—Plant in late summer or fall, 6 to 8 weeks before first fall freeze:

Beets
Collards
Kale
Mustard
Spinach
Turnips

Plant in fall in mild climates, or 4 to 6 weeks before last spring freeze:

Broccoli
Cabbage
Lettuce
Onions
Peas
Potatoes
Spinach
Turnips

Plant 2 to 4 weeks before last frost date in spring:

Beets
Carrots
Chard
Mustard
Parsnips
Radishes

Cold-tender—Plant on last frost date in spring:

Beans, snap
Corn, sweet
Okra
Squash
Tomatoes

Heat-requiring—plant 1 or more weeks after last frost date in spring:

Beans, lima
Cucumbers
Eggplant
Melons
Peppers
Sweet potatoes

Heat-tolerant—plant in early summer:

Beans, all
Chard
Corn, sweet
Squash

The distinction between warm-season and cool-season vegetables is an important one because it determines when to plant. Most cool-season vegetables can tolerate light frosts. They are usually planted as soon as the soil can be worked in spring so they will mature before the weather gets hot. They can also be planted in midsummer to late summer so they mature in the cool months of fall.

In the mild-winter climates of the West and Southeast, many cool-season vegetables are grown as winter crops. Warm-season vegetables cannot withstand frosts and grow poorly in cool weather, so are usually planted after the average date of the last spring frost. Although these planting times seem fairly straightforward, there are variations within both cool-season vegetables and warm-season vegetables. If you live in an area with a short growing season, you may be able to grow cool-season crops all summer long. Some vegetables require warmer soil than others to germinate, as shown in the chart below. In such cases, it is best to plant 1 to 2 weeks after the last frost date, when the soil has had a chance to warm up.

The chart at left gives some general recommendations for planting each type of vegetable. The map of spring frost dates on page 17 will also be helpful. Local university extension offices are the best source of exact vegetable planting dates for your area. Many seed catalogs and seed packets also contain planting information.

HOW TO PLANT

There are basically two ways to start vegetables—from seed or seedlings. Seed can be sown directly in the ground or started indoors and transplanted into the garden when conditions are right. Seedlings can be bought at a local nursery or garden center in six-packs or individual pots, and immediately planted in the garden. Which method you choose depends on several factors.

Purchasing seedlings at the nursery is often the easiest way to go. Growing your own transplants indoors from seed usually takes at least 6 to 8 weeks of constant attention, and conditions should be as close to ideal as possible.

REQUIRED SOIL TEMPERATURES FOR VEGETABLE SEED GERMINATION

Vegetable	Minimum	Optimum	Maximum
Asparagus	50F (10C)	75F (24C)	95F (35C)
Beans, lima	60F (16C)	80F (27C)	85F (30C)
Beans, snap	60F (16C)	85F (30C)	95F (35C)
Beets	40F (4C)	85F (30C)	95F (35C)
Broccoli	40F (4C)	85F (30C)	95F (35C)
Cabbage	40F (4C)	85F (30C)	95F (35C)
Carrots	40F (4C)	80F (27C)	95F (35C)
Cauliflower	40F (4C)	80F (27C)	95F (35C)
Celery	40F (4C)	70F (21C)	75F (24C)
Chard, Swiss	40F (4C)	85F (30C)	95F (35C)
Corn, sweet	50F (10C)	85F (30C)	105F (41C)
Cucumbers	60F (16C)	95F (35C)	105F (41C)
Endive	32F (0C)	75F (24C)	75F (24C)
Lettuce	32F (0C)	75F (24C)	75F (24C)
Muskmelon	60F (16C)	95F (35C)	105F (41C)
Okra	60F (16C)	95F (35C)	105F (41C)
Onions	32F (0C)	80F (27C)	95F (35C)
Parsley	40F (4C)	80F (27C)	95F (35C)
Parsnips	32F (0C)	70F (21C)	85F (30C)
Peas	40F (4C)	75F (24C)	85F (30C)
Peppers	60F (16C)	85F (30C)	95F (35C)
Pumpkin	60F (16C)	95F (35C)	105F (41C)
Radishes	40F (4C)	85F (30C)	95F (35C)
Spinach	32F (0C)	70F (21C)	75F (24C)
Squash	60F (16C)	95F (35C)	105F (41C)
Tomatoes	50F (10C)	85F (30C)	95F (35C)
Turnips	40F (4C)	85F (30C)	105F (41C)
Watermelons	60F (16C)	95F (35C)	105F (41C)

On the other hand, because nurseries usually carry only a limited number of varieties as seedlings, you may not be able to plant the variety you want unless you grow them yourself from seed. Many vegetables, including beets, radishes and corn, do not transplant well and should only be direct seeded.

You can buy vegetable seeds from a wide variety of retail sources, including supermarkets, home-improvement centers and nurseries. For a greater selection, you can buy from mail-order catalogs.

Germination—Seed catalogs, seed packets and the descriptions on the following pages list the number of days that seeds of a given vegetable take to germinate. These numbers are determined for plants grown under ideal conditions. If you're like most gardeners, you will probably have a hard time recreating ideal conditions, especially if you are sowing directly outside. Use these numbers as guidelines. Cooler soil temperatures will slow germination.

Variety Selection—Most vegetables are available in many varieties. Sometimes available varieties differ according to which grown in your area. If possible, choose varieties adapted to your area—local nurseries usually carry these, or can make recommendations. Varieties also differ in the time it takes them to reach maturity for harvesting.

Besides categorizing vegetables as being early, midseason or late, catalogs and seed packets will list the number of days it takes a variety to go from seed to harvest. Again, these numbers are only guidelines but they can be useful. By planting a combination of early, midseason and late varieties, you can extend your harvest. In short-season areas, early varieties may be the only ones to reach maturity before the first frost.

Within the basic types of vegetables, varieties will also differ in shape, size, flavor, uses, storage life, and the size and shape of plant that bears it.

Choosing a Site—Vegetables should be planted where they will receive full sun for at least 8 hours a day. A full day of sun is ideal. Some vegetables, such as lettuce and root crops, can take partial shade. The soil should be well drained. If the drainage is poor, consider planting in containers or raised beds.

In areas with long growing seasons, succession planting extends harvest period.

If planting in rows, make sure you plant the tall vegetables, such as corn, in a position where they will not shade lower-growing crops that require full sun. However, if you live in a climate where summers are extremely hot, such as the Southwest desert, a little shade may be valuable protection for some crops.

Soil Preparation—Correct soil preparation before planting is one of the most important steps toward a successful vegetable garden. Few vegetables grow well in poor soil.

Before planting, cultivate the soil thoroughly and work in generous amounts of organic matter. This is also a good time to work in an all-purpose fertilizer or one formulated especially for vegetables.

Succession Planting—In areas with average or long growing seasons, many vegetable gardeners extend their harvest season by making successive plantings every few weeks. With vegetables that mature all at once, such as corn, lettuce, and broccoli, this allows you to harvest over a longer period.

Short Growing Seasons—If your growing season is less than 150 days, it is often difficult to grow many warm-season vegetables. There just isn't a long enough warm period. However, here are a few tricks to help you make the most of your season:

● Start seeds indoors, in a greenhouse or in cold frames. Or buy established seedlings or larger transplants, so they are already growing vigorously when you put them in the ground. However, bear in mind that large transplants which are already in bloom or bearing fruit often perform poorly once they are planted.

● Try to outguess the weather and plant just before the last frost date. Use hot caps or plastic covers to protect plants during cold weather. See drawings on page 25.

● Use a black plastic mulch to warm the soil in early spring.

● Plant early varieties.

● Take advantage of any warm microclimates in your yard and plant the vegetable garden next to hot, south-facing walls or reflective surfaces such as pavement.

Edible flower of artichoke, ready to pick.

Harvest asparagus spears when 6-8" long.

PERENNIAL VEGETABLES

The popular perennial vegetables listed here will produce crops for many years if plants are properly cared for.

ARTICHOKE

Artichokes are members of the thistle family. They have large, bold-textured, prickly, silver-green leaves that form an attractive mound-shaped plant. The unopened flower, produced on thick stems and held torchlike above the foliage, is the portion harvested. It consists of leathery, overlapping leaflike bracts. If harvested at the correct time, the bottoms of the scales and the base of the flower, called the *heart,* soften when cooked and are delicious to eat. If not harvested, buds open into large, purple blooms that make stunning dried thistles for flower arrangements.

Artichokes have exacting climate requirements. Mild winters and cool, humid summers, such as are found in coastal areas of California, produce the most tender buds and long-lived plants. Plants will usually not survive where soils freeze in winter. In areas where summers are hot and dry, flowers mature quickly and have a tough texture. If you live in an area with cold winters, it's best to treat artichokes as annuals grown from seed or dig up the plants in winter and store them in a cool, dark place until spring.

How to Plant—In cool areas, plant root divisions 6 inches deep, or set out transplants, in winter or spring. In cold-winter climates, sow seed indoors 6 to 8 weeks before the last frost. Plant seed 1/2-inch deep. Germination takes 7 to 14 days. Set plants 3 to 4 feet apart in rows spaced 6 to 8 feet apart. Artichokes can also be a handsome addition to a perennial flower border.

How to Grow—Artichokes must have consistent moisture and well-drained soil that is rich is organic matter. Plant in partial shade in hot climates, otherwise full sun. Fertilize in spring or fall.

Varieties—'Green Globe' is the most common variety available as root divisions. 'Grand Beurre' is a short-season seed variety.

Harvesting—In cool climates, the first real harvest will be in 18 to 24 months. A healthy plant may produce over 30 buds from fall through spring. Seed-grown artichokes mature about 160 days after planting. Harvest buds while they are still tight and at least the size of your fist. Cut with a knife, leaving about 1 inch of stem.

ASPARAGUS

If you are patient, asparagus is a generous plant. Few vegetables ask so little yet provide so much. If you take special care when planting, you will be rewarded with many tender spears over the years.

Asparagus spears arise from underground stems called *rhizomes.* They emerge from the ground in early spring and if uncut, grow into ferny plumes of foliage up to 5 feet tall, which produce bright red berries.

How to Plant—Asparagus is usually planted as dormant rhizomes in spring. Seedlings are slow to reach transplant size and take 3 years before they produce enough spears to harvest.

Choose a planting site that won't have to be disturbed for 15 to 20 years. Work soil throughly, adding organic matter and about 1/4 pound actual nitrogen per 100 square feet.

To plant rhizomes, or *crowns* as they are often called, dig a trench 10 to 12 inches deep and 12 inches wide. Work generous amounts of composted manure or other organic matter into the bottom of the trench to a depth of at least 6 inches. Set the crowns, with buds pointing up, in the bottom of the trench, spaced about 18 inches apart. Cover with 2 inches of soil and water thoroughly. As shoots emerge, gradually cover them with soil until they reach the top of the trench. Always leave the tips exposed.

Don't harvest any spears the first year. Let the foliage develop and nourish the rhizomes. The second spring, you can cut a small sampling. The third year you can begin harvesting in earnest.

How to Grow—Water occasionally until midsummer, then let the foliage dry out naturally. Fertilize before and after harvesting. Otherwise, just make sure enough foliage develops each summer to replenish the rhizomes and keep weeds down. Once all the foliage has dried, cut it back to ground level.

Varieties—'Mary Washington' is the most popular variety.

Harvesting—Harvest spears when they reach 6 to 8 inches tall. Either snap them off or cut them with a knife just below soil level. You may have to harvest every other day for as long as 4 weeks. When you notice the spears are getting thinner—less than 1/4 inch in diameter—stop harvesting and let the rest develop into foliage.

RHUBARB

Rhubarb is a striking, leafy plant that makes a eye-catching addition to the vegetable or flower garden. Leaves are huge, up to 18 inches across and at least as long, and bright green with red stalks. The stalks are harvested and used primarily to make rhubarb pie. The green, leafy section of the foliage, which contains poisonous amounts of oxalic acid, is not used. Rhubarb grows best where the soil freezes in winter and the summers are cool. However, there are varieties adapted to mild-winter climates.

How to Plant—Plant dormant root divisions, called *crowns,* as soon as soil can be worked in early spring. Set the crowns so the tops are just below the soil surface. Space about 3 feet apart. If soil is poor, plant crowns in a 12-inch-deep trench backfilled with amended soil. Do not allow crowns to dry out.

How to Grow—Water regularly. Fertilize in early spring. Remove flower stalks.

Varieties—Look for 'MacDonald', 'Ruby' and 'Valentine Red' in cold-winter climates. 'Giant Cherry' is more reliable in mild-winter areas.

Harvesting—You may be able to harvest a few stems the second spring, much more in the third. Plants are productive for 4 to 6 years.

Harvest leaf stems when they reach about 10 inches long. They can be easily removed with a sideways twist. Don't harvest all the leaves at once. Always leave some to replenish the roots. Harvest usually lasts for about 6 to 8 weeks in spring.

COOL-SEASON VEGETABLES

BEETS

Beets are a "no-waste" vegetable. In addition to the fleshy root, you can also eat the tender greens like spinach. Although beets are technically a cool-season vegetable, they can be harvested over a long season extending into the warm months of summer if they are watered regularly and given some afternoon shade. Plant successively for longer harvest.

How to Plant—Sow seed directly in well-worked soil rich in organic matter. Either broadcast in wide bands or plant an inch apart and 1/2 inch deep in rows spaced 12 to 18 inches apart. Seeds germinate in 14 to 21 days. For spring harvest, sow 2 to 3 weeks before the last frost date. For fall harvest, sow 6 to 8 weeks before the first frost date. In mild climates, sow any time from early spring to mid-autumn.

How to Grow—Careful thinning and consistent moisture are most important. Thin seedlings to 2 to 3 inches apart when they are 2 to 3 inches tall. Do not let plants dry out.

Varieties—There are many hybrid varieties that differ in maturity dates, root color, shape and storage life. There are also varieties selected for excellent-flavored greens.

Harvesting—Most varieties are ready

Beets are a no-waste crop—both roots and greens are tasty.

Edible sprouts form along leafless stem of brussels sprouts (near hedge in rear). Sprouts are harvested when about size of golf ball.

for harvest 45 to 65 days after germination. But the roots usually get tougher as they get thicker. You can begin harvesting when roots are about 1 inch in diameter and continue until they reach 3 to 4 inches in diameter. Harvest young, tender individual leaves anytime but leave enough on each plant for root development.

BROCCOLI

There are two types of broccoli you can grow—*heading broccoli* or *sprouting broccoli*. In both types, the unopened flower cluster is harvested. Heading broccoli, the type commonly sold in supermarkets, first produces one large cluster in the top of the plant. After this cluster is cut, smaller clusters grow from leaf axils along the sides of the plant. Sprouting broccoli produces smaller heads from the very beginning and continues to produce them as long as they are harvested or until the weather gets too warm.

Whichever type of broccoli you choose, time your planting so the flower heads mature in cool weather. Hot weather causes plants to grow fast and flower clusters to bolt.

How to Plant—Broccoli is most often planted in early spring for a late spring harvest. It can also be planted in late summer or early fall for a fall harvest. It is easiest to grow from transplants started indoors 5 to 7 weeks before

planting, or from seedlings purchased from a nursery. Sow seeds 1/4 inch deep. Germination usually takes 5 to 10 days at 70F (21C). Set transplants 15 to 24 inches apart in rows spaced 24 to 36 inches apart.

How to Grow—Water regularly and keep weeds under control. As plants get larger, you may want to mound soil up against the stem to prevent top-heavy plants from falling over.

Varieties—The most commonly grown varieties are 'Premium Crop' which matures 82 days after transplanting, and 'Green Comet', which can be harvested about 55 days after transplanting.

Harvesting—Harvest heads while they are still firm and dark green, before they begin to loosen and show yellow. Use a knife to harvest, cutting 5 to 6 inches below the head. Continue to harvest smaller side clusters as they appear.

BRUSSELS SPROUTS

Brussels sprouts make a strange sight around harvest time, with their erect, leafless stems lined with miniature cabbagelike balls.

Brussels sprouts take longer to reach maturity than any other member of the cabbage family—up to 100 days from transplanting. Combine this with the fact that it is a cool-season vegetable which will only

mature in cool weather, and you will begin to see why brussels sprouts are usually planted for a fall harvest. Most areas don't have a long enough period of cool weather in spring. Commercial production of brussels sprouts is largely confined to the cooler coastal areas of California where summers remain cool.

How to Plant—For fall harvest, plant in midsummer. For spring harvest, plant 2 to 3 weeks before the first frost. Start seedlings indoors 5 to 7 weeks before transplanting time. Sow seeds 1/4 inch deep and maintain a soil temperature of 70F (21C). Germination takes about 10 days. Set out plants 2 feet apart in rows 2 feet apart. To help avoid insect and disease problems, don't plant in areas where other members of the cabbage family were grown the year before.

How to Grow—The most important thing is to keep the plants well watered. Sprouts mature from the bottom of the stalk to the top. Removing the leaves between lower sprouts will encourage buds to form along the entire stalk. Pinching the growing tip promotes ripening of the upper sprouts. Plants may need staking for support.

Varieties—'Jade Cross' is by far the most widely grown variety.

Harvesting—Sprouts mature over a long period. Some people believe flavor improves after a frost. Harvest when sprouts reach the size of a golf ball.

CABBAGE

Crinkly-leaved or smooth, bright green or deep red, cabbage is as distinctive in the garden as it is delicious in the kitchen. There are many varieties to choose from. Some are bred for storage, others mature quickly. Some are resistant to soil-borne diseases, others are are more tolerant of warm temperatures. For best results with any type, plant so the heads mature in cool weather. High temperatures cause the heads to crack.

How to Plant—Cabbage seed is slow to germinate in cold soil so it is best to start seed indoors or purchase transplants for the first planting of spring. Sow seeds 1/4 inch deep, 8 to 12 weeks before the last frost and maintain a temperature of 70F (21C). Germination takes 5 to 10 days. Seedlings will be ready for transplanting outdoors about 4 to 6 weeks before the last frost. Set out plants 1 to 2 feet apart—early varieties can be planted closer together—in rows spaced 2 to 3 feet apart. Once the soil warms outdoors, cabbage can be seeded directly in the garden for a succession of summer harvests, or for fall harvests from midsummer planting.

How to Grow—Water regularly. Apply fertilizer before planting and again in about 3 to 4 weeks. Cabbage is a shallow-rooted plant that can be easily damaged through cultivation. Use a mulch to keep soil cool and to prevent weeds.

Varieties—Many varieties are available that differ in appearance, maturity dates—from 50 to 100 days—head size and disease resistance. Favorites includes 'Stonehead', which produces 6-inch heads 70 days after transplanting; 'Red Ball', a red variety that resists cracking in hot weather and matures in 68 days; and 'Savoy Ace', a crinkle-leaf variety which is harvested in 75 days.

Harvesting—Begin when the heads reach the size of a softball. Cut just below the head with a knife.

CARROTS

The key to growing perfect carrots is to spare no expense when preparing the soil before planting and to carefully thin seedlings before they become crowded. If you neglect either of these procedures, your carrots will grow bent, knobby, cracked and often tough. If you live in an area with poor, rocky soil, plant in containers or raised beds.

How to Plant—Sow seed directly in well-worked, sandy soil that is rich in organic matter. Either broadcast in wide bands or space seeds 2 inches apart in rows spaced 12 to 30 inches apart. Cover seeds with 1/4 to 1/2 inch of soil. Germination takes 7 to 21 days. Thin seedlings to 4 to 5 inches apart when they reach 1 inch in height. For an early summer harvest, sow in early spring. For fall harvest, sow in midsummer.

How to Grow—If you have prepared the soil and thinned properly, consistent moisture is all that is really necessary.

Varieties—Many are available. They vary primarily in length and shape. Short varieties, such as 'Short'n Sweet' which grows only 3 to 4 inches long, are best if your soil is less than ideal. Longer varieties, such as 'Nantes' and 'Gold Pak', require deep, loose soil that is rich in organic

Cabbage 'Ruby Ball' in foreground, broccoli in background.

matter and on the sandy side.

Harvesting—You can begin as early as 40 to 50 days after sowing for short varieties, 60 to 70 days for longer varieties. Harvesting may last for 2 to 3 months, but the carrots will begin to get tough and woody if the weather gets hot or they are left in the ground too long. To harvest, gently lift up by the tops. If the tops break, use a hand fork to lift carrots from the soil.

CAULIFLOWER

Cauliflower is a more temperamental vegetable than its close relative broccoli, even though both plants are similar in appearance and share many cultural requirements. To be successful with cauliflower, choose healthy, vigorously growing transplants. Stunted or rootbound plants will seldom produce full heads. Also make sure you plant early enough in spring so

To have continuous supply of chard, harvest large outer leaves, leaving enough leaves in center to regenerate plant.

that the weather is still cool when the heads are maturing. Otherwise, plant in midsummer so that heads mature in the cool months of fall. Heat causes the heads to bolt or discolor.

How to Plant—For early spring planting, sow seeds indoors 10 to 12 weeks before the average last frost date. Germination should take about 10 days at 70F (21C). Transplants should be set in the ground 2 to 4 weeks before the average last frost date. Space seedlings 15 to 24 inches apart in rows spaced 24 to 36 inches apart. For fall harvest, set out transplants in midsummer.

How to Grow—Keep plants growing continuously with regular watering. Control weeds.

To ensure attractive, cloud white cauliflower, you must protect the head from sun and rain through a process called *blanching*. When the head reaches about 2 inches across, pull several leaves over the top of it and tie them with soft twine.

Varieties—'Snowball', 'Snow King' and 'Snow Crown' are popular white varieties. All mature in about 50 days. 'Purple Head', as the name suggests, produces purple heads that turn green and taste like broccoli when cooked. It matures in about 85 days. 'Self Blanche' is self-blanching, meaning that leaves naturally fold over the head.

Harvesting—Harvest when the head reaches 4 to 6 inches across and before it begins to loosen or buds begin to open. Use a knife to cut the stem 5 to 6 inches below the head.

CHARD

Chard is one of the most ornamental vegetables you can grow in your garden. It is also one of the most carefree. It is grown for its tender leaves which are either deep green with bright red stems and veins or bright green with white stems. Both types can be used as striking accents among spring flowers or other cool-season vegetables. Chard plants are hardy and able to withstand neglect. They also endure more heat and drought than most other cool-season vegetables.

How to Plant—Sow seeds directly in the ground about 2 to 4 weeks before the last frost date in spring. For an even earlier harvest, start seeds indoors 6 to 8 weeks before that and set the transplants outside several weeks before the last frost.

Plant seeds 1/2 inch deep, 1 to 2 inches apart in rows spaced 18 to 24 inches apart. Thin seedlings to 12 inches apart.

How to Grow—If planted in good soil, all you really have to do is keep the plant moist.

Varieties—'Fordhook Giant' is a popular white-veined variety. 'Ruby' and 'Rhubarb' are widely available red-veined varieties.

Harvesting—You can begin harvesting leaves about 2 months after sowing seed. Tear or cut the outside leaves just above their base, leaving the center of the plant to continue growing.

KOHLRABI

Kohlrabi is a strange-looking vegetable that is gaining in popularity because of the delicious, crisp-textured, turniplike swelling that forms just above the ground. When peeled, it can be sliced and eaten fresh or cooked like a turnip.

How to Plant—Sow seed directly in the ground about 2 to 4 weeks before the last frost date in spring. For an earlier harvest, start seeds indoors 4 to 6 weeks before that. Plant seeds 1/2 inch deep, and 1 inch apart in rows spaced 18 inches apart. Germination usually takes 8 to 10 days. Thin seedlings to 6 to 8 inches apart. Kohlrabi can also be planted in midsummer for fall harvest.

How to Grow—Water regularly and remove weeds.

Varieties—'Grand Duke' is one of the most popular varieties because it remains tender and crisp even when allowed to reach 4 inches in diameter.

Harvesting—The bulbs are most tender when they are about 2-1/2 inches in diameter, which is usually about 50 days after planting.

LETTUCE

A spring garden isn't a spring garden without lots of leafy lettuce. It comes in a variety of leaf types, colors and shapes. It is attractive in rows combined with spring flowers, or planted in containers. There should always be room for lettuce.

How to Plant—Lettuce seed can be sown outdoors as soon as the soil can be worked in spring or, for earlier crops, it can be started indoors and later transplanted outside. It can also be planted in late summer for fall harvest. The important thing is to make sure it matures in cool weather, otherwise the leaves will have a bitter flavor and plants will go to seed.

Plant seeds 1/4 inch deep, 1 to 2 inches apart in rows spaced 12 to 24 inches apart. Germination usually takes 8 to 12 days. Thin seedlings to 6 to 12 inches apart. Leaf lettuce and cos lettuce will stand spacing as close as 6 inches apart. Head lettuce should be spaced a full 12 inches apart.

How to Grow—Lettuce grows best in rich soil that is kept moist and free of weeds. If you plant in partial shade, you can sometimes harvest quality lettuce during the warmer months.

Varieties—Lettuce can be broken down into four different types, each with its own varieties. Leaf lettuce does not form heads, but instead forms a tight cluster of foliage which can be harvested one leaf at a time. Leaf lettuce is one of the easiest types of lettuce to grow because plants mature quickly—about 45 days from seed—and withstand crowding. Varieties differ in leaf color and shape.

Popular types include 'Ruby' with red leaves, 'Green Ice' with lacy green leaves and 'Salad Bowl' with bright green, lobed leaves. Butterhead lettuce forms small, loose heads of tender green leaves that are a favorite of gourmet cooks. Leaves that develop inside the head are soft yellow, and especially soft-textured and delicious. Popular varieties include the heat-resistant variety, 'Buttercrunch', and 'Bibb'. 'Tom Thumb' is a miniature variety that is excellent in small containers.

Crisp-head lettuce includes head types often referred to as *iceberg lettuce*. They are harder to grow than other types of lettuce because they take longer to mature—up to 90 days—and must be given room to develop. Favorite varieties include 'Great Lakes', 'Iceberg' and 'Thaca'.

Romaine or cos lettuce forms upright clusters of crisp leaves. It generally takes about 75 days to mature. 'Parris Island' is a popular variety.

Harvesting—Leaf lettuce can be harvested a leaf at a time as long as the center of the plant is left to grow. Other types of lettuce are best harvested by cutting the whole plant off at the base with a knife.

ONIONS

Onions have a two-stage life cycle. The first stage takes place shortly after planting, during the cool months of winter or spring. During this period, all the plant's energy is used to produce the green tops. When the days begin to get longer and warmer, a transition takes place—the onions go into a bulbing stage where all the energy is stored below ground in the

'Butter King' (front) and 'Ruby' (back) are two excellent varieties of leaf lettuce. Pick individual leaves as needed or cut off entire heads.

fleshy bulb. To grow onions successfully, you must time your plantings so the plants can complete both stages of their life cycle.

How to Plant—Onions can be planted from seed, transplants or *sets* (small, dry onion bulbs.) Whichever method you use, work the soil vigorously before planting, adding lots of organic matter and a general-purpose fertilizer. In areas where the ground freezes in winter, plant as soon as the soil can be worked in spring. In mild-winter climates plant in late fall for a spring harvest. Growing onions from seed takes the longest—as much as 12 weeks longer than transplants or sets—but offers the most varieties. Sow seeds 1/2 inch deep, 1/2 inch apart in rows spaced 18 to 24 inches apart. Germination takes 7 to 12 days at 70F (21C). Thin seedlings to 3 to 4 inches apart.

If you want to start seed indoors for transplanting outside later, begin about 12 weeks before it's time to plant. Transplants and sets are by far the most popular way to start onions. Transplants usually result in the biggest onions in the shortest period. Sets are usually reliable, but have a tendency to bolt to seed. Plant transplants 1 to 2 inches deep, 3 to 4 inches apart in rows spaced 18 to 24 inches apart. Plant sets 1 to 2 inches deep, 2 to 4 inches apart in rows spaced 18 to 24 inches apart.

Mature onions are harvested when tops fall over and start turning yellow. Spanish onions are shown here.

How to Grow—Onions are shallow-rooted plants that must be watered often to keep soil consistently moist. They must also be kept free of weeds.

Varieties—There are many onion varieties that differ in color, shape, flavor and storage life. However, climate adaptation is often the most important factor in determining which variety to grow. Check with your local

Potatoes grow best in loose organic mulch.

nurseryman or university extension agent for varieties that are best suited to your area.

Harvesting—Green onions, which are immature bulb onions, can be harvested whenever they reach acceptable size. For mature bulbs, wait until the tops turn yellow and begin to fall over. When this happens, push the remaining tops over and discontinue watering. After the tops have dried completely you can begin to harvest. To prepare onions for storage, lay the entire plant, top and all, on newspapers in a cool, dry place out of direct sunshine. After 10 days they can be trimmed and stored indoors in a cool, dry place. Best temperature for storage is between 35F to 50F (2C to 10C).

PEAS

There are basically three types of peas for the home garden—*English peas* (shelling peas), *edible-pod peas,* and *snap peas.* English peas must be shelled before eaten. Edible-pod peas are harvested when the peas themselves have not completely developed but the pods are tender and edible. These are often called snow peas, sugar peas or Chinese peas. A relatively recent introduction to the gardening world, snap peas are also edible-pod peas but the peas inside can be allowed to develop to maturity without the pod becoming tough.

All peas are borne on fragile, twining plants that are best grown with some type of support such as a twine or wire trellis, frame or fence. Most pea plants will grow between 4 to 6 foot tall. There are also dwarf types that only reach about 2 feet tall.

How to Plant—Sow seeds directly in the ground 6 to 8 weeks before the last frost date. Plant 1 to 2 inches deep, 1 inch apart in rows spaced 24 to 48 inches apart. Germination takes 1 to 2 weeks. Install supports while planting. Peas can also be planted in double rows, 6 inches apart with 36 inches between each set of rows. For fall crops, plant about 3 months prior to the first frost date.

How to Grow—Peas require regular watering and freedom from weed competition. They need only light fertilization. Too much nitrogen causes excessive foliage growth at the expense of fruit production.

Varieties—Favorite English peas include early-ripening 'Alaska', vigorous-growing 'Green Arrow', midseason 'Lincoln', heat-resistant 'Wando' and dwarf 'Little Marvel'. Popular edible-pod peas include 'Mammouth Melting Sugar' and 'Sugar Pod', and the dwarf variety 'Dwarf Grey Sugar'. 'Sugar Snap' is one of the best sugar snap peas.

Harvesting—You can begin harvesting most pea varieties between 60 and 70 days after planting seeds. Varieties are often labeled *early, midseason,* and *late*—if you live in an area with short seasons, plant early varieties.

Harvest English peas when they swell to almost round. Begin picking edible-pod peas when pods are 2 to 3 inches long and before the peas begin to swell. If harvested too late they will be tough. Harvest sugar snaps when they reach 2-1/2 to 3 inches long and after the peas have swollen. Once the plants are producing, peas must be picked every couple of days. If peas are allowed to hang on the plant, production will stop.

POTATOES

Most people, gardeners or not, know there is a big difference in taste between a supermarket tomato and one grown in a home garden. What many people do not know is that there is a similar difference between garden-grown potatoes and those bought in a store. Home-grown potatoes, no matter how they are cooked, have a silky smooth texture and a mild but delicious flavor—qualities rarely found in store-bought potatoes. And they are relatively easy to grow.

How to Plant—Potatoes require between 90 and 120 frost-free days to mature. Unlike most other cool-season vegetables, their foliage is sensitive to frost. Start with certified, disease-free *seed potatoes.* These are small potatoes or sections of potatoes that are usually slightly shriveled and coated with fungicide to help prevent deterioration. They are available at most nurseries, seed stores and mail-order catalogs. The variety 'Liberty' can be grown from seeds but it's much easier to start from seed potatoes. Don't plant potatoes purchased in the produce section of a supermarket. They are often sprayed with chemicals to prevent sprouting.

Cut the seed potatoes into chunks about 1-1/2 inches in diameter. Each chunk should have at least two *eyes* (small buds). Plant in soil that is loose and rich in organic matter. Work in a general-purpose fertilizer at a rate of about a 1/2 pound of actual nitrogen per 100 feet of row. Set the chunks, cut side down, 4 inches deep and 12 inches apart, in rows spaced 24 to 36 inches. Do this a week or two before the last frost date.

The potatoes will sprout in about 2 to 3 weeks. When the sprouts reach 4 to 5 inches high, mound soil up against the stems. Continue to mound soil against the growing stems as long as possible. The tubers will form along the stems in the mounded soil.

How to Grow—It is important to keep the developing potatoes covered because they will turn green if exposed to sunlight. The best way to do this is to apply at least a 6-inch layer of organic mulch such as straw. This will also help keep the soil cool and make harvesting easier because tubers will form closer to soil level and sometimes in the mulch itself. Potatoes must also be kept constantly moist.

Varieties—Varieties are divided into early, midseason and late, and also differ by storage capabilities and by skin color—red, white and brown (russeted). There is even a blue variety that is available in some areas. Most nurseries will carry several locally adapted varieties. They may or may not be labeled. Mail-order catalogs have a larger selection.

Harvesting—You can begin harvesting *new potatoes*—small immature tubers—when plants begin to flower. Gently feel around in the upper soil or mulch to find them. If you plan to

Radishes come in many sizes, shapes and colors—white and red kinds are most common.

store your potatoes over winter, they should be allowed to mature fully in the soil. Once the tops die down completely, gently dig up the tubers with a pitchfork or with your hands. Place them in a dark place at about 70F (21C) for about a week to heal any bruises. Then store those that are healed or bruise-free in a humid place at at temperature between 35F to 40F (2C to 4C).

RADISHES

It's a surprise to many beginning gardeners to find out how many kinds of radishes there are. Besides the familiar red types common in supermarkets, there are white, yellow, purple and black varieties. Some are small and round, others are long like carrots. Flavors range from mild and sweet to fiery hot. It is also sometimes a surprise to find out how fast radishes mature. The small red varieties can be harvested as early as 3 weeks after sowing. Larger varieties take up to 70 days.

How to Plant—Like other root crops, such as carrots and beets, it is important that radishes be planted in soil that is loose, rich in organic matter, and free of rocks and clods. Either broadcast seed in wide bands, or plant 1/2 inch deep, 1 inch apart in rows spaced 8 to 18 inches apart. Seeds usually germinate in 5 to 10 days. Thin seedlings to 3 to 4 inches apart. In

cold-winter climates, you can begin sowing most radishes several weeks before the last frost date and continue throughout spring. Larger radish varieties, which take longer to mature, are best sown in fall so they will mature in cool weather. In mild-winter areas, sow them throughout spring and then again in fall.

How to Grow—After soil preparation and thinning seedlings, the most important thing is to keep radishes moist. If they dry out or stop growing they will be uncharacteristically hot and tough.

Varieties—'Cherry Belle' (22 days) is a popular round, red variety; 'Sparkler' (25 days) is round, half red and half white; 'Burpee White' (25 days) is round and white. 'French Breakfast' (24 days) is oblong and red and white. All of these have a mild flavor. Hotter radishes include 'Round Black' (55 days), 'Icicle' (28 days) which is white and shaped like a carrot and 'China Rose' (52 days) which is also carrot shaped. Most of the oriental or daikon radishes are long and hot.

Harvesting—Begin pulling the small, round varieties when they reach about 1-1/2 inches in diameter. If left in the ground too long, they become hot and pithy. Larger varieties can be harvested when they reach acceptable size and flavor. Pulling and tasting is the best way to check maturity.

Pole beans require sturdy trellis for support.

SPINACH

Spinach is a bit more temperamental than the other popular salad green, lettuce. Plan carefully so that the plants mature while daytime temperatures stay under 75F (25C). If the temperature gets too warm, spinach will become bitter tasting and quickly go to seed. The reward of crisp, delicious spinach is well worth the effort.

How to Plant—Plant spinach as early as possible in spring—as soon as the soil can be worked. You can also plant in fall about a month before the first frost date. Sow seed directly in the ground, or for an earlier harvest, start seed indoors or purchase transplants at your local nursery. Plant seeds 1/2 inch deep, 1 inch apart in rows spaced 12 to 30 inches apart. Germination takes 14 to 21 days. Thin seedlings to about 4 to 6 inches apart.

How to Grow—Water regularly and keep free of weeds.

Varieties—'Melody' is a popular variety known for its heat resistance and disease tolerance. Other popular varieties include 'America', 'Bloomsdale Long Standing' and 'Winter Bloomsdale'.

Harvesting—Spinach can be harvested a leaf at a time as long as you leave the center of the plant intact so it can continue growing. But the best way to harvest spinach is to let the plants completely mature (about 45 days) and cut off the entire head. This way, the outer leaves supply energy to keep the plant growing vigorously, and your overall harvest is greater.

WARM-SEASON VEGETABLES

BEANS

A whole book could be, and probably has been, devoted to describing the great diversity among the family of vegetables called *beans*. They come in many shapes, sizes, textures and colors. Some kinds are eaten green, pod and all. Others are dried, shelled and used in soups and stews. Their flavors are as different and as interesting as their names—black-eyed bean, pinto bean, fava bean, kidney bean, soybean, lima bean, snap bean and so on.

Even though beans are a diverse group, they have important similarities. They are borne on one of two types of plants. One type is a twining vine, which can climb up to 10 feet. These plants require the support of a trellis or pole and are often referred to as *pole beans*. *Bush beans* are shorter, stockier plants that are self-supporting and can be grown in rows. You have a choice of varieties with either growth habit.

How to Plant—Plant beans directly in the ground after the soil has warmed in spring. If you plant too soon, beans will germinate slowly and may rot. Plant seeds of bush-type snap beans 1 to 2 inches deep, 2 inches apart in rows spaced 2 to 3 feet apart. Pole-type snap beans require more room—6 to 12 inches between plants and 3 to 4 feet between rows. Germination takes 6 to 14 days at 60F (16C). Other types of beans may require different spacing. The seed packet is your best source for such information.

How to Grow—Water regularly and remove weeds. Pole beans can be supported in a variety of ways. String or wire trellises are excellent. A single vertical pole supporting a teepee of strings also works well.

Varieties—Each type of bean has its own varieties. Popular bush snap beans include 'Bush Blue Lake', 'Tender Crop' and 'Tendergreen'. Favorite pole types include 'Kentucky Wonder', 'Blue Lake' and 'Romano'. 'Kentucky Wonder Wax' is a yellow, wax-type, snap bean. 'Fordhook' and 'Fordhook No. 242' are excellent varieties of lima beans. 'Frostbeater' is a favorite soybean.

Harvesting—Depending on type and variety, beans begin producing any-where from 50 to 100 days after planting. You can harvest most bush-type snap beans in about 60 days. Pole types will take about 10 days longer. Snap beans are ready to pick when they reach 3 to 4 inches long and the beans begin to swell along the sides of the pods.

Once plants begin producing, you must keep them picked. If you leave the pods on too long, plants will stop flowering and your harvest will be greatly reduced.

Harvest shelling or dried beans after the pod has dried on the plant. Soybeans are harvested when the beans are full size but the pod is still green.

CORN

To many people corn is more than just a vegetable—it is a celebration of warm summer days, clear blue skies and whispering breezes. A garden wouldn't be a garden without it. That's why you see corn planted so many unusual ways.

Sometimes, it's a stalk here and a stalk there. Other times, it's one straight row at the back of a flower bed. Unfortunately, these plantings will seldom bring about a satisfactory harvest. If there is one thing that prevents gardeners from enjoying a long season of fresh corn, it is lack of available space. You can plant one tomato plant here, put in some beans there, but with corn you need some room.

There are at least two reasons why. First, each stalk may produce only one or two ears. Second, corn needs to be wind pollinated from tassel to ear to produce edible kernels. You should plant at least three rows 8 to 10 feet long, to fill the air with pollen and to produce enough corn for more than just one or two meals.

How to Plant—Plant corn as soon as the soil has warmed to at least 50F (10C) in spring. Choose a planting site with at least 8 hours of full sun and where, as the stalks get taller, they won't shade other parts of the garden. After thoroughly working the soil and mixing in a nitrogen fertilizer, dig straight trenches about 6 to 8 inches deep and at least 30 inches apart. Mound the excavated soil to one side of each trench. Sow the seed 1 to 2 inches deep, 4 to 6 inches apart about half way up the mound side of each trench. You can now use the trenches to flood-irrigate without washing away the seed. Germination usually takes 6 to 10 days. Thin seedlings to 12 to 15 inches apart.

How to Grow—Water regularly and make two applications of fertilizer—one when the plants are about 1 foot tall and again when they reach about 30 inches.

Varieties—Varieties differ in kernel color, sweetness and ripening dates. 'Silver Queen' is probably the most popular variety. It has sweet, white kernels that mature late in the season, about 92 days from planting. 'Golden Cross Bantam' is a popular yellow corn that is not as sweet as 'Silver Queen' but has a more traditional corn flavor which many people prefer. It matures in 87 days. 'Sugar and Gold' is an early variety (67 days) with white and yellow kernels. There are also dwarf varieties and selections of indian corn and popcorn.

Harvesting—Corn takes 60 to 100 days from seed to harvest, depending on whether you grow early, midseason or late varieties and the degree of hot weather. Corn takes longer to grow in cooler areas. Ears are ready to harvest about 3 weeks after the silk emerges. To make sure they're ready, pull back the husk slightly and puncture a kernel with your thumbnail. If a milky white juice squirts out, it's ready.

CUCUMBERS

Cucumbers can be separated into three groups—slicers, picklers and everything else. Slicing cucumbers for use in salads are usually harvested when they reach 5 to 8 inches long. They have a smooth, tough, dark green skin. Pickling cucumbers have a soft, bumpy skin and are harvested when they are smaller, usually between 2 to 5 inches long. Use them to make pickles. The third group of cucumbers includes some unusual varieties. Slicers and picklers can be further separated into standard varieties, which bear male and female flowers on the same plant (monoecious), and all-female hybrids, which bear almost all female flowers (gynoecious).

All-female hybrids are tremendously productive because all their energy goes into producing fruit. However, because male and female flowers must be present for pollination and fruit production, some plants that produce male flowers need to be planted

These ears of corn are ready to harvest.

'Armenian' is an extra-long, light-skinned cucumber variety.

along with the females. Seed of such plants are usually mixed in the seed packet containing the all-female hybrids. They may be dyed a different color to distinguish them from the females. The seed packet will usually include pollination information, if applicable.

Cucumbers can be further divided by type of plant. Bush-type cucumbers produce fruit on compact plants that do not require a trellis for support. They are excellent container plants. Vine-type cucumbers produce fruit on sprawling vines that should be supported by a trellis or wire cage.

How to Plant—Plant cucumber seeds directly in the soil as soon as it has warmed in spring. Plant four to six seeds, 1 inch deep in a mound of soil, or sow in rows with groups of five or six seeds spaced every 12 inches. Space rows 3 to 6 feet apart. Seeds usually germinate in 7 to 10 days. Thin seedlings to two or three per hill or one per group.

How to Grow—Water regularly but avoid getting the foliage wet, which promotes disease. Tie vines to a trellis, if desired. With most varieties, this will save space and produce straighter fruit. Remove weeds.

Varieties—There are many varieties of cucumbers. 'Victory' and 'Marketer' are popular slicing types. 'Spacemaster' and 'Pot Luck'—very

compact and ideal for containers—are bush-type varieties for slicing. 'Liberty' and 'National Pickling' are favorite cucumbers for pickling. 'Lemon' cucumber produces small, yellow, round fruit which are good for pickling or slicing. Other unusual cucumbers include the extra long fruited 'Armenian' and 'Kyoto Long'.

Harvesting—Most varieties mature in 60 to 70 days. Pick slicing cucumbers when they reach 6 to 8 inches long. Picklers can be picked any time they reach acceptable size. Harvest at least two times a week to keep plants producing.

EGGPLANT

Eggplant comes in a variety of shapes and colors that are never seen in supermarkets. Besides the familiar egg-shaped, blackish-purple varieties, there are white, yellow and red types, and varieties that produce round or oblong fruit.

How to Plant—Eggplant must have warm soil. If seeds are sown directly in cold soil, germination will be slow and erratic. If plants are placed outside too early in spring, cold soil will cause them to stagnate or grow so poorly they may never recover. For this reason, it best to start seeds indoors 6 to 8 weeks before the last frost date and transplant them outside once the soil has warmed. This way the plants

Icebox watermelons are among easiest to grow. They produce small, round melons.

will grow vigorously without interruption and you will have a jump on the season. Of course, you can also buy transplants at your local nursery. Sow seeds 1/4 inch deep, 1 to 2 inches apart in flats or peat pots. Germination takes 7 to 10 days at 80F to 85F (27C to 30C). Set transplants 12 to 18 inches apart in rows spaced 3 feet apart.

How to Grow—A plastic mulch is an effective way to warm the soil and keep eggplant growing vigorously in spring. Hot caps are also a good idea if cold weather sets in. Water regularly and apply a balanced fertilizer every 3 weeks.

Varieties—'Dusky' is a popular early variety. 'Golden Egg' produces whitish-yellow, egg-shaped fruit. 'Ichiban' and 'Imperial' are oriental varieties with cylindrical, blackish-purple fruit.

Harvesting—Varieties mature in 60 to 90 days. Fruit can be harvested as soon as they reach full color. They are best picked early rather than late. Keep fruit picked so plants continue to produce.

MELONS

The sweet, juicy, brightly colored flesh of cantaloupes, watermelons, honeydew, crenshaws and the rest seems to belong in fruit salads along with apples and oranges rather than grouped with vegetables like peppers and squash. Indeed, the melons are the dessert vegetables. Refrigerated to a crisp chill, they are the finest complement to a hot summer day.

Although various types of melons look and taste remarkably different, they all have two requirements in common—they need lots of room to grow and long, hot summers to mature. If you live in a short-summer area or where summers are cool, try one or more of these suggestions:

• Choose early ripening varieties.

• Start melon seeds indoors to get a jump on the season.

• Place transplants in the hottest spot in the garden.

• Use a plastic mulch to warm the soil.

If you have limited space, consider growing some of the compact bush varieties or grow melons on a trellis.

How to Plant—Melons are most often planted in raised mounds of soil surrounded by a ditchlike basin for easy watering. Space mounds 4 to 6 feet apart. Sow four to five seeds, 1 inch deep in each mound after the soil has warmed in spring. Germination usually takes 6 to 12 days. Thin seedlings to two or three per hill. Melons can also be planted in widely spaced rows with 12 inches between plants.

How to Grow—Water consistently. Avoid overwatering, which can cause fruit to split. Try to keep the foliage and fruit dry, especially near the end of the season or in humid climates. Excess moisture promotes disease. Small-fruited melons can also be grown on a trellis if the melons are supported as they get bigger. One method of support is to hang the fruit in a nylon stocking with one end tied in a knot, the other end tied to the trellis.

Varieties—There are many types of melons and even more varieties of each type. 'Classic', 'Burpee Hybrid' and 'Ambrosia' are favorite cantaloupes with excellent flavor. The easiest watermelons to grow are *icebox* watermelons, which produce small, round fruit. Other watermelons include 'Yellow Baby' with yellow flesh and 'Sugar Baby' with red flesh. Both are incredibly sweet. 'Earlidew' is a popular honeydew melon. 'Golden Beauty' is an excellent casaba.

Harvesting—Melons ripen in anywhere from 80 to 130 days depending on type and variety. Judging maturity can be difficult. Pick watermelons when the white "ground spot" on the underside of the melon turns a rich yellow. Harvest other types of melons when they are at *full slip,* meaning when the stem separates easily from the fruit when you lift it.

PEPPERS

Peppers can be divided into two groups—sweet and hot. Sweet varieties, including the popular bell peppers, have a mild, sweet flavor and are excellent in fresh salads and in casseroles. Hot peppers, with names like 'Jalapeno' and 'Serrano', are best known for their spicy hot flavor, although many varieties are quite mild. They are favorite ingredients in spicy cuisines around the world, including China, Mexico and Southeast Asia. Although peppers are classified as warm-season vegetables, if temperatures climb too high—over 75F (18C) for sweet peppers and over 85F (30C) for hot varieties—blossoms tend to drop from the plant without setting fruit. But in most areas, spring temperatures last long enough to produce remarkably productive plants.

How to Plant—It's best to start with transplants set outside 1 to 2 weeks after the last frost date, or whenever daytime temperatures rise above 65F (18C). Sow seeds indoors 6 to 8 weeks before the last frost or purchase transplants at your local nursery. Plant seeds 1/4 inch deep and 1 inch apart. Germination will take about 10 days at 80F (27C). Set transplants 18 to 24 inches apart in rows spaced 2 to 3 feet apart.

How to Grow—Water regularly and remove weeds. Many varieties require staking to prevent the plants from falling over when laden with fruit.

Varieties—There are many varieties of sweet peppers and literally hundreds of varieties of hot peppers. Often, the best ones to grow are locally adapted, so check with your nurseryman. Favorite bell peppers include 'Bell Boy', 'Big Bertha' and 'California Wonder'. 'Yellow Banana' and 'Gypsy' are excellent yellow sweet peppers.

'Anaheim' is a large, mild-flavored hot pepper that is often used to make *chili rellenos*. 'Jalapeno', 'Serrano' and 'Fresno' are among the most fiery hot peppers.

Harvesting—Most peppers ripen in 60 to 80 days. Some hot peppers take longer. Peppers can be harvested when they reach acceptable size and color. Most, including bell peppers, turn bright red at full maturity. Bell peppers are picked green for use in salads, or can be left until they turn red, for a sweeter flavor and for use in pickling. Use a knife or pruning shears to cut the peppers from the plant.

PUMPKINS

Pumpkins are usually grown for Halloween Jack O'Lanterns, but like their close relatives squash, they have many kitchen uses. You can use pumpkins for pies, cakes, breads and even soups. Roasted and salted, the seeds make a delicious snack. Plenty of garden space is the most important thing you need to grow pumpkins. The sprawling vines can spread seemingly forever and actually make a

Many varieties of hot peppers make striking ornamental plants.

good temporary ground cover.

How to Plant—Pumpkins are easy to grow from seed sown directly in the ground. Take extra time preparing the soil, working in generous amounts of nitrogen fertilizer or composted manure, and you will be rewarded with vigorous, healthy vines and a large crop. Sow five to six seeds 1 inch deep in hills spaced 6 to 8 feet apart as soon as the soil warms in spring. Germination takes about 10 days. Thin seedlings to two or three per hill.

How to Grow—The plants need regular, deep watering to maintain large leaves and produce bumper crops. They are also heavy feeders so

apply a nitrogen fertilizer about every 3 weeks.

Varieties—These vary by size and use. 'Jack O'Lantern' is a favorite for Halloween carving. 'Big Max' produces some of the largest pumpkins but is not suitable for cooking. 'Spirit' is a compact plant for gardeners with limited space. 'Triple Treat' is a multi-purpose pumpkin grown for its hull-less seeds. It has sweet flesh and is easy to carve.

Harvesting—Most pumpkins are harvested after the first fall frost has killed the foliage. If stored in a cool, dry place, they will keep at least several weeks after harvesting.

Summer squashes pictured include yellow straightneck, yellow crookneck, zucchini and scalloped squash.

SQUASH

Reactions to growing squash for the first time usually come in two phases. After the seeds have germinated and the vines are off to a quick start, there is a tremendous feeling of satisfaction—few plants grow so well with so little effort. Once the plants begin to produce, a feeling of astonishment takes over as the gardener finds out how much squash can be harvested from just a few plants. There is usually more squash than one family can eat.

Basically, there are two types of squash—summer squash and winter squash. Both are warm-season vegetables, despite the name of the latter.

Summer squash has a soft skin, mild flavor and is eaten whole. Zucchini is the most popular type of summer squash. Winter squash takes longer to mature and has a hard shell surrounding a typically sweet, edible flesh. They come in a myriad of strange shapes and sizes and are well known for their storage capabilities. Actually, the name winter squash comes from the fact that they can be stored after harvesting and eaten during winter.

Both types of squash grow on vigorous vines, although summer squash plants are more compact. Both share the same cultural requirements.

How to Plant—Squash plants are easily started from seed sown directly in the ground after the last frost. The most common method is to plant five to six seeds in hills of soil surrounded by watering basins and spaced 5 to 6 feet apart. Be sure to add lots of organic matter to the soil before planting. Composted manure is ideal. Sow seeds 1 inch deep. Germination takes about 10 days. Thin seedlings to two or three per hill. You can also plant in rows with 18 to 24 inches between plants. Make sure you have enough room for plants to spread between rows—at least 8 feet for vigorously growing kinds.

How to Grow—Plants must have consistent moisture or they will stop producing. Apply a nitrogen fertilizer about every 3 weeks.

Varieties—Summer squash and winter squash each have a multitude of varieties. 'Aristocrat' is one of the best green zucchinis. 'Gold Rush' is a popular straight yellow zucchini. 'Golden Summer Crookneck' is a good yellow crookneck squash. 'Patty Green Tint' and 'Scallopini' are excellent scalloped squash—pie-shaped with scalloped edges. Popular winter squash include 'Buttercup', 'Early Butternut', the huge 'Hubbard' and the acorn-type 'Table Ace'.

Harvesting—You can begin harvesting most summer squash varieties in about 50 days. The smaller the fruit are when picked, the more tender and juicy they will be when cooked. Don't let zucchini and crookneck types get over 6 inches long unless you plan to stuff and bake them. Scalloped types should be less than 3 or 4 inches in diameter. Use a knife to harvest. Keep the plants picked or they will stop producing.

Winter squashes take longer to mature—usually between 80 to 120 days. If you harvest too early, they will not be full flavored. Many types develop full sweetness only after cold weather causes the vines to die down. Others turn from green to a bronze or tan. If stored in a cool, dry place, most varieties will keep up to 4 months.

SWEET POTATOES

Sweet potatoes are native to tropical countries, which should give you a hint about their most important requirement—long, hot summers. Only in the warm climates of the South and West can sweet potatoes be considered a reliable crop. In these areas, sweet potatoes are not only productive but are also ornamental. The tubers are produced on the roots of attractive, vining plants with heart-shaped leaves that are often tinged reddish purple. Under ideal conditions, the vines grow vigorously and form an attractive mat of foliage. Sweet potatoes often are mistakenly called yams. True yams are actually a different species of plant, seldom grown in American gardens.

How to Plant—Sweet potatoes are planted as rooted slips. You can purchase slips from mail-order nurseries or at local nurseries, or you can grow your own from dormant tubers. To grow your own, lay the tubers in a container, cover them with 4 inches of moist sand, perlite or vermiculite and place them in a warm location—80F to 85F (27C to 30C) is ideal. When the sprouts appear, move the container to a warm, sunny location. When the shoots reach about 4 inches long, either gently cut or pull them away from the mother tuber. Plant the slips 9 to 12 inches apart in rows spaced 3 to 4 feet apart. If drainage is poor, plant in raised ridges or beds of soil about 12 inches high.

How to Grow—Water regularly. Relatively easy to care for if correctly planted in good soil.

Varieties—Sweet potatoes are separated into two types. The varieties 'Gold Rush' and 'Centennial' have sweet, soft-textured, light orange flesh. 'Jersey Orange' and 'Nugget' have dry, white flesh.

Harvesting—Sweet potatoes can be harvested whenever they reach adequate size. This usually takes at least 4 months. Yellowing foliage is a good sign of maturity. If the tubers are cured at about 85F (30C) and 85 percent humidity for 2 weeks, they can then be stored in a cool place for up to 5 months and will actually get sweeter.

TOMATOES

Tomatoes are the most popular garden vegetable. Most people can trace their first vegetable gardening experience back to tomatoes. Many other people who don't even consider themselves gardeners still grow a few tomatoes. One main reason explains this popularity—few things taste as good as a fresh, garden-grown tomato. Supermarket tomatoes just won't do. If you want them bright red, juicy and sweet, you have to grow them yourself, and everyone knows it!

How to Plant—Setting out transplants is the best way to start tomatoes. You can grow your own indoors or purchase them at your local nursery. Start seeds indoors in flats or peat pots about 5 to 7 weeks before the last frost. Sow seeds 1/4 inch deep and 1 inch apart. Germination takes 7 to 10 days at 70F (21C). If you buy transplants, choose stocky, deep green plants which are not in flower or fruit. Plant deep, up to the first true leaves. Leave about 2 feet between plants.

How to Grow—You'll find many recommendations on how to grow tomatoes. Pinching, pruning and tying to stakes are common practices of many gardeners. However, the least time-consuming method and one that results in the least sunburned or rotten fruit, is to support tomatoes in wire cages. You can make your own or purchase one of many styles available in local nurseries and garden centers.

Tomatoes require regular deep watering and occasional application of a nitrogen fertilizer. Inconsistent watering can cause blossom-end rot, a brownish rotting on the bottom of the tomato. This problem can also be caused by insufficient calcium in the soil. Too much nitrogen causes exces-

Wire cages are best way to support tomatoes. Large mesh size of hogwire used here makes harvesting easier.

sive foliage at the expense of fruit production. Not enough nitrogen results in stunted plants with yellowish foliage.

Tomato blossoms are extremely temperature sensitive. Ideal nighttime temperatures for fruit set are between 60F and 70F (16C and 21C). Hotter weather causes the blossoms to drop from the plant without setting fruit.

Varieties—Tomato varieties come in many sizes, shapes, and colors. They can also be divided by how they are used, local adaptation, resistance to various diseases, ripening season and whether or not the vines are *indeterminate* or *determinate*. Determinate tomato vines usually ripen earlier, grow lower and produce over a shorter season. The term determinate means that the plant grows, produces fruit and dies within a given amount of time. Indeterminate vines take longer to come into bearing, but once they do, they continue to produce until killed by frost. Often, the best way to choose a tomato variety is to ask an experienced gardener in your area which are his or her favorites.

'Better Boy', 'Big Boy' and 'Early Girl' are widely adapted standard varieties. 'Pixie' and 'Tiny Tim' are small-fruited, dwarf varieties ideal for containers. 'Sweet 100' produces

huge clusters of incredibly sweet cherry tomatoes. 'Beefmaster' and 'Beefsteak' are popular beefsteak tomatoes. 'Roma' and 'Chico 111' are excellent paste tomatoes.

Harvesting—You can usually begin harvesting tomatoes after 60 to 90 days, depending on whether the varieties are early, midseason or late. Tomatoes are ready to pick when they reach full color.

FRUITS, BERRIES & NUTS

Gardeners grow fruit for many of the same reasons they grow fresh vegetables. Home-grown fruit can be allowed to ripen on the plant until it reaches flavor perfection. If you have ever compared a store-bought peach or apple with one just picked from the tree, you know what a difference this can make. If you haven't made such a comparison, you have some very pleasant experiences ahead. The flavor and quality of home-grown fruit can't be matched.

There are a number of reasons why home-grown fruit tastes so good. First, there is only one place where most fruit is meant to ripen and that's on the tree. Only there will sugar content build to a peak and important texture changes take place. Once the fruit reaches this stage, it can't be shipped long distances. Supermarket fruit is usually picked slightly hard and unripe so it can be shipped.

Home-grown fruit is also better because you can choose the best-tasting varieties—ones that are hard to find in a supermarket. Most commercial fruit varieties are developed for appearance, shipping qualities and shelf life, rather than flavor. For instance, the most important commercial apple variety, 'Red Delicious', is popular primarily because of its excellent exterior color. Ask any apple expert how its flavor compares to such varieties as 'Cox's Orange' 'Pippin' or 'Jonagold'. There's no comparison in flavor—and 'Red Delicious' is not a good cooking apple.

When you choose fruit varieties, select the ones that best satisfy your objectives. Many fruit, nut and berry plants are beautiful additions to the garden. A number of the characteristics that you would use to choose ornamental plants can also be found in fruiting plants—fragrant flowers, and brightly colored fruit and autumn foliage, to name a few. Fruiting plants can also be versatile in the landscape. Blueberries can be used as a hedge. Many fruits, including apples and pears, can be trained as espaliers. Kiwifruit or grape vines can cover an arbor. Large nut trees, such as pecans, make excellent shade or lawn trees.

No matter which fruit you want to grow or how the plants will function in your yard, the first thing to determine is whether or not a particular fruit, nut or berry is adapted to your area. Climate adaptation is one of the most important factors in ease of care, quality of harvest, and even plant survival.

ADAPTATION

The following climate factors greatly influence which fruit you can grow:

Hardiness—Each fruit-bearing plant

Left: Raspberries are closely related to blackberries but differ in that fruit readily separates from the core. Raspberry 'Meeker' is shown here.

Above: Trees in backyard fruit orchard are pruned to make picking easy.

LOW-CHILL FRUITS

This is a list of deciduous fruit varieties developed especially for mild-winter climates. All deciduous fruits require a certain number of *chilling hours* to produce fruit, as discussed on the following page. The varieties listed here require fewer chilling hours than standard fruit varieties. If you live in a mild-winter area, check with a local nursery or your university or county extension agent to find out the number of chilling hours for your area. If you can't get this information, use the conversion chart at right to figure chilling hours. To use the chart, you'll need to find out the mean (average) temperature of the coldest month of the year—usually January—from your local weather service. Then choose a variety that requires the *same or fewer* number of chilling hours in your area.

*In climates where winter days are generally sunny, a 10% to 20% reduction in the number of chilling hours should be made.

Mean Temperature Coldest Month (January)	Chilling Hours Accumulated for Season*
46F (8C)	988
48F (9C)	883
50F (10C)	778
52F (11C)	675
54F (12C)	575
56F (13C)	475
58F (14C)	355
60F (15C)	288
62F (17C)	200
64F (18C)	118
66F (19C)	58
68F (20C)	0

APPLES

Variety	Chilling Hours	Ripening Date	Remarks
'Anna'	350	L. June	Crisp, juicy, sweet-tart flavor. Green with red blush. Self-fruitful but does better with 'Dorsett Golden' as pollenizer.
'Beverly Hills'	600	September	Best in areas with mild summers. Good flavor.
'Dorsett Golden'	250	L. June	Crisp, juicy, sweet. Yellow with 10% pink blush. Self-fruitful.
'Ein Shemer'	450	July	Similar to 'Golden Delicious'. Best in areas with mild summers. Good flavor and texture.

NECTARINES

Variety	Chilling Hours	Ripening Date	Remarks
'Panamint'	400	L. June	Semifree, medium fruit. Very good flavor, widely available.
'Sunfre'	500	M. June	Semifree, very good flavor, large fruit.
'Sunred'	250	E. May	Semifree, small fruit. Excellent flavor, red color.
'Sunripe'	350	M. May	Semifree, medium fruit. Excellent flavor.

PEACHES

Variety	Chilling Hours	Ripening Date	Remarks
'Babcock'	450	E. July	White flesh, good texture, poor flavor.
'Desert Gold'	350	E. May	Semicling, good flavor, small fruit, widely available.
'Earligrand'	200	E. May	Semicling, good flavor, medium fruit.
'Flordabelle'	150	M. May	Freestone, good flavor and texture, very large fruit.
'Flordagold'	325	L. May	Semifree, very good flavor and texture, medium fruit.
'Flordaking'	400	M. May	Semicling, good flavor, large fruit.
'Flordaprince'	150	L. April	Semicling, good flavor and texture, excellent color.
'Flordared'	100	M. May	Freestone, good flavor, small fruit, lacks firmness.
'Gold Dust'	550	M. June	Semifree, very good flavor and texture.
'June Gold'	650	M. June	Semicling, large fruit, good flavor and texture. Very showy blooms.
'Rio Grande'	450	E. June	Freestone, large fruit, excellent flavor and texture.

PEARS

Variety	Chilling Hours	Ripening Date	Remarks
'Baldwin'	500	August	Good texture and flavor. Moderate resistance to fire blight.
'Flordahome'	400	M. July	Sweet, buttery textured flesh when ripe. Plant with 'Hood' or 'Pineapple' for cross-pollination.
'Hood'	400	M. July	Sweet, buttery textured flesh when ripe. Very good flavor, self-fruitful, resistant to fire blight.
'Pineapple'	500	L. July	Tart flavor, good for canning. Highly resistant to fire blight.
'Shinseiki'	400 est.	L. July	Excellent Asian pear, which seems to have a low chilling requirement. Self-fruitful.
'20th Century'	400 est.	E. August	Crisp, sweet, juicy Asian pear, which seems to have low chilling requirement.

Chart developed by Mike Burraston, Bountiful Nursery, Tucson, AZ.

has a *minimum temperature* below which its tissues will be killed. However, this is not as clear-cut as it sounds. The time of year when the cold weather occurs and the duration of cold are two climatic factors that influence whether or not the plant will be injured. Most plants are less hardy in fall than they are in the dead of winter.

The location of the tree in the garden, soil-moisture content, wind and sunlight also influence the plant's susceptibility to injury. Start by correlating a plant's hardiness with your location on the USDA climate map, page 13. Local nurseries and extension agents can also help you judge whether or not a fruit, berry or nut is hardy enough for your area.

Spring Frosts—Even if the type of fruit you want to grow is hardy enough for your area, its blossoms and small developing fruit may be susceptible to damage from spring frosts. Blossoms and fruit are much less hardy that the tree itself. Most will be damaged if temperatures fall just a few degrees below freezing. Early-blooming fruits and nuts, such as apricots, almonds and Japanese plums, are most susceptible to damage from spring frosts. If you live in an area with late-spring frosts, choose late-blooming varieties. See the last spring frost map on page 17.

Chilling Requirements—Most deciduous fruits require a certain number of hours near 45F (7C) during winter or they will not correctly break dormancy in spring. This number of hours is called a *chilling requirement.* Whereas cold hardiness is a major limiting factor for growing fruit in cold climates, chilling requirements restrict the varieties of deciduous fruits that can be grown in mild-winter climates. In many areas of the South and West, selecting varieties with a low chilling requirement (low-chill varieties) is critical to success with most deciduous fruit.

Low-Chill Varieties—Recent interest in low-chill deciduous fruits has fostered the development of many new varieties, with more being introduced each year.

If you live in a mild-winter climate and want to grow deciduous fruits, you'll first have to find out the number of *chilling hours* in your area. For information on chilling hours, contact your county extension service or university extension agent, or use the conversion chart on the facing page. Then choose varieties that have a chilling requirement equal to or less than that amount of hours. Visit nurseries that specialize in low-chill varieties. Also refer to the list of low-chill varieties and their chilling requirements on the facing page.

Heat and Humidity—Some fruits require more summer heat than others to ripen their crop. Peaches, many types of citrus, almonds, some grapes, and pecans like long, hot summers. On the other hand, some fruits are generally intolerant of high summer temperatures and prefer cooler climates. These include raspberries, many blackberries, highbush blueberries, and some apple varieties.

When high summer temperatures are combined with high humidity, many fruits are subject to severe disease problems. This is why many stone fruits, and European and American grapes, are rarely successful in the Deep South. Humidity and cool temperatures can cause problems as well. In coastal areas of the Pacific Northwest where summer fog or long, rainy periods are common, many varieties of apricots and cherries are especially susceptible to disease. In such areas, selecting disease-resistant varieties or maintaining a preventative spraying program is critical to success with some fruit.

CULTURAL REMINDERS

Standard gardening practices will play an important role in the quality of your harvest. Planting in a sunny spot where the soil is well drained, applying water regularly and, if necessary, feeding regularly with fertilizer, will help ensure healthy plants and the best possible harvest. Pollination needs are important for many tree fruits, nuts and berries. Other specific factors that must be considered for fruit trees are discussed at right.

Pollination—Most fruiting plants are either *self-fruitful* or *self-unfruitful.* Self-fruitful plants provide their own pollen for pollination and can produce fruit without any other plants present. Self-unfruitful plants require another plant nearby to provide for cross-pollination. The plant should be of the same type and bloom about the same time. Bees, insects or wind act as pollinators and carry pollen from one tree to the other. So with self-unfruitful plants you have to grow more than one plant to produce fruit. With some self-unfruitful plants, such as Japanese plums, the second plant must be a specific variety.

GROWING FRUIT TREES

Fruit that is borne on trees, such as apples, pears and cherries, have some specific requirements not shared with berries or nuts. Because each tree has a different bearing habit, correct pruning and training is important. Some trees, including peaches and nectarines, must be pruned heavily to remain productive. Others, such as apples and pears, should be pruned more selectively. Information on pruning individual fruit trees starts on page 169, with apples. Apples, apricots, peaches, nectarines and Japanese plums overproduce, meaning they will set more fruit than they can actually ripen to perfection. To correct this problem, you should reduce the number of fruit by thinning. Otherwise, you'll have a lot of small, low-quality fruit.

The best time to thin fruit is right after *June drop,* a period when most trees naturally thin themselves by dropping some of their fruit. Although called June drop, this may happen as early as April in some areas. It is often hard to notice exactly when June drop occurs, if it occurs at all. As general rule, thin fruits as soon as spring frost danger is over or when fruits reach 1/2 to 1 inch in diameter. Leave 6 to 8 inches between fruit or, with apples and Japanese plums, thin to one fruit per cluster. Thin carefully, making sure you don't damage fruiting spurs.

Most fruits and some nuts, like almonds shown here, are thinned so remaining fruit will be larger.

Carefully trained apple trees are good example of using fruit trees for landscaping.

GROWING BERRIES

Berries are remarkably productive plants. Under ideal conditions, 25 mature strawberry plants can produce up to 30 quarts of fruit per season, six mature blueberry plants can produce up to 15 quarts of fruit, 12 mature blackberry plants can produce up to 15 quarts of fruit and 24 mature raspberry plants can produce up to 30 quarts of fruit. These amounts are enough to supply a family of five with fresh fruit. If you plan to do any preserving, you may want to plant more.

Most blackberries and some grapes require a trellis for support and easy harvesting. Erect-type blackberries and raspberries need little support. Usually only a light wire or string suspended between stakes is needed to keep them upright.

When you build a trellis, make it strong. Any wood that will be in contact with soil should be pressure treated with a wood preservative. Otherwise, it will eventually rot. Pressure-treated lumber is available at lumber yards. Specify wood treated with a preservative that is non-toxic to plants.

Soil preparation prior to planting is particularly important with many berry plants. Work in ample amounts of organic matter to a depth of 6 to 12 inches.

GROWING NUTS

Most nut trees grow quite large. Avoid planting too close to the house or where the trees will eventually shade out other areas of the garden. Give nut trees plenty of room.

Most nuts must be dried in the sun several days before they can be stored. Always remove the husk first. A nut has been dried long enough if the kernel snaps in two rather than bending.

Nut trees generally do not have to be pruned as severely as fruit trees to produce quality fruit, but they do require some pruning.

VARIETY SELECTION

Fruit breeding is an advanced science. Most types of fruits, nuts and berries are available in many varieties. Often, it may appear as if a certain type of fruit is not adapted to your climate. It may not be hardy enough, it may need more chilling, or it may have disease problems. However, by doing a little homework you may find an exceptional variety that can be grown in your area. Many fruits are available in extra-hardy varieties, low-chill varieties or disease-resistant varieties. A little bit of searching through mail-order catalogs or a few short phone calls with local extension agents and nurseries that

specialize in fruit trees may greatly increase your gardening enjoyment.

Adaptation is not the only factor that should influence variety selection. Plant early, midseason, and late-ripening varieties to extend the harvest period. Also, don't forget how productive most fruiting plants can be. Select varieties of fruit that can be used in a number of ways or those that store well. Otherwise, you may have to give away or waste a lot of fruit.

Dwarf Trees—Many types of fruit and nut trees are available in dwarf varieties. The term *dwarf* refers to the size of the tree—dwarf trees bear full-size fruit. Dwarf trees are ideal where space is limited, and many are excellent choices for large containers (15-gallon size or larger). Dwarf trees are also easier to harvest, spray and prune.

There are two basic types of dwarf trees—those in which the *scion,* or fruiting part of the tree, is grown on a dwarf rootstock, and those in which the scion itself is genetically dwarf. Scions from most varieties of fruits can be grafted to a dwarf rootstock of a closely related tree. With genetic dwarfs, it is the scion that is dwarf, grafted onto standard-size rootstock. Compared to trees with dwarf rootstocks, genetic dwarfs offer fewer varieties because they must be specially bred. Many have a tendency to overbear, so they require special attention to fruit thinning.

FRUIT

This section gives basic cultural information for growing popular deciduous fruits, citrus and tropical fruit.

APPLES

Apples are by far America's favorite fruit. One variety or another can be grown almost anywhere in the United States. They are relatively easy to grow, are available in almost any size tree—thanks to the Malling dwarf rootstocks—and can be used to make some of America's favorite recipes, including apple pies, applesauce and ciders.

Important Numbers—Standard apple trees may reach over 25 feet high and usually take 4 to 8 years after planting to bear fruit. Dwarf varieties grow smaller—size depends on the rootstock—and take 3 to 4 years to bear a crop. Plant standard-size trees at least

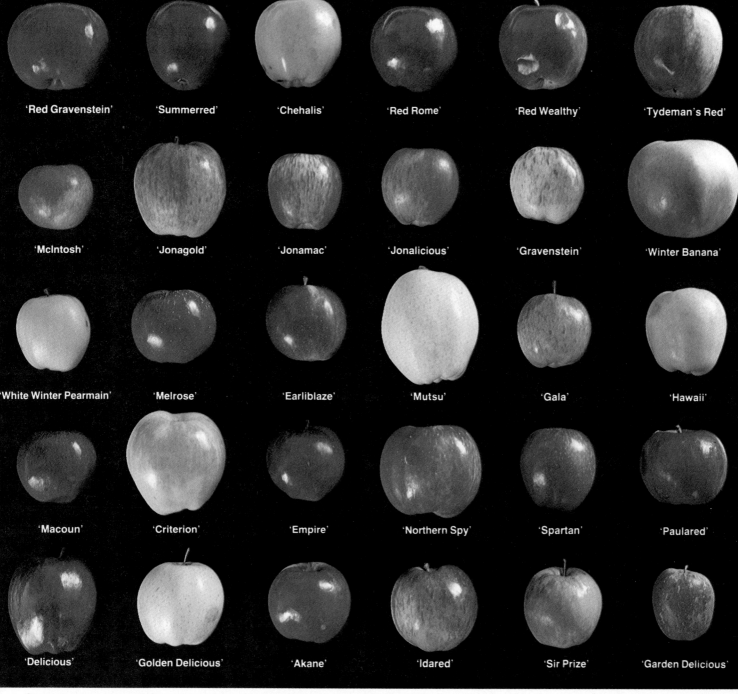

'Red Gravenstein'   'Summerred'   'Chehalis'   'Red Rome'   'Red Wealthy'   'Tydeman's Red'

'McIntosh'   'Jonagold'   'Jonamac'   'Jonalicious'   'Gravenstein'   'Winter Banana'

'White Winter Pearmain'   'Melrose'   'Earliblaze'   'Mutsu'   'Gala'   'Hawaii'

'Macoun'   'Criterion'   'Empire'   'Northern Spy'   'Spartan'   'Paulared'

'Delicious'   'Golden Delicious'   'Akane'   'Idared'   'Sir Prize'   'Garden Delicious'

Shown here are some of the many apple varieties available to gardeners. The difference in color and form may be surprising to those used to the two or three commercial varieties sold at the local supermarket.

20 feet apart. Dwarf varieties can be planted much closer.

Adaptation—Apples can be grown almost anywhere, but variety selection is important. Chilling requirements average about 900 hours, but low-chill varieties have chilling requirements as low as 250 hours. Most apple trees can withstand temperatures as low as -30F (-34C) if properly hardened-off. *Apple scab,* a fungal disease that thrives in humid areas, limits adaptation in many parts of the East.

Pollination—Most apple varieties are only partially self-fruitful, so it's best to have another variety nearby that is blooming at the same time. Because it's likely some of your neighbors have apple trees—or crabapple trees, which are also good pollinizers—you probably won't have to plant more than one tree. If there are no apple trees nearby, you can graft a scion of a good pollinator variety onto a branch of your apple tree.

Pruning—Just after planting, trees should be headed to 18 to 24 inches tall. Training main scaffold limbs begins the first summer.

Train dwarf and semidwarf apple trees to a central leader. Use a stake or wire to support espaliers. Use a temporary support only if the tree is exposed to strong wind. Spread side limbs, if necessary.

Train standard-size trees to develop three or four leaders at 20° to 30° from vertical. Head leaders annually and remove competing shoots. Spread secondary scaffolds, if necessary.

The main apple varieties differ as much in growth habits as in fruit. Each typical growth habit requires slightly different training and pruning. The many varieties of apples have been categorized into four main groups according to similarities in growth habits Type I, Type II, Type III and Type IV. If you don't know which type you have, follow general recommendations for pruning and observe the growth habit. Within a season or two, you'll probably be able to place your tree in one of the four groups described above.

Type I Apples: These are spur-types such as 'Starkrimson Red Delicious' and 'Jonagold'. They tend to be upright, develop narrow crotches and branch sparsely. Fruiting occurs on many short, long-lived spurs. Most fruit develops near the main trunk.

Head primary scaffolds to stimulate branching, or retain a large number of primary scaffold limbs from the central leader without heading. Dormant-season heading must be followed by thinning branch ends to single shoots after new growth begins.

Type I varieties require little pruning once trained. Spurs remain productive for 10 or more years. Because spurs are long-lived, they are sometimes susceptible to a disease known, appropriately enough, as dead-spur disease. It is a drastic problem because it destroys most old spurs within a short time. The only recourse is to remove stricken limbs entirely, then renew them using an available water sprout (sucker).

Type II Apples: These are non-spur varieties typified by most standard non-spur strains of 'Delicious'. They branch frequently and the fruiting zone tends to migrate away from the trunk.

Train Type IIs with few major limbs. Use spreaders on scaffold limbs to develop wide-angle crotches. Mature trees require moderate to heavy annual pruning to renew fruiting buds. Thin relatively upright replacement shoots. Head nearly horizontal branches back to 2-year-old wood so they won't break once loaded with fruit.

Type III Apples: These are spreading trees as typified by standard-size 'Golden Delicious' and 'Mutsu'. Branch angles are naturally wide, and branching is frequent. They bear on 1- to 3-year-old spurs, and the fruiting zone tends to migrate rapidly from the trunk to the outside of the tree.

Train trees to develop no more than three primary scaffold limbs. After the first fruit crop, head secondary scaffold limbs to stiffen them.

Mature Type IIIs require extensive annual thinning. To renew fruiting wood, thin upright shoots that develop from 2- or 3- year-old wood. Lighten branch ends each year by thinning to single, upright shoots.

Type IV Apples: These are tip-bearers such as 'Red Rome', 'Granny Smith' and 'Tydeman's Early Worcester'. They have upright main scaffolds, narrow crotches and extensive branching. Fruit is borne on the end of last season's shoots. The lower half of shoots may be without leaves or fruit. Fruiting wood develops at branch ends, causing the tree to spread.

Train Type IVs to no more than three leaders. To promote secondary branching and to stiffen the main branch, head leaders annually to about 2 feet from their previous head. Midsummer heading also helps in this training.

Mature Type IVs require heavy annual thinning in order to replace fruiting wood. Make all thinning cuts to upright shoots in 2- to 3-year-old wood around the outside of the tree canopy.

Varieties—There are hundreds of apple varieties, differing in climate adaptation, fruit color and shape, ripening period and how the fruit can be used. 'Anna' and 'Dorsett Golden' are favorite low-chill varieties for

Heavy crops, especially on small trees, often must be supported with props to avoid breaking branches.

areas with mild winters. 'Red Melba', 'Haralson' and 'McIntosh' are excellent varieties known for their hardiness. 'Chehalis', 'Liberty' and 'Prima' are disease-resistant varieties that are useful in areas where apple scab is a problem. 'Golden Delicious', 'Jonagold' and 'Jonathan' are delicious multipurpose apples that can be eaten fresh or cooked, or used to make cider.

Any variety can be dwarfed using the Malling (M) and Merton-Malling (MM) dwarf rootstocks. *MM-106 stock* dwarfs trees by 30% less than standard size; *M-26 stock,* by 50%; *M-9 stock,* by 60% and *M-27 stock,* by 70% to 75%. 'Garden Delicious' and 'Compact McIntosh' are genetic dwarfs. Spur varieties are also more compact, and lower growing than standard varieties.

Harvesting—Apples are ready to harvest when they reach their characteristic color and when a gentle upward twist easily separates them from the tree. When a few apples have already fallen, the rest of the crop is ready to harvest. Pick apples carefully so you do not damage the fruiting spurs.

APRICOTS

Apricots are one of the prettiest fruit trees you can grow—soft green, heart-shaped leaves fluttering in the wind, and bright pink flowers clothing branches in spring. However, apricots also have the most limited range of adaptation. They bloom early in spring, and in cold climates their blossoms and young fruit are often destroyed by spring frosts. In warm, humid areas, fungal and bacterial diseases further limit their adaptation.

Important Numbers—Standard apricot trees are large, sometimes growing as much as 25 feet high and 20 feet wide. They should be spaced at least 20 feet apart. Trees usually begin bearing 3 to 4 years after planting. No fully dwarfing rootstocks have been developed but many varieties are available as semidwarf trees that grow 12 to 25 feet high. There is also at least one genetic dwarf variety that maintains a height of 6 to 8 feet.

Adaptation—Early-blooming characteristics and susceptibility to disease limit adaptation in many areas, even though most trees are hardy to -15F (-26C). Average chilling requirements are between 600 and 800 hours, but many low-chill varieties

Apricots 'Blenheim' (top) and 'King Cot' (bottom) illustrate size difference of largest and smallest varieties.

are available. Ideal climates for growing apricots are found in dry areas of the West, Pacific Northwest, and Southwest. In other areas, fruit production will be unreliable or disease problems will be severe.

Pollination—Most apricots are self-fruitful. Varieties that are self-unfruitful can be pollinated by any other variety blooming at the same time.

Pruning—Apricot trees too often tend to spread excessively. Cutting away horizontal limbs helps direct upward growth. Head scaffold limbs to maintain desired tree height. Keep fruiting wood thinned.

Varieties—The varieties 'Moorpark'

and 'Blenheim' are excellent for the correct climate. 'Moongold' and 'Sungold' were developed for cold climates. 'Goldcot' is widely adapted and is a good choice wherever growing conditions are less than ideal. 'Goldenglo' is a beautiful genetic dwarf variety. Low-chill selections include 'Katy', 'Goldkist', 'Earligold', 'Perfection' and 'Flora Gold'.

'Plum Parfait' is a hybrid between a plum and an apricot that bears apricot-like fruit on a small tree.

Harvesting—Harvest apricots when they reach full color and begin to soften slightly. Fruit won't ripen all at once but over a period of 2 to 3 weeks.

Fruit of sweet cherry 'Jubilee' are borne in clusters. These are ready for picking.

CHERRIES

There are two types of cherries commonly grown in home gardens—*sweet cherries* and *sour cherries*. Most people are familiar with sweet cherries because these are the type grown commercially and sold in supermarkets. Sour cherries, or pie cherries as they are often called, are grown primarily in cold-winter climates and are used to make pies, pastries and juice. Sweet cherries and sour cherries also differ in the size of tree they are borne on and the areas in which they can be grown.

Important Numbers—Sweet cherries are borne on large, spreading trees that can reach 40 feet high and 30 feet wide. They should be spaced at least 35 to 40 feet apart. Sour cherries are borne on smaller trees that rarely exceed 15 feet in height but can become twice as wide. They should be spaced 15 to 20 feet apart. Both sweet and sour cherries are available as dwarfs that grow about 6 to 8 feet high. Both kinds take about 5 to 6 years to begin bearing.

Adaptation—Although sweet cherries and sour cherries differ substantially in climate adaptation, both share high chilling requirements of over 800 hours. This excludes them from much of the southern and southwestern United States. Sweet cherries also bloom relatively early and are subject to damage from spring frosts. In addition, rain close to harvest time causes the fruit to crack, and temperatures over 100F (38C) inhibit fruit development. Trees are hardy to -20F (-29C). Parts of Northern California, the Northwest and Northeast are considered the best cherry-growing regions.

Sour cherries can be grown almost anywhere they receive adequate chilling. They are extremely hardy, withstanding temperatures of -35F (-38C).

Pollination—Most sweet cherries require another cherry variety nearby to provide pollen. Almost any variety will do, however, 'Bing', 'Royal Ann', and 'Lambert' will not pollinate each other. All sour cherries are self-fruitful.

Pruning—Cherries are borne on long-lived spurs. Sweet cherries are usually trained to a central leader and are pruned heavily to keep them within bounds. Train sour cherries to a vase shape. Once mature, they require very little pruning.

Cherry, Sour: The weight of a crop of sour cherries can easily break trees because of their brittle wood and weak crotches. To help prevent such damage, head nursery trees at 18 to 24 inches. Select three or four shoots with wide crotch angles and train to a multiple leader. After the first dormant heading of scaffold limbs, further heading will not be required because of the free-branching pattern of the tree. Contain height and spread of mature trees by thinning.

Cherry, Sweet: Normally, sweet cherry trees branch only at the beginning of the growing season, if at all. Unless you prune them, these trees can rapidly become leggy.

Head nursery trees about 18 to 24 inches after planting. Head all shoots to 24 to 36 inches after the first and second year's growth. Removing terminal buds of shorter shoots promotes branching. Head only the vigorous shoots during the third and fourth year. Once fruiting begins, gradually remove a few scaffold branches until only seven or eight remain. Head all shoots annually in dormant season to encourage low, spreading trees that are easily picked.

Thin tops of mature trees as necessary to let in more light and keep upper limbs within reach. Vigor of old trees can be increased by harder pruning, using both heading and thinning.

Varieties—'Lambert', 'Royal Ann', 'Van', 'Bing' and 'Rainier' are popular sweet cherry varieties. 'Hedelfigen' and 'Ulster' are good for cold areas or those with frequent summer rain. 'Stella' is a self-fruitful variety. 'Compact Stella', 'Compact Lambert' and 'Starkcrimson' are genetic dwarf sweet cherries. 'North Star' and 'Montmorency' are popular sour cherries. 'North Star' is a small, compact tree.

Harvesting—The best way to tell if cherries are ripe is to pick a few and taste them. Pick with the stems attached if you intend to store the fruit or eat it fresh. Cherries can be picked without stems attached if you plan to use them for canning or cooking.

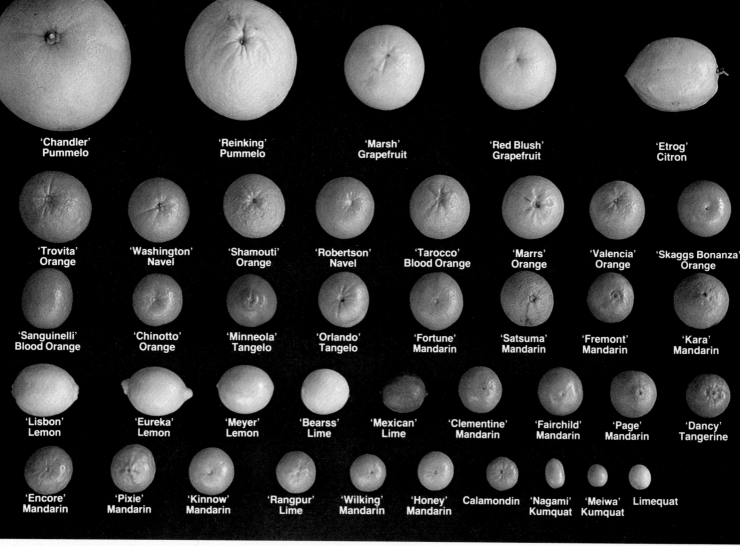

The citrus family is a large one, from giant pummelos to tiny kumquats and limequats.

CITRUS

Citrus are evergreen fruit trees that offer tremendous rewards for gardeners in mild climates of the South, Southwest and West. They are among the easiest fruit to grow and are exceedingly handsome plants with fragrant white flowers, clean green leaves, and brightly colored fruit. In many areas where they are adapted they double as ornamentals, lining the avenues as street trees or providing privacy as hedges.

Important Numbers—Types of citrus vary greatly in height. Lemons are most vigorous and can reach over 20 feet high. Grapefruit, pummelos, 'Valencia' and navel oranges, and 'Dancy' tangerines are also large trees that can reach 18 to 20 feet. Mandarins and blood oranges are smaller, reaching 12 to 15 feet. Kumquats, kumquat hybrids, and 'Meyer' lemon are naturally smaller trees that usually grow between 8 to 12 feet high.

Even within groups of citrus, varieties will differ in size and tree shape. Spacing between trees will differ according to height, but there should be at least as much distance between trees as the trees are tall. Dwarf varieties of citrus will be about 50% smaller than standard trees. Exceptions are varieties grafted to 'Flying Dragon' rootstock, which will maintain a height of 5 to 7 feet.

Adaptation—Few fruit trees are as dramatically affected by climate variations. Winter cold, heat, humidity, fluctuations between day and night temperatures, and light intensity all have strong influences on adaptation, fruit color and fruit flavor. Some varieties are only adapted to the humid South, others grow best in the coastal areas of California. Checking with your local nurserymen or university extension agent is one of the best ways to determine which types of citrus you can grow.

Hardiness is one of the most important factors in determining adaptation. Limes are the most sensitive to cold. They will usually be damaged if temperatures fall below freezing (32F, 0C). Lemons are slightly more hardy, being able to withstand temperatures as low as 28F to 30F (12C to -1C). Kumquats are the hardiest, able to withstand temperatures as cold as 18F (-8C). Hardiness of other citrus types falls somewhere between these extremes, with oranges at a midpoint of 26F (-3C). However, hardiness is a difficult factor to determine exactly. Duration of cold is also important. Also, mature fruit is often less hardy than foliage.

How warm it is where you live is also important in determining which type of citrus you can grow. Grapefruits need a lot of heat to sweeten their fruit and are best adapted to desert areas of the Southwest and to Florida. Lemons can withstand cooler temperatures and can be grown in cool coastal areas of California. Citrus is usually sweeter but less brightly colored when grown in the humid Southeast. Arid climates promote more acid in citrus and more brightly colored rinds.

Pollination—Most citrus varieties are self-fruitful. Exceptions are some varieties of mandarin that produce larger crops when other mandarin varieties are planted nearby.

Pruning—Citrus species grow, bloom and fruit at any time the weather is favorable, eliminating the need to prune for fruit renewal. They are pruned for appearance, size control, or to allow light and chemical sprays into the center of the tree.

Pruning the tops keeps trees from becoming too tall for easy picking. Do not prune lower, outer limbs because they produce most of the fruit. Thin to maintain a compact shape and ensure that early fruiting takes place on wood strong enough to support fruit weight. Thin to strong laterals or to main branches at any time in frost-free climates or after frost danger in cold climates.

Orange and grapefruit trees should be trained to develop a strong central leader. Gradually remove lower side limbs to raise the head. Train until trees are high so lower limbs can spread out and downward. Mature trees require only removal of dead, twiggy growth.

Due to their rangy nature, lemon trees require more training than other citrus trees. Head young trees at about 3 feet and select three or four main leaders. Head leaders severely to balance the top, if necessary. Thin and head as required to develop compact growth.

Lemon trees produce vigorous water sprouts that run through the center of the tree. When correctly spread, they can be used to fill gaps in the canopy of the tree. Spread apart water sprouts before they are too stiff. Tie them in place, if necessary.

Varieties—There are many types of citrus and many more varieties of each type. Popular orange varieties in the West include 'Washington' and 'Roberton' navel oranges, 'Valencia', and 'Trovita'. 'Valencia' is also grown in Florida, as are 'Hamlin', 'Parson's Brown' and 'Pineapple'. 'Eureka' and 'Lisbon' are lemon varieties grown in the West. 'Meyer' lemon grows well

in all citrus areas. 'Redblush' and 'Marsh Seedless' are red and white grapefruit varieties for the hottest climates. 'Duncan' and 'Tarocco' grapefruit are grown in Florida. 'Moro' and 'Sanguinelli' are varieties of blood orange for western gardeners. The coloration of blood oranges is less predictable in the Southeast. 'Dancy', 'Clementine' and 'Satsuma' are three of many popular mandarin varieties.

Harvesting—Most citrus varieties ripen between November and March depending on type and where they are grown. Fruit grown in warm areas will ripen before the same variety grown in cooler ones. The best way to test ripeness is to pick a sample and taste it. Fruit color is a poor indicator of ripeness. Ripe fruit of most citrus types can be left on the tree for at least 3 to 4 weeks without deteriorating.

FIGS

A mature fig tree can be a stunning sight. The branches are twisted and gnarled. They appear almost muscular. The leaves are huge with deeply cut lobes, adding a definite tropical appearance to the spreading canopy. The fruit is deliciously sweet and soft textured. Few fruit trees can have such a dramatic presence and provide such a bountiful harvest with a minimum of care.

Important Numbers—Mature fig trees can fairly quickly reach 40 feet

'Mission' is a popular fig variety in the West.

high and up to 60 feet wide. However, they can be kept much smaller by pruning. In orchardlike conditions, space trees at least 20 feet apart.

Adaptation—Lack of winter hardiness is the most important limiting factor that determines where figs can be grown. Most varieties are severely damaged or killed if temperatures reach 0F (-18C). Temperatures of 10F (-12C) can injure some varieties. Figs have a very low chilling requirement of less than 300 hours, which is seldom a limiting factor.

Pollination—All popular fig varieties are self-fruitful.

Pruning—Edible figs can be pruned to grow as trees or as bushes with multiple trunks. Bushes regenerate faster after freezes than trees do, thus are preferable for cold regions.

For bushes, plant in a depression and head 12 inches above the ground. After several branches have formed, fill in the depression, and mound soil so that the bases of the shoots are below ground. Head shoots annually at 2- or 3-foot intervals to stimulate branching pattern and ensure fruiting close to the ground.

Trees should be trained to the multiple leader system with three or four main scaffold limbs and two or three secondary scaffolds on each main scaffold. Remove suckers and sprouts at the base of tree each year.

Some fig varieties produce their first of two annual crops on wood of the previous season. Heading would remove most of this wood, so mature figs should be pruned by thinning. Varieties that produce fruit on the current-season's shoots should have all of the previous-season's shoots headed to one or two buds during the dormant season. The remaining buds produce long shoots that bear 10 to 15 figs.

Varieties—'Mission' and 'Brown Turkey' are popular varieties in the West. 'Celeste' and 'Texas Everbearing' are popular in the South. Check with your local nurserymen for other locally adapted varieties.

Harvesting—Figs usually produce two crops. The first ripens in early summer, the second in fall. In some climates, only the first crop matures. Figs are ready to pick when the *neck* of the fruit softens, causing it to droop from the branch. If any milky latex drips from the branch after the fruit is picked, its not quite ripe.

PEACHES AND NECTARINES

Peaches and nectarines are the juicy fruits of summer. Many varieties are available. With careful selection, you can begin harvesting peaches and nectarines in late spring and continue throughout summer, never experiencing a day without fresh fruit.

Peaches and nectarines have identical cultural and climatic requirements. In fact, a nectarine is simply a fuzzless peach.

Important Numbers—Peaches and nectarines are borne on relatively small trees that are easily maintained below 15 feet high. Under orchard conditions, they should be spaced 15 to 20 feet apart. Many varieties are available on partially dwarfing rootstocks that restrict growth to about 10 to 12 feet. Genetic dwarf varieties that seldom grow over 8 feet high are also available. Most peaches and nectarines will begin bearing fruit 2 to 3 years after planting.

Adaptation—Peaches and nectarines have chilling requirements that average between 600 and 900 hours. However, there are many low-chill varieties that allow these delicious fruits to be grown in even the warmest climates of the United States. Trees are hardy to about -15F (-26C) The best quality fruit is produced in hot-summer climates. Fungal and bacterial diseases, such as brown rot and bacterial canker, can be serious problems in humid areas. Peach leaf curl requires control in most areas of the country.

Pollination—Almost all peach and nectarine varieties are self-fruitful.

Pruning—These two trees require more pruning than any other fruiting tree. Those left with a central leader may grow too much at the top, losing lower limbs due to shading. Two-leader, Y-shaped trees fit into small spaces better than trees with more limbs. Three-leader trees are strong and easy to care for. More leaders are not desirable. Genetic dwarfs only require thinning to four or five scaffolds.

At planting time, head young trees 6 inches above the ground for short trees, 2 feet above the ground for gardening space underneath. Shorten side shoots to 2 or 3 inches where you want a scaffold branch, spacing branches evenly around the trunk and several inches apart vertically to help prevent weak crotches. Remove all other shoots. If you want a central-

There are literally hundreds of peach varieties. 'Cardinal' is shown here.

leader tree, remove all side limbs and do not head leader.

During summer, pinch unwanted shoots to direct cane growth into scaffolds. Head scaffold limbs at 24 to 30 inches from the trunk during the first dormant season to strengthen secondary limbs and scaffold. Remove vigorous shoots that compete with secondary scaffolds.

In the second dormant season, thin shoots again. During the third dormant season, thin fruiting wood to prepare for next season's fruiting.

Peaches and nectarines bear only on the previous season's wood, so bearing trees must be pruned annually. Head the upper, outer shoots in midsummer to late summer to bring sunlight to lower limbs and prevent dieback from shading. Remove fruiting shoots when dormant and cut back shoots of medium vigor. Prune to counteract the strong tendency of fruiting wood to move upward and outward away from the trunk.

Thin these back to more upright shoots. Upper, outside branches tend to spread too much. Thin weakest spots, leaving shoots of about pencil-

thickness spaced far enough apart for good light distribution and fruit production.

Varieties—There are hundreds of varieties. Peaches and nectarines come in white-fleshed and yellow-fleshed varieties, and with flesh that either clings to the pit (clingstone) or separates from the pit easily (freestone). Freestone varieties are best for canning or preserves. Excellent flavored midseason peach varieties include 'Fay Elberta', 'Halehaven' and 'Flavorcrest'. Outstanding midseason nectarines include 'Sunglo' and 'Flavortop'. 'Flordagold', 'Flordaking', 'Desertgold' and 'Mid-pride' are a few of many low-chill peaches. 'Fantasia' and 'Sunrise' are low-chill nectarines. 'Fantasia' has a sweet-kernel pit that can be cracked and eaten like an almond. 'Honey Babe' and 'Sensation' are popular genetic dwarf peaches. 'Honeyglo', 'Nectar Babe' and 'Sweet Melody' are excellent genetic dwarf nectarines.

Harvesting—Let peaches and nectarines ripen completely on the tree. Pick when they begin to soften slightly.

Pear in bottle makes unique gift. Attach bottle to branch as soon as tiny fruit forms.

PEARS

There are basically two types of pears—*European* and *Asian*. European pears are familiar to most people. They are picked green and ripened off the tree. They have delicious, soft-textured flesh and the classic pear shape. Asian pears are round and can be eaten right after they are picked. However, the most important difference between Asian and European pears is that Asian pears have a crisp texture that resembles an apple. In fact, Asian pears are often called apple pears. Asian pears are gaining rapidly in popularity because of their delicious flavor and unique texture.

A third group of pears called *hybrid pears* are, as the name suggests, hybrids between Asian and European varieties. They are particularly popular in the southern United States because of their low chilling requirements and greater resistance to fire blight. Their fruit resembles European varieties.

Important Numbers—All pears are borne on handsome, glossy foliaged trees that are easily maintained below 20 feet tall. At least one fully dwarfing rootstock is available—Old Homex Farmingdale No. 51—that dwarfs trees to 6 feet in height. There are also some varieties available as semidwarfs that reach 12 to 15 feet high. Space pears 18 to 25 feet apart. Trees begin bearing 4 to 8 years after planting.

Adaptation—Most pears have chilling requirements between 600 and 900 hours. However, varieties with lower chilling requirements are available. The greatest limiting factor to where pears can be grown is susceptibility to the bacterial disease *fire blight*. The disease is common almost everywhere east of the Rocky Mountains and in many areas of the West. Planting disease-resistant varieties is the best preventative measure. Most pear varieties are hardy to about -20F (-29C).

Pollination—Pears require another variety in bloom nearby to produce the biggest possible crop.

Pruning—When planting, head pear trees 24 to 30 inches above the ground. Select three well-spaced scaffold limbs and remove any shoots between them, leaving any shoots below scaffold limbs to fill in the bottom of trees. Keep central leader for 1 or 2 years to help spread permanent scaffolds before removing it completely.

Each year, head scaffolds at 2-1/2 to 3 feet above the previous year's heading. Do not head side shoots. Summer pinching of rapidly growing leaders stimulates branching. To prevent breaking young, flexible limbs, tie scaffold limbs together.

Pear trees usually require heavy pruning to stimulate fruit-set, especially when there's no cross-pollination. Pears bear on long-lived spurs. On 2- or 3-year-old wood, head only those shoots that are over 2 feet long, back to flower buds at about 18 inches. Remove wood that fruited heavily during the previous year, leaving a well-positioned, 1-year-old shoot as a replacement. Remove water sprouts and suckers to help replace fruiting wood.

Varieties—'Fan Stil', 'Moonglow', 'Orient' and 'Sure Crop' are popular hybrid or European pears with resistance to fire blight. 'Bartlett' and 'Seckel' are widely available summer pears. 'Anjou' and 'Comice' are excellent winter pears. 'Chojoro' is a good Asian pear variety. Low-chill varieties include 'Flordahome', 'Hood' and the Asian variety 'Shinseikei'.

Harvesting—European and hybrid pears must be harvested green and ripened off the tree. If left to ripen on the tree, fruit will not reach peak flavor. Summer pears ripen in about 1 week at room temperature. Winter pears must be stored in a cold place for 6 to 8 weeks before they will ripen at room temperature. Asian pears are ready to pick when they reach an even yellow color and break easily from the fruiting spur. They can be eaten immediately.

PERSIMMONS

Two types of persimmons are grown in the United States—the *Oriental persimmon* and *American persimmon*. Both require minimum care and are extremely ornamental trees with glossy, green leaves that turn colorful shades of yellow, orange or red in fall. Oriental persimmons are grown most often but the American persimmons are much hardier and can be grown in climates where Oriental types cannot.

Important Numbers—Under ideal conditions, persimmon trees grow up to 40 feet tall and 30 feet wide. They are often much smaller. Trees should be spaced about 25 feet apart. They will usually begin bearing at 3 years of age.

Adaptation—Lack of hardiness is the only factor that determines whether or not you can grow persimmons. Oriental persimmons are hardy to 0F (-18C). American persimmons are hardy to about -20F (-29C).

Pollination—American persimmons are self-unfruitful; Oriental persimmons generally self-fruitful.

Pruning—Nursery trees should be headed to 2-1/2 to 3 feet at planting time. Choose five or six shoots, spaced over a foot or more apart along the trunk, to form scaffold limbs. Prune other growth below scaffolds. After the first season's growth, head scaffolds from 1/3 to 1/2 their original length. Avoid any more pruning until the tree begins to bear fruit.

Remove occasional crossing or poorly placed limbs on mature trees. Thin to more upright shoots to lighten ends of branches. Thin out tops of old trees to stimulate growth and allow sunshine in.

Varieties—There two types of persimmon varieties—*astringent* and *nonastringent*. Astringent varieties must be allowed to soften to an almost mushlike consistency before they can be eaten. Non-astringent types can be eaten firm-ripe like an apple. Most American persimmons are grown from seedlings and all bear astringent fruit. Astringent varieties of Oriental persimmon include 'Hachiya' and 'Tamopan'. 'Fuyu' is the most popular nonastringent variety.

Harvesting—Astringent persimmons can be left on the tree until they soften, but they may be damaged by birds. You can also pick when they are still slightly hard and ripen them off the tree. Nonastringent persimmons are picked when they reach full color. Use pruning shears to harvest persimmons, leaving 1 to 2 inches of stem attached to the fruit.

PLUMS

You can probably grow at least one of the three basic plum types. In cold climates, plant *hybrid plums,* which are known for their hardiness. In most other areas of the United States you can choose between *Japanese plums* or *European plums.* Japanese plums have red-skinned fruit and are the ones commonly sold in supermarkets. European plums have deep purple, freestone fruit. Some varieties with high sugar content are often dried and called prunes. In mild-winter climates, plant low-chill varieties of Japanese plums. A fourth group, called *cherry plums,* are hybrids between an American native plum and Japanese plum. They are small trees with plumlike fruit and are widely adapted.

Important Numbers—All plums are borne on relatively small trees that are easily maintained below 15 feet.

'Stanley' is a popular European plum.

While no fully dwarfing rootstocks are available, many varieties are sold as semidwarf trees that grow between 10 and 12 feet high. Space standard plums 18 to 20 feet apart. Semidwarf trees can be planted as close as 12 feet apart. Most plums will begin bearing at 3 to 4 years old.

Adaptation—Each type of plum has its own climate requirements. Japanese plums bloom early, along with apricots, and are subject to damage from late spring frosts in many areas of the country. However, many varieties have low enough chilling requirements to be grown in the mildest winter climates. European plums bloom later but have higher chilling requirements, excluding them from many southern areas. Both Japanese and European plums are hardy to about -20F (-29C). Hybrid plums are trees for northern regions. Trees are hardy to at least -30F (-35C).

Pollination—European plums are self-fruitful, but most varieties do better if cross-pollinated. Japanese and hybrid plums need another variety to provide pollen.

Pruning—Train to a multiple leader with three or four main scaffold limbs. At planting time, head to 18 to 24 inches, selecting those shoots that will be leaders. Upright shoots with narrow crotches should be held in a spread position by spring-type clothes-pins during the first growing season.

European plums or prunes require only one light heading of scaffold limbs about 2 to 2-1/2 feet from the crotch to stimulate branching. Light pruning results in heavier and earlier fruit.

Prune bearing European plums to lighten branch ends, thus preventing breakage. Renewal of fruiting wood comes from long water sprouts that grow from the upper side of arched, fruiting limbs. Cut back to the arch of these limbs to reduce tree height and renew fruiting wood.

Japanese plums need more severe heading of scaffold limbs to strengthen them and encourage branching. Thin to retain the outside spreading limbs. To stimulate branching, keep well-positioned secondary branches and head primary scaffolds just above secondary branches about 24 to 36 inches from the crotch.

Thin third-year scaffolds during the third dormant season to one or two per secondary branch. Thinning interior shoots helps the tree to spread.

Bearing Japanese plums should have 1-year-old shoots thinned, leaving some of them to renew fruiting wood. Also remove some branches carrying old, weak spurs.

Varieties—'Pipestone', 'Tonka' and 'Superior' are popular hybrid plums. Each will pollinate the other. 'Burbank', 'Eldorado', 'Queen Ann' and 'Satsuma' are among many popular Japanese plums. 'Santa Rosa' and 'Methely' are excellent low-chill Japanese plum varieties. Both are also excellent pollinizers for most other varieties. 'Brooks', 'French Prune' and 'Stanley' are popular European plums. 'Sprite' and 'Delight' are excellent cherry plum varieties.

Harvesting—European plums ripen over a period of several weeks. They should be picked when they begin to soften. Japanese and hybrid plums are picked at a slightly firmer stage. As soon as you notice a few fruit softening, the rest of the crop is ready to pick.

TROPICAL AND SUBTROPICAL FRUIT

Areas of the Southeast and Southwest where winter temperatures rarely drop below freezing present the interesting possibility of growing tropical and subtropical fruit. Some of these fruits, such as avocados and bananas, are familiar to American palates. Others, including papayas and mangos, are less familiar but are staples in the diets of millions of people in tropical countries around the world.

Growing these fruits often means making concessions. In climates that are less than ideal, they may need special nurturing to get them to bear fruit. Being able to situate these plants in the best possible microclimate is also highly important. See page 23. Also, you must always be ready to provide protection if the weather threatens to get too cold. You might even want to grow them in containers and move them to a protected spot or a greenhouse during the cold season. But if you go to the trouble of giving these plants what they need, you can be rewarded with exciting and exotic-flavored tropical fruit.

Here are brief descriptions of some of the most popular tropical and subtropical fruit:

Avocados—These large, evergreen trees can reach over 40 feet high. There are two types—Guatamalan varieties and Mexican varieties. Guatamalan avocados include the varieties 'Hass' and 'Reed', and are generally more sensitive to cold than Mexican avocados. The foliage of Mexican avocados is hardy to about 24F (4C). Fruit and flowers are more sensitive and may be damaged if temperatures fall below freezing. Varieties include 'Mexicola', 'Bacon' and 'Zutano'. Both types of avocado will fail to set fruit if temperatures are cool during blossoming. Both must have extremely well drained soil.

Dwarf varieties include 'Whitsell' and 'Glenn', both 16 to 20 feet in height. Together, these trees provide fruit year-round.

Bananas—These trees provide large, tropical-looking leaves on tall, erect, fast-growing trunks that can grow as high as 20 feet. Plants must be protected from wind and frost. Soil should be rich and well drained. Good choice for containers. Many varieties are available, including dwarf types that only grow 5 to 6 feet high.

Guavas—There are several types of guavas, but the easiest and most attractive are *strawberry guavas* and *lemon guavas*. Both have glossy green leaves, pretty white flowers and brightly colored red or yellow fruit with a sweet, aromatic flavor. Plants are hardy to 20F to 25F (-7C to -4C).

Loquat—These are round-headed evergreen trees with heavy-textured, sharply toothed, deep green leaves. Grows 15 to 25 feet high. Foliage is hardy to 20F (-7C) but blossoms, which open in late fall to midwinter, are damaged at about 28F (-2C). Yellow fruit are juicy and sweet, and have three large seeds. Excellent for making jams and jellies.

Macadamia Nut—These glossy-foliaged evergreen trees reach 25 to 30 feet high. They produce a rich-flavored nut with an extremely hard shell. Grows best in Hawaii and coastal areas of Southern California. Hardy to about 25F (-4C).

Mango—These large, compact evergreen trees bear long sprays of yellow to red flowers. Sensitive to cold. Temperatures below 25F (-4C) may kill the tree entirely. Warm days and nights are necessary for fruit to set. Select locally adapted varieties.

Natal Plum—Widely grown as an ornamental shrub for its glossy green leaves, fragrant, white flowers and brightly colored fruit. Easy to grow. Hardy to 26F (-3C). Many varieties are available, but only 'Fancy' is recommended for fruiting quality. Plant two different varieties for cross-pollination.

Papaya—This large herbaceous plant with huge, deeply lobed, fanlike leaves can reach 25 feet high. Grows fast and may bear fruit as soon as 8 months after planting seed. Rather difficult to grow except in Hawaii. Requires exceptional soil drainage and warm weather year round. Frost sensitive. Plant male and female plants to ensure pollination. The hybrid 'Babaco' from Ecuador shows great promise for cooler climates—it is hardy to 26F (-3C).

Pineapple Guava—Not a true guava. Handsome shrub with silvery green leaves and unusual red and white flowers. Used as an ornamental in many areas of California. Fruit is pear-shaped with delicious minty flavor and drops from the plant when ripe. Shrub is easy to grow and can be trained as a hedge. Varieties selected for good fruit quality are 'Coolidge', 'Nazemetz' and 'Trask', all hardy to about 15F (-10C). Some varieties produce better when cross-pollinated with another variety.

Avocado trees can reach over 40 feet high. Because avocados bruise easily, special long-handle picking device is used.

BERRIES

BLACKBERRIES

Blackberries are known by many names—loganberries, boysenberries, olallieberries and youngberries. Actually, each of these berries is a variety of blackberry. Loganberries are a hybrid blackberry variety known as 'Logan'. Boysenberries are a hybrid variety called 'Boysen', and so on. The parentage of these hybrids is rather confusing because there are many species of blackberry native to almost every part of the United States. This means that one blackberry variety or another can probably be grown in your area.

Planting—Blackberries are borne on vigorous, thorny canes that are either erect or spreading. Both types are usually planted bare root. They are planted in trenches or individual holes, set an inch deeper than they were in the nursery. Plant erect blackberry varieties 24 to 30 inches apart in rows spaced 6 to 10 feet. Trailing blackberries require a trellis for support. The most common type is a two-wire trellis with the first wire about 30 inches above the ground and the second 5 feet above the ground. Plant trailing varieties 5 to 8 feet apart in rows spaced 8 to 10 feet. After planting, cut back canes to 8 to 10 inches above the ground.

Adaptation—Blackberries produce the best-tasting fruit in areas with mild winters and cool summers. But varieties differ dramatically in adaptation. Chilling requirements range from 100 to 1000 hours. Hardiness varies from -20F (-29C) in some erect types up to 5F (-15C) in boysenberries and some thornless varieties. To determine the best varieties for your area, consult your local nurserymen or university extension agent.

Pollination—All blackberries are self-fruitful.

Pruning—Blackberries are borne on 2-year-old canes. Pruning consists of removing canes that have fruited and tying to the trellis young canes that will fruit the following spring. Young canes grow from the base of fruited canes. Erect blackberries can be grown without a trellis by heading unfruiting canes from 4 to 6 feet above the ground.

Varieties—'Bailey', 'Darrow' and 'El Dorado' are erect varieties for cold climates. 'Dallas', 'Brazos' and

'Olallie' is a popular low-chill blackberry grown in the Southwest.

'Flordagrand' are low-chill varieties commonly grown in the Southeast. 'Olallie', 'Young' and 'Logan' are low-chill varieties commonly grown in the Southwest. Other popular varieties include 'Marion', 'Chehalem', 'Lucretia' and 'Boysen'.

Harvesting—Blackberries should be picked every 2 or 3 days for a period of 1 or 2 weeks. Pick berries when they reach full size and color and when they separate easily from the cluster.

BLUEBERRIES

Blueberries have one cultural requirement that sets them apart from most other fruits that are grown in the home garden—they must be grown in acid soil. If you can meet this requirement—see page 60 for information on altering soil pH—and if you choose varieties that are adapted to your climate, you'll be rewarded not only with a delicious crop, but also with the visual delights of what is perhaps America's most beautiful native fruit.

Blueberries are borne on clean-foliaged shrubs that bear dainty clusters of white flowers in spring and turn stunning shades of red and orange before dropping their leaves in fall.

There are two types of blueberries grown in North America. Highbush blueberries are the type seen in super-markets. Most varieties are best adapted to northern, cold-winter climates, but low-chill varieties are available. Rabbit-eye blueberries are grown in warmer climates of the South and West.

Planting—Set bare-root plants 4 to 6 feet apart in rows spaced about 10 feet apart. Blueberries can double as ornamentals and be worked into shrub borders or planted as hedges.

Adaptation—Most highbush blueberries have chilling requirements of over 800 hours and are hardy to -20F (-29C). They grow best in areas with cold winters and mild summers. Rabbit-eye blueberries have only slight chilling requirements but are only hardy to about 0F (-18C). They are more tolerant to warm summers and are widely grown in the Southeastern United States.

Pollination—Rabbit-eye blueberries are self-unfruitful. Some highbush blueberries are self-fruitful, but usually benefit by cross-pollination. To ensure adequate pollination plant at least three different varieties.

Pruning—Pruning is relatively simple. Thin plants to keep the center open and remove criss-crossing branches, especially near the base. Remove branches that are over 4 years old. If fruit is small, shorten branches that have abundant flower buds.

Varieties—There are many blueberry

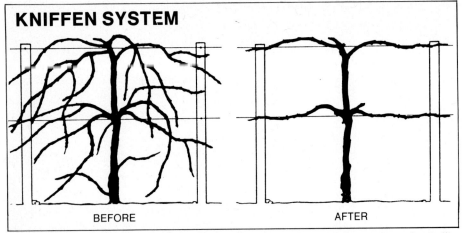

KNIFFEN SYSTEM

BEFORE

AFTER

Kniffen system is popular method of training American grape varieties on two-wire trellis. Each year, old fruited canes are removed and young, vigorous growth, which will produce fruit the following year, is cut back to six to ten buds and tied to trellis wires (left). From base of old fruiting cane, select two or three strong canes and cut back to two to three buds each (right). Growth from these buds will supply next year's fruiting canes.

varieties. 'Berkeley', 'Bluecrop', 'Collins' and 'Herbert' are a few of many popular highbush blueberries. Low-chill highbush blueberry varieties include 'Sharpebule' (under 200 hours), 'Avonblue' (400 hours) and Flordablue (200-300 hours). Popular rabbit-eye blueberries include 'Bonita', 'Woodard Delight', 'Southland' and 'Tifblue'.

Harvesting—Blueberries are ready to pick when they turn deep blue, usually in midsummer. You can pick every few days, but because ripe blueberries will last on the vine for 8 to 10 days, you can do one picking, if desired.

GRAPES

There are four types of grapes commonly grown in North America: *American, European, French hybrids* and *muscadines*. Each type has different fruit characteristics and climate adaptation. American grapes bear strong-flavored fruit with tough skins that separate easily from the flesh. Fruit color ranges from greenish yellow to red to purplish red. American grapes can be eaten fresh or used to make jelly or juice. European grapes are more delicately flavored and have thin skins. They come in white or red varieties and are used to make some of the world's finest wines. Many are also excellent table grapes.

Hybrid grapes share qualities of each parent—European and American. They make excellent wine and have greatly expanded wine-grape growing into areas where European

grapes cannot be grown. Muscadine grapes are a strong-flavored, slip-skinned fruit that come in white, red or purple varieties.

Planting—Grapes are usually planted bare root. Set American, European and hybrid grapes 8 to 10 feet apart in rows spaced 10 to 12 feet apart. Muscadine grapes should be spaced 12 to 15 feet apart in rows 18 to 20 feet apart.

Adaptation—Each type of grape has different climate requirements. American grapes are primarily grown in areas with cold winters and mild summers. They are hardy to 0F (-18C) and usually require a growing season of at least 160 days to ripen their fruit. Chilling requirements vary from 400 to 1200 hours but disease problems exclude them from the Southeast. European grapes require a long, hot, dry growing season to ripen their crop. They have chilling requirements of at least 800 hours and are only hardy to 10F (-12C). European grapes are most popular in the dry-summer areas of the western United States. Hybrid grapes are adapted to most of the same areas where American grapes can be grown. Muscadine grapes are best adapted to the hot, humid climates of the Southeast. They are hardy to 10F (-12C) and have only a slight chilling requirement. All grape varieties are susceptible to damage from late spring frosts.

Pollination—All grapes are self-fruitful, with the exception of some older varieties of muscadine grapes,

which bear only female flowers and must have a male variety nearby to set fruit.

Pruning European grapes (*Vitis vinifera)*, grown primarily for wine making, produce fruitful basal buds on the previous season's wood, while the basal buds of American species (*V. labrusca* and *V. rotundifolia*) are not fruitful. Thus, *V. vinifera* can be pruned back to two to four basal buds on each cane annually. The American natives need much longer canes.

When planting grapes, head cuttings to three buds and prune roots to about 6 inches long. Plant top buds level with the soil surface and mound loose soil over the plant to protect it from sunburn. Insert a stake to support plants as the canes grow.

During the first dormant season, remove all but one cane from each vine. Cut back single canes to two or three buds. During the second summer, save the strongest and best-positioned shoots and remove the rest. Tie shoots loosely to the stake and remove suckers from roots and old stems. Tied branches should be allowed to branch freely.

European grapes that are confined to small spaces are usually *head-pruned*. Cut off canes at the node above where the head forms, cutting through the node to destroy the bud. Tie canes securely to the top of supporting stakes and loosely about halfway to the ground.

Remove all laterals below the middle of the trunk, as well as any weak laterals in the upper half of the vine. Head two to four of the stronger laterals back to two or three basal buds each.

Mature head-trained vines are spur-pruned to restrict their size. Remove all but three to six of the strongest canes that developed in the third summer after planting vine. Head remaining cane to two, three or four basal buds—the greater the diameter of the vine, the more buds that can be left. Leave more of these fruiting spurs each year as vines mature.

A similar method of pruning that often makes European grapes more productive is *cane-pruning*. Head remaining canes to six to 18 buds depending on the vigor or diameter of the canes. Select canes to form a fan-shaped vine, rather than leaving canes spaced evenly around the trunk.

During the third dormant season,

select two canes and tie them to a support. Head two other canes at basal buds. Basal bud growth produces the next season's fruiting canes. Leave more canes as vines mature.

American grapes are usually pruned by the *Kniffen system,* which is similar to cane-pruning except that a second, higher pair of canes is selected and tied to a higher support. Keep the central leader straight by tying it to a cane. Head canes just above top vines. See drawing on the facing page.

Remove all but two canes at each level following the next season's growth. Head canes to four to eight buds and fasten canes to the support. As vines mature, remove all canes that have fruited and select vigorous new canes for the next year's fruit. Tie canes to the support and head the canes back to six to 10 buds, according to cane diameter and vigor. Choose two or three strong canes from the base of the old fruiting canes (arms) near the trunk and head each to two or three buds. Their growth produces the next season's fruiting cane.

A variation of head-pruning is *cordon-training,* in which two permanent laterals stretch in opposite directions along a support such as a wire, fence or wall. Select two strong laterals, one on the main shoot, at a point 8 to 10 inches below the support to serve as the cordon arms. Pinch back all other laterals and the main shoot, then fasten the arms to the support at least 1 foot back from their growing tips.

Varieties—There are many varieties of each type of grape. Choosing the right varieties for your area is important. Consult with your local nurseryman or university extension agent to find out which varieties do best where you live.

Harvesting—The best way to tell if grapes are ripe is to taste a few once they have reached full color. Harvest clusters with pruning shears or a sharp knife.

RASPBERRIES

Raspberries are closely related to blackberries but differ in that their fruit separates easily from its core, while blackberries are picked core and all. Raspberries also have a narrower range of adaptation, being best adapted to areas with cool summers and mild winters. Raspberries are available in varieties that produce red, yellow,

'Brandywine' is a good purple raspberry—mature berries are slightly darker than immature ones shown here.

purple or black fruit.

Planting—Raspberries are usually planted bare root. Plant red- and yellow-fruited varieties 30 to 36 inches apart in 6-inch-deep trenches spaced 6 to 10 feet apart. Plants will spread to form a solid row. Black and purple raspberry plants do not spread. Plant in individual holes 2 to 3 feet apart in rows spaced 6 to 8 feet apart. Cut back all raspberry plants to 5 to 6 inches above the ground after planting.

Adaptation—Raspberries are hardy to between -20F and -30F (-29C and -34C) and have a chilling requirement of 200 hours or more. They are best adapted to areas with cool, moist summers such as the Pacific Northwest and parts of the Midwest and Northeast. Recently developed low-chill varieties include 'San Diego', 'Oregon No. 1030' and 'Dorman'.

Pollination—All raspberries are self-fruitful.

Pruning—The easiest way to grow raspberries is to train them between a four-wire trellis with two parallel wires, spaced about 2 feet apart at a height of 3-1/2 feet, and two more

parallel wires at a height of 2 feet. Pruning involves removing canes that have fruited and selecting the most vigorous 1-year-old canes to train between the parallel wires of the trellis, for fruiting the following year.

Varieties—There are many raspberry varieties. They vary in fruit color, ripening period and climate adaptation. Most varieties bear one large crop sometime near midsummer. Everbearing varieties bear two major crops—one in spring and then another in fall. Popular red raspberry varieties for the Midwest and Northeast include 'Boyne', 'Latham' and 'Newburgh'. In the Northwest 'Puyallup', 'Sumner', 'Meeker' and 'Willamette' are popular varieties. 'September' and 'Heritage' are widely grown everbearing raspberries. 'Amber' and 'Fallgold' are popular yellow raspberries. 'Brandywine' is a good purple raspberry. 'Allen', 'Black Hawk' and 'Cumberland' are a few of many black raspberries.

Harvesting—Raspberries are ripe when a gentle pull separates them from their core. Pick every few days during the harvest period.

Bird netting protects backyard strawberry patch. Loose mulch keeps weeds down.

STRAWBERRIES

Strawberries are one of the least demanding and most adaptable fruit you can grow. One variety or another can be grown almost anywhere in North America. Their low, clumping habit allows them to fit in the smallest available spot, making strawberries perfect for containers. When given room, they will spread and form an attractive mat or ground cover.

There are two types of strawberries: *spring-bearing strawberries* and *everbearing strawberries.* Spring-bearing strawberries bear one large crop in spring. Everbearing varieties produce fruit over the entire growing season, although it doesn't amount to a lot of fruit at any one time.

Strawberries spread by *runners,* small vinelike arms that produce another plant at their tip. Often referred to as *babies,* these small plants will root and grow wherever they settle. The original plant that produced the runner is called the *mother plant.* If strawberry plants are left to send out runners at will, they will eventually create a dense mat of plants, often called a *strawberry patch.* However, strawberry plants sometimes produce runners at the expense of fruit. So by cutting off runners whenever they occur, you may get more or larger fruit per plant. These factors will influence how you plant strawberries.

Planting—Start with plants certified to be disease free. This will ensure that they are not contaminated with hard-to-detect viruses, which can be a problem if you start with babies from your neighbor's patch. Plants are usually sold bare root. They are planted in fall in mild-winter areas, spring in cold-winter areas. In some areas of the Southeast, strawberries are grown as annuals, planted in midsummer for a spring crop.

There are basically two planting schemes to follow. The first is called the *matted row,* in which plants are placed 18 to 24 inches apart in rows spaced 48 inches apart. Runners are allowed to fill in at will until rows are about 2 feet wide and solid with strawberry plants. Each year, thin out older plants and allow new babies to become established. If you don't thin, plants will loose productivity. The *hedgerow* system of planting strawberries produces the biggest fruit. Plants are grown 12 inches apart on 6-inch-high soil ridges spaced 24 to 30 inches apart. All runners are cut off as soon as they are noticed. A variation of this method is called the *selective hedgerow,* in which plants are set 24 inches apart in rows spaced 48 inches apart. Each plant is allowed to set two evenly spaced runners; all others are removed.

The hedgerow and selective hedgerow methods make it easier to use a mulch to keep berries clean and provide winter protection. Planting depth is important—not so shallow that roots are subject to drying, and not so deep that the crown is covered. To establish strong plants, remove all blossoms and runners the first growing season. Most experts also recommend replanting after the third or fourth season.

Adaptation—Varieties have been developed for almost every region of the United States and Canada. Mulching is important in cold-winter climates. In areas where late spring frosts are common, plant everbearing varieties. If frost destroys the first blossoms, everbearing strawberries will continue blooming and produce fruit. Spring-bearers may not bloom again once their flowers are destroyed.

Pollination—All strawberries are self-fruitful.

Pruning—Strawberries do not require any pruning other than to remove runners, if necessary. Replace old plants every 3 or 4 years.

Varieties—A number of varieties are available. Local adaptation is often important. Consult your local nurseryman or university extension agent to find out which varieties are best adapted to your area.

Harvesting—Pick strawberries when they reach full color. You'll have to pick every few days in spring. Leave stems attached if you plan to store the fruit in the refrigerator.

NUTS

ALMONDS

The narrow range of adaptation of almonds eliminates them from most gardens in the United States. However, if you like a challenge, select your planting spot carefully and provide protection from spring frosts, or plant a dwarf variety in a container and move it to a protected spot in spring.

Important Numbers—Almonds are medium-size trees that are easily maintained below 25 feet in height with an equal spread. They are commonly spaced 25 to 30 feet apart in orchard conditions. A few dwarf varieties can be maintained below 10 feet in height. Most almond trees will begin bearing at 3 to 4 years of age.

Adaptation—Although almonds are fairly hardy and have a relatively low chilling requirement, their early-blooming characteristics and need for long, dry summers generally limit successful nut production to warm-summer areas of California.

Pollination—With a few exceptions, all almonds are self-unfruitful and require another variety nearby to provide pollen.

Pruning—Once a sturdy, vase-shaped framework is established, little pruning is necessary.

Varieties—'Nonpareil', 'Jordanola', 'Ne Plus Ultra' and 'Hall's Hardy' are popular varieties. 'All-In-One' and 'Legrand' are self-fruitful varieties. 'Garden Prince' is a self-fruitful dwarf variety.

Harvesting—Almonds should be harvested when the hulls split open and are partially dry. Shake the tree or knock the nuts off with a stick. Remove the hulls and sun-dry for at least 2 days. When the kernels rattle in the shell the nuts are ready for storage. Stored in a cool, dry, well-ventilated place, almonds will keep up to 6 months.

Filberts are ripe when husk dries out and nuts fall to the ground. To avoid deterioration, gather nuts frequently.

FILBERTS (HAZELNUTS)

There are several species of filberts, or hazelnuts as they are often called, that can be grown in North America as ornamentals. The European filbert is the only one grown extensively for edible nuts. It is adapted primarily to the Pacific Northwest and parts of California. But some hybrid filberts—crosses between native American species and the European filbert—do produce acceptable nuts and extend filbert growing into the Midwest and Northeast.

Important Numbers—Filberts are shrubby plants that are usually maintained under 20 feet tall. Space plants 18 to 20 feet apart. Most filberts will begin bearing at 4 years of age.

Adaptation—European filberts have high chilling requirements—at least 800 hours—which excludes them from most southern climates. In addition, they flower in late winter or early spring, making them susceptible to spring frost damage. These facts, and susceptibility to a fungal blight in the East, limits their culture primarily to portions of the Pacific Northwest and California. Hybrid filberts have disease resistance and hardiness that extend their range into to parts of the Midwest and Northeast.

Pollination—Most filberts are self-unfruitful and require another variety nearby to provide pollen.

Pruning—Little pruning is necessary if they are allowed to grow in their natural shrublike form.

Varieties—'Barcelona', 'Du Chilly', 'Royal', 'Daviana' and 'Hall's Giant' are common European filbert varieties. 'Bixby', 'Buchanan', 'Potomac' and 'Reed' are common hybrid filberts.

Harvesting—Filberts are harvested when they fall to the ground. Gather nuts as often as possible to avoid deterioration. Dry in the sun and store in a cool place.

PECANS

Pecans are borne on large, beautiful trees with bright green, compound leaves that turn bright yellow before dropping in fall. They are grown as shade trees in many areas where the climate prevents the production of edible nuts.

Important Numbers—Pecans require a lot of space. At maturity, some can reach over 80 feet high and about half as wide. They should be planted no closer than 40 to 50 feet apart. Most trees will begin bearing at 4 years of age.

Adaptation—Pecans require long, warm summers of at least 200 frost-free days to produce an edible nut. The deep South and the Southwest desert are ideal climates, but pecans can also be grown in warmer areas of central and northern California and in parts of the upper South. There is little known about the chilling requirements of pecans, but trees have been known to provide good crops with as low as 100 hours. Trees are hardy to about 0F (-18C). Pecan trees are susceptible to zinc deficiency. Affected trees respond well to foliar applications of chelated zinc.

Pollination—Solitary pecan trees will produce a crop, but for maximum production, plant two varieties for cross-pollination.

Pruning—Once an initial sturdy framework is established, pecans require little pruning.

Varieties—'Choctaw', 'Cheyenne' and 'Mohawk' are widely adapted varieties. 'Western Schley' is popular in the West.

Harvesting—Pecans are knocked from the tree with poles or long sticks. They are ready to harvest when the hulls begin to split and the shells are well filled with meat.

WALNUTS

There are two types of walnuts commonly grown in the United States: the *English or Persian walnut* and the *Eastern black walnut*. Both are large, stately trees that can double as lawn or shade trees. The widely grown English walnut is the type found in supermarkets and known for its thin shell and large, sweet meat. The Eastern black walnut has a harder shell but is an equally delicious nut. In fact, many people consider it more flavorful than English walnuts. A close relative of the walnuts, the butternut, is a similarly beautiful tree, grown in many cold-winter climates.

Important Numbers—All walnuts are borne on large trees that need a lot of room to grow. English walnuts can grow over 60 feet high with an equal spread. The Eastern black walnut can grow over 100 feet high with about half the spread. Neither should be planted closer than 50 feet apart. Grafted varieties of either type will begin bearing at about 5 years of age.

Adaptation—Choosing the right variety is one of the most important factors when growing English walnuts. In many areas, early-blooming varieties are subject to frost damage and severe disease or insect problems. Most have chilling requirements of between 500 and 1000 hours, but low-chill varieties, such as 'Placentia', are available. However, severe disease problems prevent success in most areas of the Southeast. English walnuts are hardy to at least -35F (-37C).

The Eastern black walnut is widely adapted and can be grown over most of the United States and Canada. It has a relatively low chilling requirement and is hardy to at least -20F (-29C).

Pollination—Most walnuts will produce larger crops if a different variety that blooms at the same time is planted nearby. However, many gardeners harvest sufficient crops with only one tree.

Pruning—Head nursery trees at planting time to four or five buds and tie leader to a 6-foot-tall stake. Pinch back all shoots that compete with the central leader.

At the end of the first growing season, head the leader about three buds above the stake and remove all side limbs. Break off buds on short stems to encourage strong scaffold limbs from secondary buds below. If the leader failed to grow enough, head it back to last season's growth. Continue training and staking the leader through the second summer.

During the second dormant season, select four to six wide-angled crotched scaffold limbs about 5 to 7 feet above ground, avoiding those that are horizontal. Remove lateral branches below the lowest scaffold limb and cut lower branches on the trunk to short stubs.

For newer varieties that bear laterally, prune and head scaffolds each dormant season.

Most young bearing trees do not need pruning. However, some new, heavy-bearing varieties stop growing or break apart if shoots aren't headed 25% to 50% each year. All mature trees benefit from thinning to let light into the canopy. You'll probably need to call in tree or landscape service to prune large trees.

Varieties—The best advice on variety selection is to consult your local nurseryman or university extension agent. Some of the popular varieties of English walnuts grown in the western United States include 'Payne', 'Franquette', 'Placentia' and 'Spurgeon'. 'Hansen' and 'Adams' are popular in the eastern United States. 'Thomas' is a widely planted variety of black walnut.

Harvesting—Walnuts are ready to harvest when the hulls split and the nuts begin to fall from the tree. When a few start to fall, knock the rest off with a pole or long stick, being careful not to break branches. Remove the hulls and wash the nuts with water to remove tannins, which will stain the shells. Dry in the sun as you do almonds. Walnuts will keep many months if stored in a cool, dry place.

Immature English walnuts have bright green hulls. Walnuts are ready to harvest when hulls split open and nuts begin to fall to ground. If hulls of some ripe nuts are not easily removed, soak nuts in water overnight, then use pocketknife to remove hull.

English walnut makes a beautiful shade tree.

HERBS

Herbs are an important part of gardening antiquity. People have been growing them for centuries. Most herbs are deeply entrenched in religious, mystical, medicinal and historical legend and fact. Today, growing herbs blends modern practices with ancient tradition.

Above all, herbs are useful. They enhance the flavor of food and can also be used to make fragrant candles, sachets, potpourris, perfumes, soaps, cosmetics, dyes, dried bouquets, teas and much more.

Herbs are also versatile in the garden. Besides traditional herb beds where many types of herbs are grouped together, most herbs are ornamental enough to double as landscape plants. Rosemary is commonly seen as a ground cover, as are various forms of mint and thyme. Chives and parsley are distinctive accents in flower gardens and perennial borders. Many herbs make ideal container plants. Try matching plant habits with a particular style of container, or blend your favorite kitchen herbs in

one container. Make a hanging basket of spaghetti herbs—oregano and basil—or a combination box of several colorful varieties of thyme or mint. There are hundreds of possibilities.

Many herbs can be grown indoors as well as outdoors. A bright, sunny kitchen window filled with kitchen herbs is attractive and practical. If a sunny window isn't available, try herbs indoors under artificial light. Fluorescent light systems developed for plants are widely available, and they are simple enough to install yourself.

HOW TO GROW HERBS

As a group, herbs represent almost every type of plant imaginable. Some are tender annuals or perennials, others are hardy perennials, shrubs or bulbs. This means each herb has its own growing requirements. However, there is one requirement most herbs have in common. Aromatic oils in the leaves of herbs, which give them their characteristic flavor, are usually strongest when plants are not overstimulat-

ed by excess nitrogen. Fertilize just enough to keep plants looking healthy. In cold-winter climates, most herbs should be covered with a protective mulch to prevent winter damage. Grow tender herbs as annuals or plant them in containers and move plants indoors in winter. Many herb growers in cold climates dig up their plants each winter and store them in a basement or cold frame.

STORING HERBS

Some herbs are most flavorful when used fresh, others are best after they have been allowed to dry in a cool, dry place. Whatever the case, you'll want to have a year-round supply in the kitchen.

A common method of drying herbs is to pick sprigs, branches or entire plants, tie them together and hang them upside down in a relatively cool, dry place, such as a pantry or basement. Avoid drying herbs in direct sunlight. For drying small-leaved plants, flowers or chopped herbs, make a drying screen from

Left: Formal herb garden lends Old World touch to landscape.

Above: Herb vinegars make attractive, useful gifts. It's easy—place fresh herbs in fancy jars or bottles, pour in ordinary white vinegar and store in a cool, dark place for several months.

Puerto Rican basil is popular type of sweet basil, excellent in spaghetti sauces.

Chives are often interplanted with flowering plants in beds or borders.

ordinary window-screen material and attach it to a wood frame. Dried herbs are stored in airtight containers.

Freezing fresh herbs is done much like storing other foods in the freezer. The herbs are washed, patted dry, then stored in an airtight plastic freezer bag. The following descriptions of common herbs include suggestions for storing them.

POPULAR HERBS

Growing herbs can quickly change from a fancy to an obsession. On the following pages we describe the most common and useful kitchen herbs. But this is just the tip of the iceberg. To fully appreciate the wonderful world of herbs, read *Herbs, How to Select, Grow and Enjoy* by Norma Jean Lathrop, published by HPBooks.

Basil—If you decide to grow just one cooking herb, it should probably be basil *(Ocimum basilicum)*. Many cooks consider fresh basil essential and it is relatively easy to grow. Basil is an annual which can either be started from seed or from transplants, commonly available in nurseries. Plant as early in spring as possible because as

soon as weather warms and days get longer, basil will begin to produce flowers at the expense of foliage. You can keep flowers pinched to favor foliage but your best harvest of leaves will be in cooler months of spring. In cold climates, start seeds indoors 6 to 8 weeks before the last frost. Plants will be ready to go outside early.

There are a number of different types of basil. Most will reach 12 to 18 inches in height and grow about as wide. If you want enough for drying or freezing, plant at least six plants. However, basil is most flavorful when used fresh. Pick leaves as you need them, or else cut the plants back completely three or four times over the growing season. Basil grows best in full sun.

Besides common sweet basil, you may also want to try lettuce-leaf basil *(0. basilicum crispum)* which has large, crinkled leaves. Purple basil *(0. basilicum 'Dark Opal')* has reddish-purple leaves. Both are attractive complements to sweet basil. Basil is a must for Italian cooking. It is a main ingredient in *pesto* sauce, and really shows off in tomato sauce. Basil is also excel-

lent with fresh vegetables and in salads.

Basil is best used fresh, but also can be dried or frozen for future use. To dry or freeze, pick whole branches just before the plant flowers. Wash, remove dead or discolored leaves and hang upside down in paper bag to dry. Store dried leaves in cool, dry place.

Chives—Members of the onion family, chives *(Allium schoenoprasum)* are attractive, grasslike, perennials that are favorites in flower gardens and containers indoors or out. Used in cooking and as a garnish, their leaves add a mild onionlike flavor. Chives form small clumps of foliage that reach about 12 inches high. In early summer they bear small round pinkish flowers, held nicely above the foliage.

In early spring, start chives from seed or increase plants by dividing clumps. Transplants are also available at nurseries. Grow in full sun or partial shade. Divide clumps every 3 or 4 years to keep them growing vigorously. To collect seeds, pick flowers after they have dried.

Chinese or garlic chives *(Allium tuberosum)* are similar to common

Garlic is harvested when tops die down in summer. It can be used fresh or dried for storage.

Peppermint is small-leaved, grows about 12" high. It has cooling menthol aroma.

chives but they have mild garlic flavor. They are also a little taller and have a flattened leaf.

Try using a small container of chives as a centerpiece on the kitchen or garden table. They can be an attractive, easy-to-reach herb for baked potatoes.

Chives are eaten fresh in salads or as a garnish, or can be dried or frozen for use in cooking. To freeze, chop chives into small pieces and store in freezer bag. To dry, place chopped or whole chives on drying screen, then store in cool, dry place.

Garlic—Everyone has a favorite piece of folklore concerning this popular member of the lily family. Whether it's to ward off vampires or give soldiers strength, garlic *(Allium sativum)* is also one the world's favorite cooking herbs. It has an unmistakably rich flavor that complements a wide variety of foods, and it's relatively easy to grow.

Garlic is a perennial herb planted in early spring or fall. Space individual cloves, pointed side up, 2 inches deep and at least 3 inches apart. Give full sun. Plants prefer a loose soil rich in organic matter and slightly on the sandy side. Water regularly and keep the soil free of weeds.

Harvest garlic when the tops die down in summer. Braid leaves of plants together and hang to dry. Because garlic dries slowly, the clusters of cloves last for many weeks and can be stored like onions. However, garlic is most flavorful just after harvest. It can also be peeled and stored in olive oil.

Mints—The mints are a greatly varied group of plants that have been grown for centuries for the aromatic oils contained in their foliage. The leaves are used for teas, perfumes, medicinal purposes and in a wide range of recipes from salads to soups. Each mint has its own distinctive flavor, aroma and plant habit.

Apple mint *(Mentha suaveolens)* is an erect plant reaching 24 to 30 inches high with green leaves clothed in grayish wool. Leaves have a fruity apple scent.

Orange bergamot mint *(M. piperita)* grows 12 to 24 inches high and has citrus-scented, green leaves with red edges.

Corsican mint *(M. requienii)* is a ground-hugging plant that grows only 1 to 2 inches high. It has tiny green leaves with a peppermint flavor and makes a highly attractive small-scale ground cover.

Pennyroyal *(M. pulegium),* also low growing and spreading plant, may reach 6 to 12 inches high. Shiny green leaves have a strong mint flavor.

Peppermint *(M. piperita)* is an erect plant reaching about 12 inches high. Light green leaves have a cooling menthol aroma.

Spearmint *(M. spicata),* also erect, may reach 36 inches high. Crinkly, bright green leaves borne on red stems have a distinctive minty aroma.

Choose a planting spot carefully. Mints spread rapidly by underground stems, and if not controlled can quickly overtake an entire bed. You may want to grow mints in containers, which greatly reduces their maintenance by restricting root growth. Otherwise, be prepared to cut back plants often.

Most mints will grow just about anywhere, but do best with partial shade and lots of water. Many people grow mint under outdoor water faucets next to the house.

Most mints are hardy to at least 10F (-12C). Plants will easily survive winter in a cool, well-lighted spot indoors. Most mints are easily grown from rooted cuttings or root divisions.

Mints can be harvested any time. Use them fresh in salads, for cooking

Marjoram (Origanum marjorana) is closely related to oregano. They have similar flavor.

Curled parsley makes attractive low border. Often interplanted with flowers or vegetables.

and garnish. They can also be dried for a variety of uses. Hang upside down in bunches, crush dried leaves and store like you would other herbs.

Oregano and Marjoram—Oregano *(Origanum vulgare)* and marjoram *(Origanum majorana)* are closely related members of the mint family. The two are often confused because of their similarity and because many herbs either look or taste like them. Both are indispensable in cuisines from Italy to Mexico.

Common marjoram is an upright shrub which will reach about 2 feet in height. It has reddish stems and fuzzy leaves. The flavor of marjoram is a little sweeter and milder than oregano. Plants are tender and will need to be protected or brought indoors in cold-winter areas.

Common oregano is a little taller than marjoram, sometimes reaching 3 feet high. It is a hardy perennial. Both marjoram and oregano are available in a number of interesting varieties. Creeping golden marjoram and Crete dittany *(0. dictamnus)* are two worthy low-growing cousins.

Grow oregano or marjoram in full sun from seed or transplants. Flavor will be at its peak just before flowering, which is usually in late spring or summer. Oregano leaves can be used fresh, but are considered more flavorful when dried. Small-leaved kinds are best dried on a drying screen. Sweet marjoram does not freeze as well as oregano.

Parsley—The finely cut, frilly leaves of parsley *(Petroselinum crispum)* make it as distinctive in the garden as it is in fine foods. Its compact, mounding habit makes parsley an excellent ornamental plant for flower beds, small containers and hanging baskets. It can be grown indoors or out.

Parsley is a biennial, producing foliage the first year and flowers the second, but it is usually treated as an annual because the leaves lose their peppery flavor as the flowers appear. Seeds are difficult to germinate so parsley is best started from transplants in spring. Plants will tolerate light frosts—in mild-winter climates parsley can be planted in fall and harvested throughout winter. Parsley grows best in partial shade with ample moisture.

Many varieties of parsley are available. Some have extra-curly or dark green foliage. Others have a compact growing habit. Chinese parsley or cilantro *(Coriandrum sativum)* is a similar, but unrelated plant, and the two are sometimes confused. Its leaves are not as finely cut and curled as those of true parsley. The seeds of cilantro are known as the herb coriander.

You can harvest parsley leaves individually if you are careful not to damage the inner growing point. Leaves are best preserved by freezing, although their flavor is most pleasing when used fresh. Parsley can also be dried for use in soups, stews and sauces.

Rosemary—A member of the mint family, rosemary *(Rosmarinus officinalis)* is famous for the sweet, piney aroma of its leaves and the distinctive and delicious flavor it imparts to food. It is also widely grown as an evergreen ornamental shrub. Its narrow, needle-like leaves are dark green above and silvery gray beneath. Small white or blue flowers are borne in winter or early spring.

Many varieties of rosemary are available, but there are basically two plant forms—spreading and erect. Spreading types, such as 'Lockwood de Forest' and 'Prostratus', make beautiful ground covers about 18 inches high. They will also trail over the edge of walls and containers. Erect types, of which there are many, may grow as high as 4 feet.

Rosemary is an evergreen, ornamental shrub with many landscape uses. Here it trails over low wall next to steps.

Golden sage has beautiful variegated leaves.

'Narrowleaf English' common thyme is one of more than 400 species of this herb. Plant at left is typical nursery size, one at right after 6 weeks' growth.

Once established, rosemary is drought tolerant and hardy to 0F (-18C). In areas with sub-zero temperatures, plant in a protected location, or plant in containers and bring indoors during winter. Seeds are difficult to germinate, but plants are easily started as cuttings and are widely available in nurseries as transplants. Grow rosemary in full sun and hold back on water once plants are established.

Rosemary leaves can be used fresh, or can be dried or frozen for storage. Leaves are most flavorful just before the plant flowers. Hang branches upside down to dry, remove dried leaves and store in a cool, dry place.

Sage—The aromatic sages *(Salvia)* are known for their great variety of foliage form and color and for the distinctive flavor they add to foods of all types. There are many species and varieties.

Garden sage *(S. officinalis)* is the most common and frequently grown sage. It is a hardy perennial that grows 24 to 30 inches high. Leaves are grayish green. Violet flowers are borne on large spikes in early summer. Some of the varieties of garden sage add striking color to flower borders or as backgrounds. 'Aurea' has a compact habit and yellow variegated foliage. 'Purpurea' has purplish-red variegated leaves. 'Tricolor' has variegated leaves of white, purplish red and pink. Pineapple sage *(S. elegans)* is well known for its strong pineapple aroma. It is more tender than garden sage and will be damaged if temperatures drop below 20F (-7C). Leaves are light green.

Sages prefer full sun and dry conditions. They can be grown from seeds or cuttings, or bought as nursery transplants. Trim plants often to keep them compact. Leaves can be used fresh, dried or frozen.

Thyme—The variety of form, foliage and fragrance of the *Thymus* species present numerous opportunities for gardeners and cooks. Common thyme *(T. vulgaris)* grows 6 to 8 inches high. The small leaves, borne on erect stems, provide a familiar flavor cooks like to use. Lemon thyme *(T. citriodorus)* bears bright green to yellow-green foliage that has a rich, lemony scent.

'Argenteus' has silver variegated leaves. 'Aureus' has green-and-yellow variegated leaves. Both form a compact, spreading plant about 6 inches high that drapes nicely over the edge of a container.

Two low-growing forms of thyme are 3- to 6-inch Mother-of-Thyme *(T. praecox arcticus)* and 2- to 3-inch woolly thyme *(T. pseudolanuginosus)*. Both form dense, ground-hugging mats and make excellent small-scale ground covers or container plants. Planted between stepping stones, they release their pungent aroma when stepped on. There are many other low-growing varieties.

Thyme can be started from seed, but seedlings grow slowly. Plants can easily be grown from cuttings or divisions, and transplants are available at most nurseries.

Grow thyme in full sun. Provide protection in cold-winter climates. Use leaves fresh, dried or frozen.

GARDENER'S GUIDE

COMMON/BOTANICAL NAME CROSS-REFERENCE

The following list includes a large selection of common garden and landscape plants.

Common Name	Botanical Name
A	
African boxwood	*Myrsine africana*
African corn lily	*Ixia maculata*
African daisy	*Arctotis, Gazania, Osteospermum*
African iris	*Dietes vegeta*
African sumac	*Rhus*
African violet	*Saintpaulia*
Alder	*Alnus*
Almond	*Prunus dulcis* var. *dulcis*
Althaea	*Hibiscus syriacus*
American arborvitae	*Thuja occidentalis*
Amur maple	*Acer ginnala*
Anise	*Pimpinella anisum*
Apple	*Malus*
Apricot	*Prunus armeniaca*
Arborvitae	*Thuja*
Artichoke	*Cynara scolymus*
Ash	*Fraxinus*
Asparagus	*Asparagus officinalis*
Australian fuchsia	*Correa*
Australian tree fern	*Alsophila australis*
Australian willow	*Geijera*
Autumn crocus	*Colchicum*
Avocado	*Persea americana*
Azalea	*Rhododendron*
B	
Baboon flower	*Babiana*
Baby's breath	*Gypsophila*
Baby's tears	*Soleirolia soleirolii*
Bachelor's button	*Centaurea cyanus*
Bald cypress	*Taxodium distichum*
Bamboo	*Bambusa, Sasa,* others
Bamboo palm	*Chamaedorea erumpens*
Banana	*Musa*
Banana tree	*Ensete*
Banyan tree	*Ficus benghalensis*
Barberry	*Berberis*
Basket-of-gold	*Aurinia saxatilis*
Basil	*Ocimum*
Bean	*Phaseolus*
Bearberry	*Arctostaphylos uva-ursi*
Bear's breech	*Acanthus*
Beautybush	*Kolkwitzia amabilis*
Bee balm	*Monarda didyma*
Beech	*Fagus*
Belladonna lily	*Amaryllis belladonna*
Bellflower	*Campanula*
Bentgrass	*Agrostis*
Birch	*Betula*
Bird-of-paradise	*Strelitzia*
Bird's-eye bush	*Ochna*
Bird's-nest fern	*Asplenium nidus*
Bittersweet	*Celastrus*
Blackberry	*Rubus*
Black-eyed Susan	*Rudbeckia hirta*
Black-eyed Susan vine	*Thunbergia alata*
Black gum	*Nyssa sylvatica*
Bleeding-heart	*Dicentra*
Blueberry	*Vaccinium*
Blue hibiscus	*Alyogyne huegelii*
Boston ivy	*Parthenocissus tricuspidata*
Bottlebrush	*Callistemon*
Bottle tree	*Brachychiton*
Boxwood	*Buxus*
Brake fern	*Pteris*
Bramble	*Rubus*
Breath-of-heaven	*Diosma ericoides*
Bridal-wreath	*Francoa ramosa, Spiraea*
Brisbane box	*Tristania conferta*
Broccoli	*Brassica oleracea*
Broom	*Cytisus, Genista, Spartium*
Brush cherry	*Syzygium paniculatum*
Buckthorn	*Rhamnus*
Bunya-bunya	*Araucaria bidwillii*
Bush anemone	*Carpenteria californica*
Buttercup	*Ranunculus*
Buttercup shrub	*Potentilla*
Butterfly bush	*Buddleia*
C	
Cabbage	*Brassica oleracea*
Cabbage palm	*Sabal palmetto*
California buckeye	*Aesculus californica*
California fan palm	*Washingtonia filifera*
California fuchsia	*Zauschneria*
California lilac	*Ceanothus*
California poppy	*Eschscholzia californica*
Calla lily	*Zantedeschia*
Camphor tree	*Cinnamomum*
Candytuft	*Iberis*
Cantaloupe	*Cucumis melo*
Cape honeysuckle	*Tecomaria capensis*
Cape primrose	*Streptocarpus*
Carambola	*Averrhoa carambola*
Carob tree	*Ceratonia*
Carolina jasmine	*Gelsemium*
Carpet bugle	*Ajuga reptans*
Carrot wood	*Cupaniopsis*
Cast-iron plant	*Aspidistra elatior*
Cat's-claw	*Macfadyena unguis-cati*
Cedar	*Cedrus, Cryptomeria*
Celery	*Apium graveolens dulce*
Chamomile	*Chamaemelum nobile, Matricaria*
Chaste tree	*Vitex Agnus-castus*
Cherimoya	*Annona cherimola*
Cherry-of-the Rio-Grande	*Eugenia aggregata*
Chervil	*Anthriscus*
Chestnut	*Castanea*
Chilean jasmine	*Mandevilla laxa*
Chilean guava	*Ugni molinae*
Chilean wine palm	*Jubaea chilensis*
Chinese gooseberry	*Actinidia chinensis*
Chinese ground orchid	*Bletilla striata*
Chinese lantern	*Abutilon hybridum*
Chinese plumbago	*Ceratostigma willmottianum*
Chinese tallow tree	*Sapium sebiferum*
Cilantro (coriander)	*Coriandrum sativum*
Cineraria	*Senecio hybridus*
Cinquefoil	*Potentilla*
Clover	*Trifolium*
Coast redwood	*Sequoia sempervirens*
Columbine	*Aquilegia*
Comfrey	*Symphytum officinale*
Confederate jasmine	*Trachelospermum*
Confederate rose	*Hibiscus mutabilis*
Coralbells	*Heuchera sanguinea*
Coral tree	*Erythrina*
Coral vine	*Antigonon leptopus*
Corn	*Zea mays*
Cottonwood	*Populus*
Coyote brush	*Baccharis pilularis*
Crabapple	*Malus*
Cranesbill	*Geranium*
Crape myrtle	*Lagerstroemia indica*
Crocus	*Crocus*
Cup-and-saucer vine	*Cobaea scandens*

Common Name	Botanical Name
Currant	Ribes
Cypress	Chamaecyparis, Cupressocyparis, Cupressus

D

Common Name	Botanical Name
Daffodil	Narcissus
Daisy	Arctosis, Chrysanthemum, Dyssodia, Gerbera, Felicia, Venidium
Daisybush	Olearia
Date palm	Phoenix dactylifera
Dawn redwood	Metasequoia glyptostroboides
Daylily	Hemerocallis
Dogwood	Cornus
Douglas fir	Pseudotsuga menziesii
Dracaena palm	Cordyline australis
Dragon tree	Dracaena draco
Dusty-miller	Senecio cineraria
Dwarf karo	Pittosporum crassifolium 'Compactum'
Dwarf periwinkle	Vinca minor

E

Common Name	Botanical Name
Easter-lily vine	Beaumontia grandiflora
Eggplant	Solanum melongena var. esculentum
Elderberry	Sambucus
Elephant-foot tree	Beaucarnea recurvata
Elm	Ulmus
Empress tree	Paulownia tomentosa
English fern	Polystichum setiferum
English laurel	Prunus laurocerasus
European fan palm	Chamaerops humilis
Evening primrose	Oenothera biennis
Evergreen pear	Pyrus kawakami

F

Common Name	Botanical Name
False cypress	Chamaecyparis
False holly	Osmanthus heterophyllus
Fennel	Foeniculum vulgare
Ferns	Alsophila, Angiopteris, Asplenium, Cyrtomium, Dicksonia, Dryopteris, Microlepia, Nephrolepis, Polystichum, Pteris, Rumohra
Fernleaf yarrow	Achillea filipendulina
Fescue	Festuca
Fig, edible	Ficus carica
Filbert	Corylus
Fir	Abies
Firethorn	Pyracantha
Fishtail palm	Caryota
Flame bottle tree	Brachychiton acerifolius
Flannel bush	Fremontodendron
Fleur-de-lis	Iris germanica
Floss flower	Ageratum houstonianum
Floss silk tree	Chorisia speciosa
Flowering maple	Abutilon hybridum
Flowering quince	Chaenomeles
Forget-me-not	Myosotis
Fortnight lily	Dietes vegeta
Foxglove	Digitalis
Franklin tree	Franklinia
Fringe tree	Chionanthus
Fuchsia	Fuchsia

G

Common Name	Botanical Name
Garlic	Allium sativum
Gasplant	Dictamnus albus
Geraldton wax flower	Chamelaucium uncinatum
Geranium, hardy	Geranium
Geranium, tender	Pelargonium
Germander	Teucrium
Giant sequoia	Sequoiadendron giganteum
Gill-over-the-ground	Glecoma hederacea
Gillyflower	Matthiola incana
Ginger	Zingiber officinale
Gloxinia	Sinningia speciosa

Common Name	Botanical Name
Gold dust plant	Aucuba japonica
Golden bells	Forsythia
Goldenchain tree	Laburnum anagyroides
Golden larch	Pseudolarix
Golden-rain tree	Koelreuteria
Golden shrub daisy	Euryops
Golden wattle	Acacia
Gooseberry	Ribes
Gooseberry vine	Actinida chinensis
Gourd	Cucurbita
Goutweed	Aegopodium
Granadilla	Passiflora quadrangularis
Grape	Vitis
Grape hyacinth	Muscari
Grape ivy	Cissus rhombifolia
Grapefruit	Citrus paradisi
Grecian pattern plant	Acanthus
Guadalupe palm	Brahea edulis
Guava	Psidium
Guava, pineapple	Feijoa
Guinea gold vine	Hibbertia
Gum tree	Eucalyptus

H

Common Name	Botanical Name
Hackberry	Celtis
Hawthorn	Crataegus
Hazel, Japanese witch	Hamamelis japonica
Hazelnut	Corylus
Heath	Erica
Heavenly bamboo	Nandina domestica
Heliotrope	Heliotropium
Hemlock	Tsuga
Hibiscus, tropical	Hibiscus rosa-sinensis
Himalayan sweet box	Sarcococca
Holly	Ilex
Holly fern	Cyrtomium falcatum
Honey locust	Gleditsia
Honeysuckle	Lonicera
Hop, common	Humulus lupulus
Hopseed bush	Dodonaea
Hornbeam	Carpinus
Horsechestnut	Aesculus
Horsetail	Equisetum
Huckleberry	Vaccinium

I

Common Name	Botanical Name
Ice plant	Carpobrotus, Cephalophyllum, Delosperma, Drosanthemum, Lampranthus, Malephora, Mesembryanthemum, Oscularia
Incense cedar	Calocedrus decurrens
Indian bean tree	Catalpa
Indian hawthorn	Raphiolepis
Indigo	Indigofera
Ironbark	Eucalyptus
Ivy	Hedera

J

Common Name	Botanical Name
Jade plant	Crassula
Japanese aralia	Fatsia
Japanese cedar	Cryptomeria
Japanese maple	Acer palmatum
Japanese plum	Eriobotrya
Japanese sword fern	Dryopteris erythrosora
Jasmine (Jessamine)	Cestrum, Gelsemium, Jasminum, Mandevilla, Murraya, Stephanotis, Trachelospermum
Jojoba	Simmondsia chinensis
Joe-Pye weed	Eupatorium
Jonquil	Narcissus jonquilla
Jujube	Ziziphus
Juniper	Juniperus
Jupiter's beard	Centranthus ruber

K

Common Name	Botanical Name
Kaffirboom	Erythrina
Kaffir lily	Clivia

Common Name	Botanical Name
King palm	*Archontophoenix*
Kinnikinick	*Arctostaphylos uva-ursi*
Kiwi	*Actinidia*
Kumquat	*Citrus fortunella*

L

Common Name	Botanical Name
Lace fern	*Microlepia, Polystichum*
Lady fern	*Athyrium filix-femina*
Lady palm	*Rhapis*
Larch	*Larix*
Laurel	*Cordia, Ficus, Laurus*
Lavender	*Lavandula*
Lavender cotton	*Santolina*
Leatherleaf fern	*Rumohra*
Leek	*Allium*
Lemon	*Citrus*
Lemon balm	*Melissa officinalis*
Lemongrass	*Cymbopogon citratus*
Lemon verbena	*Aloysia triphylla*
Lettuce	*Lactuca*
Lilac	*Buddleia, Ceanothus, Syringa*
Lily-of-the-Nile	*Agapanthus*
Lily-of-the-valley	*Convallaria*
Lily-of-the-valley shrub	*Pieris*
Lily turf	*Liriope, Ophiopogon*
Lime	*Citrus aurantifolia*
Linden	*Tilia*
Locust	*Robinia*
Loquat	*Eriobotrya japonica*
Love-in-a-mist	*Nigella damascena*
Love-lies-bleeding	*Amaranthus caudatus*
Lychee	*Litchi chinensis*

M

Common Name	Botanical Name
Macadamia	*Macadamia*
Madagascar jasmine	*Stephanotis*
Madagascar periwinkle	*Catharanthus roseus*
Maidenhair fern	*Adiantum*
Maidenhair tree	*Ginkgo*
Manzanita	*Arctostaphylos*
Maple	*Acer*
Marguerite	*Chrysanthemum frutescens*
Marguerite, blue	*Felicia*
Marigold	*Tagetes*
Marjoram	*Origanum majorana*
Matilija poppy	*Romneya coulteri*
Medlar	*Mespilus, Mimusops elengi*
Mesquite	*Prosopis*
Mexican cycad	*Dioon*
Mexican fan palm	*Washingtonia robusta*
Mexican orange	*Choisya ternata*
Mimosa	*Albizia*
Mint	*Mentha*
Mock orange	*Philadelphus, Pittosporum*
Mole plant	*Euphorbia*
Mondo grass	*Ophiopogon*
Montbretia	*Crocosmia*
Morning glory	*Ipomoea*
Mother fern	*Asplenium bulbiferum*
Mother-in-law's tongue	*Sansevieria trifasciata*
Mountain ash	*Sorbus*
Mulberry	*Morus*
Mum	*Chrysanthemum morifolium*
Mustard	*Brassica*
Myrtle	*Myrtus, Vinca*

N

Common Name	Botanical Name
Naked lady	*Amaryllis belladonna*
Nasturtium	*Tropaeolum*
Natal plum	*Carissa*
Night-blooming jasimine	*Cestrum nocturnum*
Norfolk Island pine	*Araucaria heterophylla*

O

Common Name	Botanical Name
Oak	*Quercus*
Oleander, common	*Nerium oleander*

Common Name	Botanical Name
Olive	*Olea europaea*
Onion	*Allium*
Orange, sweet	*Citrus sinensis*
Orange jasmine	*Murraya paniculata*
Orchid	*Cattleya, Cymbidium, Oncidium, Paphiopedilum, Phalaenopsis*
Orchid tree	*Bauhinia*
Oregano	*Origanum vulgare*
Oregon grape	*Mahonia*
Oriental arborvitae	*Platycladus orientalis*

P

Common Name	Botanical Name
Palm	*Archontophoenix, Arecastrum, Brahea, Caryota, Chamaedorea, Chamaerops, Cycas, Dioon, Phoenix, Rhapis, Sabal, Trachycarpus, Washingtonia*
Palo verde	*Cercidium floridum*
Pampas grass	*Cortaderia*
Pansy	*Viola wittrockiana*
Parlor palm	*Chamaedorea*
Passion flower, vine	*Passiflora*
Pea	*Pisum sativum*
Peach, nectarine	*Prunus persica*
Pear	*Pyrus communis*
Pecan	*Carya illinoinensis*
Peony	*Paeonia*
Pepper	*Capsicum, Piper*
Peppermint	*Mentha × piperita*
Pepper tree	*Schinus*
Piggy-back plant	*Tolmiea menziesii*
Pimpernel, scarlet	*Anagallis arvensis*
Pine	*Pinus*
Pineapple	*Ananus comosus*
Pinks	*Dianthus*
Pistachio	*Pistacia*
Plane tree	*Platanus*
Plum, prune	*Prunus*
Plumbago	*Ceratostigma*
Pomegranate	*Punica*
Poplar	*Populus*
Poppy	*Eschscholiza, Meconopsis, Papaver, Romneya*
Poppy-flowered anemone	*Anemone coronaria*
Powder puff	*Calliandra*
Princess flower	*Tibouchina urvilleana*
Privet	*Ligustrum*
Pumpkin	*Cucurbita*
Purpleblow maple	*Acer truncatum*
Pussy willow	*Salix discolor*

Q

Common Name	Botanical Name
Quaking aspen	*Populus tremuloides*
Queen palm	*Arecastrum romanzoffianum*
Queen's wreath	*Antigonon*
Quince	*Cydonia*
Quince, flowering	*Chaenomeles*

R

Common Name	Botanical Name
Rain lily	*Zephyranthes*
Raspberry	*Rubus idaeus*
Redbud	*Cercis*
Red-hot poker	*Kniphofia*
Red maple	*Acer rubrum*
Redwood	*Metasequoia, Sequoia, Sequoiadendron*
Rice paper plant	*Tetrapanax*
Rockcress	*Arabis*
Rockrose	*Cistus*
Rose	*Rosa*
Rose mallow	*Hibiscus moscheutos*
Rose-of-Sharon	*Hibiscus syriacus*
Rosemary, culinary	*Rosmarinus officinalis*
Rubber plant	*Ficus elastica*
Rupturewort	*Herniaria glabra*

Common Name	Botanical Name
S	
Sage	*Salvia*
Sagebrush	*Artemisia*
Sago palm	*Cycas*
Saltbush	*Atriplex*
Sand verbena	*Abronia*
Sapote	*Casimiroa*
Sassafras	*Sassafras albidum*
Satinwood	*Murraya paniculata*
Savory	*Satureja*
Scholar tree, Chinese	*Sophora japonica*
Scotch broom	*Cytisus*
Scotch heather	*Calluna vulgaris*
Scotch moss	*Sagina subulata*
Sea lavender	*Limonium*
Sego lily	*Calochortus nuttallii*
Serviceberry	*Amelanchier laevis*
Service tree	*Sorbus*
Shadbush	*Amelanchier laevis*
Shaddock	*Citrus maxima*
Shallot	*Allium cepa*
Shrimp plant	*Justicia brandegeana*
Siberian pea shrub	*Caragana arborescens*
Siberian wallflower	*Erysimum*
Silk oak	*Grevillea robusta*
Silk tree	*Albizia*
Silverberry	*Elaeagnus*
Silver dollar gum	*Eucalyptus polyanthemos*
Silver lace vine	*Polygonum*
Sloe	*Prunus*
Smoke tree	*Dalea spinosa*
Snail vine	*Vigna caracalla*
Snapdragon	*Antirrhinum majus*
Snowball, Chinese	*Viburnum macrocephalum*
Snow-in-summer	*Cerastium tomentosum*
Solomon's-seal	*Polygonatum*
Sorrel	*Rumex*
Sour gum	*Nyssa sylvatica*
Sourwood	*Oxydendrum arboreum*
South African honeysuckle	*Turraea obtusifolia*
Southernwood	*Artemisia abrotanum*
Spanish bayonet	*Yucca aloifolia*
Spanish broom	*Spartium*
Spearmint	*Mentha spicata*
Spicebush	*Lindera benzoin*
Spider lily	*Lycoris radiata*
Spruce	*Picea*
Squash	*Cucurbita*
Squirrel's foot fern	*Davallia trichomanoides*
St. Catherine's lace	*Eriogonum giganteum*
St. John's bread	*Ceratonia siliqua*
St. Johnswort	*Hypericum calycinum*
Star jasmine	*Trachelospermum jasminoides*
Star pine	*Araucaria heterophylla*
Stock	*Matthiola incana*
Stonecrop	*Sedum*
Strawberry	*Fragaria*
Strawberry tree	*Arbutus unedo*
Sugar maple	*Acer saccharum*
Sumac	*Rhus*
Summer lilac	*Buddleia davidii*
Sunflower	*Helianthus*
Sunrose	*Helianthemum*
Sweet alyssum	*Lobularia maritima*
Sweet bay	*Laurus nobilis*
Sweetbrier	*Rosa eglanteria*
Sweet broom	*Cytisus*
Sweet gum, American	*Liquidambar*
Sweet marjoram	*Origanum majorana*
Sweet olive	*Osmanthus fragrans*
Sweet pea	*Lathyrus odoratus*
Sweet potato	*Ipomoea batatas*
Sweet William	*Dianthus barbatus*
Sweet woodruff	*Galium odoratum*
Sword fern	*Nephrolepis*
Sycamore	*Platanus*
T	
Tangelo	*Citrus tangelo*
Tangerine	*Citrus reticulata*
Tarragon	*Artemisia dracunculus*
Taro	*Alocasia*
Tasmanian tree fern	*Dicksonia antarctica*
Tea	*Camellia sinensis*
Tea tree	*Leptospermum scoparium*
Texas ranger	*Leucophyllum frutescens*
Texas sage	*Salvia coccinea*
Thrift	*Armeria*
Ti plant	*Cordyline terminalis*
Tomato	*Lycopersicon lycopersicum*
Toyon	*Heteromeles arbutifolia*
Trailing African Daisy	*Osteospermum fruticosum*
Transvaal Daisy	*Gerbera jamesonii*
Tree tomato	*Cyphomandra betacea*
Tree-of-heaven	*Ailanthus altissima*
Trident maple	*Acer buergeranum*
Trumpet creeper	*Campsis radicans*
Trumpet tree	*Tabebuia*
Trumpet vine	*Anemopaegma, Campsis, Clytostoma, Disticus, Macfadyena, Pandorea, Pyrostegia*
Tulip	*Tulipa*
Tulip tree	*Liriodendron*
Tupelo	*Nyssa sylvatica*
Turnip	*Brassica rapa*
U	
Umbrella plant	*Schefflera*
V	
Vinca	*Vinca, Catharanthus*
Vine maple	*Acer circinatum*
Virginia creeper	*Parthenocissus*
W	
Wallflower	*Cheiranthus, Erysimum*
Walnut	*Juglans*
Water lily	*Nymphaea*
Wattle	*Acacia*
Wax flower	*Hoya*
Wax leaf privet	*Ligustrum japonicum*
Western red cedar	*Thuja plicata*
Wheat	*Triticum*
White clover	*Trifolium repens*
White sapote	*Casimiroa edulis*
Wild buckwheat	*Eriogonum*
Wild ginger	*Asarum, Costus*
Willow	*Salix*
Willow-leaved peppermint	*Eucalyptus*
Windflower	*Anemone*
Windmill palm	*Trachycarpus*
Wintergreen	*Gaultheria procumbens*
Woad	*Isatis*
Woodruff, sweet	*Galium odoratum*
Woodwaxen	*Genista tinctora*
Woolly yarrow	*Achillea tomentosa*
Y	
Yam	*Dioscorea*
Yarrow	*Achillea*
Yellow oleander	*Thevetia peruviana*
Yellow poplar	*Liriodendron tulipifera*
Yellowwood	*Cladrastis lutea*
Yesterday-today-and-tomorrow	*Brunfelsia*
Yew	*Taxus*

GUIDE TO SELECTING ORNAMENTAL PLANTS

On the following pages, you'll find lists and brief descriptions for many popular ornamental plants. Included in each category are plant lists grouped by use or function. Plants are organized by general use, habit and cultural requirements into the following main categories:

1. Flowering annuals, bulbs and perennials, pages 198-202.
2. Vines, pages 203.
3. Ground covers, pages 204-205.
4. Woody ornamental shrubs, pages 206-208.
5. Azaleas, camellias, rhododendrons, pages 209-212.
6. Roses, page 213.
7. Ornamental trees, pages 214-217.

Popular varieties of vegetables and of fruits, berries and nuts are discussed in their respective chapters—vegetables, pages 147-163 and fruits, berries and nuts, pages 165-185.

FLOWERING ANNUALS, BULBS AND PERENNIALS

The following flowering plants bring splashes of color to the garden throughout the growing season. All are used as foreground plants in beds and borders. Annuals are reseeded each year. Bulbs are either left in the ground or dug up and stored each winter. Perennials are more permanent, being left in place to bloom year after year.

ANNUALS

Botanical Name/ Common Name	Habit/Adaptation	Bloom	Remarks
Ageratum houstonianum Flossflower	5-10" mounds. Warm season. Full sun. Space 6-8".	Tight clusters of fuzzy soft blue, lavender or white flowers in summer.	Excellent edging. Avoid overhead watering.
Antirrhinum majus Snapdragon: See page 112.			
Begonia × semperflorens-cultorum Fibrous begonias	4-18" mounds. Warm season. Shade. Space 8-10".	Abundant clusters of small white, pink or red flowers.	One of the most popular annuals for shade. Succulent foliage is bright green, bronze or red (red-flowering varieties). Bronze can take more sun. Start with transplants.
Calendula officinalis Calendula	12-18" mounds. Cool season. Sun. Space 12".	Short stemmed, marigoldlike flowers in shades of yellow. and orange.	Reseeds itself invasively—pick spent blooms to avoid this.
Coleus × hybridus Coleus	6-18", erect. Warm season. Shade. Space 10-15".	Grown for brightly colored foliage. Flowers insignificant.	Available in almost every foliage color combination imaginable. Leaves round or deeply cut, smooth-edged or crinkly. Keep flowers picked to encourage dense branching.
Lobularia maritima Sweet alyssum	3-8", spreading. Cool season. Sun. Space 6-10".	Tiny flowers in tight clusters that cover plants. White, pink and purple.	Beautiful low edging. Drapes nicely over walls and edges of containers. Easily grown from seed. Reseeds readily. Good small-scale ground cover. Will bloom in heat if well watered.
Impatiens wallerana Impatiens	8-20" mounds. Warm season. Shade. Space 12-18".	Abundant 1-2 inch blooms in almost every shade but blue and yellow.	The most popular annual for shady gardens. Great in containers or hanging baskets. New Guinea impatiens have variegated foliage.
Lathyrus odoratus Sweet pea	9-30" bush or 6' climbing vine. Cool season. Sun. Space 4-10".	Wonderfully fragrant, pea-shaped flowers in every shade but yellow.	Available in climbing or bush types. Climbing varieties need support. Easy from seed.
Lobelia erinus Edging lobelia	4-6", upright or spreading. Warm season. Sun. Space 4 to 8".	Small deep blue, light blue, pink or white flowers produced in abundance.	Available in clumping or trailing forms. Ideal for edgings or hanging baskets.
Myosotis sylvatica Forget-me-not	6-12" mounds. Cool season. Partial shade. Space 12".	Tiny clusters of soft blue flowers.	Excellent woodland annual. Beautiful when combined with spring-flowering bulbs. Self sows.
Petunia × hybrida Petunia: See page 112.			

ANNUALS, CONT'D.

Botanical Name/ Common Name	Habit/Adaptation	Bloom	Remarks
Portulaca grandiflora Rose moss	2-10", spreading. Warm season. Sun. Space 8-18".	Single or double, 2 to 3 inch flowers in every shade but true blue.	Sprawling, succulent plants best suited to hot, dry spots. Good small-scale ground cover.
Primula malacoides Fairy primrose	10-12" mounds. Cool season. Shade. Space 8-12".	Tall spikes of tiny flowers in pastel shades of white, pink and lavender.	Flower spikes arise from compact rosettes of hairy, green leaves. Delicate appearance.
Salvia splendens	12-36" mounds. Warm season. Sun. Space 8-12".	Tall spikes of fiery red flowers. White, pink and purple sometimes available.	Many varieties—vary by height. Make a brilliant-colored flower bed.
Tagetes species Marigolds: See page 111			
Viola species Pansies and violas	6-12" mounds. Cool season. Sun or light shade. Space 6-10".	Brightly colored, facelike, 1-5 inch flowers in every shade. Single and bicolors.	Closely related plants. Pansies generally have fewer but much large flowers. Violas have many small flowers. Great in containers.
Zinnia hybrids: See page 113			

BULBS

Botanical Name/ Common Name	Habit/Adaptation	Bloom	Remarks
Agapanthus orientalis Lily-of-the-Nile	Zones 9-10. 12-48" mounds. Sun to light shade.	Huge clusters of blue or white funnel-shaped flowers held high above foliage in summer.	Cover rhizomes with 1/2 inch of soil. Straplike, deep green foliage of species reaches 48 inches. 'Peter Pan' grows to 12 inches.
Amaryllis belladona Naked lady	Zones 7-10. 2-3' mounds. Sun to light shade.	Large, funnel-shaped flowers atop tall stems in late summer. Usually pink but also white and red. Fragrant.	Plant bulbs 2 inches deep. Flowers appear after foliage has died down. Can be grown in colder climates if planted deeper.
Begonia × tuberhybrida Tuberous begonia	Zones 9-10. 12-18", erect or pendulous. Shade.	Large or small, single or double summer flowers in every shade except blue.	Barely cover tubers with soil. A favorite shade flower. Must be stored dry during winter. Can be grown anywhere in containers. Varieties differ in flower size, color and form.
Caladium × hortulanum Fancy-leaved caladium	Zone 10. 12-24", erect. Shade.	Grown for large, colorful, heart-shaped leaves, variegated in shades of white, bronze, red and green.	Cover tubers with 1 inch of soil. Can be grown anywhere if kept dry and warm in winter. Excellent container plant.
Crocus species Crocus	Zones 3-10. 3-5", erect. Sun to light shade.	Small, cup-shaped flowers in shades of white, yellow and purple. Bloom late winter or early spring.	Plant corms 2-3 inches deep. Perform best in cold winter climates. Best displayed in groups. Good in small containers.
Dahlia hybrids	Zones 9-10. 10-60", erect. Sun.	Great variety of flower forms from button size to huge, 10-inch mammoths. All colors except blue. Single and bicolors. Bloom from midsummer to fall.	Plant tubers 2-3 inches deep. Versatile plants come in all sizes. In cold climates, dig and store tubers over winter. Low-growing varieties often treated as annuals.
Gladiolus × hortulanus Gladiolus	Zones 9-10. 30-60", erect. Sun.	Long spikes of trumpet-shaped flowers in all shades except true blue. Single or double. Spring and summer.	Plant corms 2 inches deep. Stake flowers to prevent breaking. Excellent cut flower.
Hyacinthus orientalis Hyacinth	Zones 7-10. 8-15", erect. Sun to light shade.	Upright spikes completely surrounded with fragrant, bell-shaped flowers in shades of white, pink, yellow and purple. Midspring.	Plant bulbs 5 to 6 inches deep. Excellent in containers or planted in large groups.
Iris species and hybrids	Zones 3-10. 3-48", erect. Sun to light shade.	Many types of artistically formed flowers in shades of white, yellow, orange and purple. Single and multicolors. Spring into summer.	Plant bulb types 2 to 3 inches deep, rhizomes just under the soil. One type or another can be grown anywhere. Beautiful cut flowers.

BULBS, CONT'D.

Botanical Name/ Common Name	Habit/Adaptation	Bloom	Remarks
Lilium species Lily	Zones 4-10. 1-7', erect. Partial shade.	Many variations of the standard six-petalled, trumpet-shaped flower. All shades except blue. Bloom from from late spring to fall depending on type.	Plant bulbs 4 inches deep. Amazing diversity of flower form among many species available. Most bear flowers atop erect stems with grass-like leaves. Tall varieties may need staking.
Muscari species Grape hyacinths	Zones 3-10. 6-12" mounds. Full sun to partial shade.	Short stalks of blue or purple, fragrant flowers that look like grape clusters. Early spring.	Plant bulbs 3 inches deep. Several species of similar plants. Increase fairly rapidly.
Narcissus species Daffodils, Narcissus	Zones 5-10. 5-20", erect. Full sun to partial shade.	Single or clusters of white, yellow and orange blooms atop a single stem. Many bicolors. Spring.	Plant twice the depth of the bulb. An all-time favorite family of bulbs. Many species and varieties, some fragrant. Daffodils generally have one flower per stem. Narcissus are borne in clusters. Beautiful in containers or as cut flowers.
Ranunculus asiaticus Ranunculus	Zones 8-10. 12-18", erect. Sun.	Multipetaled, ball-shaped flowers held singly atop tall stems. Shades of white, yellow, orange and red. Bloom over a long period in spring.	Plant tuberous roots 1 to 2 inches deep. Often sold as spring bedding plants. Makes an exceptionally colorful spring flower bed.
Tulipa species Tulips	Zones 5-9. 8-30", erect. Sun	Basically urn-shaped flowers atop straight stems although there is great variation. Single and multicolors including all shades but blue. Spring.	Plant bulbs 4 to 6 inches deep. A huge family of bulbs that could fill a book. Require winter chill. Store in refrigerator for 6 weeks in mild climates. Great in containers.

PERENNIALS

Botanical Name/ Common Name	Habit/Adaptation	Bloom	Remarks
Achillea species Yarrow	Zones 3-10. 10-60", upright or spreading. Sun.	Flat-topped clusters of white, yellow and sometimes red flowers over a long period from late spring into summer.	Several species of valuable hot-weather plants with attractive, deeply divided, feathery leaves. Long-lived, drought-tolerant. Propagated by seed or division. Low-growing types make good ground covers.
Aquilegia × hybrida Columbine	Zones 3-9. 18-36", upright clumps. Partial shade.	Dramatic, cup-shaped blooms with back-sweeping, often spurred sepals. Many bicolor shades. Spring.	Soft-textured, lacy green foliage. Needs soil high in organic matter. Plant from seed or transplants.
Aster hybrids	Zones 4-10. 6-72", upright clumps. Sun.	Colorful, daisylike blooms in shades of purple, pink, red, and white, all with a bright yellow center. Midsummer to frost.	Many varieties available, ranging from low and spreading to tall and upright. Tall varieties may need staking. Grow from transplants or divisions. Divide established plants every few years. Avoid splashing water on foliage.
Bellis perennis English daisy	Zones 3-10. 4-6" clumps. Partial shade.	Small, buttonlike blooms in shades of pink, red, white and purple. Yellow centers. Early spring.	Often grown as a spring annual. Will bloom during winter in mild climates. Grow from seed or transplants. Divide every 2 or 3 years.
Bergenia cordifolia Heartleaf bergenia	Zones 2-10. 12-18", spreading. Sun to shade.	Clusters of white, pink or lavender, bell-shaped flowers held above foliage on strong stems. Mid spring.	Forms an attractive ground cover of large, round, glossy green leaves. Plant from transplants or divisions.
Campanula species Bellflower	Zones 3-8. 6-36" mounds. Partial shade.	Bell- or star-shaped flowers in shades white, pink, blue and purple. Primarily in summer.	Large family of versatile flowering plants with attractive foliage. Vary in height and time of bloom. Can take full sun in cool climates. Start from seed or transplants. Divide plants every 3 or 4 years.
Centaurea cineraria Dusty Miller	Zones 5-10. 12-18" mounds. Full sun.	Small, purple flowers in summer but grown primarily for silvery foliage.	Lacy, whitish gray leaves provide a striking contrast to green-foliaged plants. Best in dry soils. Start from seed or transplants.
Chrysanthemum species	Zones 4-10. 5-60" mounds or erect. Sun.	A great variety of flower shapes, sizes, colors, and time of bloom. From small buttons to white daisies to dramatic mums.	A large family of plants with enough variation to landscape a whole yard. Vary in adaptation. Includes marguerites (*C. frutescens*), Shasta daisy (*C. × superbum*) and common garden mums (*C. × morifolium*). Great cut flowers. Start with transplants.

PERENNIALS, CONT'D.

Botanical Name/ Common Name	Habit/Adaptation	Bloom	Remarks
Coreopsis grandiflora Coreopsis	Zones 5-10. 24-36" mounds. Sun.	Bright yellow, single or double, daisylike flowers held one to a long stem in spring and summer.	Easy-to-grow plants with a long season of color. Pick spent blooms often. Good cut flower. Reseeds readily. Start with seeds or transplants.
Delphinium elatum Delphinium	Zones 2-10. 24-48" mounds. Partial shade.	Stunning spikes (up to 8 feet high) of five petaled, often spurred flowers in shades of white, pink, purple and blue. Summer.	Harder to grow than most. Best in areas with cool, moist summers. Tall varieties may need staking but make excellent backgrounds. Start with transplants. Sometimes treated as an annual.
Dianthus species Sweet William Carnations, pinks	Zones 3-9. 3-24" mounds or erect. Sun to partial shade	Colorful and often sweetly scented Most useful garden types are dainty, flattened, often frilly flowers, in all shades but blue. Many bicolors.	Large family of useful plants. Best garden types are low-growing sweet Williams (clusters of small flowers) and pinks (single, often frilly flowers). Start with transplants.
Digitalis purpurea Foxglove	Zones 4-10. 24-60", erect. Sun to partial shade.	Tall spikes lined with rows of tubular white, pink, purple, or yellow flowers with purple-spotted throats. Early summer.	Actually biennials, producing flowers the second year. Beautiful background plants. Start with seed or transplants.
Felicia amelloides Blue marguerite	Zones 8-10. 12-36" mounds. Sun.	Beautiful blue, daisylike flowers with yellow centers. Spring to summer.	Can be used as an annual in cold-winter climates. One of the prettiest blue flowers. Pick spent flowers. Cut back in fall. Start with transplants.
Gaillardia × grandiflora Blanketflower	Zones 3-10. 12-36" mounds. Sun.	Striking daisylike blooms with multi-colored bands of red, maroon, bronze and yellow. Early summer to fall.	One of the best plants for a long season of color. Takes heat and drought. Plant seed, transplants or divisions.
Gerbera jamesonii Gerbera daisy	Zones 8-10. 12-18" mounds. Sun to partial shade.	Huge, perfectly formed daisylike in pastel shades of red, orange and pink. Long stems. Summer to fall.	Used as an annual in cold-winter climates. Wonderful cut flower. Attractive dark green foliage. Plant transplants. Divide every 3 to 4 years.
Hemerocallis hybrids Daylily	Zones 3-10. 12-48" mounds. Sun to partial shade.	Trumpetlike flowers in yellow, orange, pink or red shades. Some bicolors. Held on tall stalks. Late spring to fall.	One of the most carefree and rewarding flowering plants you can grow. Handsome, dark green, grasslike leaves. Plant transplants or divisions. Divide when crowded.
Iberis sempervirens Edging candytuft	Zones 4-10. 4-12" mounds. Sun to partial shade.	Small but abundant clusters of intense white flowers in early spring.	One of the brightest whites. Ideal companion for spring bulbs. Small, dark green leaves. Plant from seeds or transplants.
Paeonia hybrids Peony	Zones 5-9. 24-48", shrubby. mound. Sun to light shade.	Incredible 4- to 8-inch blossoms in many shades of white, pink, red and purple. Some with yellow centers or bicolored. Fragrant. Spring.	Real eye-catchers in the spring garden. Glossy green leaves with deep lobes turn red before dropping in fall. Plant transplants or divisions.
Papaver species Poppies	Zones 3-10. 12-36" mounds. Sun.	Large, delicate, silky blooms on tall stems in many colors. Spring.	Two species, *P. nudicaule* and *P. orientale*, which are often grown as annuals. Both have attractive lobed foliage. Plant from seed or transplants.
Pelargonium species Pelargoniums (Geraniums)	Zones 9-10. 10-36" mounds or spreading. Sun to partial shade.	Beautiful, round clusters of white, pink, salmon, red and purple flowers in spring. Some bicolors.	Extremely useful and popular garden plants, grown as annuals in cold winter areas. Attractive, lobed foliage, often variegated and fragrant. Some forms trailing. Great in containers. Hardy geraniums (*Geranium* species) are different plants.
Phlox species Phlox	Zones 3-9. 6-48", spreading or erect. Sun to partial shade.	Colorful clusters of trumpet-shaped flowers with flared lobes. Many colors. Spring and summer.	Several species. Mostly low-growing forms, ideal for rock gardens or as edgings. Easy care once established. Plant by seed, transplants or division.
Salvia species Sage	Zones 4-10. 24-60", erect. Sun.	Tall spikes of small white, blue or purple flowers from summer to fall.	Many species of varying hardiness and and adaptation. Tender types often used as annuals. Long season of color, low maintenance. Plant from seed or transplants. Some species used as cooking herbs.
Verbena × hybrida Verbena	Zones 9-10. 6-12", spreading. Sun.	Round clusters of tiny flowers with small white eyes. Many colors. Summer to fall.	Blooms in summer. Well adapted to poor, dry soils. Used as an annual in cold climates. Good ground cover. Plant transplants.
Viola odorata Sweet violet	Zones 6-10. 5-8", spreading clumps. Shade.	Dainty white, blue, purple or pink flowers in spring. Delightfully fragrant.	A delicate gem for shady spots around the base of trees or shrubs. Attractive, deep green, heart-shaped foliage. Start from seed, transplants or divisions.

USES FOR PERENNIALS, ANNUALS AND BULBS

PERENNIALS FOR ALL SEASONS

Blooming Season
Sp=Spring
Su=Summer
A=Autumn
W=Winter

Common Name/Botanical Name	
Aster (Aster species and hybrids)	Su, A
Baby's breath (Gypsophila paniculata)	Su, A, W
Basket-of-gold (Aurinia saxatilis)	Sp, Su
Beard tongue (Penstemon species)	Sp, Su
Bear's breech (Acanthus mollis)	Sp, Su
Bergenia (Bergenia cordifolia)	Sp, W
Bishop's hat (Epimedium species)	Sp
Black-eyed Susan (Rudbeckia fulgida)	Su, A
Blanketflower (Gaillardia × grandiflora)	Su, A
Blazing star (Liatris spicata)	Su, A
Bleeding heart (Dicentra species)	Sp, Su, A
Blue plumbago (Ceratostigma plumbaginoides)	Su, A
Candytuft (Iberis sempervirens)	Sp, Su
Columbine (Aquilegia species)	Sp, Su
Coral bells (Heuchera sanguinea)	Sp, Su
Coreopsis (Coreopsis lanceolata)	Sp, Su, A
Cottage pinks (Dianthus plumarius)	Su, A
Christmas rose (Helleborus niger)	Sp, W
Daylily (Hemerocallis hybrids)	Sp, Su
Delphinium (Delphimium elatum)	Su, A
False spirea (Astilbe species and hybrids)	Su
Forget-me-not (Myosotis scorpioides)	Su
Foxglove (Digitalis species)	Sp, Su, A
Geranium (Pelargonium species)	Su, A
Goldenrod (Solidago hybrids)	A
Chrysanthemums (Chrysanthemum hybrids)	Su, A
Japanese anemone (Anemone hybrida)	A
Lupine (Lupinus species)	Sp, Su
Maltese cross (Lychnis chalcedonica)	Sp, Su
Oriental poppy (Papaver orientale)	Sp, Su
Peachleaf bellflower (Campanula persicifolia)	Sp, Su, A
Peony (Paeonia hybrids)	Sp
Phlox (Phlox paniculata)	Sp, Su
Plantain lily (Hosta species)	Su
Pincushion flower (Scabiosa caucasica)	Su, A
Primrose (Primula species)	Sp, Su, A
Purple coneflower (Echinacea purpurea)	Su
Red-hot poker (Kniphofia hybrids)	Sp, Su
Rose mallow (Hibiscus moscheutos)	Su, A
Salvia (Salvia x superba)	Su, A
Shasta daisy (Chrysanthemum × superbum)	Su, A
Speedwell (Veronica hybrids)	Sp
Stonecrop (Sedum species)	Su, A
Verbena (Verbena species)	A
Viola (Viola species)	Sp, Su
Wake robin (Trillium species)	Sp
Yarrow (Achillea species)	Su

ANNUALS FOR SHADE

Because most annuals prefer full sun, we've included a list of those that grow well in some degree of shade. Those most tolerant of shade are marked with an asterisk.

Baby blue-eyes (Nemophila menziesii)
Black-eyed Susan vine (Thunbergia alata)
Browallia (Browallia speciosa)
*Coleus (Coleus blumei)
Flowering tobacco (Nicotiana alata)
Forget-me-not (Myosotis sylvatica)
*Impatiens (Impatiens wallerana)
Lobelia (Lobelia erinus)
*Monkey flower (Mimulus hybridus)
Primrose (Primula species)
Scarlet sage (Salvia splendens)
Summer forget-me-nots (Anchusa capensis)
Viola (Viola cornuta)
*Wax begonia (Begonia semperflorens)
*Wishbone flower (Torenia fournieri)

BULBS FOR NATURALIZING

The following bulbs can be used for permanent beds or borders in many situations.

Allium (Allium species)
Apennine anemone (Anemone apennia)
Autumn crocus (Colchicum autumnale)
Belladonna lily (Amaryllis belladonna)
Bluebells (Scilla species)
Calla lily (Zantedeschia aethiopica)
Camass (Camassia species)
Checkered lily (Fritillaria meleagris)
Crocus (Crocus species)
Erythronium (Erythronium species)
Grass nut (Brodiaea laxa)
Greek anemone (A. blanda)
Glory-of-the-snow (Chionodoxa species)
Grape hyacinth (Muscari species)
Hardy cyclamen (Cyclamen species)
Miniature iris (Iris reticulata)
Snowdrops (Galanthus species)
Snowflakes (Leucojum species)
Narcissus (Narcissus species)
Winter aconite (Eranthis species)

BULBS FOR CONTAINERS

Amaryllis (Hippeastrum species)
Blood lily (Haemanthu katharinae)
Calla lily (Zantedeschia species)
Cyclamen (Cyclamen persicum)
Gloxinia (Sinningia speciosa)
Kaffir lily (Clivia miniata)
Lily-of-the-Nile (Agapanthus africanus)
Magic flowers (Achimenes species)
Oxalis (Oxalis species)
Scarborough lily (Vallota speciosa)
Tuberous begonia (Begonia tuberhybrida)

VINES

Botanical Name/ Common Name	Adaption	Habit	Remarks
Bougainvillea species Bougainvillea	Zones 9-10. Sun. Best in hot, dry climates.	Evergreen to partially deciduous. Vigorous, sprawling plant to over 30' with support. Many forms.	Spectacular bloom in all shades but blue. Blooms all year in mild winters. Available in many plant forms with a variety of uses. Some make good ground covers.
Clematis species Clematis	Zones 4-10. Sun. Adaptation varies.	Evergreen or deciduous. Twining vine with beautiful form. Needs support.	One of the classiest flowering vines. Beautiful, divided leaves. Attractive flowers in bright shades of white, pink, lavender and blue. Several species with a variety of flower forms, from large-petaled giants to small, bell-shaped flowers.
Euonymus fortunei Wintercreeper	Zones 4-9. Sun or partial shade. Widely adapted.	Evergreen. Climbs almost anything, holding on with rootlike holdfasts. Attractive, glossy green leaves form dense mat.	Extremely useful vine ideal for covering walls or as a ground cover. 'Colorata' turns purple in fall and winter. Variegated forms also available.
Ficus pumila Creeping fig	Zones 9-10. Partial shade.	Evergreen. Clings to anything, holding on with rootlike holdfasts. Forms a tight, hugging cover over walls. Small, deep green leaves.	Ideal for tight spaces. Can be difficult to remove once attached.
Hedera helix English ivy	Zones 5-10. Sun or shade. Widely adapted.	Evergreen. Vigorous vine that climbs on and over anything, attaching with small rootlets. Dark green, lobed leaves.	Good large scale ground cover. Many varieties with variegated or unusually shaped foliage. Most varieties are better behaved than the species, which can be invasive.
Jasminum polyanthum Chinese jasmine	Zones 8-10. Partial shade.	Evergreen. Climbs by twining. Handsome, deep green foliage.	Large clusters of wonderfully scented flowers in shades of white and pink in spring. Good fence cover.
Lonicera species Honeysuckle	Zones 4-10. Sun or shade.	Semideciduous. Rampant growing, twining vines with dark green leaves.	Several species of incredibly tough plants for large, open areas. Clusters of yellow-to-red tubular flowers, sometimes fragrant. Use carefully or prune heavily. Good ground cover for large, difficult spots.
Parthenocissus species Virginia creeper, Boston ivy	Zones 4-10. Sun or shade.	Deciduous. Fast-growing plants attaching with small adhesive discs. Pretty, deeply lobed leaves that turn bright colors in fall.	Two species of slightly different plants loved for the soft texture and bright fall color—fiery red and yellow—they add to walls. Good ground covers.
Rosa species Climbing rose: See page 140.			
Trachelospermum jasminoides Star jasmine	Zones 8-10. Sun or partial shade.	Evergreen. Well behaved, twining vine with shiny green foliage. Needs support.	One of the most valuable vines for mild climates. Intensely fragrant, white flowers cover plants in late spring to summer. Beautiful 1- to 2-foot ground cover.
Vitis species Grapes: See page 180.			
Wisteria sinensis Wisteria	Zones 5-9. Sun or partial shade.	Deciduous. Twining vine requiring strong support. Large, deeply divided leaves.	Loved for its intensely fragrant, white, pink or purple spring flowers, hanging in long, grapelike clusters. Great for covering a strong arbor or fence.

GROUND COVERS

Botanical Name/ Common Name	Adaptation	Habit/Spacing	Remarks
Aizoaceae (carpetweed) family Ice plant	Zones 8-10. Full sun. Heat and drought tolerant.	6-18" high. Spreading succulents. Space 12-18".	A large family of dense-growing ground covers. Grows on slopes and near the coast. Many have colorful flowers.
Ajuga reptans Carpet bugle	Zones 4-10. Light shade. Best in moist soil.	2-4" high. Herbaceous perennial Space 6-12".	Ground-hugging rosettes of shiny, bright green leaves topped with blue flower spikes in late spring and early summer. Varieties with silvery or pink and white variegated foliage also available.
Arctostaphylos uva-ursi Kinnikinick	Zones 2-8. Full sun or partial shade. Drought tolerant. Acid soil.	12" high. Evergreen shrub Space 36".	Shiny green leaves turn reddish in winter. White flowers and red berries not very showy. Great in poor, sandy soils.
Baccharis pilularis Coyote brush	Zones 8-10. Full sun. Drought tolerant.	1-2' high. Evergreen shrub. Space 30-36".	Valuable western native with bright green foliage. Useful on slopes or near the coast. Mow annually to keep compact.
Convallaria majalis Lily-of-the-Valley	Zones 3-9. Shade. Poor in hot, dry climates.	6-8" high. Herbaceous perennial. Space pots 12-18".	Forms a lush, deep green carpet in shady conditions. Dies to the ground in winter. Fragrant, white flowers in spring. Spreads by underground stems called *pips*. Space individual pips 6-8 inches apart.
Festuca glauca Blue fescue	Zones 5-10. Sun. Heat and drought tolerant.	4-10" high. Grasslike perennial. Space 6-12".	Soft, silver-blue mounds of grasslike leaves topped with small, feathery flowers in summer. Best as small-scale ground cover. Cut back often to keep full.
Fragaria chiloensis Wild strawberry	Zones 4-8. Full sun in cool areas. Partial shade in hot climates.	6-12" high. Herbaceous perennial. Space 6-12".	Forms a dense mat of dark green, lobed leaves. White flowers in spring followed by red, edible but tasteless, strawberries. Spreads rapidly by surface runners.
Gazania rigens Gazania	Zones 9-10. Full sun. Drought and heat tolerant.	6-8" high. Herbaceous perennial. Space 6-12".	Brilliant spring flowers in shades of yellow, orange and red. Silvery or gray-green foliage. Available in clumping or spreading varieties.
Hypericum calycinum Aaron's beard	Zones 5-10. Full sun to shade. Widely adapted.	12-18" high. Evergreen subshrub. Space 12-18".	Soft green leaves on erect stems. Bright yellow flowers all summer. Spreads rapidly by underground stems, Can become a pest in flower beds and lawns. Best in large areas.
Lantana montevidensis Trailing lantana	Zones 9-10. Full sun. Heat and drought tolerant.	12" high. Evergreen shrub. Space 24".	Spectacular flowering ground cover with sticky, green leaves. Blooms all summer in single or bicolor shades of white, yellow, orange, red and purple. Shear to keep compact.
Liriope species and *Ophiopogon* species Mondo grass, lily turf	Zones 5-10. Shade.	12-36" high. Grasslike perennials Space 6-18", depending on species.	Two similar shade-loving plants with grasslike leaves. Liriopes are slightly hardier and have showier flowers. Bloom in shades of white or purple during summer. All make a lush ground cover. Space taller species farther apart.
Osteospermum fruticosum African daisy	Zones 9-10. Full sun. Drought and heat tolerant.	6-12" high. Herbaceous perennial. Space 12-14".	One of the most beautiful flowering ground covers. Bright white or purple, daisylike blooms in spring and fall, some year-round. Lush green foliage. Mow annually for best bloom.
Pachysandra terminalis Japanese spurge	Zones 4-9. Partial shade.	6-10" high. Herbaceous perennial. Space 6-12".	Lush, dark green leaves arranged in whorls on erect stems. Creamy white flowers in summer. Good for large or small areas.
Rosmarinus officinalis Rosemary	Zones 7-10. Full sun or partial shade.	18-24" high. Evergreen shrub. Space 24-36".	Choose low-growing varieties such as 'Lockwood de Forest'. Small, needlelike, silvery green foliage. Light blue or white flowers in spring. Will drape over walls. Popular kitchen herb.
Vinca minor Periwinkle	Zones 5-10. Light shade. Moist soil.	4-6" high Herbaceous perennial. Space 6-12".	Forms an even mat of dark green leaves. Bright blue or white flowers in spring. Much more useful than its close cousin, *V. major,* which is very invasive and only useful in large areas.

GROUND COVERS FOR SPECIAL USES

Drought Resistant
Blue fescue (*Festuca ovina* 'glauca')
Broom (*Genista* and *Cytisus* species)
Capeweed (*Arcotheca calendula*)
Dwarf rosemary (*Rosmarinus officinalis* 'Prostratus')
Ice plant (several genera in *Aizoaceae* family.
Juniper (*Juniperus* species)
Lavender cotton (*Santolina chamaecyparissus*)
Perennial verbena (*Verbena peruviana*)
Rock rose (*Cistus* species)
Stonecrop (*Sedum* species)
Trailing African daisy (*Osteospermum fruticosum*)

Erosion Control on Slopes
Aaron's beard (*Hypericum calycinum*)
Bearberry (*Arctostaphylos uva-ursi*)
Carmel creeper (*Ceanothus griseus* 'Horizontalis')
Cotoneaster (*Cotoneaster* species, low growing)
Dwarf rosemary (*Rosmarinus officinalis* 'Prostratus')
Honeysuckle (*Lonicera* species)
Ice plant (Several genera in *Aizoaceae* family.)
Ivy (*Hedera* species)
Lantana (*Lantana montevidensis*)
Parrot's beak (*Lotus berthelotii*)
Periwinkle (*Vinca major* and *V. Minor*)
Pyracantha (*Pyracantha koidzumii* 'Santa Cruz')
Rose (*Rosa* species, low-growing)

Shade Tolerant
Baby's tears (*Soleirolia soleirolli*)
Dwarf periwinkle (*Vinca minor*)
English ivy (*Hedera helix*)
Five-finger fern (*Adiantum pedatum*)
Japanese painted fern (*Athyrium goeringianum*)
Japanese spurge (*Pachysandra terminalis*)
Lily-of-the-valley (*Convallaria majalis*)
Sweet sarcococca (*Sarcococca humilis*)
Sweet violet (*Viola odorata*)
Sweet woodruff (*Galium odoratum*)
Wood fern (*Dryopteris* species)
Wood sorrel (*Oxalis* species)

For Large Areas
Capeweed (*Arctotheca calendula*)
Cinquefoil (*Potentilla* species)
Dwarf coyote brush (*Baccharis pilularis* 'Twin Peaks')
Gazania (*Gazania* species)
Ivy (*Hedera* species)
Japanese spurge (*Pachysandra terminalis*)
Lippia (*Phyla nodiflora*)
Maiden pink (*Dianthus deltoides*)
Periwinkle (*Vinca major* and *V. minor*)
Star jasmine (*Trachelospermum jasminoides*)
Spreading juniper (*Juniperus* species)
Wild strawberry (*Fragaria chiloensis*)

Heavy Traffic Areas
Blue rug juniper (*Juniperus horizontalis* 'Blue Rug')
Bugleweed (*Ajuga* species)
Chamomile (*Chamaemelum nobile*)
Corsican sandwort (*Arenaria balearica*)
Creeping speedwell (*Veronica repens*)
Irish or Scotch moss (*Sagina subulata*)
Mock strawberry (*Duchesnea indica*)

Herbal Carpets
Catmint (*Nepeta mussinii*)
Chamomile (*Chamaemelum nobile*)
Corsican mint (*Mentha requienii*)
Dwarf germander (*Teucrium chamaedrys*)
Dwarf rosemary (*Rosmarinus officinalis* 'Prostratus')
English lavender (*Lavendula angustifolia*)
Lamb's-ears (*Stachys byzantina*)
Lavender cotton (*Santolina chamaecyparissus*)
Thyme (*Thymus* species)
Woolly yarrow (*Achillea tomentosa*)
Wormwood (*Artemisia* species

Low Maintenance
Aaron's beard (*Hypericum calycinum*)
Baby's tears (*Soleirolia soleirolli*)
Bearberry cotoneaster (*Cotoneaster dammeri*)
Bugleweed (*Ajuga reptans*)
Carmel creeper (*Ceanothus griseus* 'Horizontalis')
Chamomile (*Chamaemelum nobile*)
Common thrift (*Armeria maritima*)
Creeping lily turf (*Liriope spicata*)
Creeping mahonia (*Mahonia repens*)
Creeping speedwell (*Veronica repens*)
Dwarf rosemary (*Rosmarinus officinalis* 'Prostratus')
Evergreen candytuft (*Iberis sempervirens*)
Forget-me-not (*Myosotis scorpioides semperflorens*)
Green carpet natal plum (*Carissa macrocarpa* 'Green Carpet')
Ground morning glory (*Convolvulus mauritanicus*)
Ground pink (*Phlox subulata*)
Ivy (*Hedera* species)
Japanese spurge (*Pachysandra terminalis*)
Mock strawberry (*Duchesnea indica*)
Periwinkle (*Vinca major* and *V. minor*)
Scotch heather (*Calluna vulgaris*)
Stonecrop (*Sedum* species)
Star jasmine (*Trachelospermum jasminoides*)
Sun rose (*Helianthemum nummularium*)
Sweet woodruff (*Galium odoratum*)
Trailing African daisy (*Osteospermum fruticosum*)
Trailing gazania (*Gazania uniflora*)
Virginia creeper (*Parthenocissus quinquefolia*)
Wild strawberry (*Fragaria chiloensis*)
Woolly yarrow (*Achillea tomentosa*)
Yerba buena (*Micromeria chamissonis*)

ORNAMENTAL SHRUBS

The following list groups shrubs by height. A list of shrubs for specific uses appears on page 208.

LOW SHRUBS: 18" TO 3'

Botanical Name/ Common Name	Adaptation	Remarks
Azalea: See pages 209-211.		
Berberis thunbergii 'Atropurpurea Nana' Dwarf Red-leaf Barberry	Zones 4 to 9. Full sun. Drought tolerant. Good in hot climates.	Deciduous, fine textured foliage turns bright red. Good ground cover.
Buxus species Boxwood	Zones 5-10. Full sun to partial shade. Needs moisture.	Evergreen. Small-foliaged, compact plants. Ideal for low hedges. *B. microphylla koreana* is most hardy.
Cotoneaster species Cotoneaster	Zones 5-10. Full sun to partial shade. Tough plants.	Many species of deciduous and evergreen plants. *C. dammeri* and *C. horizontalis* are two low growers. Small, attractive foliage, white spring flowers and bright red berries in winter. Good ground covers.
Euonymus fortunei Euonymus	Zones 5-8. Full sun to partial shade. Heat tolerant.	Evergreen. Many varieties of glossy-foliaged, compact shrubs. Some with variegated leaves. Good accent, hedge or ground cover, depending on variety.
Ilex species Hollies	Zones 5-10. Full sun to partial shade. Best in acid soils.	Evergreen. *I. cornuta* and *I. crenata* varieties make best low shrubs. Shiny foliage, bright red berries. Make good hedges or container plants.
Juniperus species Junipers	Zones 2-10. Full sun. Tough and drought tolerant. Not good in wet climates.	Evergreen. Many species and varieties of versatile landscape plants. Scalelike foliage in many hues of green, yellow and blue. Many are excellent ground covers for hot, dry climates.
Nandina domestica 'Compacta' Dwarf heavenly bamboo	Zones 6-10. Full or partial shade.	Evergreen. Airy foliage, white spring flowers and red berries. Good low hedge.
Pittosporum tobira 'Wheeler's Dwarf' Wheeler's dwarf pittosporum	Zones 8-10. Full sun to partial shade.	Evergreen. Dense, light green, whorled foliage. Fragrant white flowers in spring. Excellent low hedge, container plant or accent.
Pyracantha species Firethorn	Zones 6-10. Full sun. Drought tolerant.	Evergreen. Several low-growing, compact varieties. Flat clusters of white flowers in spring followed by red or orange berries that last into winter. Good hedges, accents or ground covers, depending on variety.
Rhaphiolepis indica Indian hawthorn	Zones 8-10. Full sun. Drought tolerant.	Evergreen. Dwarf varieties have compact, leathery foliage. Pinkish white flowers in spring. Black berries in winter. Can be used as a ground cover.
Spiraea × bumalda 'Anthony Waterer' Dwarf pink bridal wreath	Zones 3-9. Full sun. Needs moisture.	Deciduous. Compact, small foliage. Rose-pink flowers in spring. Excellent hedge.

MEDIUM SHRUBS: 3' TO 6'

Botanical name/ Common name	Adaptation	Remarks
Abelia grandiflora Glossy abelia	Zones 6-10. Full sun or partial shade.	Evergreen in warm climates. Partially deciduous in cold areas. Glossy green foliage turns bronzy red in fall. Abundant whitish pink flowers during summer. Excellent hedge.
Berberis species Barberry	Zones 4-10. Full sun to partial shade. Drought tolerant. Good in hot climates.	Evergreen or deciduous. Many species with attractive foliage. Some turn bright colors in fall, others have berries. Good screens or hedges.
Chaenomeles species Flowering quince	Zones 5-9. Full sun to partial shade.	Deciduous. Glossy foliage on thorny branches Bright red, pink or white flowers on bare branches in early spring. Good hedge.
Euonymus species Euonymus	Zones 3-9. Full sun to partial shade. Heat tolerant.	Evergreen. Compact, shiny-foliaged plants, many with brightly colored variegation. Hardiness varies by species. Fine clipped hedge.
Fatsia japonica Japanese aralia	Zones 8-10. Partial to full shade. Needs moisture.	Evergreen. Bold, tropical foliage. Leaves up to 12 inches wide and deeply divided. White flowers in fall. Good accent.
Grevillea 'Noell' Noell grevillea	Zones 8-10. Full sun. Poor in wet soils. Drought tolerant.	Evergreen. Forms arching mounds of needlelike foliage. White flowers in spring.

MEDIUM SHRUBS: 3' TO 6', CONT'D.

Botanical name/ Common name	Adaptation	Remarks
Hebe species Hebe	Zones 9-10. Full sun to partial shade. Poor in hot climates.	Evergreen. Shiny, mound-shaped plants. White or purple flowers in summer; some fragrant. Neat hedges.
Hydrangea arborescens Hills-of-snow	Zones 5-9. Partial shade.	Deciduous. Mound-shaped plant with large, deep green leaves and huge clusters of white, pink or blue flowers in summer.
Ilex species Hollies	Zones 6-10. Full sun to partial shade. Best in acid soils.	Mostly evergreen. Many species. Shiny, often spined foliage. Bright colored berries. Versatile landscape plants.
Juniperus chinensis Chinese juniper	Zones 4-9. Full sun. Drought tolerant. Poor in wet-summer climates.	Evergreen. Many varieties differing in height and foliage color (shades of green, yellow and blue). Many can be used as tall ground covers.
Mahonia aquifolium Oregon grape	Zones 5-9. Partial shade. Best in cool-summer climates.	Evergreen. Distinctive shiny foliage—large, toothed and deeply divided—turn purple in cold climates. Yellow flower spikes in spring followed by deep blue berries.
Myrtus communis True myrtle	Zones 9-10. Full sun to partial shade. Tolerates heat.	Evergreen. Compact, small foliaged plant with fragrant white flowers and purplish fruit. Excellent hedge.
Nandina domestica Heavenly bamboo	Zones 6-10. Full sun to shade. Widely adapted.	Evergreen. Airy plant with oriental feel. Deeply divided, light green leaves are bronzy pink when new, red and purple in cold weather. White flowers in summer followed by bright red berries. Best as informal shrub.
Pittosporum tobira 'Variegata' Variegated mock orange	Zones 8-10. Full sun to partial shade.	Evergreen. Neat whorls of gray-green leaves edged white. Fragrant, creamy yellow flowers followed by capsules containing orange seeds. Good hedge or accent.
Potentilla fruticosa Shrubby cinquefoil	Zones 2-9. Full sun. Extremely cold-hardy and tough.	Deciduous. Grown for its toughness and long bloom of yellow flowers in summer.
Rhododendron: See page 212.		
Spiraea species Spirea	Zones 3-9. Full sun to partial shade. Needs moisture.	Deciduous. Many species of versatile plants. Neat foliage and bloom of white, pink or red flowers in late spring or early summer. Excellent hedges.
Viburnum species Viburnum	Zones 3-10. Full sun to partial shade. Widely adapted.	Evergreen and deciduous. Large family of plants with a variety of beautiful habits. Grown for its often fragrant spring and summer flowers, brightly colored fruit and stunning fall color.
Xylosma congestum Shiny xylosma	Zones 8-10. Full sun to light shade. Drought tolerant.	Evergreen. Shiny, light green foliage is tinged red when new. Excellent hedge.

LARGE SHRUBS 7' TO 15'

Botanical name/ Common name	Adaptation	Remarks
Aucuba japonica Japanese aucuba	Zones 7-10. Shade.	Evergreen. Large, glossy green leaves, usually with bright yellow spots.
Callistemon citrinus Lemon bottlebrush	Zones 8-10. Full sun. Drought tolerant.	Evergreen. Narrow, green leaves have copper tinge when young. Bright red, bottlebrushlike flowers bloom from spring through summer.
Camellia: See page 211.		
Caragana arborescens Siberian pea shrub	Zones 2-7. Full sun to partial shade. Very hardy.	Evergreen. Feathery, yellow-green foliage. Bright yellow flowers in late spring. Good informal hedge.
Dodonaea viscosa Hopbush	Zones 8-10. Full sun.	Evergreen. Willowy, olive-green foliage. Good for a fast-growing screen.
Elaeagnus pungens Silverberry	Zones 7-10. Full sun. Drought and heat tolerant.	Evergreen. Silver-speckled, grayish-green leaves have silvery undersides. Leaves sparkle in the sun, Inconspicuous but fragrant flowers followed by red berries.
Euonymus japonica Euonymus	Zones 6-9. Full sun to partial shade. Widely adapted.	Evergreen. Handsome foliage plant that adapts well to pruning. Many varieties have variegated foliage.
Hamamelis × intermedia Witch hazel	Zones 6-8. Full sun to partial shade. Moist, rich soil.	Deciduous. Large, rounded leaves turn bright orange-red in fall. Wonderfully fragrant orange-to-red flowers on bare branches in spring.
Hibiscus syriacus Rose-of-Sharon	Zones 5-10. Full sun to partial shade. Takes heat. Best with regular water.	Deciduous. Bright green, toothed foliage. Beautiful, large flowers in shades of white, pink, red and purple in late summer. Many varieties.
Hydrangeas *Hydrangea* species	Zones 6-10. Partial shade. Regular water.	Deciduous. Large, bright green leaves on mound-shaped plants. Stunning ball-shape flower clusters in shades of white, pink and purple, borne in late summer. Several species available.
Ilex species Hollies	Zones 6-10. Full sun. Prefer acid soil.	Evergreen. Many species get quite large. Grown for shiny foliage and bright red berries.

Botanical name/ Common name	Adaptation	Remarks
Ligustrum japonicum Japanese privet	Zones 7-10. Full sun to partial shade. Heat and drought tolerant.	Evergreen. Bright, glossy green leaves. White flowers in summer followed by blue-black berries. Grown primarily because of its toughness and ability to make a quick screen or hedge.
Myoporum laetum 'Carsonii' Myoporum	Zones 8-10. Full sun. Drought tolerant.	Evergreen. Valued for bright green foliage and fast growth in coastal conditions. Good screen.
Nerium oleander Oleander	Zones 8-10. Full sun. Heat and drought tolerant.	Evergreen. Tough and fast growing. Bright summer flowers in shades of white, yellow, pink, and red. Excellent screen.
Philadelphus species Mock orange	Zones 4-8. Full sun to partial shade. Widely adapted.	Deciduous. Several species of handsome plants with intensely fragrant late-spring or early-summer flowers. Can be pruned or sheared.
Photinia fraseri Red-tip photinia	Zones 7-10. Full sun to partial shade. Drought tolerant.	Evergreen. Exceptionally long season of color. New growth is fiery red. Bright white flowers in late spring. Shiny green leaves all summer. Excellent hedge or screen.
Pyracantha coccinea Firethorn	Zones 7-9. Full sun. Heat and drought tolerant.	Evergreen. Large, rangy shrub with white spring flowers followed by bright red berries. Many varieties with easier-to-control habits.
Rhododendrons: See page 212		
Syringa vulgaris Lilac	Zones 3-8. Full sun Best with regular water. Not for warm-winter climates.	Deciduous. Famous for their intensely fragrant spring flowers in shades of purple, pink and white. Handsome dark green, heart-shaped leaves.
Viburnum species Viburnum	Zones 3-10. Full sun or partial shade. Widely adapted.	Deciduous or evergreen. Several species grow quite large. Grown for their excellent form, often fragrant white-to-pink spring flowers and brightly colored berries. Some deciduous types have stunning fall color.

SHRUBS FOR SPECIFIC PURPOSES

Evergreen
Arborvitae (*Thuja* species)
Boxwood (*Buxus* species)
Cotoneaster (*Cotoneaster* species)
English laurel (*Prunus laurocerasus*)
Euonymus (*Euonymus* species)
Heath (*Erica* species)
Heavenly bamboo (*Nandina domestica*)
Holly (*Ilex* species)
India hawthorne (*Raphiolepis indica*)
Japanese aucuba (*Aucuba japonica*)
Mountain laurel (*Kalmia latifolia*)
Myrtle (*Myrtus communis*)
Oleander (*Nerium oleander*)
Oregon grape (*Mahonia* species)
Photinia (*Photinia* species)
Pittosporum (*Pittosporum* species)
Privet (*Ligustrum* species)
Rhododendron (*Rhododendron* species)
Scarlet firethorn (*Pyracantha coccinea*)
Viburnum (*Viburnum* species)
Yew (*Taxus* species)

Fall Color
Burning bush (*Euonymus alatus*)
Heavenly bamboo (*Nandina domestica*)
Japanese barberry (*Berberis thunbergii*)
Laceleaf Japanese maple (*Acer palmatum dissectum*)
Oakleaf hydrangea (*Hydrangea quercifolia*)
Oregon grapeholly (*Mahonia aquifolium*)
Red chokeberry (*Aronia arbutifolia*)
Rhododendron (*Rhododendron* species)
Sumac (*Rhus* species)
Sweet azalea (*Rhododendron arborescens*)
Viburnum (*Viburnum* species)
Virginia rose (*Rosa virginiana*)
Witch hazel (*Hammamelis* species)

Fragrance
Carolina allspice (*Calycanthus floridus*)
Common lilac (*Syringa vulgaris*)
Daphne (*Daphn* species)

Elaeagnus (*Elaeagnus* species)
Escallonia (*Escallonia* species)
Gardenia (*Gardenia jasminoides*)
Honeysuckle (*Lonicera* species)
Manchu cherry (*Prunus tomentosa*)
Mock orange (*Philadelphus* species)
Pittosporum (*Pittosporum* species)
Summer lilac (*Buddleia davidii*)
Star magnolia (*Magnolia stellata*)
Viburnum (*Viburnum* species)
Wild lilac (*Ceanothus* species)

Ornamental Fruits or Berries
Note: Fruits or berries of some of these shrubs are poisonous. Check with local nursery personnel or a university extension agent.

Barberry (*Berberis* species)
Cotoneaster (*Cotoneaster* species)
Elaeagnus (*Elaeagnus* species)
Flowering quince (*Chaenomeles speciosa*)
Heavenly bamboo (*Nandina domestica*)
Japanese aucuba (*Aucuba japonica*)
Manzanita (*Arctostaphylos* species)
Photinia (*Photinia* species)
Pomegranate (*Punica granatum*)
Sargent's crabapple (*Malus sargentii*)
Scarlet firethorn (*Pyracantha coccinea*)
Sumac (*Rhus* species)
Tartarian honeysuckle (*Lonicera tatarica*)
Viburnum (*Viburnum* species)
Winterberry (*Ilex verticillata*)

Hedges
Barberry (*Berberis* species)
Boxwood (*Buxus* species)
Camellia (*Camellia* species)
Cotoneaster (*Cotoneaster* species)
Euonymus (*Euonymus* species)
Glossy abelia (*Abelia ×grandiflora*)
Holly (*Ilex* species)
Myrtle (*Myrtus communis*)

Natal plum (*Carissa grandiflora*)
Oleander (*Nerium oleander*)
Privet (*Ligustrum* species)
Yew (*Taxus* species)

Low Maintenance
Broom (*Cytisus* species)
Burning bush (*Euonymus alatus*)
Cotoneaster (*Cotoneaster* species)
Flowering quince (*Chaenomeles speciosa*)
Holly (*Ilex* species)
Indian hawthorne (*Raphiolepis indica*)
Juniper (*Juniperus* species)
Mock orange (*Philadelphus* species)
Myrtle (*Myrtus communis*)
Oleander (*Nerium oleander*)
Pittosporum (*Pittosporum* species)
Privet (*Ligustrum* species)
Spirea (*Spiraea* species)
Sumac (*Rhus* species)
Viburnum (*Viburnum* species)
Witch hazel (*Hamamelis* species)
Yew (*Taxus* species)

Shade Tolerant
Azalea, Rhododendron (*Rhododendron* species)
Camellia (*Camellia japonica*)
English laurel (*Prunus laurocerasus*)
Euonymus (*Euonymus* species)
Fuchsia (*Fuchsia* species)
Gardenia (*Gardenia jasminoides*)
Heavenly bamboo (*Nandina domestica*)
Holly (*Ilex* species)
Japanese aucuba (*Aucuba japonica*)
Mexican orange (*Choisya ternata*)
Myrtle (*Myrtus communis*)
Pittosporum (*Pittosporum* species)
Privet (*Ligustrum* species)
Viburnum (*Viburnum* species)
Yew (*Taxus* species)

AZALEAS, CAMELLIAS AND RHODODENDRONS

Azaleas, camellias and rhododendrons have been grouped together because of similar habit and cultural requirements. All require acidic soil and the same general climatic conditions. See pages 134-137 for more information.

EVERGREEN AZALEAS

Kaempferi Hybrids—Descendents of the tall Japanese *Rhododendron kaempferi* and the Malvatica hybrids, these are the most cold-hardy azaleas, taking temperatures as low as −10F (−24C).

Name	Plant Height	Flower	Bloom Season
'Alice'	6'	Salmon-red fades to pink.	Early to mid.
'Fedora'	6'	Pink or violet-red single.	Early.
'Herbert'	Under 6'	Reddish-violet hose-in-hose.	Midseason.
'Palestrina'	3-5'	White with chartreuse blotch.	Mid to late.

Girard Hybrids—Bred from Gable hybrids crossed with several species including *R. mucronatum* and *R. poukhanense*. They are cold hardy to −5F (−21C).

Name	Plant Height	Flower	Bloom Season
'Girard Crimson'	Under 6'	Crimson-red, single.	Mid.
'Hot Shot'	3-5'	Orange-red, double.	Mid to late.
'Rene Michelle'	Under 3'	Pink, single.	Mid.
'Roberta'	Under 6'	Pink, double.	Mid.

Gable Hybrids—A group of hybrids crossed from numerous other hybrids and species, including the Korean *R. poukhanense*.

Name	Plant Height	Flower	Bloom Season
'Campfire'	Under 6'	Bright red with dark blotch, hose-in-hose.	Mid.
'Kathy'	Under 3'	White, frilled single.	Mid to late.
'Lorna'	Under 3'	Pale pink, double hose-in-hose.	Late.
'Purple'	Under 6'	Lavender with dark blotch.	Mid.
'Splendor'	Under 6'	Ruffled hose-in-hose.	
'Rose Greeley'	Under 3'	White with chartreuse blotch, single hose-in-hose, fragrant.	Early to mid.

Glenn Dale Hybrids—The largest group of evergreen azaleas was bred from a number of Japanese species and hybrids for survival in mid-Atlantic states. Hardy to 5F (−15C).

Name	Plant Height	Flower	Bloom Season
'Cooperman'	3-5'	Orange-red, single.	Late.
'Delaware Valley White'	Under 6'	White, single, fragrant.	Late.
'Fashion'	Over 5'	Orange-red, single hose-in-hose.	Early to mid.
'Gaiety'	3-5'	Rose-pink with dark blotch, single.	Late mid.
'Helen Close'	3-5'	White with yellow blotch, single.	Mid.
'Martha Hitchcock'	3-5'	White with magenta margins, single.	Late.
'Treasure'	3-5'	White with pink blotch, single.	Early to mid.

Satsuki/Macrantha Hybrids—Hybridized by 17th-century Japanese breeders, these late-blooming azaleas are cold hardy to 5F (-15C). Sometimes known as Indica hybrids. Favorites for bonsai due to their dwarf, often pendant form.

Name	Plant Height	Flower	Bloom Season
'Beni-Krishima'	3-5'	Orange-red with dark blotch, double.	Late.
'Chinzan'	Under 3'	Salmon, single.	Late.
'Flame Creeper'	Under 3'	Orange-red, single.	Late.
'Gumpo White'	Under 3'	White with occasional red spots, single.	Late.
'Linda R.'	Under 3'	Pale pink, single.	Mid.
'Salmon Macrantha'	Under 3'	Salmon to purple, single.	Mid to late.

Kurume Hybrids—Bred in the early 19th century from Japanese natives, these cold-hardy hybrids (to 5F, −15C) were introduced to the U.S. at the Panama Pacific Exposition in San Francisco in 1915 and have remained favorites of American gardeners.

Name	Plant Height	Flower	Bloom Season
'Christmas Cheer'	3-5'	Bright red, hose-in-hose.	Early to mid.
'Coral Bells'	Under 3'	Shell-pink, single hose-in-hose.	Early to mid.
'Hershey's Red'	Under 3'	Bright red, double.	Mid.
'H.H. Hume'	Under 6'	White, single hose-in-hose.	Mid.
'Hinodegiri'	3-5'	Violet-red, single.	Early to mid.
'Orange Cup'	Under 6'	Reddish-orange.	Late.
'Pink Pearl'	6' or more	Salmon-rose, double.	Mid.
'Sherwood'	3-5'	Violet-red with dark blotch.	Mid.
'Orchid'	Under 6'	Single.	Mid.
'Snow'	Under 6'	White, hose-in-hose.	Mid.

Rutherfordiana Hybrids—Cold hardy to 20F (−7C), these small plants with flowers larger than Belgian Indicas were developed for greenhouse forcing of flowers.

Azalea	Plant Height	Flower	Bloom Season
'Alaska'	Under 3'	White with chartreuse blotch, mostly single, some double.	Mid to late.
'Dorothy Gish'	Under 3'	Orange-red, frilled single, hose-in-hose.	Mid to late.
'Gloria'	3-6'	Salmon and white variegated, hose-in-hose.	Early to mid.
'Redwing'	Under 6'	Red, hose-in-hose.	Mid.

Southern Indica Hybrids—These favorites of the Deep South were the first evergreen azaleas introduced to America, in the mid-1800s. Cold hardy to 20F (−7C).

Name	Plant Height	Flower	Bloom Season
'Brilliant'	3-5'	Red, single.	Mid to late.
'Coccinea Major'	Under 3'	Orange-red, single.	Late.
'Fielder's White'	3-5'	White with chartreuse blotch, frilled single.	Early to mid.
'Formosa'	6' or more	Lavender-magenta.	Mid to late.
'Pride of Dorking'	Under 6'	Orange-red, single.	Late.
'Pride of Mobile'	6' or more	Deep rose-pink, single.	Mid to late.
'Southern Charm'	6' or more	Pink, single.	Mid.

Belgian Indica Hybrids—Bred for greenhouse forcing from Japanese and Chinese species in Belgium and other western European countries in the early 1930s, these tender evergreens are hardy only to 20F (−7C). They remain favorites of the florist trade and Southern gardeners.

Name	Plant Height	Flower	Bloom Season
'Albert and Elizabeth'	Under 3'	White with salmon edging, double.	Mid
'Avenir'	Under 3'	Coppery pink, double.	Early to mid.
'Blushing Bride'	Under 3'	Pale pink, double.	Late.
'Chimes'	Under 3'	Deep red, semidouble.	Early to mid.
'Violacea'	Under 3'	Violet-purple, double.	Early to mid.

DECIDUOUS AZALEAS

Gardeners in the North, Midwest and other cool areas should look at these azaleas that are more cold hardy than their evergreen relatives. In addition to the named hybrids that follow, check your nursery sources for Asian and North American native species from which these have been bred.

Knap Hill and Exbury Hybrids—Descendents of 19th-century breedings of Chinese and North American natives, these azaleas are cold hardy to −20F (−29C). They produce the largest flowers of all deciduous azaleas.

Name	Plant Height	Flower	Bloom Season
'Aurora'	Under 6'	Salmon with orange blotch.	Mid.
'Balzac'	Under 6'	Red-orange, star-shaped, fragrant.	Late.
'Brazil'	Under 6'	Tangerine-red, frilly.	Late.

'Fireball'	Under 6'	Bright red.	Mid.
'Gold Dust'	Under 6'	Gold.	Mid.
'Royal Lodge'	Under 6'	Dark red.	Very late.
'Toucan'	Under 6'	Creamy yellow with pink edges.	Mid to late.

Mollis Hybrids—Produced from crossings of Chinese, Japanese and North American species during the 1870s.

Name	Plant Height	Flower	Bloom Season
'Adrian Koster'	4-5'	Deep yellow, star-shaped.	Late.
'Christopher Wren'	Over 6'	Yellow with tangerine blotch.	Mid to late.
'Koster's Brilliant Red'	Over 6'	Orange-red, single.	Mid to late.

Ghent Hybrids—Probably the hardiest of all azaleas, many survive temperatures of −25F (−32C) or below. Hybridized in late 1820s from several American natives.

Name	Plant Height	Flower	Bloom Season
'Coccinea Speciosa'	5-6'	Orange-red with yellowish blotch.	Early to mid.
'Daviesii'	Over 6'	Pale yellow to white.	Late.
'Narcissiflora'	Over 6'	Yellow, double, fragrant.	Late.

Occidentale Hybrids—Results of crossings of *R. occidentale* from along mountain streams of the West Coast with Mollis hybrids, these azaleas are cold hardy to -25F (−32C).

Name	Plant Height	Flower	Bloom Season
'Graciosa'	5-6'	Pale yellow with hint of rose.	Early to mid.
'Irene Koster'	5-6'	Rose-pink with yellow blotch.	Early to mid.
'Magnifica'	Over 6'	Rose-red with orange-yellow blotch.	Late.
'Westminster'	Under 6'	Almond-pink.	Early.

POPULAR CAMELLIAS

This list includes camellias of the *C. japonica* and *C. sasanqua* groups, subgrouped by flower color.

Camellia japonica

White
'Alba Plena'. Early, double.
'Nuccio's Gem'. Early to midseason, double.
'Lulu Belle'. Early to midseason, semidouble.
'Emmett Barnes'. Early, semidouble.
'Purity'. Midseason to late, double.
'Swan Lake'. Midseason to late, double.

Pink
'Berenice Boddy'. Midseason, semidouble.
'Kumasaka'. Midseason to late, semidouble.
'Moonlight Sonata'. Midseason to late, semidouble.
'Guilio Nuccio'. Midseason, semidouble.
'Rosea Superba'. Midseason to late, double.
'Show Time'. Early to midseason, semidouble.

Red
'Adolphe Audusson'. Midseason, semidouble.
'Blood of China'. Late, semidouble.
'Glen 40'. Midseason to late, double.
'Grand Slam'. Midseason, semidouble.
'Kramer's Supreme'. Midseason, semidouble.
'Reg Ragland'. Early to late, semidouble.
'Te Deum'. Midseason to late, double.

Bicolors
'Alta Gavin'. White, edged in red. Midseason to late, semidouble.
'Betty Sheffield Supreme'. White, edged pink-red. Midseason, double or semidouble.
'Brushfield's Yellow'. White with yellow center. Midseason to late, semidouble.

'Chandleri Elegans'. Rose with white. Early to midseason, semidouble.
'Elizabeth Dowd Silver'. Blush pink, edged white. Midseason, semidouble.
'Gee Homeyer'. Pine with red veins. Midseason, double.
'Prairie Fires'. Deep red, mottled white. Early to late, double.
'Ville de Nantes'. Red blotched white. Midseason to late, semidouble.

Camellia sasanqua

White
'Little Pearl'. Pink in bud. Semidouble.
'Setsugekka'. Ruffled, semidouble.
'Snowflake'. Single.
'White Frills'. Semidouble.

Pink
'Cleopatra'. Semidouble.
'Jean May'. Double.
'Pink Showers'. Semidouble.
'Tanya'. Single.

Red
'Australian Hiryu'. Semidouble.
'Bonanza'. Semidouble.
'Shishi Gashira'. Double.
'Yuletide'. Single.

Bicolors
'Apple Blossom'. White blushed pink. Single.
'Hana Jiman' White tipped pink. Semidouble.
'Momozona Nishiki'. Pink with red border. Semidouble.
'Narumigata'. White tinged pink. Single.
'Rainbow'. White bordered red. Single.

RHODODENDRONS

Here are recommended species and hybrids grouped in order of cold hardiness, beginning with those that can tolerate the lowest temperatures.

Name	Plant Height	Flower	Bloom Season
Cold Hardy to −25 F (−32C)			
'Boule de Neige'	5'	White, round trusses.	Mid.
R. carolinianum	4'	White to rose or purple-rose.	Mid.
R. catawbiense	6'	Lilac-purple with green or brownish spots.	Mid to late.
R. maximum	4-40'	White, flushed pink.	Mid to late.
'Nova Zembla'	5'	Dark red, round trusses.	Mid.
'Roseum Elegans'	6'	Rosy lilac, dome-shaped trusses.	Mid to late.
Cold Hardy to −20F (−29C)			
'America'	5'	Red, ball-shaped trusses.	Mid.
'English Roseum'	Over 6'	Rose-pink, tinged lavender, large trusses.	Mid to late.
'Ignatius Sargent'	5-6'	Rose-red, slightly fragrant.	Mid to late.
'Lee's Dark Purple'	6'	Dark purple, large trusses.	Mid to late.
'Purple Gem'	2'	Deep purple-violet.	Early to mid.
Cold Hardy to −15F (−26C)			
'Caroline'	6'	Orchid-pink, fragrant.	Mid to late.
R. chryseum	1'	Bright yellow, bell-shaped.	Early to mid.
'Dora Amateis'	3'	White with green spots, fragrant.	Early to mid.
R. fastigiatum	1'	Lilac-purple, small trusses.	Mid.
R. mucronulatum	5-8'	Orchid-pink.	Very early.
Cold Hardy to −10F (−24C)			
'Anah Kruschke'	6'	Lavender-purple, ball-shaped trusses.	Late.
'Cunningham's White'	4'	White with greenish blotch, upright trusses.	Mid to late.
R. keleticum	1'	Rose to purple with red specks.	Mid.
'Purple Splendor'	5'	Dark purple with black blotch.	Mid to late.
'Sappho'	6'	White with blackish-purple blotch, dome-shaped trusses.	Mid.
'Scintillation'	5'	Pale pink with bronze and yellow throat, large dome-shaped trusses.	Mid.
'Yaku King'	Under 3'	Deep pink with lighter blotch, ball-like trusses.	Mid to late.
Cold Hardy to −5F (−21C)			
'Arthur Bedford'	6'	Lavender-blue with dark blotch, dome-shaped trusses.	Mid to late.
'Antoon van Welie'	5'	Deep pink, big trusses.	Mid to late.
'Carmen'	1'	Lavender to deep red.	Early to mid.
'Pink Pearl'	6'	Rose-pink, large trusses.	Mid.
R. keiskei	3'	Lemon-yellow, bell-shaped trusses.	Early to mid.
Cold Hardy to 0F (−18C)			
'Bow Bells'	3'	Deep pink opening to lighter-colored loose trusses.	Early to mid.
'Kluis Sensation'	5'	Dark red, tight trusses.	Mid to late.
'Moonstone'	3'	Creamy yellow, bell-shaped trusses.	Early to mid.
'Mother of Pearl'	6'	Pink fading to pearly white, slightly fragrant.	Mid.
'Unique'	4'	Light pink fading to creamy yellow flushed with peach. Dome-shaped trusses.	Early to mid.
Cold Hardy to 5F (−15C)			
'Barto Blue'	6'	Blue, three-flower trusses.	Early to mid.
'Bric-a-brac'	2'	White or pink with brown anthers.	Very early.
'General Eisenhower'	6'	Deep red, large trusses.	Mid.
'Mrs. Betty Robertson'	4'	Pale yellow with red blotches, dome-shaped trusses.	Mid.
Cold Hardy to 20F (−7C)			
'Fragrantissimum'	10'	White tinged with pink, fragrant.	Mid.
'Lady Alice Fitzwilliam'	Under 6'	White, fragrant.	Mid.

HIGH-RATED ROSES

The rose varieties in each of the following categories are listed in order of ratings given them by the American Rose Society. The ARS rates roses on a scale of 1 to 10. Those listed here received ratings of 7.6 or above.

HYBRID TEAS

Name	Rating	Flower
'First Prize'	9.0	Large, double, pink outside, ivory inside.
'Peace'	9.0	Large, double, golden yellow tipped pink.
'Granada'	8.9	Large, double, red and yellow bicolor.
'Tiffany'	8.8	Large, double, silvery pink with yellow base.
'Tropicana'	8.8	Large, double, orange-red.
'Mister Lincoln'	8.7	Large, double, glowing red.
'Garden Party'	8.6	Large, double, creamy ivory-yellow with a touch of pink.
'Double Delight'	8.5	Large, double, rich cream edged red.
'Paradise'	8.5	Large, double, silvery lavender edged ruby-red.
'Lady X'	8.4	Large, double, soft lavender.

MINIATURES

Name	Rating	Flower
'Starina'	9.4	Double, orange-red with yellow base. Borne singly or in small clusters.
'Beauty Secret'	9.0	Double, bright red. Borne in clusters.
'Cinderella'	8.9	Double, white with a touch of pink. Borne in clusters.
'Toy Clown'	8.9	Semidouble, white edged pink or red. Borne singly or in clusters.
'Magic Carrousel'	8.9	Double, white with red or pink edge. Borne singly or in small clusters.
'Judy Fischer'	8.8	Double, rose-pink. Borne singly or in small clusters.
'Mary Marshall'	8.7	Double, coral-orange with yellow base. Borne in clusters.
'Simplex'	8.6	Single, white. Borne in clusters.
'Starglo'	8.6	Double, white. Borne in clusters.
'Chipper'	8.5	Double, salmon-pink. Borne in clusters.
'Holy Toledo'	8.5	Double, apricot with yellow base. Borne singly or in clusters.
'Over The Rainbow'	8.5	Double, red and pink bicolor with yellow base and reverse. Borne in clusters.

GRANDIFLORAS

Name	Rating	Flower
'Queen Elizabeth'	9.0	Large, double, clear pink.
'Pink Parfait'	8.4	Large, double, pink and cream bicolor.
'Sonia'	8.0	Large, double, coral-pink.
'Montezuma'	7.7	Large, double, salmon-orange.
'Ole'	7.7	Large, double, vermilion-red with unusual, frilled petals.
'Camelot'	7.7	Large, double, pale salmon.
'Mount Shasta'	7.7	Large, double, pure white.
'Carrousel'	7.6	Large, double, deep red.

FLORIBUNDAS

Name	Rating	Flower
'Europeana'	8.8	Double, cardinal-red. Borne in large clusters.
'Little Darling'	8.8	Double, yellow and salmon-pink bicolor. Borne in large clusters.
'Iceberg'	8.6	Double, crystal white. Borne in large clusters.
'Walko'	8.5	Double, dark crimson. Borne in medium clusters.
'Gene Boerner'	8.4	Double, true pink. Borne singly or in clusters.
'Sea Pearl'	8.4	Double, pink with peach overtones. Borne in small clusters.
'Betty Prior'	8.3	Single. Bright pink. Borne in medium clusters.
'Floradora'	8.3	Double, cinnabar-red. Borne in large clusters.

CLIMBERS

Name	Rating	Flower
'Altissimo'	8.8	Large, single, blood-red with bright yellow stamens. Borne in small clusters.
'Don Juan'	8.6	Large, double, deep red. Borne singly or in small clusters.
'Handel'	8.6	Large, double, pale pink edged deep pink. Usually borne singly.
'Dortmund'	8.6	Large, single, red with white center. Borne in large clusters.
'May Queen'	8.4	Large, double, pink.
'Royal Flush'	8.3	Large, semidouble, cream edged pink. Borne in small clusters.
'Royal Sunset'	8.1	Large, double, apricot. Borne singly.
'America'	8.0	Large, double, deep red. Borne in small clusters.

ORNAMENTAL TREES

The following ornamental trees are grouped into three basic categories: *Small patio trees* generally have a compact, non-invasive habit and are used where space is limited or a small tree is desired. Those listed here are deciduous, with the exception of evergreen pear, which is partially deciduous (remains evergreen in mild climates). *Shade trees* are large, spreading trees that provide full or partial shade over a wide area. Choose trees with large, dense leaves for deep shade; trees with sparse, narrow, feathery leaves, such as silk tree or jacaranda, for light, filtered shade. *Evergreen trees* listed on page 216 include needled evergreens (conifers) and broadleaf evergreens. These are used for permanent greenery in the landscape and most make excellent year-round windbreaks. For more information on selecting landscape trees, see pages 129-133. See pages 46-53 for planting information.

SMALL PATIO TREES

Botanical Name/ Common Name	Adaption	Habit	Remarks
Acer palmatum Japanese maple	Zones 6-8. Full sun in cool-summer climates. Partial shade where hot.	Deciduous. 15-20' high. Spreading, multi-trunked.	Divided leaves turn stunning shades of red, often orange or yellow. Many varieties with unique shapes. Picturesque, twisting branching habit.
Betula pendula European white birch	Zones 2-9. Full sun. Needs summer water.	Deciduous. 40-50' high. Upright, often multi-trunked.	Dramatic white, papery, peeling bark. Bright yellow fall color.
Cercis canadensis Eastern redbud	Zones 4-7. Full sun or partial shade.	Deciduous. 25-40' high. Spreading crown, often multi-trunked.	Bare branches clothed in purplish-pink, pea-shaped flowers in spring. Heart-shaped leaves unfold reddish purple, turn dark green then yellow before dropping in fall.
Cornus florida Flowering dogwood	Zones 5-9. Best in partial shade.	Deciduous. 20-30' high. Wide-spreading.	Long bloom of beautiful white flowers in spring followed by red berries. Leaves turn crimson-red in fall.
Crataegus species Hawthorns	Zones 3-9. Full sun. Widely adapted, tough trees.	Deciduous. 15-30' high. Spreading to round-headed.	Several species of colorful, small trees. Shiny green leaves often turn bright colors in fall. White, pink or red spring flowers followed by red berries that last long into winter. Some have thorny branches.
Koelreuteria paniculata Golden-rain tree	Zones 5-9. Full sun. Widely adapted.	Deciduous. 20-30' high. Round-headed.	Bright yellow flower clusters in midsummer followed by unusual papery seed pods that resemble Japanese lanterns. Deeply divided green leaves turn various shades of yellow before dropping in fall.
Lagerstroemia indica Crape myrtle	Zones 7-9. Full sun. Best in hot, dry-summer climates.	Deciduous. 10-30' high. Vase-shaped. often multi-trunked.	Always attractive. Crepelike clusters of midsummer flowers in shades of white, pink, red and purple. Bright red fall color. Muscular branches with shiny, peeling brown bark.
Magnolia species Deciduous magnolias	Zones 5-10. Full sun. Best with summer water.	Deciduous. 20-25' Spreading or vase-shaped. Often multi-trunked.	*M. stellata* or *M. soulangiana* are best choices. Each bears stunning spring blooms on bare branches. Handsome foliage all summer.
Malus species Flowering crabapples	Zones 2-8. Full sun.	Deciduous. 12-30' high. Habits vary in species and varieties.	Many species and varieties available. Vary by size, habit and fruit color. All bear white spring flowers followed by brightly colored fruit in shades of red, yellow or orange. In wet-summer climates, choose disease-resistant varieties.
Oxydendrum arboreum Sourwood	Zones 6-9. Full sun. Needs acid soil and summer water.	Deciduous. 20-30' high. Upright.	Long clusters of creamy white flowers in summer followed by interesting seed pods. Rich green leaves turn orange to red in fall.
Prunus species Deciduous flowering plums and cherries	Zones 5-9. Full sun. Most need some winter chill.	Deciduous. 12-30' high. Variable habit.	Includes some of the finest spring-flowering trees—the flowering plums and cherries. Some have colorful foliage or fragrant flowers. Others are fruitless.
Pyrus kawakami Evergreen pear	Zones 9-10. Full sun to light shade.	Partially deciduous. 20-30' high. Round-headed.	Shiny-foliaged tree with masses of fragrant, white flowers in spring. Scattering of red leaves in fall.

SHADE TREES

Botanical Name/ Common Name	Adaption	Habit	Remarks
Acer rubrum Red maple	Zones 4-9. Full sun. Best with summer water.	Deciduous. 50-60' high. Broad pyramid.	One of the most colorful maples. Stunning red fall color. Reddish new growth and seed pods. Many varieties with different habits available.
Albizia julibrissin Silk tree	Zones 7-10. Full sun. Drought tolerant.	Deciduous. 25-35' high. Broad-spreading.	Fast-growing tree with finely cut, featherlike leaves. Pink powder-puff flowers held above foliage. Good for quick shade. Seed pods messy.
Celtis species Hackberry	Zones 5-9. Full sun. Widely adapted.	Deciduous. 50-60' high. Upright, rounded.	Three similar species adapted to different areas. Consult nurserymen for correct type. Extremely tough trees for difficult situations.
Fraxinus species Ash	Zones 2-10. Full sun. Widely adapted.	Mostly deciduous. Upright, rounded.	A large family of fast-growing trees known for toughness, pleasant shade cast by divided leaves and brilliant fall color. *F. oxycarpa* 'Raywood' and *F. holotricha* 'Moraine' are just two of many excellent varieties.
Ginkgo biloba Maidenhair tree	Zones 4-9. Full sun. Widely adapted.	Deciduous. 60-100' high. Spreading.	Ancient tree with unusual fan-shaped leaves that turn bright yellow before dropping in fall. Beautiful winter silhouette. Needs room to spread. Plant only seedless, male varieties to avoid smelly seeds.
Gleditsia triacanthos inermis Thornless honey locust	Zones 4-10. Full sun. Widely adapted.	Deciduous. 60-90' high. Spreading.	Deeply cut, fernlike leaves cast light shade; filter into lawns after falling. No raking needed. 'Moraine' has deep green leaves and a round head. 'Sunburst' has bright yellow new growth.
Jacaranda mimosifolia Jacaranda	Zones 9-10. Full sun.	Partially deciduous. 25-40' high. Spreading.	Spectacular purplish-blue flowers in spring. Finely cut, feathery leaves. Interesting branch pattern.
Liriodendron tulipifera Tulip tree	Zones 5-9. Full sun. Best in moist soils.	Deciduous. 80-100' high. Pyramidal when young, becoming rounded.	Yellow-green, lyre-shaped leaves turn yellow over a long period in fall. Green, tuliplike flowers are interesting but not showy. Aphids can be a serious problem.
Magnolia grandiflora Southern magnolia	Zones 7-10. Full sun.	Evergreen. 80-100' high. Pyramidal to rounded.	Classic tree of the South. Large, leathery, deep green leaves. Huge, fragrant white flowers in summer. 'Majestic Beauty' and 'Saint Mary' are smaller versions.
Morus alba Mulberry	Zones 5-9. Full sun. Drought and heat tolerant.	Deciduous. 40' high. Spreading.	Valued for its fast growth in harsh climates. Large mitten-shaped leaves. Fruiting and fruitless varieties available.
Nyssa sylvatica Black gum	Zones 5-9. Full sun. Tolerates wet soils.	Deciduous. 30-50' high. Broad pyramid.	Shiny green, oval leaves turn striking shades of scarlet, orange and yellow in fall. Interesting bark and branching pattern.
Pistacia chinensis Chinese pistache	Zones 7-10. Full sun. Drought tolerant.	Deciduous. 50-60' high. Broad-spreading.	Casts delightful shade below deeply divided, clean green leaves that are tinged pink when unfolding. Brilliant yellow, red-orange or scarlet fall color.
Platanus acerifolia 'Bloodgood' Bloodgood London plane tree	Zones 5-10. Full sun. Heat and drought tolerant.	Deciduous. 80-100' high. Upright to rounded.	A disease-resistant selection of a popular fast-growing tree. Pointed, lobed leaves. Flaking bark. Good for tough situations.
Quercus species Oaks	Zones 4-10. Full sun. Adaptation varies by species.	Deciduous or evergreen. 20-100' high. Upright to rounded.	A large family of beautiful trees. Many native to North America. Variety of qualities to choose from, including fall color, interesting branching patterns and leaf shapes. Check local adaptation.
Sophora japonica Japanese pagoda tree	Zones 5-8. Full sun. Takes heat and drought.	Deciduous. 30-60' high. Round-headed.	Tough tree clothed in bright yellow bloom in midsummer. Fernlike leaves cast pleasant shade. Interesting bark and artistic branching.
Sorbus aucuparia European mountain ash	Zones 2-7. Full sun to partial shade. Poor in heat and drought.	Deciduous. 35-45' high. Upright to spreading.	Colorful tree for mild-summer climates with ample moisture. Beautiful clusters of white flowers in spring followed by bright red berries. Divided leaves turn yellow to red in fall.
Tilia cordata Little-leaf linden	Zones 4-8. Full sun. Widely adapted.	Deciduous. 35-50' high. Rounded pyramid.	Fairly dense crown of small, deep green leaves with silvery undersides. Small clusters of white, fragrant flowers attract bees and are followed by small, round seed clusters. 'Chancellor' is an excellent upright cultivar.
Zelkova serrata Saw-leaf zelkova	Zones 5-9. Full sun. Needs moisture.	Deciduous. 75-100' high. Rounded to vase-shaped.	Soft green, toothed leaves turn rust-colored in fall. 'Village Green' is an improved form that leafs-out all at once. Some seedling trees leaf-out branch by branch.

EVERGREEN TREES

Botanical Name/ Common Name	Adaption	Habit	Remarks
Abies concolor White fir	Zones 5-8. Full sun or partial shade. Best in cool, moist climates.	Needled. 80-100' high. Pyramidal with tiered limbs.	Blue-green needles. Cones held upright. Stiff, formal appearance.
Acacia baileyana Bailey acacia	Zone 9. Full sun. Heat and drought tolerant.	Broadleaf. 20-30' high. Wide-spreading.	Very fast-growing tree for California. Masses of yellow flowers in early spring. Small, fernlike leaves. Good screen. Not for gardens.
Arbutus unedo Strawberry tree	Zones 7-10. Full sun to partial shade. Drought tolerant.	Broadleaf. 10-30' high. Rounded, usually multi-trunked.	Handsome plant that needs pruning to form a tree. Clusters of small, white, urn-shaped flowers in spring followed by bright red, ball-shaped, edible fruit. Smooth, shiny red, flaking bark.
Calocedrus decurrens California incense cedar	Zones 6-10. Full sun. Widely adapted.	Needled. 85-100' high. Pyramidal with sweeping lower limbs.	Tough tree with scalelike leaves in flat sprays. Deeply furrowed, reddish bark. Fragrant foliage and bark. Good screen or buffer.
Cedrus species True Cedars	Zones 6-10. Full sun.	Needled. 60-80' high. Pyramidal.	Two popular species: *C. atlantica* has stiff, bluish-green needles in short clusters. *C. deodar* has soft, green needles and branches with weeping tips. It is slightly less hardy than *C. atlantica.*
Ceratonia siliqua Carob	Zones 9-10. Full sun. Drought tolerant.	Broadleaf. 20-40' high. Round-headed.	Deep green, divided leaves with rounded edges. Casts dense shade. Male trees have flowers with unpleasant odor. Females have large (12-inch) seed pods used to make a chocolate substitute.
Chamaecyparis species False cypress	Zones 5-9. Full sun. Needs moisture.	Needled. 20-75' high. Rounded pyramids.	A large family of soft-textured plants with needles or scalelike foliage. Some are weeping, others have yellow- or blue-tinged foliage. Dwarf forms, such as *C. obtusa nana* are popular shrubs. Avoid windy sites.
Cinnamomum camphora Camphor Tree	Zones 9-10. Full sun.	Broadleaf. 20-50' high. Spreading, round-headed.	Clean, light green foliage. Scattered leaves sometimes turn red. Dense when young, more open with age. Roots can be invasive. Can be sheared as a hedge.
× *Cupressocyparis leylandii* Leyland cypress	Zones 5-10. Full sun. Widely adapted.	Needled. 70-100' high. Broad, columnar.	Compact, upright branches. Gray-green foliage in horizontal sprays. Tall, fast-growing screen or hedge.
Cupressus species Cypress	Zones 7-10. Full sun. Adaptation varies by species.	Needled. 40-60' high. Forms vary.	Three species with scalelike foliage and different adaptation. *C. arizonica* is a pyramidal, light green tree, good for a screen or windbreak in hot climates. *C. macrocarpa* is a spreading, usually windswept tree for coastal California. *C. sempervirens* is a narrow, columnar tree grown as a formal accent.
Eucalyptus species Eucalyptus	Zones 7-10. Full sun. Heat and drought tolerant.	Broadleaf. 20-100' high. Mostly upright and open.	A large family of trees native to Australia. Species vary in hardiness, form and foliage. All are fast growing. Some have colorful flowers. Others make good screens. Choose species carefully.
Grevillea robusta Silk oak	Zones 8-10. Full sun or partial shade. Heat and drought tolerant.	Broadleaf. 50-60' high. Narrow pyramid.	Fast-growing tree, valuable as a quick screen or hedge. Otherwise messy and weak wooded. Yellowish-green, divided leaves and unusual yellow flowers in summer.
Ilex species Hollies	Zones 6-9. Full sun. Best in acid soil.	Broadleaf. 15-40' high. Pyramidal.	Two species reach tree height— *I. aquifolium* and *I. opaca.* Both have shiny green leaves and bright red berries.
Juniperus species Junipers	Zones 4-10. Full sun. Most are heat and drought tolerant.	Needled. 15-40' high. Narrow, pyramidal.	Many species reach tree height. *J. scopularum* is particularly tolerant to heat and drought. *J. virginiana* is widely adapted to Eastern climates.
Ligustrum lucidum Glossy privet	Zones 8-10. Full sun or partial shade. Heat and drought tolerant.	Broadleaf. 15-30' high. Narrow, upright.	One of the toughest trees you can grow. Adapts to almost anything. Bright green leaves. White flowers in summer followed by black berries. Great hedge, screen or buffer.
Olea europaea Olive	Zones 9-10. Full sun. Heat and drought tolerant.	Broadleaf. 25-30' Round-headed. Often spreading and multi-trunked.	Fruit-producing tree with silvery foliage and small creamy yellow flowers. Distinctive, gnarly habit well-suited to desert landscapes. Large trees easily transplanted. Messy unwanted fruit can be controlled with sprays.

EVERGREEN TREES, CONT'D.

Botanical Name/ Common Name	Adaption	Habit	Remarks
Pinus species Pine	Zones 3-10. Full sun or partial shade. Adaptation varies by species.	Needled. 5-100' high. Form varies by species.	There is probably one pine or another to fit almost every landscape need. Most species are pyramidal, but some are spreading and distinctive. Some are short needled and stiff, others are long needled and weeping. Check local adaptation.
Podocarpus species Yew pine	Zones 8-10. Full sun to partial shade.	Needled. 50-60' high. Upright, irregular.	Two very distinctive plants. Deep green needles from 3 to 4 inches long. Plants have oriental feel. *P. gracilior* is more weeping; *P. macrophyllus* is better adapted to hot climates. Beautiful plants for containers, patios or entryways.
Pseudotsuga menziesii Douglas fir	Zones 4-9. Full sun. Needs moisture. Check adaptation carefully.	Needled. 50-100' high. Conical and weeping.	Attractive Western native with soft green needles. Beautiful as specimen or in grove.
Sequoia sempervirens Coast redwood	Zones 7-10. Full sun or partial shade. Best adapted to Pacific coast.	Needled. 60-100' high. Narrow pyramid.	Dark green needles. Soft, deeply furrowed red bark. Poor in hot or dry climates. Fast-growing screen or grove. Can be clipped as a hedge.
Sequoiadendron giganteum Giant redwood	Zones 6-10. Full sun.	Needled. 60-100' high. Pyramidal. Stiffer texture. Loses lower branches with age.	Blue-green, scalelike foliage. Broader adaptation than coast redwood but fewer landscape uses.
Tsuga canadensis Canadian hemlock	Zones 5-9. Full sun or shade. Best in moist climates.	Needled. 60-90' high. Broad pyramid.	Soft textured, graceful tree with swooping branches. Two rows of shiny, deep green needles. Good hedge. Many dwarf varieties.

TREES FOR SPECIFIC USES

Fall Color
American sweetgum (*Liquidambar styraciflua*)
Ash (*Fraxinus* species)
Birch (*Betula* species)
Chinese pistache (*Pistacia chinensis*)
Common persimmon (*Diospyros virginiana*)
Japanese larch (*Larix leptolepis*)
Maidenhair tree (*Ginkgo biloba*)
Maple (*Acer* species)
Sassafras (*Sassafras albidum*)
Serviceberry (*Amelanchier canadensis*)
Smoke tree (*Cotinus coggygria*)
Sourwood (*Oxydendrum arboreum*)
Tulip tree (*Liriodendron tulipifera*)

Fast Growing
Ash (*Fraxinus* species)
Black locust (*Robinia pseudoacacia*)
Catalpa (*Catalpa* species)
Empress tree (*Paulownia tomentosa*)
Eucalyptus (*Eucalyptus* species)
Poplar (*Populus* species)
Pine (*Pinus* species)
Red oak (*Quercus rubra*)
River birch (*Betula nigra*)
Sycamore (*Platanus* species)
Tulip tree (*Liriodendron tulipifera*)

Fragrance
Amur maple (*Acer ginnala*)
Black locust (*Robinia pseudoacacia*)
Citrus (*Citrus* species)
Crabapple (*Malus* species)
Eucalyptus (*Eucalyptus* species)
Japanese lilac tree (*Syringa reticulata*)
Japanese pagoda tree (*Sophora japonica*)
Plums (*Prunus* species)
Russian olive (*Elaeagnus augustifolia*)

Snowdrop (*Halesia carolina*)
Southern magnolia (*Magnolia grandiflora*)
Sweet bay (*Laurus nobilis*)
Sweet olive (*Osmanthus fragrans*)
Victorian box (*Pittosporum undulatum*)

Flowering
Acacia (*Acacia* species)
Cape chestnut (*Calodendrum capense*)
Catalpa (*Catalpa* species)
Coral tree (*Erythrina* species)
Crabapple (*Malus* species)
Crape myrtle (*Lagerstroemia indica*)
Dogwood (*Cornus* species)
Flowering plums (*Prunus* species)
Goldenchain (*Laburnum* species)
Golden trumpet (*Tabebuia chrysotricha*)
Horse chestnut (*Aesculus* species)
Magnolia (*Magnolia* species)
Red-flowering gum (*Eucalyptus ficifolia*)
Silk tree, mimosa (*Albizia julibrissin*)
Tea tree (*Leptospermum* species)

Tolerate Wet Soil
Alder (*Alnus* species)
American arborvitae (*Thuja occidentalis*)
American sweet gum (*Liquidambar styraciflua*)
Birch (*Betula* species)
Cottonwood, Poplar (*Populus* species)
Cypress (*Taxodium* species)
Elderberry (*Sambucus caerulea*)
Oregon ash (*Fraxinus latifolia*)
Pear (*Pyrus communis*)
Red maple (*Acer rubrum*)
Southern magnolia (*Magnolia grandiflora*)
Sour gum (*Nyssa sylvatica*)
Sycamore (*Platanus* species)
Swamp white oak (*Quercus bicolor*)

RETAIL SUPPLIERS OF PLANTS AND GARDEN SUPPLIES

Abundant Life Seed Foundation
P.O. Box 772
Port Townsend, WA 98368
Specialists in seeds of North Pacific plants. Many unusual herbs. One-year membership for $2.

Armstrong Nurseries
P.O. Box 4060
Ontario, CA 91761
Rose specialists, but also many fruit trees.

Caprilands Herb Farm
Silver Street
North Coventry, CT 06238
Long-established herb specialists. Send self-addressed, stamped envelope for free catalog.

Clyde Robin Seed Company Inc.
P.O. Box 3855
Castro Valley, CA 94566
Seeds of many woody plants and wildflowers. Informative catalog, $1.

Comstock, Ferre & Company
263 Main Street
Wethersfield, CT 06109
Herbs and vegetables.

DeGiorgi Company Inc.
Council Bluffs, IA 51502
Many unusual vegetable varieties. Catalog 66¢.

Farmer Seed & Nursery Company
Fairbault, MN 55021
Most vegetables including unusual midget varieties.

Four Winds Growers
42186 Palm Avenue
P.O. Box 3538
Fremont, CA 94538
Specialists in dwarf citrus trees. Many varieties.

Geo. W. Park Seed Company Inc.
Greenwood, SC 29647
Useful and widely distributed garden catalog includes vegetables, fruits and many ornamentals.

Gurney Seed & Nursery Company
1448 Page Street
Yankton, SD 57078
Interesting and complete list of edible and ornamental garden plants.

H. G. Hastings Company
P.O. Box 4274
Atlanta, GA 30302
Complete list of vegetables, fruits and ornamental plants especially for Southern States.

Henry Field Seed & Nursery Company
Shenandoah, IA 51602
Informative and complete catalog of vegetables and other plants.

Jackson & Perkins
1 Rose Lane
Medford, OR 97501
Primarily roses, also some vegetables, fruits and ornamental plants.

Johnny's Selected Seeds
Albion, ME 04901
Many vegetables and herbs, and helpful information. Catalog 50¢.

Joseph Harris Company
Moreton Farm
Rochester, NY 14624
or
Box 432
Gresham, OR 97073
Informative and complete list of vegetables.

Miniature Plant Kingdom
4125 Harrison Grade Road
Sebstopol CA 95472
Hundreds of miniature rose varieties. Catalog 25¢.

Necessary Trading Company
623 Main Street
New Castle, VA 24127
Complete line of products and services for successful biological agriculture. Catalog $2.

New York State Fruit Testing
Cooperative Association
Geneva, NY 14456
Catalog of fruit trees available for $5 membership fee.

Nichols Garden Nursery
1190 North Pacific Highway
Albany, OR 97321
Informative catalog listing many unusual kinds of vegetables and many good ideas.

Nor'East Miniature Roses
58 Hammond Street
Rowley, MA 01969
Many varieties of miniature and microminiature roses. Catalog upon request.

Pacific Tree Farms
4301 Lynnwood Drive
Chula Vista, CA 92010
Extensive list of tropical and subtropical fruit trees. Also many pines. Catalog on request.

Redwood City Seed Company
P.O. Box 361
Redwood City, CA 94064
Wide variety of seeds, including many unusual kinds. Catalog $1.

Roses by Fred Edmunds Inc.
6235 S.W. Kahle Road
Wilsonville, OR 97070
Rose specialists. Catalog upon request.

Roses of Yesterday & Today
802 Brown's Valley Road
Watsonville, CA 95076
Many old-fashioned roses and many modern shrub roses.

Seeds Blum
Idaho City Stage
Boise, ID 83706
Seeds of heirloom vegetables and flowers. Catalog $2.

Stark Brothers Nurseries
Box B4225A
Louisiana, MO 63353
Extensive list of fruits, nuts and berries.

Stocking Rose Nursery
785 North Capitol Avenue
San Jose, CA 95133
Rose specialists. Free catalog upon request.

Sunnybrook Farms Nursery
P.O. Box 6
9448 Mayfield Road
Chesterland, OH 44026
Complete list of herb plants.

Taylor's Herb Gardens Inc.
1535 Lone Oak Road
Vista, CA 92083
Complete list of herb seeds and plants.

Thompson & Morgan
P.O. Box 1308
Jackson, NJ 08527
Complete list of vegetables including many unusual varieties.

Wayside Gardens
503 Garden Lane
Hodges, SC 29695
Beautiful catalog includes many choice perennials, shrubs and other ornamentals. Catalog $1.

W. Atlee Burpee Company
300 Park Avenue
Warminster, PA 18974
Widely distributed, deservedly popular general garden catalog.

W. H. Perron & Company, Ltd.
515 Labelle Boulevard
Chomedey, P. Que.
Canada H7V 2T3
Complete garden catalog, $1.

Well-Sweep Herb Farm
317 Mt. Bethel Road
Port Murray, NJ 07865
Extensive list of herb seeds and plants. Catalog 50¢.

Wonder Crops Natural Foods Institute
Box 185 WMB
Dudley, MA 01570
Catalog ($3.) lists sources of more than 200 fruits nuts, grains and vegetables with post-resistant or hardy character.

White Flower Farm
Litchfield, CN 06759
Beautiful and informative catalog of many choice annuals, perennials, conifers and bulbs.

EXTENSION SERVICES AND AGENTS

The following is a list of agricultural colleges and land grant universities in the United States and Canada that have cooperative extension services or experiment stations. These agencies provide consultation and literature on gardening, horticulture and agriculture. Also, many counties have extension services or agents that provide these services. Check the County Government listing in your phone book.

University of Alaska
School of Agriculture and Land Resources Management
Agriculture Experiment Station
Fairbanks, AK 99701

University of Arizona
Cooperative Extension Service
Tucson, AZ 85721

University of Arkansas
Cooperative Extension Service
1201 McAlmont
P.O. Box 391
Little Rock, AR 72203

Auburn University
Alabama Cooperative Extension Service
Auburn, AL 36830

University of California
Agricultural Sciences Publications
1422 S. 10th Street
Richmond, CA 94804

Clemson University
Agricultural Publications
Clemson, SC 29631

Colorado State University
Extension—Experiment Station
Publications Office
Fort Collins, CO 80523

University of Connecticut
Cooperative Extension Service
College of Agriculture
and Natural Resources
Storrs, CT 06268

Cornell University
Mailing Room
7 Research Park
Ithaca, NY 14853

University of Delaware
Mailing Room
Agricultural Hall
Newark, DL 19711

University of Florida
Cooperative Extension Service
Gainesville, FL 32601

University of Georgia
Extension Editor
Athens, GA 30602

University of Hawaii
College of Tropical Agriculture
Cooperative Extension Service
Honolulu, HI 96822

University of Idaho
Agricultural Science Building
Moscow, ID 83843

University of Illinois
Agricultural Publications Office
123 Mumford Hall
Urbana, IL 61801

Iowa State University
Publications Distribution
Printing and Publications Building
Ames, IA 50010

Kansas State University
Extension Horticulture
Waters Hall
Manhattan, KA 66506

University of Kentucky
Bulletin Room
Experiment Station Building
Lexington, KY 40506

Louisiana State University
Publications Librarian
Knapp Hall, Room 192
Baton Rouge, LA 70803

University of Maine
Department of Public Information
PICS Building
Orono, ME 04473

University of Maryland
Information and Publications
College Park, MD 20742

University of Massachusetts
Cooperative Extension Service
Stockbridge Hall
Amherst, MA 01002

Michigan State University
Department of Information Services
East Lansing, MI 48824

University of Minnesota
Bulletin Room, Coffey Hall
St. Paul, MN 55108

Extension Horticulture Department
Mississippi Cooperative Extension Service
Mississippi State University
Mississippi State, MS 39762

University of Missouri
College of Agriculture
Extension Programs
214 Waters Hall
Columbia, MS 65201

Montana State University
Cooperative Extension Office
Bozeman, MT 59717

University of Nebraska
Department of Agricultural Communications
Lincoln, NE 68583

University of Nevada
Cooperative Extension Service
Reno, NV 89507

University of New Hampshire
Cooperative Extension Service
Plant Science Department
Durham, NH 03924

New Mexico State University
Department of Agricultural Information, Drawer 3-Al
Las Cruces, NM 88003

North Carolina State University
Publications Office, Department of Agricultural Information
Box 5037
Raleigh, North Carolina 27607

North Dakota State University
Agricultural Experiment Station
University Station
Fargo, ND 58105

Ohio State University
Extension Office of Information
2120 Fyffe Road
Columbus, OH 43210

Oklahoma State University
Central Mailing Service
Cooperative Extension Office
Stillwater, OK 74704

Oregon State University
Bulletin Mailing Service,
Industrial Building
Corvalis, OR 97331

Pennsylvania State University
Agricultural Mailing Room
Agricultural Administration Building
University Park, PA 16802

University of Puerto Rico
Box A
Rio Piedras, P.R. 00928

Purdue University
Mailing Room
Agricultural Administration Building
West Lafayette, IN 47907

University of Rhode Island
Resource Information Office
24 Woodward Hall
Kingston, RI 02881

Rutgers University
Publications Distribution Center
Cook College, Dudley Road
New Brunswick, NJ 08903

South Dakota State University
Bulletin Room
Extension Building
Brookings, SD 57007

University of Tennessee
Agricultural Extension Service
P.O. Box 1071
Knoxville, TN 37901

Texas A & M University
Texas Agricultural Extension Service
College Station, TX 77843

Utah State University
The Bulletin Room
Logan, UT 84322

University of Vermont
Publications Office
Morrill Hall
Burlington, VT 05401

Virginia Polytechnic Institute and
State University
Extension Division
Blacksburg, VA 24061

Washington State University
Bulletin Department
Cooperative Extension
Publications Building
Pullman, WA 99164

West Virginia University
2104 Agricultural Sciences Building
Evansdale Campus
Morgantown, WV 26506

University of Wisconsin-Madison
Extension Service
College of Agricultural and Life Sciences
432 North Lake Street
Madison, WI 53706

University of Wyoming
Box 3354, University Station
Laramie, WY 80271

Canada
University of Alberta
O. S. Longman Building
6906 116 Street
Edmonton, Alberta
T6G 2E1

University of British Columbia
Vancouver, British Columbia
V6T 1W5

Department of Agriculture
Parliament Building
Victoria, British Columbia
V8W 2Z7

University of Guelph
Guelph, Ontario
N1G 2W1

Universite Labal
Cite Universitaire
Quebec, Quebec
G1K 7P4

McGill University
P.O.B. 6070
Montreal, Quebec
H3C 3G1

University of Manitoba
Winnipeg, Manitoba
R3T 2N2

Nova Scotia Agricultural College
Truro, Nova Scotia

University of Saskatchewan
Saskatoon, Saskatchewan
S7N 0W0

PESTICIDES

Common garden pesticides listed here include *fungicides* (kill fungi) *insecticides* (kill insects), *miticides* (kill mites) and molluskicides (kill snails and slugs.) Common herbicides (weedkillers) are described on page 224.

SOME COMMON FUNGICIDES

Generic or Common Name	Trade Name(s)	Toxicity* LD50(Oral)	Use**
Benomyl	Benlate, Tersan 1991	9,950	Controls *Botrytis* and *Sclerotinia* diseases, *Septoria* leaf spots, smuts, *Rhizoctonia* diseases. Protects against powdery mildew. Absorbed by foliage or roots.
Captan	Orthocide	9,000	Controls fungus and leaf spots.
Chlorothalonil	Daconil 2787, Bravo	10,000	Controls *Botrytis, Alternaria* and other leaf spots; also *Rhizoctonia.*
Copper, fixed (inorganic copper)	Tribasic copper sulfate	Non-toxic	General-purpose fungicide. Effective on peach leaf curl.
Copper, organic		Low toxicity	Derived from copper salts of fatty and rosin acids. Controls fungus leaf spots. Does not spot leaves.
Cycloheximide	Acti-dione PM	10,000	Controls powdery mildew and rusts on roses and other plants. Some eradicant action.
Dinocap	Karathane	980	Specifically for powdery mildews. Eradicant with little residual.
Ferbam	Carbamate, Fermate	1,000	Controls fungus leaf spots, rusts.
Folpet	Phaltan	10,000	Similar to captan. Effective on powdery mildew of begonias.
Mancozeb	Dithane M-45, Fore, Manzate 200	8,000	Controls fungus leaf spots, *Botrytis.*
Maneb	Dithane M-22 Manzate, Manzeb	6,750	Controls fungus leaf spots, *Botrytis.*
Sulfur	Flowers of sulfur	Non-toxic	Protects against powdery mildew, no eradicant activity.
Thiram	Arasan, TMTD	780	Seed protectant. Controls fungus leaf spots, *Botrytis.*
Triforine	Funginex	6,000	Controls powdery mildew, rust and black spot on roses and other plants.
Zineb	Dithane Z-78	5,200	Controls fungus leaf spots, rusts, *Botrytis.*

*LD50—Lethal dose required to kill 50% of test animals. Numbers represent milligrams of *technical* (undiluted) material per kilogram of body weight (mg/kg) when taken orally. The higher the LD50 number, the safer the fungicide. However, different products will vary in toxicity, depending on the amount of active ingredients. Read label precautions carefully.
**Read the label of the specific product you use. Active ingredients may be formulated differently by different manufacturers for different purposes. Recommendations here are general.

INSECTICIDES, MITICIDES, MOLLUSCICIDES

Generic or Common Name	Trade Name(s)	Toxicity* LD50 (Oral)	LD50 (Dermal)	Class and Use**
Acephate	Orthene	886	2,000	Organophosphate. Systemic. Residual of 3 to 5 weeks. Caterpillars, many other pests.
Allethrin		680	11,200	Synthetic pyrethrum. No residual. Flies and mosquitoes.
Bacillus popillae	Doom, Japidemic	Non-toxic		Microbial insecticide for Japanese beetle grubs.
Bacillus thuringiensis	Dipel, Thuricide	Non-toxic		Microbal insecticide. No residual. Caterpillars only.
Carbaryl	Sevin	307	2,000	Carbamate. Short (2 to 3 day) residual. Wide specturm—caterpillars, many insects, pets. Highly toxic to honey bees—do not use on flowering plants.
Chlordane		283	580	Chlorinated hydrocarbon. Long residual. Ants, termites.
Chlorpyrifos	Dursban	97	2,000	Organophosphate. Turf pests, mosquito larve and adults.
Diazinon	Spectracide	66	379	Organophosphate. Relatively long (15 days) residual. Wide spectrum—red spider mites, aphids, mealybugs, adult whiteflies, fungus gnats, leafhoppers, cutworms, grubs.
Dichlorvos	DDVP, Vapona	25	59	Organophosphate. Pest strips and pet collars, rarely on plants. Flies, mosquitoes, fleas, ants.
Dicofol	Kelthane	575	4,000	Chlorinated hydrocarbon. Miticide for fruit, vegetables, ornamentals. Long residual.
Dimethoate	Cygon	250	150	Organophosphate. Systemic. Long residual (4 weeks). Aphids, mites, thrips.
Disulfoton	Di-Syston	2	20	Organophosphate. Systemic. Granules are spread around plant roots, which absorb the insecticide. Aphids, scale.
Endosulfan	Thiodan	18	74	Chlorinated hydrocarbon. Whiteflies, mites, especially fuchsia mite.
Fluvalinate	Mavrik	5,150		Synthetic pyrethroid. Contact poison. Residual 1 week or less. Aphids, thrips, whiteflies, caterpillars.
Malathion	Cythion	885	4,000	Organophosphate. Short (3 to 4 day) residual. Wide spectrum—scales, aphids, mites, other sucking and chewing insects. One of safest organophosphates.
Mercaptodimethur	Mesurol	130	2,000	Carbamate. Molluskicide. Effective, long-lasting control of snails and slugs. Also registered bird repellent.
Metaldehyde		630		Molluscicide. Controls slugs and snails. Works best in hot weather.
Methoprene	Altosid	34,600	5,000	Insect growth regulator. Prevents normal development and reproduction of some insects.
Methoxychlor	Marlate	5,000	2,820	Chlorinated hydrocarbon. Caterpillars, fleas, beetles.
Mexacarbate	Zectran	15	500	Carbamate. Molluskicide (slugs, snails) on many ornamentals.
Nicotine (sulfate)	Black Leaf 40	50	140	Alkaloid. Botanical, derived from tobacco. Aphids, thrips, leafhoppers, whiteflies. Highly toxic to animals.
Oxydemetonmethyl	Meta-Systox-R	65	100	Organophosphate. Systemic. Aphids, thrips.
Propoxur	Baygon	95	1,000	Carbamate. Mole crickets, cockroaches, other household insects.
Pyrethrins		200	1,800	Botanical. Derived from *Chrysanthemum cinerariaefolium*. Broad spectrum—many garden insects and household insects—flies, mosquitoes, fleas, earwigs. Relatively safe. No waiting between application time and harvest of food crops. Quick knock-down properties.
Rotenone		350		Botanical. Broad spectrum. Beetle, caterpillars, aphids, thrips, spider mites, ants, whiteflies, cutworms. Short (1 to 3 day) residual. Relatively safe. No waiting between application time and harvest of food crops.
Sabadilla		4,000		Botanical. Considered safest of all botanicals. Grasshoppers, caterpillars, thrips, scale, true bugs (chinch bugs, stink bugs, squash bugs). No waiting between application time and harvest of food crops. Short residual.

*LD50—Lethal dose required to kill 50% of test animals. Numbers represent milligrams of *technical* (undiluted) material per kilogram of body weight (mg/kg) when taken orally or dermally (through skin contact). The higher the LD50 number, the safer the pesticide. However, different products will vary in toxicity, depending on the amount of active ingredients. Read label precautions carefully.
**Read the label of the specific product you use. Active ingredients may be formulated differently by different manufacturers for different purposes. Recommendations here are general.

GUIDE TO NATURAL/BIOLOGICAL INSECT PEST CONTROL

DETERRENT ACTIONS				TRAPS		COMMON INSECT PESTS	BIOLOGICALS		MINERALS, OILS				BENEFICIALS		BOTANICALS			
Variety Selection	Planting Date	Crop Rotation	Trapping Crops[1]	Pheromone Traps[2]	Catch traps[3]		Bacillus thuringiensis	Other Pathogens	Dormant Oil Spray[4]	Insecticidal Soap	Miscible Oil[5]	Diatomaceous Earth (DE)[5]	Parasites	Predators	Ryania	Rotenone	Pyrethrins	Nicotine
						Alfalfa Caterpillar	X						X	X				
						Alfalfa Looper	X						X	X				
X		X			X	Aphids				X				X			X	X
						Asparagus Beetle								X		X	X	
						Bagworm	X											
X		X				Cabbage Butterfly	X				X							
X		X				Cabbage Looper	X							X		X	X	
						Cockroaches						X				X	X	
				X	X	Codling Moth	X	X	X		X		X	X	X	X		
X	X		X		X	Corn Earworm		X			X		X	X	X	X		
X	X	X	X			Cucumber Beetle										X	X	X
X		X				Diamondback Moth	X											
X	X	X				European Corn Borer								X	X	X	X	
						Fall Webworm	X											
						Flea Beetles						X				X	X	X
						Fleas						X				X	X	
X						Grasshoppers		X						X				
						Green Cloverworm	X											
			X			Gypsy Moth	X							X		X		
						Hornworm	X						X	X				
			X		X	Housefly								X	X	X	X	X
	X		X			Japanese Beetle		X								X	X	
					X	Leafhopper				X		X						
						Leafroller	X						X	X				
						Mealybug		X	X	X				X				
X	X		X			Mexican Bean Beetle								X		X	X	
X						Mites		X	X	X				X		X	X	X
						Oriental Fruit Moth		X					X	X	X		X	
						Pear Psylla		X	X	X				X				
						Scale		X	X	X				X				
						Spruce Budworm	X										X	
	X					Stinkbugs						X				X	X	
					X	Tent Caterpillar	X										X	
						Thrips				X		X					X	
						Tobacco Budworm	X						X	X			X	
						Tomato Fruitworm	X						X	X			X	
						Tussock Moth	X									X		
					X	Whitefly				X	X					X	X	

[1]Plants or crops planted specifically to lure pests away from desirable crops, and trap them. A trapping crop is one that is more attractive to the pest than the crops being protected. An example is planting French marigolds to attract nematodes, which get "trapped" in the root system of the plant. Infested plants are then disposed of.
[2]Sex-attractor traps.
[3]Sticky traps, usually yellow.
[4]Horticultural or superior oil applied during plant's dormant period.
[5]See Glossary.

Chart courtesy of Necessary Trading Company, New Castle, VA. Adapted with permission.

RETAIL SUPPLIERS OF BENEFICIAL ORGANISMS

Associates Insectary
P.O. Box 969
Santa Paula, CA 93060
(805) 933-1301
Decollate snail and mealybug destroyer.

Beneficial Biosystems
1603 63rd Street
Emeryville, CA 94608
(415) 655-3928
Specializes in fly control.

Beneficial Insectary
245 Oak Run Road
Oak Run, CA 96069
(916) 472-3715
Various fly parasites, biological controls for grasshoppers and mosquitoes.

Beneficial Insects Ltd.
P.O. Box 154
Banta, CA 95304
Green lacewings, egg wasps, various fly parasites.

Bio-Control Company
P.O. Box 247
Cedar Ridge, CA 95924
(916) 272-1997
Green lacewings, ladybugs, praying mantids, egg wasps, various fly parasites.

Biotactics Inc. Sales
22142 Pico St.
Grand Terrace, CA 92324
(714) 685-7681
Various predatory mites.

Bo-Biotrol
54 S. Bear Creek Drive
Merced, CA 95340
(209) 722-4985
Green lacewings, egg wasps, various fly parasites.

BR Supply Company
P.O. Box 845
Exeter, CA 93221
(209) 732-3422
Various parasitic nematodes.

Burpee Seed Company
300 Park Avenue
Warminster, PA 18974
Ladybugs, praying mantids.

Foothill Agricultural Research Inc.
510 West Chase Drive
Corona, CA 91720
(714) 371-0120
Ladybugs, egg wasps, black scale parasite, decollate snail, various fly parasites, mealybug destroyer, red scale parasite.

Fountain's Sierra Bug Company
P.O. Box 114
Rough & Ready, CA 95975
(916) 273-0513
Ladybugs.

Gothard Inc.
P.O. Box 370
Canutillo, TX 79835
(505) 874-3125
Egg wasps.

Gurney Seed & Nursery Company
Yankton, SD 57079
Ladybugs, praying mantids, egg wasps, grasshopper parasite.

Integrated Pest Management
305 Agostino Road
San Gabriel, CA 91776
(818) 287-1101
Green lacewings, ladybugs, praying mantids, egg wasps, black scale parasite, decollate snail, various fly parasites, grasshopper parasite, greenhouse whitefly parasite, mealybug destroyer, various predatory mites, red scale parasite.

King's Natural Pest Control
224 Yost Avenue
Spring City, PA 19475
Green lacewings, ladybugs, praying mantids, egg wasps, milky spore (Bacillus popilliae), various fly parasites, mealybug destroyer.

Mellinger's Nursery
2310 W. South Range Road
North Lima, OH 44452
(216) 549-9861
Ladybugs, praying mantids, egg wasps, milky spore (Bacillus popilliae), grasshopper parasite.

Natural Pest Controls
9397 Premier Way
Sacramento, CA 95826
(916) 362-2660
Green lacewings, ladybugs, praying mantids, egg wasps, black scale parasite, various fly parasites, greenhouse whitefly parasite, mealybug destroyer, various predatory mites, red scale parasite.

Nature's Control
Box 35
Medford, OR 97501
(503) 773-5927
Various predatory mites.

Pacific Agricultural Labs Inc.
P.O. Box 439
San Luis Rey, CA 92068
(714) 439-6921
Decollate snail.

Pacific Tree Farms
4301 Lynnwood Drive
Chula Vista, CA 92010
(619) 422-2400
Decollate snail.

Peaceful Valley Farm Supply
11173 Peaceful Valley Road
Nevada City, CA 95959
(916) 265-3339
Green lacewings, ladybugs, praying mantids, egg wasps, milky spore (Bacillus popilliae), black scale parasite, decollate snail, various fly parasites, grasshopper parasite, greenhouse whitefly parasite, mealybug destroyer, mosquitofish (Gambusia sp.), navel orangeworm parasite, nuclear polyhedrosis virus, various predatory mites, predatory nematodes, red scale parasite.

Rincon-Vitova Insectaries Inc.
P.O. Box 95
Oak View, CA 93022
Specialize in fly predators.

Spalding Laboratories
760 Printz Road
Arroyo Grande, CA 93420
(805) 489-5946
Green lacewings, egg wasps, various fly parasites, greenhouse whitefly parasite, mealybug destroyer.

Unique Insect Control
P.O. Box 15376
Sacramento, CA 95852
(916) 961-7945
Green lacewings, ladybugs, praying mantid egg cases, egg wasps, various fly parasites, Trichogramma, greenhouse whitefly parasite, predatory mites.

Whitefly Control Company
P.O. Box 986
Milpitas, CA 95035
(408) 295-1444 ext. 520
Greenhouse whitefly parasite.

SOME COMMON HERBICIDES

Generic or Common Name	Trade Name(s)	Toxicity* LD50 (Oral)	Class and Use**
AMS	Ammate, Ammate-X Weed and Brush Killer	3,900	Postemergence, non-selective, systemic. Weed and brush killer. Brambles, poison ivy, poison oak, poison sumac, tree sprouts, other woody and herbaceous weeds.
Benefin	Balan	10,000	Pre-emergence. Controls grasses and several broadleaf weeds—Chickweed, carpetweed, knotweed, pigweed, others.
Bensulide	Betasan, Scott's Halts Crabgrass	5,000	Pre-emergence. Controls crabgrass, annual bluegrass, redroot pigweed, watergrass, lambsquarters, shepherd spurse, others.
Bromoxynil	Buctril, NuLawn Weeder	190	Postemergence, selective, systemic. Controls many broad leaf weeds. In NuLawn Weeder, does not affect desired grasses in new lawns.
Cacodylic acid	Phytar 138, Acme Weed-N-Grass Killer	830	Postemergence, non-selective, contact weed killer.
2, 4-D+MCPP+dicamba	Miller's Lawn & Turf Weed Killer		Postemergence, selective. Controls wide range of broadleaf weeds in established grass lawns when applied at low rates.
Dalapon	Dowpon M, Green-light Dowpon M Grass Killer	6,500	Postemergence, selective. Controls grasses, including Bermudagrass, Johnsongrass, quackgrass, annual bluegrass, in dichondra lawns and ivy.
DCPA	Dacthal	3,000	Pre-emergence. Many grasses and broadleaf weeds in grass lawns, and around many woody and herbaceous ornamentals.
Dichlobenil	Casoron	3,160	Pre-emergence. Many grasses and broadleaf weeds around many established woody ornamentals.
Diphenamid	Enide	1,000	Pre-emergence. Controls many grasses and broadleaf weeds around woody ornamentals, annual and perennial flowers, ground covers, vegetables, fruit and nut trees, dichondra and Bermudagrass lawns.
DSMA	Ansar 184	1,800	Postemergence, selective. Controls grasses—crabgrass, foxtail and barnyardgrass in grass and dichondra lawns.
EPTC	Eptam	1,652	Pre-emergence. Controls a wide range of annual and perennial grasses and broadleaf weeds around flowers, ground covers, woody ornamentals and some vegetables.
Glyphosate	Roundup, Kleenup	4,320	Postemergence, systemic. Broad-spectrum herbicide controls deep-rooted perennial weeds. Useful in lawn renovation, non-crop areas along fences, sidewalks, driveways, buildings; also for spot treatment around trees and shrubs.
Metham	Vapam	820	Soil fumigant used to kill germinating seeds, rhizomes, tubers, roots and stems of weeds in soil. Controls many weeds, also some soil insects and nematodes. Use to clean heavily infested soils before planting or using as potting soil.
MSMA	Ansar 529	700	Postemergence, selective. Grasses such as crabgrass and dallisgrass in dichondra lawns.
Napropamide	Devrinol	5,000	Pre-emergence. Controls many annual broadleaf and grass weeds in dichondra lawns, ground covers and other desired plantings.
Oryzalin	Surflan	10,000	Pre-emergence. Controls many grasses and broadleaf weeds in many situations, including around ground covers and fruit trees.
Siduron	Tupersan	7,500	Pre-emergence, selective. Controls crabgrass, barnyard grass, foxtail and Bermudagrass in germinating grass lawns of bluegrass, fescue, perennial ryegrass, zoyzia and some bentgrasses.
Simazine	Princep	5,000	Pre-emergence. Controls a wide range of grasses and broadleaf weeds in many situations.
Trifluralin	Treflan	3,700	Pre-emergence. Controls most grasses and many annual broadleaf weeds in ground covers, vegetables, and ornamentals.

*LD50—Lethal dose required to kill 50% of test animals. Numbers represent milligrams of *technical* (undiluted) material per kilogram of body weight (mg/kg) when taken orally. The higher the LD50 number, the safer the herbicide. However, different products will vary in toxicity, depending on the amount of active ingredients. Read label precautions carefully.

**Read the label of the specific product you use. Active ingredients may be formulated differently by different manufacturers for different purposes. Recommendations here are general.

GLOSSARY

This glossary defines many of the botanical and horticultural terms used in this book, along with some that you may encounter in other gardening literature, and in conversations with nursery personnel, extension agents and other gardeners.

A

Acaricide (miticide): Pesticide that kills mites and ticks.

Accent plant: A plant that attracts attention to itself, usually because its form, foliage, texture or color is in contrast to its surroundings.

Acid soil: A soil with a pH less than 7.0. In practice, slightly acid soils are desirable for most plants, and only soils with a pH less than 6.5 are too acid for most plants. Rhododendrons and azaleas are notable exceptions, preferring soils with a pH of 4.5 to 5.5. Acid soils tend to be more spongy and open but less fertile than alkaline soils.

Active ingredient: In pesticides, the portion of the material that has the pesticidal effect.

Actual nitrogen: The actual amount of nitrogen in a bag of fertilizer. For instance, a 100 pound bag of fertilizer that is 10% nitrogen—as in 10-0-0— contains 10 pounds of nitrogen, as does a 50 pound bag of 20% fertilizer. Fertilizer recommendations in pounds of actual nitrogen are useful because they are independent of the brand and concentration of fertilizer you use.

Adobe soil: Heavy clay soil.

Adventitious growth: Bud, shoot, or root produced in an abnormal position or at an unusual time of development. An example is suckers or water sprouts at the trunk of a shrub or tree.

Aeration: The condition of plentiful oxygen supply on which roots and soil microorganisms thrive. Accomplished by cultivating or turning soil, *coring* lawns, turning compost and so forth. Air in well-aerated soils is very similar in composition to air above the soil. Air in poorly aerated soils contains more carbon dioxide and less oxygen.

Aerial bulb: See *Bulbil.*

Aerobic bacteria: Bacteria living or active only in the presence of oxygen. *See Anaerobic bacteria.*

Agricultural Extension Service: A government organization that provides information and consultation on gardening, as well as home economics and agriculture. Usually based at the Land Grant University of each state. Most counties in the United States also have an agricultural extension service or agent. Addresses of Land Grant Universities are listed on pages 219-220.

Air layering: Method of propagation by which aboveground stems develop roots while they remain attached to the mother plant. See page 103 for instructions.

Alkali soil: Soil with a pH of 8.5 or higher, and containing enough sodium to interfere with plant growth. High-sodium soils may be reclaimed by applications of gypsum followed by heavy leaching with water.

Alkaline soil: A soil with a pH higher than 7.0. Common in low-rainfall areas where mineral elements such as calcium and magnesium are not washed from soil. See *Acid soil.*

Alkalinity: A condition in which *basic elements* (hydroxyl or OH-ions) in a solution are more abundant than *acid elements* (Hydrogen or H+ ions).

Alpine garden: A garden of plants that are native to alpine or high-elevation areas.

Alternate leaves: Leaves arranged singly at different heights and on different sides of the stem.

Alternate bearing: Production of heavier and lighter crops of flowers or fruits in successive years.

Ammonia: A colorless, pungent gas composed of one nitrogen atom and three hydrogen atoms. A primary component of many nitrogen fertilizers.

Ammoniacal: Containing ammonia. On fertilizer labels, the term indicates the nitrogen component based on ammonia. Ammoniacal fertilizers are acid-forming.

Ammonium: A crystalline salt containing one atom of nitrogen and four atoms of hydrogen. A basic component of many fertilizers, such as ammonium sulfate, which is used to acidify soil.

Anaerobic bacteria: Bacteria living or active in the absence of free oxygen. Gardeners encounter anaerobic bacteria in smelly compost piles and sulfurous, waterlogged soils. The smell of anaerobic bacteria is the gardener's warning to change conditions—whether in compost pile or soil—so air can circulate more freely.

Angiosperm: One of two main divisions of all seed-producing plants. These produce seeds in an enclosed ovary (carpel) within a flower. Includes all flowering plants. See *Gymnosperm.*

Annual: A plant whose entire life cycle is completed in a single growing season—germinating from seed, producing seed and dying.

Anther: The upper portion of a stamen that contains the pollen of a flower.

Anthracnose: A fungus disease that creates dead areas on leaves, stems or fruit.

Antidesiccant: A material that prevents or retards water loss in plants.

Antitranspirant: A plasticlike spray that coats leaves, thus slowing transpiration, or the loss of water vapor through leaves. Used on established plants that must endure a period of extreme drought, also on recently transplanted plants.

Apical dominance: Hormonal influence exerted by terminal bud in suppressing growth of lateral buds.

Arbor: An open structure, usually a horizontal framework supported by upright posts or columns, on which vines or other plants are trained.

Arborescent: Treelike or tending to become a tree.

Arboriculture: The practice of growing and caring of trees for ornamental purposes.

Arborist: Individual practiced in art of arboriculture—pruning, limb and tree removal, prevention and cure of tree diseases.

Arcure: A single cordon espalier in which whips are planted at slight angle, then new growth bent over to center of adjoining whip to form arches. See drawing on page 228.

Aroid: A plant of the Araceae family such as Lords-and-Ladies.

Asexual propagation: Propagation by utilizing a part of the body tissue of the parent plant as opposed to growing a plant from seed. Same as *vegetative propagation.*

Atrium: Generally a small, roofless, planted courtyard within a building.

Auxin: Natural plant hormone (indole-3-acetic acid) that promotes plant growth by cell enlargement when used in extremely low concentrations.

Available moisture: Amount of water in soil that can be absorbed by plant roots.

Available nutrient: The portion of total nutrient in the soil that is in a form plant roots can absorb.

Avenue tree: A relatively large evergreen or deciduous tree planted along wide avenues. Larger than a street tree, it should be tolerant of pests, dust and smog, have deep roots and be nonfruiting.

B

Backfill soil: The soil used to fill a planting hole; sometimes amended with organic material.

Background plant: A large shrub or small tree with attractive, evergreen foliage. It should not require frequent attention and usually does not have showy flowers or fruit.

Balanced crotch: Two branches of a tree growing from the same point at the same rate. Undesirable because balanced crotches are weak and break easily.

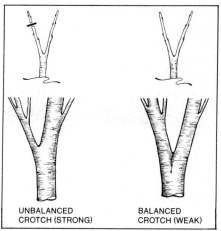

UNBALANCED CROTCH (STRONG)   BALANCED CROTCH (WEAK)

Balled-and-burlapped (B&B): Plant with a wrapped, compact mass of earth left around the roots. Larger nursery trees are often sold this way.

Bare-root transplanting: Usually dormant plants moved from one location to another with no soil around roots. Many nursery trees and shrubs are sold bare-root during their dormant period.

Bark graft: Grafting method in which a scion is inserted between the bark and xylem of stock.

Basal: Refers to the base or the lowest part of a plant or plant part.

Bedding plant: Flowering plants planted for seasonal color; commonly planted in masses or flower beds.

Berm: An elongated mound of earth.

Biennial: A plant that requires two growing seasons to complete its life cycle. Vegetative growth occurs the first season, flowering and seed production the second. Plant dies after flowering.

Biological pest control: The use of living organisms, such as bacteria or predatory insects, to control plant-destructive insects, mites or fungus. Suppliers of biological controls are listed on page 223.

Blanching: Covering a plant or part of a plant from light so that chlorophyll and associated cellular changes do not develop and tissues are more tender.

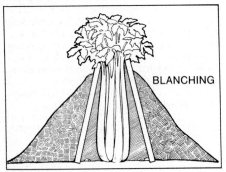

BLANCHING

Blind shoot: A shoot that fails to produce flowers, fruit or seeds as expected.

Blossom-end rot: Common disease of tomato fruit believed to be caused by calcium deficiency, drought or both. The flower end of the fruit cracks and develops a dry rot.

Bole: A strong, unbranched trunk.

Bolting: Premature flower and seedstalk growth. Often affects annual vegetables, such as lettuce or cabbage, and biennial herbs such as parsley or coriander (cilantro). Exposed to temperatures too cool or warm at critical stages of growth, these plants may produce flowers and seeds before useful vegetative growth.

Bone meal: Crushed or finely ground bones used as a fertilizer. The most common natural source of phosphorus.

Bonsai: Mature, even ancient-looking, miniature trees or shrubs. Size and growth are controlled by container size, pruning and feeding.

Border plant: Generally synonymous with herbaceous or flowering perennials. Usually annuals and perennials grouped for their colorful effect. Lower plants are situated to the front and taller ones to the rear of the border.

Botanical pesticide: Pesticides such as pyrethrum, nicotine, rotenone and ryania that occur naturally in certain plants.

Botanical variety: In botanical nomenclature, the category of plant classification after species. Example: *Juniper chinensis* var. *chinensis*. See *Cultivar*.

Boundary plant: A dense, compact, often thorny plant used to define boundaries or direct pedestrian traffic.

Bottom heat: Heat applied to the bottom of hot beds, benches or flats to speed or aid germination of seeds, or rooting of cuttings.

Bracts: Modified leaves at the base of some flowers. Also, leaves that serve as flower petals. Poinsettia and bougainvillea "flowers" are actually brightly colored bracts surrounding a small, insignificant flower.

Bramble: Usually wild relatives of blackberry, raspberry or dewberry, though the term sometimes refers to all plants of that genus *(Rubus)*.

Bridge graft: A graft utilizing long scions to bridge a severe wound, such as girdling in the lower trunk of a tree. Scions are inserted into healthy bark above and below the wound.

Broadcast: To scatter seed or fertilizer uniformly over an area rather than in rows.

Broadleaf: Generally, any plant with wide leaves. More specifically, any plant with two cotyledon seed leaves (dicots). Characterized by netted rather than parallel leaf veins. Generally includes all trees except conifers and most flowering plants except grasses.

Broad-spectrum pesticide: Pesticides such as diazinon, malathion and sevin that are effective on a wide variety of plant pests.

Bud: Growing point or protrusion on a stem where a leaf, shoot or flower arises.

Budding: Method of grafting using a single bud as a scion, placed under the bark of the stock.

Bud sport: A cultivar arising from a natural bud mutation. A bud sport may differ in shoot length, leaves, flowers or fruit from other shoots of the same plant.

Bulb: A general term describing the underground storage parts of various plants. See *Corm, Rhizome, Tuber* and *Tuberous roots*. True bulbs, including daffodils, onions, lilies and tulips, resemble enlarged buds with many overlapping, fleshy leaf bases.

Bulbil: A small bulb produced above ground in the flower head or leaf axil of some bulbous plants. Small bulbs produced on the underground portion of plants are called *bulblets*.

C

Caliche: An essentially cemented layer of calcium carbonate (lime) at or just beneath soil surface. One of the many forms of hardpan. Often a problem in arid regions with alkaline, calcareous soils.

Caliper: The diameter of a nursery tree measured 6 inches above the soil level. Trees larger than 4 inches are measured 12 inches above the soil. In forestry, large trees are measured 4-1/2 feet above the soil. Also referred to as *diameter breast height*, abbreviated *DBH*.

Callus: Healing growth that covers plant wounds.

Calyx: The lowest or most outer flower parts. Usually green and leaflike, sometimes colored and petal-like.

Cambium: Microscopic layer of living, dividing cells beneath bark from which new wood and bark develops. Best visualized as a thin cylinder just under the bark of trees.

Cane: Any hollow or pithy jointed stem, including the stems of reeds, bamboos, large grasses and small palms. Commonly refers to stems of raspberry, blackberry, grape and rose.

Cane fruit: Fruit of blackberry, raspberry, dewberry, boysenberry, gooseberry and currant.

Canker: Disease-caused trunk or stem lesion in which bark and sometimes cambium and wood are killed.

Canopy: The overhanging part of a tree which shades the ground.

Catkin: The drooping flower cluster, which looks something like a cat's tail, that appears in spring on walnut, pistache, hickory, oak and other wind-pollinated trees.

Caution: As relates to pesticides, the "signal" word on a pesticide label that indicates a slight toxicity. See page 96.

Cell: Basic structural unit of plants and animals. Plant cells are surrounded by rigid cell walls.

Cellulose: Principal component of cell walls or fiber of plant tissue. Used to make paper, cellophane, explosives and other products.

Central leader: Dominant central branch of a tree. Also a method of training fruit and ornamental trees whereby pruning encourages a dominant central leader to develop.

Chelate: An organic molecule that binds to certain plant nutrients (in metal ion form) and prevents their conversion to an insoluble form, maintaining their availability to plant roots. The micronutrients iron, manganese and zinc are readily "locked up" in soil with an alkaline pH. This lock-up is prevented by chelates.

Chilling requirement: The minimum exposure to cold weather required by many deciduous plants to grow and develop correctly in spring. In general, 600 to 1,000 hours of temperatures between 32F and 45F (0C and 7C) are necessary to fully break a plant's dormancy. Chilling requirements are especially important in selecting deciduous fruit and nut trees, as described on page 167.

Chimera: A plant composed of two genetically distinct tissues as a result of mutation, irregular cell division or grafting.

Chlorophyll: Green pigment within plant cells responsible for photosynthesis.

Chloroplast: Organ in plant cell that contains chlorophyll.

Chlorosis: Lack of chlorophyll, indicated by yellowing between veins of leaves. Chlorophyll does not develop because of a nutritional imbalance or deficiency, such as iron or manganese for example, or because of disease.

Chromosome: Microscopic structures that carry genetic information in the nucleus of all living cells. See *Diploid, Polyploid, Tetraploid,* and *Triploid*.

Clay: Microscopic-sized mineral particles. Clay soils contain 40% or more clay particles, less than 45% sand and less than 40% silt. Soils high in clay are noted for plasticity when wet, and for water and nutrient-holding capacity.

Cleft graft: A large tree serves as the stock. One or more main branches are sawed squarely, then split. Scions are inserted into the split or cleft. See page 107 for instructions.

Climber: A plant with long, usually thin and flexible branches that grow upwards, using tendrils, aerial roots or other means to hold onto a trellis, stake or other plant. Includes many vines.

Cloche: A temporary protective cover for young, delicate plants set outdoors early in the season. It is removed when danger of late frosts passes.

Clone: One of a group of asexually propagated plants all from one "mother" plant.

Cold frame: A low, unheated greenhouselike box used to propagate or acclimatize plants. Helps protect plants from climate extremes.

Cole crop: Any of the vegetables of the cabbage family, including broccoli, cabbage, kohlrabi and cauliflower.

Companion planting: Growing crops in the same area at the same time. Also, growing certain plants together because they are thought to benefit each other in some manner. Examples are squash with dill, tomatoes with basil and corn with beans.

Complete fertilizer: Any fertilizer than contains all three primary plant nutrients absorbed by roots—nitrogen, phosphorus and potassium.

Compost: Soil-improving and nutrient-rich material resulting from decomposition of organic materials.

Cone: A mass of scales or bracts bearing pollen or ovules; the seed-bearing fruit of pines and cycads. See *Gymnosperm.*

Conifer: Generally, plants that bear seeds in a cone. Conifers are usually evergreen, with the exception of bald cypress and larches and have needle-shaped or scalelike leaves. Wood of conifer trees is referred to as *softwood.*

Contact herbicide: Herbicides that kill only those portions of plants contacted by the spray. The herbicide is not systemic. Many perennial weeds will easily recover from such a spray, while annual weeds will not.

Container plant: Usually a shrub or tree of modest size that tolerates container conditions for many years. Also any plant—vegetable, herb, annual or perennial—grown in a pot or container.

Cool-season plants: Annual plants that grow best in cool, moderate temperatures of spring and fall, or winter in mild-winter climates. Examples are primroses, cole crops, calendulas, stocks, and pansies.

Cordon: A tree, usually a fruit tree such as an apple, with all branches removed so that only one main stem remains.

Corm: Flattened, underground plant part that stores plant food (carbohydrate). A type of bulb. Corms develop from the swollen base of a main stem. Gladiolus are an example.

Cormel: A small corm that forms at the base of a larger corm. Shallowly planted corms tend to develop a number of cormels.

Cornell mix: Artificial container-soil mix based on peat moss and vermiculite. Similar to but lighter weight than U.C. mix (page 234.)

Corolla: Second series of floral parts, counting from the bottom of the flower.

Cotyledons: The first one or two leaves of a seedling, also called seed leaves, that store food during early growth. See *Dicotyledons* and *Monocotyledons.*

Cover crop: Grass or legume crop grown to improve soil by adding organic matter or to protect soil from erosion.

Cross-pollination: The exchange of pollen from the pollen-producing anthers of one flower to the pollen-receptive stigma of another. Occurs naturally via wind, bees or other insects, or is done intentionally by gardeners to produce a new hybrid or to increase fruit set of some crops, such as squash.

Crown: The point on a plant at soil level where stem tissue becomes root tissue. Also, the topmost portions of the leafy canopy of a tree.

Crucifer: Any plant belonging to the cabbage family (*Cruciferae*).

Cucurbit: Any plant of the squash family (*Cucurbitaceae*), including cucumbers, melons, squash and gourds.

Cultivar: Abbreviation of *cultivated variety.* A group of plants within a species that are of horticultural origin. Cultivars are distinguished by certain significant characteristics that are retained when the plant is reproduced, either sexually or asexually. The same as horticultural or agricultural varieties, but distinct from botanical varieties. In botanical nomenclature, the cultivar name is capitalized and set off by single quotes. Example: *Hemerocallis multiflora* 'Golden Chimes'.

Cultivate: Loosening soil surface around plants to destroy competing weeds and promote air circulation around roots.

Cut flower: Any flower that remains attractive long after being removed from the plant. Also a flower useful in arrangements.

Cutting: A section of plant—leaf, stem or root—that can be cut off and grown into a new plant.

D

Damping-off: A disease of emerging or newly emerged seedlings. The cause is one or more of several soil-borne fungi, all of them encouraged by excessive moisture. Sterilized soils are free of these fungi. Prevented with fungicides such as captan.

Danger-Poison: As relates to pesticides, a *signal word* on pesticide labels indicating a highly toxic compound. See page 96.

Day-neutral plants: Plants whose development, flowering or fruiting are not influenced by relative lengths of light and dark periods.

Dead-heading: Removing flowers as soon as they fade to improve plant appearance and to redirect plant energy spent on seed development into encouraging additional blooms. Also done to prevent self-sowing of potentially invasive plants.

Deciduous: Trees or shrubs that drop their leaves at the end of the growing season and remain leafless during the winter or dormant period. Also occasionally applied to herbaceous plants that die to the ground in winter and return in spring.

Deflocculated soil: Soil lacking a well-aggregated structure. Caused by soft water (from sodium conditioning).

Dispersed soil: Soil in which clumped aggregates are separated into individual components. If caused by excessive sodium salts, dispersed soil can be recovered by gypsum. See *Flocculate.*

Defoliation: Unnatural loss of a plant's leaves, caused by weather, pests or herbicides.

Degree-day: A unit of heat energy representing one degree of temperature above a certain average daily temperature. Average daily temperatures are based on requirements of the plant being grown.

Delayed foliation: When leaf buds of deciduous trees grow slowly in spring. Fruit set from spring flowers may drop due to lack of leaf-supplied energy. Usually caused by a winter too warm to fully chill and break dormancy of leaf buds. See *Chilling Requirement.*

Determinate: Fixed or self-limiting growth habit that results in a plant of a definite maximum size. In many determinate plants, stem growth is terminated by a flower or fruit at outermost growing tips. Example: Determinate tomato plants only grow to a certain height and are usually short and bushy. They bear all their fruit at one time, then die. Indeterminate tomato plants continue to grow in size and produce fruit until killed by frost or old age.

Diatomaceous Earth (DE): Earthy deposit formed by skeletal remains of microscopic marine organisms called *diatoms.* When ingested by insects in pulverized form, DE punctures the insect's stomach, causing dehydration and death. Safe but relatively expensive nonchemical control for a number of insects.

Dibble: A pointed implement of wood, metal or plastic used to make holes for seeds or small plants.

Dicotyledon (dicot): Any plant with two cotyledon leaves. See drawing below.

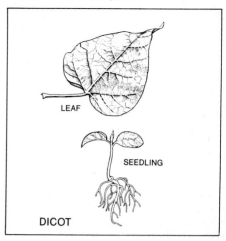

Dieback: When branches die from tips downward toward the trunk or main branch.

Dioecious: Plants with male and female flowers on separate plants. Female individuals bear pistillate (fruiting) flowers and fruit, and male individuals bear staminate (pollinating) flowers.

Diploid: Cells with two sets of chromosomes (2*n*).

Disbudding: Snipping or pinching off flower buds or shoot buds.

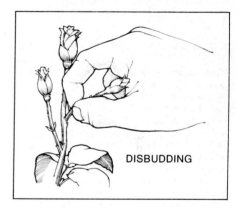

Diurnal: A plant with flowers that open during the day and close at night.

Division: A method of propagating clumping perennial plants by physically separating the crown of the plant to form two or more separate plants.

Dormant: Seeds, bulbs, buds, whole plants or plant parts in a period of inactivity, but capable of growth once conditions become favorable. Winter dormancy is triggered by cold weather, summer dormancy by hot weather.

Dormant spray: Pesticide applied during a plant's dormant period, usually "horticultural" or superior oil or lime-sulfur.

Double digging: Method of preparing soil whereby subsoil is replaced with topsoil. A process of deep cultivation, usually accomplished by digging and amending soil to a depth of two shovel blades (about 18 inches.)

Double flowers: Flowers with more than the natural number of petals common to the species found in the wild. Wild roses have five petals while modern garden roses have 25 to 60 petals. Additional petals are usually encouraged mutations that cause stamens or other flower parts to become petal-like.

Double nose: Bulbs capable of producing more than one flower.

Drip line: The imaginary line on the soil directly underneath the outermost leaves of a plant.

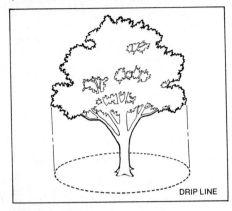

DRIP LINE

Dust: An extremely fine powder used as a pesticide carrier. Applied with squeeze bottles or one of a variety of special applicators.

Dwarf: A plant smaller at maturity than others of the same kind. Usually produced by grafting.

E

Edging plant: Low, compact, herbaceous or woody plant planted along walks or lawn borders.

Epiphyte: Nonparasitic plant, such as some orchids and bromeliads, that grows on another plant.

Ericaceous: Plants of the *Ericaceae* family, including the heathers, azaleas and rhododendrons, manzanitas and many others.

Espalier: A tree or shrub, ornamental or edible, trained to grow on a single plane, such as against a wall or fence.

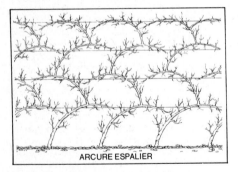

ARCURE ESPALIER

Established plant: A plant that is fully adjusted to its environment and rooted into the soil.

Etiolation: Result of growing plants in darkness, preventing the development of chlorophyll. Seedlings grown in low light are often pale in color and excessively tall.

Evapotranspiration: Total loss of water from plant and surrounding area, including both evaporation from soil surface and transpiration through leaves.

Everbearing: Fruit plants, such as many strawberry varieties, that produce fruit throughout the growing season rather than only in spring or fall.

Evergreen: Any plant that retains leaves year-round. Individual leaves may or may not last longer than one growing season. Leaves drop and are replaced intermittently rather than all at once. See *Deciduous*.

Everlasting flower: A flower that maintains its character and color after being cut and dried. Strawflowers and sedums are examples.

Eye: A visible bud or growing tip, usually in a modified root or tuber. The term is often applied to potatoes and peony divisions.

F

F hybrids: Refers to the generations of hybrids following a cross-pollination. Fl hybrids are the first generation of breeding from a cross between parents of two different true-breeding cultivars within a species. Fl hybrids are commonly more vigorous and productive than their parents. F2 hybrids are produced by interbreeding the Fl hybrids and are less vigorous than their parents. Neither Fl nor F2 hybrids reproduce true from seed (true to type). F3 hybrids are the third generation from a cross.

Facer plant: A low plant positioned in front of taller plants or structures.

Fairy ring: Conspicuous, generally circular group of mushrooms common in lawns. Caused by several kinds of fungus, they live on decaying organic matter in the soil, such as dead tree roots, and do not directly damage the lawn.

Family: A botanical classification that is one step more broad than genus.

Fasciation: A growth abnormality in which two or more stems fuse forming one enlarged, flattened, often curved stem.

Fastigiate: A narrow, erect growth habit due to closely positioned vertical branches.

Fence plant: A plant well adapted to growing against, along, or on top of a fence.

Fertilize: To apply materials that contain essential plant nutrients to soil or plant foliage. Also used to mean *pollinize*.

Fertilizer: Any material that contains one or more essential plant nutrients. A commercial fertilizer must contain at least 5% plant nutrients, such as a 3-1-1.

Fertilizer burn: Damage to or death of plant tissues, resulting from the direct or excessive application of concentrated dry fertilizer to plant foliage or roots.

Fertilizer grade (analysis): The guaranteed analysis expressed in whole numbers as percent nitrogen (N), percent phosphorus oxide (P_2O_5), and percent potassium oxide (K_2O). These percentages are always shown on fertilizer labels in the order given above. Usually abbreviated N-P-K. For example, 10-5-5 fertilizer contains 10% nitrogen, 5% phosphorus and 5% potassium.

Fibrous roots: Many-divided root systems that branch hundreds of times near the crown. Azaleas and rhododendrons, ferns and other plants adapted to loose, forest humus soil, have fibrous roots. Fibrous-rooted plants are generally easier to transplant than plants with taproots.

Filament: Stalklike part of stamen that supports anther in flower.

Flat: Shallow plastic, metal or wood box for sowing seeds or rooting cuttings. Flats of ground-cover plants contain 64 to 100 plants each, depending upon the size and growth rate of the ground cover.

Flocculate, soil: To cause soil particles, especially clay particles, to clump together. See *Deflocculated soil*.

Flower: The reproductive organ of seed-bearing plants. Usually colorful. Because flowers are uniquely characteristic, they are used as the most important basis of distinction between plants.

Flowering, new wood: Flowers develop on growth that occurs the same season as the flowers. These are mostly summer- to fall-flowering plants and should be pruned in late winter or early spring before growth begins.

Flowering, old wood: Flowers develop on wood formed during the previous growing season. These are usually spring-flowering plants and should be pruned immediately after the period of bloom.

Foliar feeding: Spray applications of nutrients that have a low burn potential and can be absorbed through leaves.

Foot-candle: A measure of light energy. 1 foot-candle equals the amount of light falling on an object placed 1 foot from a standard, 1-candlepower light source.

Forcing: Reproducing natural conditions of day length, temperature or both, to initiate a plant's natural flowering process.

Foundation plant: A shrub or small tree used to soften the right angles where the house or other structure meets the soil surface.

Friable soil: Soil with good structure. Loose, well-aggregated soil that is easy to work, usually indicating plentiful organic matter.

Frond: Foliage of ferns and palms.

Fruit: Botanically, a fruit is a distinct organ that develops from the ovary of a flower—and sometimes nearby tissues—and encloses or includes the maturing seeds. In this sense, a green bean is as much a fruit as a peach. Horticulturally, a fruit is a sweet, fleshy, ripened ovary of a woody plant, used as food.

Full slip: Vernacular description of the easy separation of a melon fruit from the vine. Harvest melons when they are at "full slip".

Fumigation: Exposing soil, any enclosed area and sometimes plants to a volatile and poisonous gas to eliminate pests.

Fungi: An order of plants that have no chlorophyll, roots, stems or leaves. Because they lack chlorophyll for photosynthesis, fungi must derive energy from other plant and animal tissue, living or dead. Fungi that parasitize living plants cause *disease* conditions in that plant. Mushrooms and toadstools are fungi that typically derive energy from decaying organic matter.

Fungicide: A pesticide that kills fungi.

Furrow: A trench in soil for planting, carrying water or reducing erosion.

G

Gall: An abnormal growth on a plant, usually in response to a bacteria such as crown gall or an insect egg or larva in the stem or root.

Genus: A grouping of related plants including at least one species. One category more general than species in the system of plant classification. It is the first part of the two-part (binomial) Latin plant name used to identify a plant. The genus and species names are written in italics, with the first letter of the genus name capitalized. Example: *Ilex aquifolium*.

Germination: Sprouting of a seed and beginning of active growth.

Gibberellic acid (GA$_3$): A substance used to regulate or modify growth characteristics of some plants. Gibberellin makes bush peas or beans into pole peas or beans. Also, camellia growers "gib" flower buds to induce larger blooms.

Girdling: Cutting around a plant through the bark and cambium. Girdling completely around a plant eventually kills it. Partial girdling is sometimes done intentionally to promote flowering and fruiting of certain trees. Often occurs accidentally as a result of rodents or wood-boring insects.

Graft: Connecting part of one plant to part of another so that both will unite and grow as one plant. Successful grafts are usually between closely related plants. With trees, a branch or growing shoot, called a *scion*, is taken from one variety and grafted to the *stock* (branch or trunk) of another.

Graft hybrid: A grafted plant that shares characteristics of both stock and scion.

Granule: A particle of fertilizer or pesticide.

Greenhouse: A building with translucent sides and roof in which temperature and humidity are made more beneficial to certain plants. Used for growing delicate or out-of-season plants.

Greenhouse plant: A tender plant that requires protection from temperatures below 50F (11C) and from temperatures above 90F (32C).

Green manure: Usually a legume crop, such as clover, grown to be incorporated into the soil for its nutrient and organic matter benefits.

Grex: A collective term for cultivars of the exact same hybrid origin.

Ground cover: Turf grasses and hundreds of other low-growing plants of all types that cover and protect the soil from weed invasion and erosion. Nonliving ground covers include stone, mulch, paving and decking.

Growth regulator: Any natural or synthetic plant hormone that affects plant growth when used in extremely small amounts. See *Gibberellic acid (GA₃)*, *Indole-3-acetic acid (IAA)* and *Indole-3-butyric acid (IBA)*.

Gymnosperm: One of two main divisions of all seed-producing plants. These produce seeds on open scales, usually in cones. Includes cone-bearing trees such as pine, fir and spruce. See *Angiosperm*.

Gynoecious: Plants that produce female flowers only. Gynoecious plants require a nearby male plant of the same species for pollination in order to set seed or fruit. See *Monoecious*.

H

Half-hardy plant: A plant that is marginally cold-hardy in a given area. It is tolerant of average minimum winter temperatures, but must be protected during periods of extreme cold.

Hardening off: Gradual adjustment of tender plants recently moved from a greenhouse or indoors to a more rigorous outdoor environment. Cold frames or other protective devices are often used to harden-off such plants.

Hardiness: Generally refers to a plant's ability to survive low temperatures. The USDA climate map on page 13 shows the various *hardiness zones* of continental United States and Canada. As an example, a plant that is hardy to Zone 6 will survive minimum temperatures between -10F to 0F (-24C to -18C).

Hardpan: A hardened layer of soil that does not allow water drainage or root penetration. Caused by a number of factors, including mineral buildup at a certain soil level (see Caliche), soil compaction by heavy equipment—common in new housing developments—and cultivating to the same depth over a long period of time (plowpan).

Hard water: Water with abundant to excessive dissolved calcium and magnesium salts. Hard water improves soil structure but tends to increase the work plant roots must perform to absorb water. "Hard water makes soil soft; soft water makes soil hard" goes an old farmer's truism.

Hardwood: Dicot trees that include a certain cell structure conifers lack. Includes all broadleaf deciduous trees. Term does not refer to hardness or density of wood, though hardwoods usually have denser wood than softwoods. An exception is balsa (a hardwood) being "softer" than fir, a softwood. Ash, birch, hickory, oak and walnut are familiar North American hardwood trees.

Hardwood cutting: Mature, hardened section of stem removed in fall or winter to be used for propagation.

Hardy: A plant that needs no protection from cold during winter. Term is sometimes used to describe certain plants that can survive extremely cold winters, but is more often used in relative sense, as in *hardy to -25F (-32C)*. See *Hardiness*.

Heading back: A basic pruning cut, opposite of *thinning*. Shortening a branch by cutting back to a bud or side branch. Useful for changing direction of growth or for promoting more dense growth.

Heaving (frost heaving): Lifting of plants (or stones) out of the ground, caused by alternate freezing and thawing of water in the soil. Often responsible for the springtime death of shallow-rooted plants.

Heavy soil: A dense soil composed primarily of clay.

Hedge: Shrubs or other plants growing close to each other in a row to form a continuous mass of foliage. A "formal" hedge is pruned to a definite geometrical shape. An "informal" hedge is kept within certain bounds but allowed to assume a more-or-less natural or freeform shape.

Hedgerow: A large hedge, usually of several kinds of plants. Used in Great Britain since the Middle Ages to define field ownership and contain livestock. Hawthorn *(Crataegus monogyna)*, field maple *(Acer campestre)* and beech *(Fagus sylvatica)* are three traditional hedgerow plants.

Heel cutting: A stem cutting taken with a piece or *heel* of 2-year-old wood attached.

Heeling-in: Storing bare-root plants in a favorable location, packed in soil or sawdust, until planting time.

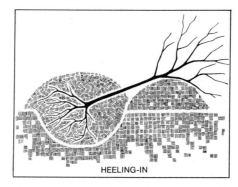

HEELING-IN

Herb: Commonly any plant valued for flavor, aroma or medicinal qualities.

Herbaceous plant: Generally, any plant with soft, nonwoody stems, such as annuals, perennials and bulbs. Specifically, any perennial plant that dies back to the roots in winter and regrows in spring.

Herbicide: Pesticide that kills plants. Some herbicides are formulated to kill certain undesirable plants without harming desirable plants, provided they are used correctly. Others kill all vegetation.

Honeydew: Sweet substance exuded by aphids, scale and related insects. It attracts ants and supports growth of black sooty mold.

Horticulture: Cultivation of fruits, vegetables, ornamental trees, shrubs and herbaceous plants.

Horticultural variety: A variety or cultivar originating as a result of controlled pollination, selective breeding or hybridization.

Hose-in-hose flower: A type of double flower, common to azaleas and primroses, that seems to include a tubular shaped flower within another flower.

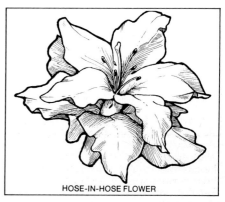

HOSE-IN-HOSE FLOWER

Host: Any organism, such as a plant, on which other organisms live. A rose plant is a frequent host of aphids.

House plant: Any plant that can adapt to indoor environmental conditions, notably light and humidity. Many plants can be raised as house plants, but certain kinds, usually tropicals, are used especially for this purpose.

Humus: Dark colored, relatively stable remains of soil organic matter after most of it has decomposed.

Hybrid: Offspring of an intentional or natural cross between two plants with different genetic makeups. A primary or interspecific hybrid is the result of crossing plants of two different species. Although rare, hybrids have been developed by crossing two plants of different genera. Hybrids are often sterile and never reproduce true from seed. In botanical nomenclature, hybrids are indicated by the symbol "×," as in *Photinia × fraseri*.

Hybrid tea rose: The most favored modern rose. These moderate-size plants produce large, usually double flowers on long stems.

Hybrid vigor: Certain plants (corn, tomatoes) display significantly extra vigor in the F1 generation when certain specific parent varieties are crossed. Hybrid vigor tends to diminish in succeeding hybrid generations. See *F hybrids*.

Hydroponics: Growing plants without soil, utilizing a carefully controlled, nutrient-rich solution. One method uses a sterile medium, such as vermiculite, to hold roots and nutrient solution, in other cases, the roots are growing directly in the liquid nutrient solution. Can be done in a greenhouse or outdoors.

I

Inarching: Grafting method in which a plant is attached to another while still attached to its own roots.

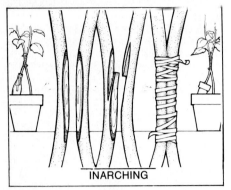

INARCHING

Indeterminate: Plants with a continuous growth pattern, or no fixed maximum size. Plant will continue to grow or bear fruit until killed by pests, disease, frost or other adverse conditions. See *Determinate.*

Indole-3-acetic acid (IAA): Plant hormone that promotes cell elongation.

Indole-3-butyric acid (IBA): Synthetic plant hormone used to promote root formation.

Inorganic: Any chemical or substance composed of matter that is not animal or vegetable, usually derived from mineral sources. Used in gardening vernacular to identify soil amendments, fertilizers and other garden chemicals not derived from plants or animals, also those that are synthetic in nature.

Insecticide: Pesticide that kills insects.

Integrated pest management: System of pest management (insects, weeds, diseases) that utilizes all methods of control—cultural techniques, predators, parasites and pesticides. The goal is to maintain pest populations below the level that causes unacceptable damage. Favored pesticides are narrow-spectrum, killing only specific pests.

Internode: Space on a stem between nodes or growing points.

Interstock: Section of stock grafted between a rootstock and scion.

J

June drop (fruit drop): Natural shedding of immature fruit in early summer.

Jute netting: A woven net made of jute fibers. Used for erosion control and seedling establishment on slopes. Biodegradable.

Juvenile growth: Growth of different character that occurs in immature (not capable of flowering) plants of a species. Some mature plants may produce juvenile growth near their bases (eucalyptus, acacia). Juvenile growth of English and Algerian ivy are more common than flowering, mature growth.

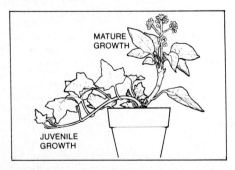

MATURE GROWTH

JUVENILE GROWTH

K

Kitchen garden: Any garden—indoors or out—producing herbs, salad greens, fruits, or cut flowers for home use.

Kniffen system: A two-wire support system for training grape vines. See page 180 for details.

Knot garden: English term for a garden design based on patterns used by weavers and lacemakers. Popular from 16th Century to late 18th Century. Knot gardens were made on level ground, usually in front of a house, with low hedge plants such as germander, dwarf lavenders, common thyme and lavender cotton.

L

Landscape: Surrounding terrain and its features. Used as a verb, the process of improving, personalizing, or making more attractive the property surrounding a residence or other building.

Landscape architecture: Designing and planning the arrangement of land, and the plants and objects upon it for the use and pleasure of people.

Landscape construction: The practice of installing landscape elements, usually according to a landscape plan or drawing. Physically creating the changes in the landscape envisioned and planned by others.

Lawn tree: A tree adapted to high moisture of a lawn and able to compete with grass roots for nutrients. Also, a lawn tree should be deep-rooted, have an attractive, clean habit and cast a light shade that permits grass to grow underneath.

Layering: Propagation method whereby stems still attached to plant are covered with moist soil, encouraging root formation. See *Air layering* and *Mound layering.*

LC50: The "lethal concentration" of active ingredient in a pesticide that kills 50% of the organisms being tested.

LD50: The "lethal dose" that kills 50% of the test organisms when testing a pesticide. Always measured in terms of milligrams of "technical" or undiluted material per kilogram of body weight (mg/kg). Rates vary for source of dose, oral (through the mouth) and dermal (through the skin). For example: malathion has an LD50 of 885mg/kg. An "average" lethal dose for a 150-pound person would be 66,375 milligrams (66.375 grams or 2.34 ounces).

Leaching: Applying up to 10 times the amount of water normally required to wet soil, to wash excessive amounts of soluble salts from the root zone.

Leader: Main stem or trunk. See *Central leader.*

Leaf cutting: A leaf or portion of a leaf removed from the parent plant and inserted in soil mix to grow a new plant. See page 102 for directions. To grow a *leaf bud cutting,* the leaf, its petiole and bud are removed from the plant and the bud is covered with moist soil until roots form.

Leaflet: An apparently separate, leaflike division of a leaf. It is not attached to a stem with a petiole and bud.

Leaf mold: A mulch or soil amendment composed of partially decayed leaves.

Leaf scar: Distinct part of a stem where a leaf and petiole were attached.

Leggy: The condition of plants with little foliage at their base or excessively long, thin stems. Usually caused by insufficient light. See *Etiolation.*

Legume: Any plant included in the family Leguminosae—acacia, peas, wisteria, alfalfa and clover.

Limestone: Sedimentary rock of calcite (mostly calcium carbonate), sometimes with significant quantities of magnesium carbonate (dolomite). Ground limestone is sometimes used to make soil more alkaline.

Loam: Technically, a textural class of soil that represents a compromise between characteristics of clay and sand soils. Loam contains less than 27% clay, 28% to 50% silt, and less than 52% sand.

Long-day plant: A plant that begins to flower when days are longer (nights shorter) than a minimum number of hours. Chrysanthemums are an example.

Loppers: Long-handled pruning shears used for branches 3/4 to 1-1/2 inches in diameter.

M

Macroclimate: Average weather patterns or climate conditions over a wide area. See *Microclimate.*

Manure: Composted animal excreta used to fertilize, enrich or improve soil.

Mellow soil: A soft, friable soil.

Meristem: Undifferentiated tissue at growing tips.

Microclimate: Small areas with a climate distinctly different than the surrounding climate, or macroclimate. Microclimates of various sizes are caused by slight differences in elevation, slopes and the direction they face (north, south, east, west) and proximity to large bodies of water. On an even smaller scale, a house, tree, wall, patio overhead, or even the type of soil mulch can influence temperature, humidity and exposure to sun and wind, creating several distinct microclimates within a single yard.

Micronutrient: A mineral element that plants require in only minute quantities. Also called *trace elements.* Although extremely small amounts are used, their absence will prevent proper plant growth.

Mildew: A surface-growing fungus, visible to the naked eye.

Miscible oil: An oil combined with an *emulsifier,* a material that allows it to mix with water and be applied as a spray. Used as an insecticide to control mites, scale, mealybugs and other insects. Kills by suffocation.

Mist propagation: Method of germinating seeds or rooting cuttings utilizing periodic fine-mist sprays over the area.

Mite: Tiny spider-like arachnids, several of which are common plant pests. Many are beneficial predators.

Miticide: Pesticide that kills mites.

Modified central leader: A training system preferred for upright and closed-center trees, which include apples, pears and some stone fruits. Develop a leader from a central axis and keep it in place until the basic tree framework is established—usually for 5 to 6 years. Then head back the central leader. This temporary central leader helps develop well-spaced, wide-angle scaffold limbs.

Molluscicide: A pesticide that kills snails and slugs.

Monocotyledon (monocot): A plant with one cotyledon in seedling stage. Grasses and conifers are monocots.

Monoecious: Plants that have separate male and female flowers but on the same individual plant. Plants of the cucumber family are usually monoecious.

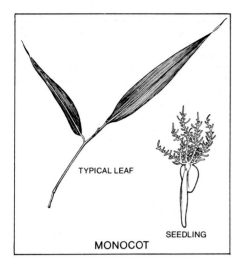

TYPICAL LEAF

SEEDLING

MONOCOT

Mosaic: A virus disease that causes mottling of leaves. One type, tobacco mosaic, affects tomatoes and some other food crops.

Mound layering: Similar to layering, but branches are left upright and moist soil or rooting media is mounded around them. Once roots form, branches are cut away from parent plant and transplanted.

Mulch: Any of a large number of materials, organic or inorganic, that are used to make a protective layer over soil to prevent weed growth, control erosion, maintain an even soil temperature or conserve moisture.

Mycorrhiza: The association of a fungus with the roots of a higher plant for mutual (symbiotic) benefit.

N

Native: A plant that is natural to an area or region.

Naturalized: An introduced plant that has established itself in a region or area but is not native. For instance, Bermudagrass has naturalized in many gardens, much to the dismay of their owners.

Nematocide: Pesticide that kills nematodes.

Nematode: Mostly microscopic worms, several of which parasitize plant roots. Beneficial nematodes are a part of integrated pest-control programs.

Nitrification: Conversion of ammonia ions to nitrate ions, accomplished by soil bacteria known as *Nitrosomonas* and *Nitrobacter*.

Nitrogen-fixing bacteria: Bacteria of the genus *Rhizobium* inhabit roots of legumes, consume atmospheric nitrogen and convert it to a form usable to plants.

N-P-K: The nutrient ingredients of common complete fertilizers. N is nitrogen, P is phosphorus, and K is potassium or potash. Where these letters appear on a fertilizer package, they are always followed by a number indicating the percentage of those nutrients in the fertilizer.

Node: The areas along a stem where a bud is present and a leaf or secondary stem may develop.

Nomenclature: A system of names. *Botanical nomenclature* refers to the usually two Latin names (genus name first, species name second) given to identify plants.

Nonselective herbicide: Chemicals that kill plants regardless of type. Used in areas where no plant growth is desired.

Nut: Hard-shelled fruit with one, usually edible, seed or kernel.

O

Offset: A short, lateral growth from the base of a plant, either as a scaly bud or with a rosette of terminal leaves. Most offsets readily form roots so are a convenient means of propagation.

Offshoot: A branch or lateral shoot arising from a main stem that is used for propagation.

Open-pollinated: Plant varieties produced by uncontrolled, natural cross-pollination in seed fields of parent varieties. Open-pollinated vegetable varieties are generally less expensive than hybrids and they produce true-to-type seeds.

Opposite leaves: Leaves that occur in matched pairs at each bud.

Orangery: Earliest "greenhouse" created by Romans and later Europeans to protect citrus through cold winters.

Organic: Any material of plant or animal origin. In gardening, many organic materials are used as fertilizer, mulch, or pesticides.

Organic gardening: A gardening technique that allows use of only natural or organic, rather than synthetic, fertilizers and pesticides.

Osmotic pressure: The negative pressure that influences the rate of diffusion of water through a semipermeable membrane such as a cell wall. High levels of salt in soil (from fertilizers or water) increases the soil's osmotic pressure, causing water to diffuse from roots into the soil. Plant shows drought symptoms even though soil is moist (physiological drought).

Ovicide: Pesticide that kills eggs of pests.

P

Parasite: Any organism (plant, insect, mite, fungus, nematode) that lives part or all of its life cycle at the expense of a host organism. Beneficial parasites are used to control many kinds of insect pests.

Parthenocarpic fruit: Fruit that develops without pollination (fertilization).

Pathogen: An organism or virus capable of causing disease in a host plant or animal. Beneficial pathogens, such as *Bacillus thuringiensis,* are used to control insect pests.

Pathology, plant: A special area of study within botany concerned with plant diseases and disorders.

Peat moss: Slightly decomposed remains of plants found in existing or former lakes, swamps, or marshes. Extremely water retentive and generally acid pH.

Peat pellet: A pellet of dried, compressed peat moss that expands with moisture and is used for starting seeds or cuttings. These and peat pots can be placed directly in the ground at planting time, reducing transplant shock.

Perennial: In the broadest sense, any plant that commonly lives 3 years of more. Perennial plants do not naturally die after flowering, as do annuals and biennials. Though all trees and shrubs are perennial, the term is commonly used to describe herbaceous (soft-stemmed) plants that die back to the roots in winter and regrow the following spring. Some perennials do remain evergreen in mild-winter climates.

Perfect flower: A flower that includes both male (stamens) and female (pistil) parts.

Perlite: Heat-treated volcanic material that is light and porous. Used as a component of artificial soil mixes and as a rooting medium.

Petiole: Stem that connects a leaf blade to a branch.

pH: A scale indicating relative acidity and alkalinity of a substance or solution. The symbol "pH" is the abbreviation of *potential hydrogen*

and represents the negative logarithm of the concentration of hydrogen ions in gram atoms per liter. The scale ranges between 0 and 14. Midpoint 7 represents a neutral condition, neither acid nor alkaline. Below 7 is acidic, above 7 is alkaline. Most plants prefer a slightly acidic soil, around pH 6.5.

Pheromone: Sex attractant produced by insects. Synthetic pheromones are sometimes used in pest-control systems, such as Japanese beetle traps.

Phloem: Special cells in plants that carry food manufactured in leaves throughout the plant. Phloem is just under the bark.

Photoperiodism: The response of some plants to light exposure, natural or artificial, or specific lengths of time. Length of light and dark periods trigger plants to begin flowering or form tubers, bulbs or runners.

Photosynthesis: The name of the process occurring in plant chlorophyll that begins with simple minerals and gases and, in the presence of sunlight, produces a carbohydrate that plants use for food.

Phototropism: The characteristic of plants to grow toward a light source. The part of the plant exposed directly to light grows more slowly and the shaded part grows faster, thus the plant curves toward the light.

Physiological drought: This occurs when a plant suffers from drought although plenty of water is available in the soil. It happens if the water in the soil is frozen, or if the roots are unable for some reason to absorb the water. See *Osmotic pressure.*

Pistil: Principle female organ of a flower including the ovary in which seeds develop.

Pistillate: Flowers with only female parts. Also called *imperfect flowers.*

Pith: The center tissues of a stem.

Pleach: Training tops of usually small trees to interlace.

PLEACHED TREES

Plugging: Vegetative propagation of turf by planting small blocks or plugs of sod at certain intervals. See page 120 for instructions.

Poisonous plants: Poisons and toxins are widely distributed throughout nature, including many plants. Most ominous are the fruits of castor bean *(Ricinus)* or precatory bean *(Abrus).* One or two of either type, when chewed and swallowed, can be fatal to a child. The fruits and berries of some ornamental shrubs and trees are poisonous. Poison hemlock *(Conium maculatum)*—popularized by Socrates—is as deadly as its reputation. Ornamental plants with toxic properties include: bulbs—*Colchicum, Convallaria, Galanthus, Hyacinthus, Narcissus, Ornithogalum;* perennials and shrubs; *Aconitum, Aleurites, Atropa, Buxus, Celastrus, Daphne, Datura, Delphinium, Dicentra, Digitalis, Hypericum, Hyoscyamus, Iris, Kalmia, Leucothoe, Ligustrum, Lupinus, Nerium,*

Pieris, Rhododendron, Solanum, Taxus and *Wisteria*. In some plants, toxic properties are in specific locations only, such as the leaves of rhubarb but not the stems, which are edible. Cassava *(Manihot)* becomes nontoxic after cooking. Poison ivy, poison oak and nettles produce allergic skin reactions as do *Primula obconica*, some of the spurges *(Euphorbia)* and dumbcanae *(Dieffenbachia)*. There are many more plants with poisonous properties than those listed here. Children are the usual victims of these plants. Learn about native poisonous plants in your area. Teach children not to eat anything but real food. Find out from the nursery if the plants you're buying (or parts thereof) have poisonous properties.

Pollard: A tree whose scaffold branches are repeatedly cut back to points near the main trunk to form a crown of many small, dense branches. Pollarding is severe pruning treatment for most trees—sycamore is one of the most tolerant.

Pollen: Dustlike grains containing male sex cells produced by anthers in flowers.

Pollination: The transfer of pollen from anthers of one flower to the receptive stigma of the same or different flower.

Pollinator: A variety of a plant grown only as a source of pollen.

Polyploid: A plant with more than the normal number of chromosomes.

Pome: The botanical term for a fleshy fruit with thin, leathery skin such as apple.

Pomology: The study of growing and handling fruit plants.

Postemergence herbicide: Herbicides applied after weeds appear.

Predator: In gardening terms, an insect or mite that consumes another insect. Predators that kill garden pests are important components of integrated pest-control systems.

Preemergence herbicide: An herbicide applied to soil before weeds germinate.

Preplant herbicide: An herbicide applied to soil months or days before planting.

Pruning: Pinching, thinning, heading or shearing plants to direct growth, promote flowering or fruiting, improve health or appearance or avoid obstructions.

Pseudobulb: Bulblike base of some orchids and other plants in which moisture and food is stored.

Q

Quiescence: Plant dormancy imposed by external conditions, such as low temperatures.

R

Relative humidity: The amount of water vapor in the air compared to the amount required to saturate the air at a given temperature.

Remontant: Blooming a second time in one season, also called *repeat bloom*.

Repellent: Any material that repels but does not kill insects or other pests. Garlic is a natural insect repellent.

Reproductive phase: The stage of plant growth dedicated to producing flowers, fruit and seeds.

Respiration: In plants, the metabolic process in which stored carbohydrate is oxidized to produce energy and compounds necessary for growth. Opposite of photosynthesis, the process that creates carbohydrate or "food" for plant growth.

Rhizome: Spreading underground stem or runner.

Rock garden: Gardens established on slopes around natural or man-made rock out-

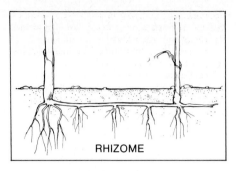

RHIZOME

croppings. Rock-garden plants are usually low growing, drought tolerant, and dependant upon fast drainage.

Roguing: Physically pulling or otherwise destroying undesirable individuals from plantings raised for seed. Usually done to obtain disease-free stock or true-to-type stock.

Roof garden: A garden of any size or description situated on a rooftop.

Root: Underground portion of plant that serves to anchor it and absorb water and minerals necessary for growth.

Rootbound: A condition with container-grown plants when roots have become crowded and establish a pattern conforming to the shape of the container. Rootbound nursery plants are not desirable because roots may never adjust to new growing environment. When planting rootbound plants, gently separate roots, cutting some if necessary, and redirecting them.

Root hair: Minute branches just behind growing tip of root, which are thin and permeable enough to allow water and mineral ions to pass through.

Root hardy: Plants with roots hardy enough to survive a rigorous winter although top portion of plant may be destroyed.

Root sucker: A branch that sprouts from a root, usually just around the base of the trunk, but sometimes several feet away from it.

Rooting hormone: A fine powder containing a plant hormone, such as a-Naphthalene-acetic acid (NAA), that aids in rooting of cuttings. Very little is needed—lightly dust the cut end of the cutting before inserting it in soil mix.

Runner: Horizontal shoot or branch that roots at tips.

Russeting: Roughened, brown areas on skins of fruit and commonly on potatoes.

S

Saline soil: A soil so saturated with soluble salts that most plants are unable to survive in it. See *Alkali soils*.

Sand: All mineral particles in a soil that are finer than gravel but larger than silt particles. A "sand" soil contains at least 85% sand and less than 10% clay.

Sapwood: Younger, outer layer of tissues in a trunk or stem that conducts and stores plant food.

Scalping: Mowing a lawn so low that green foliage is removed and only brown lower stems remain.

Scaly bulb: Bulbs with overlapping leaves that resemble scales.

Scarification: Conditioning a hard seed coat by scratching or sanding so that it will more readily absorb water and begin germination.

Scion: A branch or shoot of a woody plant used for grafting to a rootstock, sometimes to an interstock. Scions are chosen for desirable top growth, flowers, fruit, leaf color or pest resistance.

Screen, plant: A single plant or grouping of plants used to exclude the view of certain parts of the landscape.

Secateurs. Scissor- or anvil-type hand pruning shears.

Secondary pest: A potential pest of usually little importance that becomes a serious pest because predators and parasites that normally keep it in check are destroyed. Spider mites are a frequent secondary pest after use of the pesticide Sevin.

Seed: Embryonic plant in dormant state with food supply and protective covering. Swelling and then growth begin with favorable conditions of soil, moisture and temperature.

Selective pesticide: A pesticide that destroys specific kinds of insect pests while not interfering with beneficial insects.

Self-branching: Plants, usually annuals, that naturally develop side branches, becoming dense and compact. Self-branching plants usually do not require pinching.

Self-fruitful: A plant able to set and mature fruit without pollen from another plant.

Self-unfruitful: A plant unable to set and mature fruit without pollen from another plant. Self-unfruitful trees can be made self-fruitful by adding a graft of a variety that will pollinate it.

Semidouble flower: A flower with more than the minimum number of petals common to the species, but with fewer than a fully double flower.

SEMIDOUBLE

DOUBLE

Sexual propagation: Propagation by seed.

Shade tree: An evergreen or deciduous tree, fairly large in size, with dense foliage.

Shelter belt: Large-scale windbreaks of several rows designed to reduce wind velocity and protect plants and people from wind.

Shield budding: Grafting by inserting a bud or scion into a T-shaped opening in rootstock bark. Also called T-budding. See drawing on page 106.

Short-day plant: A plant that begins flowering when daylight periods are shorter (nights longer) than a specific minimum.

Short-season plant: A plant such as radish that begins growth and matures over a relatively short time.

Shrub: A woody perennial plant, usually smaller than a tree, with several stems arising from the base (multiple trunk).

Sidedressing: An application of fertilizer applied just to the side of a row of plants, usually when plants reach a certain stage of growth, such as knee-high stage of corn.

Side graft: This type of graft is used when topworking a tree or whenever the stock is much larger in diameter than the scion. The scion is inserted into the side of the stock, not the cut end.

Silt: A mineral particle of soil midway in size between smaller clay particles and larger sand particles. Silt soils contain 80% or more silt and less than 12% clay.

Single flower: A flower with the minimum number of petals for its type. Usually found in the species, or the plant, as it grows in the wild. See *Double and Semidouble flowers.*

Slip: Cutting of a soft-stemmed plant (African violet or geranium) that readily roots, perhaps in a cup of water.

Sludge: Organic solid remains after sewage treatment. When composted into manure, it is often useful as soil amendment and sometimes as a fertilizer.

Sodding: Planting by rolling or setting out sod that was recently cut.

Sodic soil: A soil that contains enough sodium to prevent proper plant growth.

Softwood: Immature soft stem of a woody plant. Term also applied to wood of conifers.

Soil: A complex mixture of weathered minerals, decomposing organic matter, air spaces and a multitude of living organisms.

Soil texture: Relative proportions of the mineral components of soil—sand, silt and clay.

Solanaceous: Any plant of the family Solanaceae, including nightshade, pepper, potato, tomato and eggplant.

Sphagnum moss: A type of bog moss used by gardeners for packing plants, lining wire baskets, and occasionally as a rooting medium and soil amendment.

Sphagnum moss fibers: Stems and leaves of sphagnum moss with characteristic fibrous structure.

Sphagnum peat moss: Oven-dried peat containing at least 67% sphagnum peat fibers by weight.

Species: A group of plants that resemble each other in minute details and interbreed freely. Usually the most specific category of plant classification, although some species are further divided into subspecies and varieties or cultivars. A hybrid is a cross between two species.

Specimen plant: A plant with a particularly attractive habit of growth, suitable for displaying alone.

Sport: A mutation, a suddenly appearing marked deviation from type, also a bud or seed variation.

Spreader-sticker: A soapy, plastic material added to sprays to improve spreading and adhesion of sprays to plant surface.

Sprig: Small shoot or twig.

Sprigging: Method of planting lawns using cuttings or stolons of desired grass. See page 120 for instructions.

Spur: Short, fruit-bearing branch of some fruit trees, especially apples and cherries.

Spur-type fruit tree: A tree that forms more fruit-bearing spurs than nonspur trees, spaced more closely together.

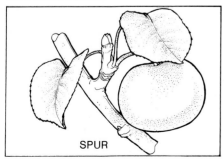

SPUR

Stamen: Male component of a flower consisting usually of a stalk or *filiment* and the anther where pollen is produced.

Staminate: A flower that has male stamen parts but not female or pistillate parts. An imperfect flower.

Standard: A naturally shrubby plant trained to a single, erect, treelike trunk. Also, the erect, inner petals of an iris flower.

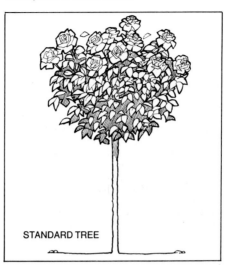

STANDARD TREE

Stele: The central vascular tissue in root and stem of a plant.

Stem: Basic aboveground part of plants, sometimes becoming woody, bearing buds from which leaves or secondary shoots arise.

Stem cutting: Part of a stem used for propagation.

Sterile soil: Usually a potting soil rendered free of plant-damaging organisms and weeds by heat treatment.

Stigma: The uppermost part of a pistil on which pollen grains settle and germinate.

Stipule: One of the pair of appendages at the base of the leaf in many plants.

Stolon: An underground stem that develops roots at nodes. Stoloniferous grasses such as Bermudagrass spread by means of stolons.

Stone fruit: A fruit whose single seed (kernel) is surrounded by a large, hard shell (pit) and is covered by fleshy pulp. Examples are plums, peaches and cherries.

Strain: A group of plants of one species that may not be technically distinct from other members of the species but are distinguishable on the basis of physical characteristics or environment.

Stratification: Storing seeds at cool temperatures—between 35F and 45F (2C and 7C) to overcome natural dormancy.

Street tree: A tree of modest height and clean appearance that is adapted to growth along streets under city conditions. Should have a high-heading habit and deep root system, and be pest free and non-fruiting.

Stress, plant: Pests, drought, heat, cold or other condition that slows or retards plant growth. Plant death often occurs when several stress factors add up to more than the plant can tolerate. Stress signs are the gardener's clue to specific plant needs.

Strip sodding: Planting 2- to 4-inch-wide strips of sod in rows 12 inches apart. Firm contact with surrounding soil is essential.

Style: Stalk connecting the stigma to the ovary in flowers.

Suberization: Conversion of cell walls into cork tissue by development of *suberin*, as when callus forms over a wound.

Subshrub: Term occasionally used to denote partially woody perennials.

Subsoil: Soil below usual depth of cultivation, usually more dense than topsoil and containing little or no organic matter.

Subspecies: Group of plants within a species that differs from other members of the same species by subtle characteristics.

Subtropical plant: Plant that tolerates more cold than a tropical plant but not as much as a hardy plant. Approximate minimum temperature tolerance of about 25F (4C).

Succession planting: Planting short-season crops such as radishes so plants mature at different times, extending harvest period.

Succulent plant: Usually drought-tolerant plant with leaves or stems that store considerable water.

Sucker: A fast-growing, upright secondary branch arising from roots, crown or main branches.

Summer-deciduous: Plant that loses leaves in summer to survive drought, rather than in winter to survive cold.

Surfactant: A spray additive that enhances spreading and effectiveness of sprays.

Sward: Turf. A dense ground cover of short grasses.

Systemic: A material that is absorbed by and moves throughout the vascular system of a plant. Several pesticides are systemic.

T

T-budding: Method of grafting, also called *shield budding*. See drawing on page 106.

Taproot: Large, deep-growing main root from which lateral roots develop.

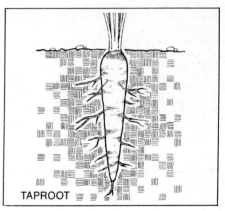

TAPROOT

Taxonomy, plant: Specialty within botany dealing with describing, naming and classifying plants.

Tender plant: A plant that most likely will not survive the expected winter of the climate where it is being grown.

Tensiometer: An instrument that measures moisture tension in soil. A plastic tube with a ceramic, porous cap at one end and a pressure gauge at the other end. Sometimes called an "artificial root."

Terminal bud: The bud at the end of a branch or stem.

Terrace: A level or defined, usually raised, paved or planted area that is a part of the garden, often the central part.

Terrarium: Miniature garden enclosed by glass.

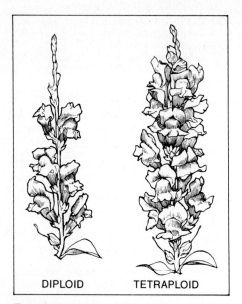

DIPLOID   TETRAPLOID

Tetraploid: A plant with cells that contain four sets of chromosomes. Double the normal number of chromosomes. Tetraploid plants are frequently more vigorous than diploid plants with larger or more dramatic flowers or other features.

Texture, soil: Relative amounts of mineral particles—sand, silt, and clay—in a soil.

Thatch: Spongy layer of dead stems and runners at soil level of lawn.

Thinning: Method of pruning that involves removing an entire branch to its point of origin. Also the selective removal of buds, flowers or immature fruit to encourage remaining fruit to grow healthier or larger.

Thorn: A special type of twig plants use as defense from grazing animals.

Tiller: A sprout or stalk, usually from a root or underground stem.

Tilth: The physical condition of a soil related to the ease with which it is worked and ease with which seedlings emerge and roots penetrate.

Tip layering: Method of propagation whereby growing tip is bent to the ground and covered with soil until it roots. Used with bramble fruits.

Top dressing: Soil amendment such as manure, sand or compost—applied to the soil surface and not incorporated. Used to cover seeds as when planting a lawn.

Topiary: Specialized pruning whereby shrubs are pruned or vines trained into specific, recognizable geometric forms.

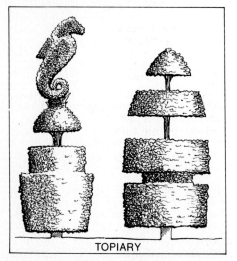

TOPIARY

Topsoil: Usually darker colored soil beginning at soil surface and extending downward a few inches to several feet. Usually a fertile soil rich in organic matter and conducive to plant growth

Topworking: Changing the variety of a mature tree, especially a fruit tree, by grafting the new variety into scaffold branches of stock.

Trace element: Essential mineral nutrients needed in minute amounts. See *Micronutrient.*

Transpiration: Movement of vaporized water from plant leaves into surrounding air.

Transplant: To move a plant from one growing area to another.

Tree: Tall, woody plant with a single trunk, generally 10 feet or taller.

Triploid: Plant with cells that contain one and one-half the normal number of chromosomes. Vigorous but usually sterile.

Tropicals (tropical plants): Plants native to tropical regions of the earth. Generally requiring high humidity, they are damaged by temperatures that approach freezing.

True from seed: Plants whose seeds grow into plants identical to the parent. Also called *true to type.*

Tuber: Enlarged portion of underground stem (rhizome) such as a potato.

Tuberous root: Enlarged portion of a root such as dahlia or sweet potato.

Tunicate bulb: Bulbs with fleshy scales in series of concentric layers.

Turf: A lawn. Dense growth of lawn grasses that forms a living carpet.

U

U.C. mix: A container soil mix of peat moss and fine sand, devised by University of California (and other) researchers in the 1940s. U.C. mix consistently approximates characteristics of ideal loam soil without complications and variability of field soils.

Urea: A soluble, high-nitrogen (45%N) fertilizer.

V

Variegated leaves: Leaves that are naturally edged, splotched, spotted or colored. Usually caused by harmless virus.

Variety: A group of plants of one species with particular characteristics in common not shared by other plants of the same species.

Vase shape: Plants with shape spread outward toward the top.

Vase system: Method of training trees, especially fruit trees. The tree is headed at 18 to 30 inches above the ground at planting. Scaffold limbs originate 1 to 2 feet above ground level, are evenly spaced around the trunk, and are about 7 inches apart vertically. Apricots and peaches are commonly trained to the vase system.

Vegetable: Mostly annual plants cultivated for succulent, edible leaves, roots, flowers or fruits.

Vegetative propagation: Method of propagating plants using any part of the parent plant except seeds. Includes root, stem or leaf cuttings, division and grafting. Asexual propagation.

Vein: Grouping of cells in a leaf that carries water and food, as well as provides structural support for leaf tissue.

Vermiculite: Micalike mineral that expands like an accordion when exposed to extremely high temperatures. In gardening, vermiculite is useful as a seed-germination medium, rooting medium or soil-mix component because it is sterile and holds water and nutrients.

Vernal: Occurs in spring.

Vernalization: Exposing seeds or plants to low temperatures to imitate their natural dormant period, then warming plants to initiate flower development. An important process in forcing bulbs.

Vine: A woody or herbaceous plant that requires support of a trellis or other plants to grow upright.

Virus: In gardening terms, a common parasitic organism smaller than bacteria that retards growth of host plant, sometimes causing death.

Viticulture: Practice of growing grapes.

Volatile: Vaporizing or evaporating quickly, such as alcohol.

W

Warm-season plant: Plant of subtropical or tropical origin that requires high temperatures to grow and is killed by low temperatures. Warm-season vegetables are those usually grown during summer months.

Water sprout: A fast-growing shoot arising from an adventitious bud on the trunk of one of the main branches.

Weed: Usually a fast-growing volunteer plant competing with desirable plants. Any undesirable plant.

Wettable powder: Extremely fine powder that mixes with water and can be sprayed on plants.

Wetting agent: A soaplike material that modifies water, increasing its ability to wet a surface. Reduces surface tension of water.

Whip: A young, unbranched, flexible tree shoot usually growing from a recently budded or grafted rootstock.

Wilting: When leaves and soft stems lose stiffness and hang in limp fashion. Usually due to lack of water but also caused by pests, diseases or poor root function.

Windbreak: Anything that slows or redirects the wind, such as a row of trees or shrubs.

Winter annual: Plant that begins growth in cool weather of fall, survives winter, then sets and spreads seeds the following spring.

Witches broom: Tree or shrub branches that are unusually tufted, dwarfed, and closely set. Usually caused by a fungus disease recurring at the same location during the same stage in the plant's growth cycle.

X

Xerophyte: Plant adapted to growing in a region of extreme drought.

Xylem: Special plant cells that conduct water and dissolved mineral ions from roots to leaves.

Y

Yellows: Virus disease that stunts growth and yellows leaves. Aster yellows is a common example.

USEFUL CONVERSION FORMULAS AND TABLES

LENGTH
1 foot	12 inches
1 yard	3 feet
1 mile	5,280 feet 1,760 yards

AREA
1 square foot	144 square inches
1 square yard	1,296 square inches 9 square feet
1 acre	43,560 square feet 4,840 square yards

VOLUME
1 tablespoon	3 teaspoons 1/2 fluid ounce 1/16 cup
1 fluid ounce	6 teaspoons 2 tablespoons 1/128 gallon 1.805 cubic inches 1/8 cup 0.0625 fluid pint
1 cup	16 tablespoons 48 teaspoons 8 fluid ounces 0.237 liter
1 pint	32 tablespoons 2 cups 16 fluid ounces 67.2206 cubic inches appx. 1 pound water
1 quart (liquid)	64 tablespoons 32 ounces 4 cups 2 pints 57.75 cubic inches 1/4 gallon
1 quart (dry)	1.1012 liters 67.2 cubic inches 0.125 peck 1/32 bushel
1 gallon	128 fluid ounces 16 cups 8 pints 4 quarts 268 cubic inches 231 cubic inches water .155 cubic feet .134 cubic feet water 8.35 pounds water
1 peck	8 quarts 2 gallons 16 pints
1 bushel	2 pecks 32 quarts 64 pints 8 gallons
1 cubic foot	0.8036 bushels 7.5 gallons 1,728 cubic inches 62.4 pounds of water
2 cubic feet	1.61 bushels 15 gallons
1 cubic yard	27 cubic feet 22 bushels

To Find:
Volume of cube:	Multiply side by side by side.
Volume of cylinder:	Multiply squared diameter by height by 0.524.

FLOW RATE
1 gallon per minute	0.134 cubic feet per minute.
1 cubic foot per second	450 gallons per minute 1 acre-inch per hour
1 cubic foot per minute	7.5 gallons per minute
10.4 gallons per minute	1,000 square-foot-inch per hour

FLOW VOLUME
1 acre-inch	3,630 cubic feet 27,154 gallons
1 acre-foot	43,560 cubic feet 325,851 gallons
1000 square-foot-inch	624 gallons

WEIGHT
1 ounce	1/16 pound
1 pound	16 ounces
1 ton	2,000 pounds
1 cubic-foot soil	92 pounds
1 acre-foot soil	2,000 tons

Conversion to Metric Measure

When You Know	Symbol	Multiply By	To Find	Symbol
VOLUME				
teaspoons	tsp.	4.93	milliliters	ml
tablespoons	tbsp.	14.79	milliliters	ml
fluid ounces	fl. oz.	29.57	milliliters	ml
cups	c.	0.24	liters	l
pints	pt.	0.47	liters	l
quarts	qt.	0.95	liters	l
gallons	gal.	3.79	liters	l
board feet	bd. ft.	0.002	cubic meters	m^3
cubic feet	cu. ft.	0.03	cubic meters	m^3
cubic yards	cu. yd.	0.76	cubic meters	m^3
MASS (WEIGHT)				
ounces	oz.	28.35	grams	g
pounds	lb.	0.45	kilograms	kg
LENGTH				
inches	in.	2.54	centimeters	cm
feet	ft.	30.48	centimeters	cm
yards	yd.	0.91	meters	m
acres	ac.	0.40	hectares	ha
miles	mi.	1.61	kilometers	km
AREA				
square inches	sq. in.	6.45	square centimeters	cm^2
square feet	sq. ft.	0.09	square meters	m^2
square yards	sq. yd.	0.84	square meters	m^2
SPEED				
miles per hour	mph	1.61	kilometers per hour	km/h
PRESSURE				
pounds per square inch	psi	68974.76	pascals	Pa
TEMPERATURE				
Fahrenheit	F	0.56 (after subtracting 32)	Celsius	C

INDEX